RATIONAL CHOICE MARXIS

Also by Terrell Carver

THE CAMBRIDGE COMPANION TO MARX
ENGELS
FRIEDRICH ENGELS: His Life and Thought
MARX: Later Political Writings
MARX'S SOCIAL THEORY

Also by Paul Thomas

ALIEN POLITICS: Marxist State Theory Retrieved
KARL MARX AND THE ANARCHISTS

Rational Choice Marxism

Edited by

Terrell Carver
Reader in Political Theory
University of Bristol

and

Paul Thomas
Professor of Politics
University of California, Berkeley

The Pennsylvania University Press
University Park, Pennsylvania

Selection, editorial matter and introduction © Terrell Carver and
Paul Thomas 1995
Chapters 1–11 © Macmillan Press Ltd 1995

First published in the United States and Canada 1995 by
The Pennsylvania State University Press, 820 North University Drive,
University Park, PA 16802

All rights reserved

Printed in Hong Kong

ISBN 0–271–01463–6 (cloth)
ISBN 0–271–01464–4 (paper)

Library of Congress Cataloging-in-Publication Data
Rational choice Marxism / edited by Terrell Carver and Paul Thomas.
    p.   cm.
    Includes bibliographical references and index.
    ISBN 0–271–01463–6 (alk. paper)   ISBN 0–271–01464–4 (pbk. : alk. paper)
    1. Socialism. 2. Rational choice theory. 3. Social choice.
  I. Carver, Terrell. II. Thomas, Paul, 1943–   .
HX73.R367 1995
335.4—dc20   94–41149
                                                                                     CIP

It is the policy of The Pennsylvania State University Press to use
acid-free paper for the first printing of all clothbound books. Publications
on uncoated stock satisfy the minimum requirements of American National
Standard for Information Sciences—Permanence of Paper for Printed Library
Materials, ANSI Z39.48–1984.

Contents

Notes on the Contributors vi

Acknowledgements viii

1. Introduction 1
   Terrell Carver and Paul Thomas
2. What is Analytical Marxism? 11
   Erik Olin Wright
3. Rational Choice Marxism 31
   Alan Carling
4. Rational Choice Marxism: Is the Game Worth the Candle? (with a Postscript 1994) 79
   Ellen Meiksins Wood
5. Marxism without Micro-Foundations 136
   Michael Burawoy
6. Class, Production and Politics: A Reply to Burawoy 167
   Adam Przeworski
7. Mythological Individualism – The Metaphysical Foundation of Analytical Marxism 191
   Michael Burawoy
8. Social Democracy and Rational Choice Marxism 200
   Desmond King and Mark Wickham-Jones
9. Marx and Methodological Individualism 231
   Mark E. Warren
10. Philosophical Foundations of Analytical Marxism 258
    Graeme Kirkpatrick
11. The Limits of Rational Choice Theory 275
    Michael Goldfield and Alan Gilbert
12. Rational Choice Marxism and Postmodern Feminism: Towards a More Meaningful Incomprehension 301
    Alan Carling

References and Select Bibliography 324

Index 336

Notes on the Contributors

Michael Burawoy is Professor of Sociology at the University of California, Berkeley. His most recent book is the coauthored *The Radiant Past: Ideology and Reality in Hungary's Road to Capitalism*, 1992.

Alan Carling is Senior Lecturer in Sociology at the University of Bradford, and is the author of *Social Division*, 1991. He has recently published articles on the theory of history and on class division.

Terrell Carver is Reader in Political Theory at the University of Bristol. His most recent book is the edited collection *The Cambridge Companion to Marx*, 1991. His new translations of classic texts will be appearing as *Marx: Later Political Writings* in late 1995.

Alan Gilbert is Professor at the Graduate School of International Studies at the University of Denver. He is the author of *Marx's Politics: Communists and Citizens*, 1981, and *Democratic Individuality*, 1990. He has also published articles on moral realism and ethics in relation to Marx.

Michael Goldfield is Professor at the College of Urban, Labor and Metropolitan Affairs of Wayne State University, Detroit. He is the author of *The Decline of Organized Labor in the United States*, 1987.

Desmond King is Fellow and Tutor in Politics at St. John's College, Oxford. His most recent publications are *Actively Seeking Work? The Politics of Unemployment and Welfare Policy in the United States and Britain*, 1995, *Separate and Unequal: Black Americans and the US Federal Government*, 1995, and the coedited book *Preferences, Institutions and Rational Choice*, 1995.

Graeme Kirkpatrick is researching at Birkbeck College, London, into questions of intentional explanation and the methodology of social science.

Adam Przeworski is Martin A. Ryerson Distinguished Service Professor of Political Science at the University of Chicago. Among his recent books is *Democracy and the Market: Political and Economic Reforms in Eastern Europe and Latin America*, 1991.

Notes on the Contributors

Paul Thomas is Professor at the Department of Political Science at the University of California, Berkeley. His most recent book is *Alien Politics*, 1994.

Mark E. Warren is Professor in the Department of Government at Georgetown University, Washington DC. He is the author of *Nietzsche and Political Thought*, 1988, as well as articles on Weber, Habermas, and democratic theory.

Mark Wickham-Jones is Lecturer in Politics at the University of Bristol. He is the author of articles on social democracy and rational choice, and is working on an analysis of economic policy-making in the British Labour Party 1970–83.

Ellen Meiksins Wood is Professor in the Department of Political Science, York University, Toronto. Her most recent book is *The Pristine Culture of Capitalism: A Historical Essay on Old Regimes and Modern States*, 1991.

Erik Olin Wright is Professor of Sociology at the University of Wisconsin, Madison. He is the author of *Interrogating Inequality: Essays on Class Analysis, Socialism, and Marxism*, 1994, and editor of *The Debate on Classes*, 1989.

Acknowledgements

Material from the following articles is reprinted by kind permission of the authors and journals as follows:

Erik Olin Wright, 'What is Analytical Marxism?', *Socialist Review*, Vol. 19, no. 4 (1989), pp. 35–56.

Alan Carling, 'Rational Choice Marxism', *New Left Review*, no. 160 (November/December 1986), pp. 24–62.

Ellen Meiksins Wood, 'Rational Choice Marxism: Is the Game Worth the Candle?' *New Left Review*, no. 177 (September/October 1989), pp. 41–88.

Michael Burawoy, 'Marxism without Micro-Foundations', *Socialist Review*, Vol. 19, no. 2 (1989), pp. 53–86.

Adam Przeworski, 'Class, Production and Politics: Reply to Burawoy', *Socialist Review*, Vol. 19, no. 2 (1989), pp. 87–111.

Desmond King and Mark Wickham-Jones, 'Social Democracy and Rational Workers', *British Journal of Political Science*, Vol. 20, no. 3 (1990), pp. 387–413.

Mark Warren, 'Marx and Methodological Individualism', *Philosophy of the Social Sciences*, Vol. 18, no. 4 (1988), pp. 447–76.

1 Introduction
Terrell Carver and Paul Thomas

As recently as 1978 Leszek Kolakowski orchestrated his ambitious, three-volume survey of Marxist theory around the claim that it was possible to 'schematise with precision' what Marxism's 'main currents' had been (Kolakowski 1978, 1:6–7). However, Kolakowski's claim was belied by his signal failure to achieve it. What he uncovered, despite himself, was the very pluralism and heterogeneity in Marxism that Erik Olin Wright stresses in the present volume (below, pp. 11–14). Kolakowski's claim was also vitiated by his failure to perceive what was already on the horizon – another attempt to 'schematise with precision'.

G. A. Cohen's *Karl Marx's Theory of History: A Defence* appeared in the same year and under the same imprint. This book seemed to be a theoretical reconstruction of Marx's own arguments, and anything but an attempt to interpret Marxist theory as it was. It self-consciously 'signalled the emergence of a group of theorists who sought to use the kind of philosophical approach embodied in the analytic tradition in order to elucidate and resolve problems within Marxism' (Callinicos 1989, p. 2). Cohen's attempted reconstruction of Marxism was governed, in his own words, by two constraints: 'on the one hand, what Marx wrote, and, on the other, those standards of clarity and rigour which distinguish much twentieth-century analytical philosophy' (Cohen 1978, p. ix).

Predictably there was little agreement between Cohen and his critics about either the meaning of 'what Marx wrote', or what Cohen's criteria of 'clarity and rigour' actually comported. Even so, many of those who regarded Cohen as more successful in elucidating than resolving problems within Marxist theory still shared his declared commitment to standards of 'clarity and rigour'. These were said to be derived from non-Marxist analytical philosophy. Thus Cohen invented 'analytical Marxism' (hereafter AM).

One of the reasons why AM needs further definition is that its proponents at first, and ever afterwards, actually agreed among themselves about very little, as Ellen Meiksins Wood delineates in the present volume (below, pp. 79–83), beyond the need for the ever-elusive 'clarity and rigour'. There were times when Cohen, John Roemer and Jon Elster – at their most irritating – appeared to value clarity and rigour in a way that suggested they had invented the terms. The question – clarity and rigour *about what?* – was answered by them individually in radically different and sometimes incompatible ways, when they bothered to address it, which was infrequently.

Yet as Wright argues (below, pp. 23–4), Roemer and Cohen both maintained that AM 'reject[s] claims about the methodological distinctiveness of Marxism[,] ... [adopts] the full repertoire of "bourgeois" social scientific practice, and question[s] the core concepts and traditional theses of Marxism'. Roemer, indeed, did not shrink from insisting that AM is distinguished by its use of 'state of the art methods of analytical philosophy and "positivist" social science' (Roemer 1986, 1–2). That characterisation was a deliberately provocative way of posing the issue, in view of the long hostility among western Marxists not just to '"positivist" social science' but also to its extension – analytical philosophy as represented by the Vienna Circle.

Much of this hostility was not lost upon Kolakowski, the author of a fine critique of positivism (Kolakowski 1969). This was written at a time when he was much less hostile to Marxism than he was when he wrote *Main Currents*. Positivist social science and analytical philosophy had long been regarded as prime instances of 'instrumental reason', and Marxists, far from subscribing to those tenets, had long been trying to subvert them. In view of this long and marked pattern of hostility, Roemer's insistence that there is nothing of value to distinguish Marx's method – suitably purged of supernumerary assumptions, to be sure – from what Marxists had excoriated as 'bourgeois' social science, certainly broke new ground. It looked calculated to outrage social scientists and Marxists alike.

One of those offended was – presumably – Cohen himself. Roemer's understanding of Marx, and of the all-important 'clarity and rigour', differs greatly from Cohen's. It is well worth examining the differences between Cohen on the one hand, and Roemer (and his kindred spirit Elster) on the other, in order to map out the distinction between AM as a general category and rational choice Marxism (hereafter RCM) as a subset (see Wright, below, pp. 21–3).

It is RCM, not AM, that is the subject of the present volume. RCM is not, however, just a subset of AM, but is rather a variant on it in certain respects. It took shape in opposition to the methodological collectivism and explicit functionalism of AM, or at least AM as expressed by Cohen. In the first instance RCM was characterised by an assertion of methodological individualism (hereafter MI) as the basis of its own, distinctive outlook.

However, many of the contributors to the present collection take RCM to represent AM as a whole. This is no oversight on their (or their editors') part. All RCM is AM, so the synecdoche is defensible, but not all AM is RCM, as Cohen's certainly was not. As Graeme Kirkpatrick pertinently reminds us (below, pp. 267–71), both AM, which can be methodologically collectivist, and RCM, which in its earliest stages embraced an unqualified form of MI, have something basic in common. What they have in common may well turn out to be more interesting and more important than the much-debated questions concerning MI and its supposed opposite, methodological collectivism or holism. AM and RCM, in Kirkpatrick's words, attempt 'to make Marx's thought "clear" with a methodology drawn from one tendency within contemporary analytical philosophy which is fundamentally corrosive to the practical, active meaning of [Marx's] thought' (below, pp. 271–3).

For Cohen, Marx's thought is concerned in the first instance not with behaviour, action, practice or *praxis*, as Kirkpatrick and Wood understand those terms (see below, pp. 114–16), but with the forces and relations of production that frame and limit human activity. Thus, in Cohen's view, structure takes analytical priority over agency in the explanation of historical change. Elster argued *per contra* that the sort of functionalist explanation mounted by Cohen in order to explain the relationship between forces and relations of production rests ultimately on a teleological conception of history.

In that teleological conception the basic explanatory principle is some underlying long-term tendency – expressed by Cohen as 'the development thesis' – for the productive forces to develop over the course of history. We would hasten to point out that Cohen had to endure considerable criticism of his 'development thesis' on historical as well as methodological grounds, and that he modified his views to some extent (Levine 1989; Brenner 1986).[1] According to Elster, Cohen's use of functional explanation – the existence of something is explained by the function it exercises after it actually comes into existence – results in 'an objective teleology', a process that has no subject, yet has a goal (Elster 1983, p. 61). Thus certain relations of production are said to come into existence *because* they tend to promote the development of a given set of productive forces – an 'explanation' that has biologistic, indeed almost providential overtones (Callinicos 1988, p. 60).

Elster's animus is directed against what he describes as a 'Hegelian' tendency to attribute explanatory power to supra-individual actors (such as humanity, capital, class or history), none of which in fact 'acts' in the way an individual human being can act. In his 'Reply to Elster' Cohen insisted that 'if functional explanation is unacceptable in social theory, then historical materialism cannot be reformed and must be rejected' (quoted in Callinicos 1989, pp. 88–9). Elster argues that while large sections of Marx's writings are indeed functionalist and teleological, Marx was 'nevertheless committed to methodological individualism, at least intermittently' (Elster 1985, p. 7)

At first this seems a surprising assertion, partly because Karl Popper, once the premier proponent of MI, had famously used the doctrine in *The Open Society and its Enemies* to excoriate Marx and not – horror of horrors – to assign the hated adversary credentials as an exponent of MI in his own right. It seems surprising also because there appears to be no need, on the face of it, to assert MI (*anyone's* MI), in order to criticise functionalism and teleology. These are assailable, after all, on quite separate grounds. Whether up-to-date 'scientific' foundations for Marxism can be erected once we have dispensed with teleology and functionalism is another question altogether. This is the question that is begged by Elster's advocacy of MI as the cornerstone of social science.

At this stage we offer a number of observations. One is that the 'intermittent' nature of Marx's purported commitment to MI appears to pose no real problem to Elster, since he exhibits no interest whatsoever in the unity, integrity or coherence of Marx's central arguments and *oeuvre*. For Elster, Marx's writings can simply be mined for whatever they contain, and what is not considered valuable can be consigned to the slag-heap. Elster's object was to reformulate what 'insights' there are in Marx on an analytically sounder basis than Marx himself had provided, and conversely, he aimed to resolve 'interesting' ambiguities in Marx by salvaging from them a consistent and rigorous version of MI. The least that can be said here is (1) that Elster's contest is with irrationality rather than capitalism, whereas Roemer comes much closer to connecting the two; (2) that 'what Marx wrote' does not operate as a 'constraint' on Elster even to the extent that it limited Cohen in his assertions; and (3) that this very fact was enough in the eyes of some Marxist stalwarts to condemn Elster's efforts once and for all.

It seemed to the stalwarts, even the thoughtful ones, that if Elster's stress on individualism could be regarded as an extreme reaction against a once-fashionable Althusserian structuralism, then Elster had merely substituted for the 'epistemological break' another break of his own devising, albeit a 'break' that shattered the integrity of Marx's writing and got us no further than had Althusser himself. In adjudicating on this we should surely bear in mind the necessity to combat functionalism and teleology as such. One of the editors of the present volume is himself on record, after all, as arguing on Marxological grounds that 'Hegelian' Marxism is largely a metaphysics unhelpfully erected by the older Engels, and he is also on record as arguing that Marx's work is 'eclectic and very complex' and cannot be reduced to a single method. Elster would disagree here, even though each contender would for different reasons take issue with Cohen's claim that 'Marx's conception of history preserves the structure of Hegel's but endows it with fresh content' (Cohen 1978, p. 26; Carver 1989).

We should also bear in mind that there are more important things for us to do than indulge in a slavish and anachronistic fidelity to the letter and spirit of Marx's every word. The point remains, however, that Elster's 'intermittence' is, above all else, a temporal category. If used as a criterion it has the effect not of misapplying but of misrepresenting what Marx had said. Elster believes that 'historical materialism' as a method formulated by Marx is logically incoherent, but that Marx's views on technical change, class struggle, and belief formation retain a validity beyond their status as components of 'historical materialism'. It follows from this conclusion that an analytical method should be applied to Marx's writings, not in order to understand how these cohere, but as a way of working out which ideas and theories in them can be incorporated into a modern social science. The utility and methodology of this social science, which owes little or nothing to Marx, is presumed by Elster to be understood and valued already.

There are costs as well as benefits in what Elster attempts to do, regardless of any commitment to the unity and integrity of Marx's *oeuvre*. For one thing, there is the danger that relations of production will be considered, in Wood's words, to be 'not so much the conditions of rational choice as its product' (below, pp. 112–13). In particular, the fact that Elster does not elaborate MI in the context of Marx's own ideas, but applies it pre-formed to Marx's thoughts as *the* criterion of judgement, speaks ill of him as an exploratory intellect. In the present volume (below, pp. 233–5) Mark Warren argues against Elster that MI is not finally all of a piece, that there are not just different shades of emphasis but actually different *senses* of the term, and that Elster slips impatiently but unaware from one to another. Thus he is in one sense at least *less* rigorous than Marx, who deployed his eclecticism with more self-consciousness.

Why does it matter so much to Elster, Roemer and others to extract a version of MI from Marx's writings, or some selection of them? It matters because of their underlying belief – articulated most immediately against Cohen – that individual human action is always the analytical *ne plus ultra* of social scientific explanation. Here proponents of RCM tend to follow a formulation of MI typified by J. W. N. Watkins: 'We will not have arrived at rock-bottom explanations of such large-scale phenomena [as inflation or full employment] until we have deduced an account of them from statements about the dispositions, beliefs, resources and interrelations of individuals' (1968, p. 271). Compare Elster, who says that MI is 'the doctrine that all social phenomena – their structure and their change – are in principle explicable in ways that only involve subjects – their properties, their goals, their beliefs and their actions' (1985, p. 5).

In one sense this might seem too narrow a criterion for explanation, since classes in Marxist theory are collective not individual actors. Yet in another sense MI may turn out to be broader than it appears at first sight: 'Disposition, beliefs, resources and interrelations' are discrete categories that do not in any obvious sense admit of reduction to a crude and 'slippery' Benthamite notion of the individual as the maximiser of preferences – although this is what 'the individual' becomes in some, less thoughtful rational choice accounts (Pitkin 1990; Bhargava 1992). Amartya Sen's wonderfully-phrased words are altogether pertinent here: 'If you are consistent, then no matter whether you are a single-minded egoist, a raving altruist or a class-conscious militant, you will appear to be maximizing your utility in the enchanted world of definitions' (Sen 1982, p. 89, quoted in Callinicos 1988, p. 118).

Michael Burawoy observes (below, pp. 149–50), in words which Alan Gilbert and Michael Goldfield would also endorse (below, pp. 275–300), that those rational choice theorists who 'reduce voting behaviour to individual traits without explaining why those traits are important' are producing 'a theory of voters without a theory of voting'. Individual choice is as capable of being fetishised and absolutised as any other concept. As Goldfield and Gilbert point out (below, pp. 295–6), to designate voting behaviour as 'irrational' (as some rational choice theorists were wont to do), without reference to the nature or spread of choices offered by the political or electoral system, can hardly be regarded as very sensible. What is at issue, as Wood recognises, is whether RCM *necessarily* operates around a conception of 'individuals with (fixed and static) "resources" or "endowments" plus "rationality" (with magically available options)', and a conception of capitalism either as 'a game between consenting adults ... in which the stakes are no more compelling than a desire for "optimization"', or as 'an inert "constraint" on individual choices (which happens to be) very permissive on the latitude of choices it allows' (see below, pp. 88–91). Wright is very sensible on this issue when he comments that:

Introduction

[M]ost Analytical Marxists take seriously the problem of understanding the relationship between individual choice and social processes. This does not imply that social processes can be *reduced* to problems of individual intentionality, nor does it imply that instrumental rationality is the ubiquitous basis for intentional action, but it does mean that social theory should systematically incorporate a concern with conscious choice. One way of doing this is through rational actor models ... (below, p. 21).

What follows from this is the illegitimacy of any attempted reduction of social structure to matters of individual agency and choice. In Callinicos's words: 'explanation of social events necessarily involves premises referring to both structures and individuals' (1988, p. 84). That is to say, structures can be both unacknowledged conditions and unanticipated consequences of individual human actions, actions which these structures both enable and constrain (Giddens 1979, pp. 69–70).

But rational actor models in game theory do not necessarily imply MI, as Gilbert and Goldfield point out (below, pp. 282–5). As Adam Przeworski states:

[O]n paper we can put people in any boxes we please, but in political practice one encounters real people, with their interests and their consciousness of these interests. And these interests, whether or not they are real, are not arbitrary; their consciousness is not arbitrary; and the very political practice that forges these interests is not arbitrary' (below, pp. 141–2).

These are words to ponder, whether or not one subscribes to Burawoy's charge that Przeworski fails to live up to them. They point back, not so much to Elster as to Roemer, who introduced the concept of exploitation into a neoclassical framework. 'In seeking to provide microfoundations for behaviour which Marxists think are characteristic of capitalism', Roemer writes, 'I think the tools *par excellence* are rational choice models: general equilibrium theory, game theory and the arsenal of modelling techniques developed by neoclassical economics' (1986, p. 192). These do not necessarily imply MI as the be-all and end-all of social analysis, since they can apply to class action as well as to individual action. This may well be an advance, as Burawoy argues. But these models do not necessarily imply any particular emphasis on production (let alone *praxis*) either, and for that reason Burawoy criticises Przeworksi and Roemer alike. Distributional questions concerning who *gets* what tell us nothing, *prima facie*, about who *does* what in society, and it is the latter question, not the former, that is constitutive of Marxism. Burawoy, too, seeks 'microfoundations' but these, he insists, must be 'grounded in production and the lived experience it generates' (below, pp. 143–4).

Whatever the rights and wrongs of Burawoy's position here – a position that Przeworski for one would not accept – Burawoy does acknowledge that Przeworski has produced a real development in the brief but intense history of RCM. Przeworski has insisted that social actors, individual and collective, do not march around with predispositions which they simply execute. He asks how capitalist relations of production shape the interests of capital and labour, and so refuses to sacrifice Marxism entirely on the altar of MI. Yet according to Burawoy, the possibility of an emergent commitment to socialism through participation in struggles is marginalised by Przeworski's embrace of a neoclassical conception of strategic action. And again, preferences are taken as given rather than made and remade through participation in the world, even if these are the preferences of collective actors, classes.

Mark Wickham-Jones and Desmond King do not agree with Burawoy that Przeworski's 'critique of the social-democratic road to power' – the conclusion of which is that 'the electoral road to socialism is self-defeating' — is either 'illuminating' or 'devastating'. Whereas Burawoy would reject Przeworski's position as having told us little about the transition to socialism – which does not in Burawoy's view depend on the social-democratic route anyway – Wickham-Jones and King dispute Przeworski's depiction of the social-democratic route itself (below, pp. 228–9).

In 1989 Callinicos wrote that 'whether analytical Marxism represents a development of, or an exit from, the revolutionary socialist tradition ... remains to be seen' (1989, p. 16). Our contributors disagree on this issue. Burawoy and Przeworski raise it once again, this time in a new and much more politically-charged register. They remind us in effect that debates of the kind that have animated RCM since its comparatively recent inception take us back to the Marxist agenda. People make their own history, but not always, or not yet, as they please. Marx's aphorism still awaits a further specification, and the present volume explores the issues. Can Marx's views on the social construction of individuals generate a plausible individualism, ethical or methodological? Do his writings employ concepts that can be used theoretically to reconcile the social construction of individuals with the question of individual agency? These are complex matters, the complexity of which Marx acknowledged through his work.

With respect to the 'individual', Marx's starting point was neither putatively biological nor 'strictly' behavioural. It was logical. The important transformations in human behaviour that have produced a world where there are 'Benthams' is possible only because of a logic traceable within the concepts through which individuals are constructed and through which they then construct themselves. It is here perhaps that the relevance of RCM to Marx's own work – which is by no means as insubstantial a question as Elster once claimed – can best be established. It could well be that the application of analytical methods – strategic analysis, equilibrium theory, collective action theory, and decision-making theory – is an obvious way to develop the theory of the commodity-owner (including the wage-labourer) already begun by Marx. Roemer distinguished 'analytical' from 'conventional' Marxism by stressing the 'unabashed commitment to abstraction' exhibited by the former, but not by the latter. But abstraction is the very method that Marx recommended in *Capital* (1986, p. 90)! Indeed, what Roemer calls 'microfoundations' and 'mechanisms at the level of preference-formation' are precisely what Marx explored in his lifelong project – a critique of political economy.

There is of course a further concept of agency at work in the pages of *Capital* and elsewhere in Marx's writings. This concept of agency has a creative, open-ended character (hence the term *praxis*) in that it does not represent human beings as necessarily conforming to some biologically or psychologically inherent rationality, as some, though not all, rational choice theory does. The claim that a critical and creative power of reason is at the root of human agency – a species-claim – begins to bridge the gap between the way in which the mode of production of material life conditions the social, political and intellectual life-process in general, on the one hand, and the claim that proletarians and communists could exercise the sort of agency that the overthrow of capitalism might require, on the other. If offers us a way through the tenacious grip that the logic of commodity-production exercises on contemporary minds, not least through the sheer necessity it imposes on us to be agents of the utility-maximizing type. Marx's specific prescriptions may have been flawed, and his politics underdeveloped, but it is still worth being told that commodity-production is a logical structure and not the outcome of biological 'drives' or psychological 'preferences' – which we could hardly hope to dislodge (Carver 1992).

NOTES

1. The thrust of Brenner's work has been to emphasise the differences between pre-capitalist and capitalist modes of production in a way that points up the *absence* of any general form of the development of productive forces over the span of human history. Wood (see below, pp. 106–9) believes that 'Brenner's history of capitalist development puts in question nearly every point in Roemer's imaginary scenario.' Alan Carling, on the other hand, thinks that it is possible to reconcile Brenner and Roemer (see below, p. 59).

2 What is Analytical Marxism?
Erik Olin Wright

It is commonplace these days to speak of a crisis of Marxism. The evidence is easy enough to find:

First, there are the extraordinary changes taking place in societies ruled by communist parties under the ideological banner of Marxism. A decade ago it seemed that Marxist orthodoxy in one form or another was firmly in place as the ruling ideology of these societies. Now, with the success of Solidarity in Poland, the development of *perestroika* in the USSR and the emergence of widespread private enterprise in China, it is no longer clear what set of ideological principles actually guides the development of these societies.

Second, when we look at the policies and practices of communist, socialist, and social democratic parties in the advanced capitalist world, it is often very difficult to discern coherent programs for progressive social reform, let alone for revolutionary transformation. And it is certainly unclear whether or not the politics of most of these parties have even vestigial linkages to Marxism as a social theory.

Finally, when we look more narrowly at Marxist theory itself, one is struck both by the rapid exit of many radical intellectuals from Marxism in recent years towards something that is often called post-Marxism, as well as by the decline in consensus among the remaining Marxist intellectuals over the core theoretical postulates of Marxism itself.

Of course, there has always been deep and often bitter debate within the Marxist tradition. Such divisions in the past, however, generally revolved around a common core of theoretical, if not political, agreement – the labor theory of value as the basis for analyzing capitalism; historical materialism as the basis for analyzing epochal historical development; class structure and class struggle as the basis for understanding the state and ideology. At the present this core itself is much harder to discern, and there is certainly sharp disagreement over every one of its elements. There are now many theorists who consider themselves to be Marxists who nevertheless reject the labor theory of value as a satisfactory way of understanding capitalism, who are skeptical that historical materialism constitutes a plausible theory of history, and who see classes as only one of a variety of determinants of the state and ideology.

Now, one might argue that those who reject these classical core elements of Marxist theory should not rightfully call themselves Marxist. There is, after all, a venerable tradition in the history of Marxism to draw lines of demarcation between true Marxists and phony Marxists. The latter might use Marxist rhetoric, but they have abandoned Marxism itself. Alternatively, and I think more constructively, it could simply be recognized that Marxism is not a unified theory with well-defined boundaries, but a family of theories united by a common terrain of debate and questions. There has always been a plurality of Marxisms; what is new, perhaps, is the degree of theoretical and methodological heterogeneity that exists on this intellectual terrain.

Given this decline in intellectual consensus among Marxists over many of the core elements of their own theoretical tradition, it is certainly easy to see why many commentators consider this a period of profound theoretical crisis within Marxism, if not necessarily of the kind of mortal crisis proclaimed by the right. However, it is equally a period of considerable theoretical vitality and innovation in which significant progress is being made in clarifying a whole set of problems. While it may at times be difficult to distinguish 'crisis' from 'dynamic change', I believe that the Marxism which will emerge from the present period of theoretical transformation will not only be more powerful theoretically than the Marxism of the heyday of the New Left, but also of more political relevance as well.

In this paper I want to look at one particular strand of new theoretical development that has emerged rather forcefully as a tendency in the context of this internal turmoil in the Marxist tradition, particularly in the United States and Great Britain. This is a tendency that has come to be known as 'Analytical Marxism'. While Analytical Marxism is by no means the only vibrant intellectual current in contemporary Marxism, it does offer, in my judgement, the most promising general strategy for reconstructing Marxism.

THE EMERGENCE OF ANALYTICAL MARXISM

In the aftermath of the student movement and radical politics of the 1960s and early 1970s, Marxism entered the university in the developed capitalist democracies in an unprecedented way. Although with few exceptions Marxism never became a dominant perspective in academic departments, nevertheless it gained intellectual influence and even a measure of respectability in a wide variety of academic fields – history, sociology, education, political science, and economics, among others.

Analytical Marxism emerged in the late 1970s as one intellectual tendency within this newly influential academic Marxism.[1] It grew out of a belief that Marxism continued to constitute a productive intellectual tradition within which to ask questions and formulate answers, but that this tradition was frequently burdened with a range of methodological and metatheoretical commitments that seriously undermined its explanatory potential. The motivation for trying to rid Marxism of this burden was the conviction that the core ideas of Marxism, embodied in concepts like class, exploitation, the theory of history, capitalism, socialism, and so on, remained essential for any emancipatory political project.

As a self-conscious school of thought, Analytical Marxism began in 1979 when G. A. Cohen, a Canadian philosopher working in Britain, Jon Elster, a Norwegian political scientist, and a number of other scholars from several countries organized a meeting in London to discuss a range of theoretical issues in contemporary Marxism. This gathering subsequently became an annual event. After the third or fourth year, basically the same people have attended each year, with occasional additions and subtractions, to discuss each other's work. Currently, the group consists of G. A. Cohen, John Roemer, Jon Elster, Adam Przeworski, Robert Brenner, Philippe Van Parijs, Robert Van der Veen, Pranab Bardhan, Hillel Steiner, Sam Bowles, and myself.[2] In a somewhat self-mocking way, the group called itself the NBSMG – the 'No Bullshit Marxism Group'. The term 'Analytical Marxism' was first publicly used by the group in 1986 with the publication under that title of an anthology of essays written largely by members of the group (Roemer 1984).[3]

The substantive concerns of this collection of people are quite wide-ranging – including issues such as class structure, the theory of history, the problem of ideology, normative political theory, basic concepts of Marxian economics, social democracy and electoral politics, economic crisis, trade unions, and the state. Theoretically, there is considerable internal disagreement over virtually all issues within this group. In the course of the group's first ten years of meetings, there have been debates over the relevance of the concept of exploitation, methodological individualism, the ethical critique of 'capitalism between consenting adults', the centrality of class struggle to historical transitions, and the economic feasibility of reforming the welfare state through a system of unconditional grants of income to all citizens. On none of these theoretical problems was there thorough consensus in the group. And, equally, the political positions are quite diverse – from fairly traditional commitments to revolutionary democratic socialism to the Greens to what might be termed left-wing libertarianism.[4] Given such substantive, theoretical, and political diversity, what is it that unites this group of theorists and defines the essential core of Analytical Marxism?

WHAT IS 'ANALYTICAL' ABOUT ANALYTICAL MARXISM?

There are four specific commitments that I think characterize Analytical Marxism and justify considering it a distinct 'school' of contemporary Marxist thought:

(1) A commitment to *conventional scientific norms* in the elaboration of theory and the conduct of research.
(2) An emphasis on the importance of *systematic conceptualization*, particularly of concepts that are at the core of Marxist theory. This involves careful attention to both definitions of concepts and the logical coherence of interconnected concepts.
(3) A concern with a relatively *fine-grained specification of the steps in the theoretical arguments linking concepts*, whether the arguments be about causal processes in the construction of explanatory theories or about logical connections in the construction of normative theories.
(4) The importance accorded to *the intentional action of individuals* within both explanatory and normative theories.

It would be arrogant to suggest that Marxism lacked these elements prior to the emergence of Analytical Marxism as a self-conscious school. There have certainly been Marxists attentive to each of these issues, and there are Marxists attentive to them today who for one reason or another distance themselves from Analytical Marxism. What makes Analytical Marxism distinctive, then, is the extent to which these principles are brought to the forefront and systematically applied to the construction and reconstruction of theory.

In what follows, we will look at each of these points in turn, illustrating them with examples of specific work by Analytical Marxists. This will help to clarify what is analytical about Analytical Marxism. After this, we will briefly turn to the problem of what remains Marxist about it.

The Commitment to Conventional Scientific Norms

Marxism as a theoretical tradition has always had a rather peculiar relation to 'science'. On the one hand, there has always been a strong current within Marxism which is quite hostile to the canons of conventional science. Particularly in the strand of Marxism associated with the tradition of critical theory, positivism and claims to scientificity are often looked upon as instruments of ideological domination rather than emancipatory knowledge. On the other hand, the type of Marxism that has enthusiastically embraced the label 'scientific socialism' and claimed the status of a full-fledged 'science of society' has often been guilty of the most serious abuses of scientific norms. Self-styled 'Scientific Marxism' has often taken the form of a rigid ideology with pre-given answers to all questions, functioning more like a secular theology than a scientific discipline: Marxism became Marxology; classical texts were canonized; and the central arguments of the 'science' were impervious to transformation. Instead of constituting a theoretical apparatus capable of learning new things about the world – the hallmark of a scientific theory – scientific Marxism has often been a closed system of thought continually reaffirming itself through its own selective observations and interpretations. Marxism has thus either been hostile to science or adopted a particularly distorted and unscientific identification with science.

Analytical Marxists are committed to the view that Marxism should, without embarrassment, aspire to the status of a genuine social science. Marxism should not be absolved from the standards of science even if it accepts other standards of evaluation and relevance in addition to strictly scientific ones.

Such a commitment to scientificity leaves unspecified exactly what is meant by 'science', and this is, of course, a hotly contested issue in philosophy. Generally speaking, I think, most Analytical Marxists adopt what can be loosely described as a *realist* view of science.[5] This involves the following basic view of the scientific enterprise: science attempts to identify the *mechanisms* which generate the empirical phenomena we experience in the world. Our observations of those phenomena are simultaneously shaped by two kinds of mechanisms: mechanisms internal to the process of observation and mechanisms which directly generate the phenomenon in question. Because of this duality, it is in general impossible to inductively discover truths about mechanisms simply from raw empirical 'facts', since those facts are necessarily selected by the observation process itself. This implies a rejection of what might be called the naive empiricist view that we can gather facts about the world and use them to generate scientific knowledge without theoretically informed principles of selecting the objects of our observation. In this specific sense, observations cannot be theory-neutral, and therefore our theories cannot simply be inductive generalizations from raw 'facts'.[6] But Analytical Marxists would also reject the anti-realist view that our observations are wholly constituted by the categories of thought, by the discourses we use in describing the world. Scientific theories attempt to construct explanations based on real mechanisms that exist in the world independently of our theories even though the selection of observations of those mechanisms and their effects depend in part upon the theories themselves.

There are three important implications of the general acceptance of conventional scientific norms by Analytical Marxists: first, Analytical Marxists tend to be quite skeptical of traditional Marxist claims to a distinctive 'Marxist Methodology'; second, they tend to emphasize the importance of empirical research joined to systematic theoretical models for the advance of scientific knowledge; and third, they try to be open to continual reassessment of their own theoretical positions, acknowledging their theoretical failures as well as arguing for their successes.

There is a long tradition among Marxists which claims that Marxism has a distinctive method which differentiates it radically from 'bourgeois social science'. Such claims involve a familiar list of contrasts: Marxism is dialectical, historical, materialist, antipositivist, holist, while bourgeois social theory is undialectical, ahistorical, idealist, positivist, and individualist. Analytical Marxists are quite skeptical of the value of such claims.[7] This is not to say that all of the specific elements that are traditionally subsumed under the expression 'Marxist method' are rejected out of hand. Analytical Marxists, for example, have found ways of including notions of contradiction and even dialectics in their arguments. But when they do so they are generally quite careful to show how these complex ideas can be translated into a language of causes, mechanisms, and effects.

Take the notion of 'contradiction'. One way of explicating this concept is to treat it as a situation in which there are multiple conditions for the reproduction of a system which cannot all be simultaneously satisfied. Or, alternatively, a contradiction can be viewed as a situation in which the unintended consequences of a strategy subvert the accomplishment of its intended goals.[8] In either case, 'contradiction' is not treated as a philosophically driven way of interpreting the essence of a process, but as a way of explicating the interactions among a set of causal mechanisms.

What is Analytical Marxism? 17

This kind of translation of an element of Marxist method into a language of causal mechanisms would be characteristic of Analytical Marxism.

The second implication of the embrace of conventional scientific norms is a commitment to the importance of systematic empirical research. This is not to say that all Analytical Marxists are themselves directly engaged in empirical research. Some are primarily concerned with normative political theory and do not engage in empirical research at all. Others are concerned with explanatory models, but are primarily preoccupied with the elaboration of the logic of the models themselves. Nevertheless, most Analytical Marxists feel that an essential element in the elaboration of theories is the systematic confrontation with empirical research. This has led to the development of a number of substantial research projects by Analytical Marxists. My own research, for example, has involved conducting closely replicated social surveys on class structure, class biography, and class consciousness in eleven capitalist democracies: the United States, Sweden, Norway, Finland, Denmark, Britain, West Germany, Canada, Australia, New Zealand, and Japan. The central objective of this research has been to develop strictly comparable microlevel data on class and its effects in this set of countries so that we could systematically explore variations in the causal interconnections among class related variables across different macro-historical contexts.[9] Other empirical research projects by Analytical Marxists include Robert Brenner's research on the transition from feudalism to capitalism; Adam Przeworski's project on social democratic party politics; Joel Rogers's research on the interaction of the state and the labor movement in American history. While none of these projects is based on a belief in simple empirical 'tests' of complex theoretical ideas, they all affirm the conventional scientific view that theoretical advances depend in part on their engagement with relevant data from empirical research.

Finally, one of the striking properties of the work of Analytical Marxists is the extent to which they take seriously the problem of revising their own theoretical positions in the light of debate and criticism. Cohen's work on the Marxist theory of history has gone through a number of significant transformations in the light of issues raised in discussions of his original formulations. Roemer first developed a comprehensive concept of exploitation and then, in the context of critical discussions of this framework, moved on to question the very relevance of exploitation so defined for understanding and criticizing capitalism. And in my own work, my treatment of class structure has gone through at least two significant reconstructions in response to debates within class analysis.[10] The commitment to science, therefore, means that Analytical Marxists treat their arguments as needing to be continually subjected to criticism and revision rather than as constituting definitive embodiments of 'truth'.

Conceptualization

One of the distinctive signatures of work by Analytical Marxists is the amount of energy devoted to the elaboration of basic concepts. A great deal of time is spent defending specific definitions, discussing alternative criteria, examining the logical interconnections of concepts, puzzling over inconsistencies, and so on. Let me give an example from my own work, the definition of the 'middle class', to illustrate this concern with conceptualization.

Here is the problem: Marxian class concepts are built around a polarized notion of class relations. There are capitalists and workers, lords and serfs. What does it mean to occupy a middle-class location within such polarized relations? Traditionally, Marxists have dealt with this problem by treating the 'middle' class as a residual – any location that cannot be firmly situated within the bourgeoisie or the proletariat is, by default, in the 'middle class'. I wanted a positive specification of this kind of class location. In my work, I proposed two basic solutions. The first was to treat the middle class as those locations in the class structure which were simultaneously in two or more classes. Managers, for example, could be thought of as simultaneously in the bourgeoisie and the proletariat. I referred to such positions as 'contradictory class locations'. The second solution argued that capitalist societies consisted of multiple forms of exploitation, not simply capitalist exploitation proper. For example, following the work of John Roemer, I argued that the control over certain kinds of skills could constitute a mechanism of exploitation. The middle class, then, was defined as locations which were exploited capitalistically but were exploiters through some subordinate mechanism of exploitation.[11]

Many other examples of this kind of intensive work on concept formation could be given: John Roemer's work on exploitation; G. A. Cohen's analysis of forces of production or the meaning of 'proletarian unfreedom'; Jon Elster's discussion of the concept of 'solidarity'; Joel Rogers and Joshua Cohen's analysis of 'democracy'; Andrew Levine's analysis of 'freedom'.[12] In each case there is the assumption that a necessary condition for the development of powerful theories is the elaboration of logically coherent concepts. It is in part from this preoccupation that Analytical Marxism gets its name: the analytical coherence of concepts is essential for the explanatory power of theories.

Elaboration of Explicit Models

One of the striking characteristics of Analytical Marxism has been the use of explicit abstract models, sometimes highly formalized as in game theory, other times somewhat less formalized as causal models. Many Marxists (as well as non-Marxist radicals) find such models objectionable on the grounds that they involve such dramatic simplifications of the complexity of real world situations that they cannot possibly deepen our knowledge of the world. Analytical Marxists counter such objections on several grounds:

First, the fact that models constitute simplifications of complexity is not in and of itself a failing, but a virtue. This is precisely what we want a good theory to do: to get to the heart of a complex problem by identifying the central mechanisms involved.

Second, the essential structure of a formal model is to create a thought experiment of some process. That is, one is forced to specify the underlying assumptions of the model, the conditions which are treated as parameters, and the ways in which the mechanisms work. The clarity forced upon a theorist by making explicit such assumptions and arguments is desirable. Furthermore, since in real-life social situations it is generally hard to construct real experimental conditions for revealing the operation of causal mechanisms (or even, through comparative methods, quasi-experimental designs), thought experiments are essential to give plausibility to the causal claims we actually make about any concrete problem.

Finally, it is generally the case that lurking behind every informal causal explanation is a tacit formal model. All explanatory theories contain assumptions, claims about the conditions under which the explanations hold, claims about how the various mechanisms fit together. The difference between what Analytical Marxists do and what many historical and empirical Marxist researchers do, then, may be basically a question of the extent to which they are prepared to put their cards on the table and articulate the causal models in their theories.

To get a sense of how Analytical Marxists actually use these kinds of models to engage Marxist questions, it will be useful to look in some detail at two prominent examples: Adam Przeworski's analysis of social democracy, which relies on elements of rational choice theory, and G. A. Cohen's reconstruction of Marx's theory of history, which is built around functional explanations.[13]

Adam Przeworski develops a general theoretical model of the historical trajectory of social-democratic politics in capitalist societies. He argues that once bourgeois democratic institutions are in place, social-democratic parties face a series of dilemmas when selecting a political strategy. The first dilemma is whether or not to participate in elections at all. If they participate, they risk incorporation into the machine of state domination; if they abstain from participation, they risk political marginalization. Second, if they decide to participate, they face a dilemma rooted in their electoral base. If they attempt to be a pure working-class party, then they can adopt a consistent set of pro-working-class policies, but they will never get an electoral majority (since the working class is never a majority of the population); if they seek alliances with various segments of the middle class, then they dilute their working-class base and ultimately alienate their working-class support.[14]

Przeworski then shows, using formal mathematical models, that: (a) given the distribution of the population into the class structure, and (b) the historical legacy of past strategies on the patterns of loyalty to and defection from parties by people in different classes, then (c) it is possible to define the maximum and minimum levels of the total vote that are available to the social-democratic party at any given time. These define what could be called the 'Gramsci bounds' on electoral strategies: the limits of what is possible under the historically embodied constraints. The cumulative effect of past strategies and current structures, then, is an historical trajectory of changing possibilities. Przeworski develops both mathematical models of this trajectory of limits for various countries, and then an empirical investigation of the actual trajectory of electoral outcomes that occur within these limits.

A second example is G. A. Cohen's analysis of classical historical materialism. Cohen's task is to try to see what kind of explanation is represented by the Marxist theory of history. He wants to reconcile a number of distinct theses: (1) the level of development of the forces of production determines the form of social relations of production; (2) the economic structure (the totality of all relations of production) determines the political superstructure; (3) the relations of production explain the development of the forces of production; (4) the superstructure explains the persistence of the economic structure. Cohen argues that these propositions can be made consistent only if they are linked together through a series of functional explanations. Thus, for example, he argues that for statements (2) and (4) above both to be true, the word 'determines' in statement (2) must mean 'functionally explains'. The superstructure must be functionally explained by the economic base in the following way: the superstructure takes the form that it does because the economic base needs it in order to be reproduced. This may or may not, of course, be a plausible theory either of the relationship between economic and noneconomic institutions or of historical development; but it is the necessary form of the argument if the specific elements of the theory as developed by Marx are to be internally consistent.

What is striking in both of these examples is not mainly the abstract substantive claims which they make. After all, Przeworski's argument could be basically viewed as an example of Marx's famous statement that 'Men make their own history, but under circumstances not of their choosing', applied to the specific problem of socialist electoral politics. And Cohen's analysis is directly based on Marx's analysis of the 'dialectical relation' between forces and relations of production. What is novel in this work is the rigor of the effort at specifying the details of the mechanisms which underlie these more abstract claims. This not only enhances the depth of our understanding of the abstract arguments themselves, but makes it much easier to identify their weaknesses and reconstruct them in light of empirical research.

The Importance of Choice
The feature of Analytical Marxism that has caused the most controversy, perhaps, is the self-conscious use by certain Analytical Marxists of rational-actor models, including mathematical game theory.[15] This has led some people to rename Analytical Marxism 'Rational Choice Marxism',[16] and to characterize it as embodying a general commitment to methodological individualism (i.e., to the methodological claim that all social phenomena are in principle explainable exclusively with reference to individuals and their attributes).

This identification of Analytical Marxism with methodological individualism is, I believe, mistaken. Indeed, a number of Analytical Marxists have been explicitly critical of methodological individualism and have argued against the exclusive reliance on models of abstract rationality as a way of understanding human action.[17] What is true, however, is that most Analytical Marxists take quite seriously the problem of understanding the relationship between individual choice and social processes. This does not imply that social processes can be *reduced* to problems of individual intentionality, nor does it imply that instrumental rationality is the ubiquitous basis for intentional action; but it does mean that social theory should systematically incorporate a concern with conscious choice. One way of doing this is through rational-actor models of various kinds.

Now, it is certainly possible to acknowledge the usefulness of the intellectual discipline of constructing formal models, and yet reject rational choice models as simply being stupid models. Particularly given the historical identification of rational actor theory with neoclassical economics, what is the attraction of this particular kind of model to many Analytical Marxists? I think the attraction lies in the importance most Analytical Marxists give to a particular analytical task, namely elaborating what is sometimes called the *micro-foundations* of macro-structural theory – that is, analyzing the mechanisms through which individuals come to act the way they do within a set of structurally defined social relations. Whatever else one might want of a social theory, if we want to understand the mechanisms through which a given social cause generates its effects, we must try to understand why individuals act the way they do. And in this context, rational actor models and game theory provide a systematic strategy for analyzing one particularly salient aspect of individual action: action that results from conscious choices in which the costs and benefits are assessed over a range of feasible alternatives within a set of social constraints. If you believe (a) that at least in some important social contexts actors make conscious choices, and (b) that when they make choices they take into consideration the expected consequences of their actions, and finally, (c) that in assessing such consequences they take into consideration the choices of other actors – that is, that they act strategically, not just rationally – then something like game theory and rational choice theory would be an appropriate part of one's repertoire of analytical techniques.

The difference between the way Analytical Marxists deploy these kinds of models and the way neoclassical economists and political scientists deploy them lies not in the internal logic of the models themselves, but in the kinds of problems they are used to address and the ways in which the 'conditions of existence' of the models are specified. Thus, for example, John Roemer uses rational choice theory to explore the problem of exploitation. In his analysis, the central conditions faced by actors are particular systems of property relations which give different actors monopolies over particular kinds of resources. He then uses the formal mathematical models of rational choice theory to show how exploitation is generated out of such conditions. Thus, while Roemer adopts the formal mathematical apparatus of 'bourgeois' models in his work, he asks different questions from neoclassical economists and he characterizes the environment of rational choice in a very different way. As a result, he comes to very different conclusions: far from generating optimal distributional consequences in a market environment, Roemer concludes that individual optimizing strategies systematically generate exploitation and classes.

To be sure, there are limits to the explanatory capacity of formal models built around rational action. Thus, most Analytical Marxists would agree that these kinds of models need to be supplemented in a variety of ways with other kinds of explanations in the construction of social theory.

Examples include such things as functional explanations in G. A. Cohen's analysis of the theory of history; subintentional causal explanations in Jon Elster's analysis of the cognitive underpinnings of ideology; and institutional-structural explanations in my work on class formation and Robert Brenner's work on economic crisis. One of the innovations of Analytical Marxism, then, is the attempt to systematically link, within a Marxist theoretical agenda, these sorts of explanatory strategies with the analysis of individual rationality and choice.

WHAT IS 'MARXIST' ABOUT ANALYTICAL MARXISM?

I have stressed in these comments what is 'analytical' about 'Analytical Marxism'. One might ask, when all is said and done, what about it remains 'Marxist'. Analytical Marxists reject claims about the methodological distinctiveness of Marxism; they adopt the full repertoire of 'bourgeois' scientific practices; and they constantly question the core concepts and traditional theses of Marxism. What, then, is Marxist about this theoretical enterprise? I would emphasize three things in answer to this question:

First, most of the work of Analytical Marxists self-conciously works on Marxism as a theoretical tradition. The typical intellectual strategy is to take some core theme or argument in Marxism, establish the necessary conditions for this argument to be sustainable, and then reconstruct the argument in light of the plausibility of those conditions.

Second, the broader agenda of theoretical and empirical questions which Analytical Marxists pose are generally firmly rooted in the discourse and traditions of Marxism. The topics of research – the transition from feudalism to capitalism, the relationship of class structure to class consciousness, the dilemmas of socialist politics, the conditions for solidarity and fragmentation of the working class – clearly take their intellectual coordinates from the Marxist tradition. Even if the *answers* to these questions may deviate considerably from classical Marxist answers, the questions themselves are characteristically Marxist.

Third, the language used to frame answers to these questions is also deeply embedded in Marxist discourse. Class, ideology, consciousness, exploitation, the state, and so on constitute the conceptual repertoire of Analytical Marxism much as they do of Marxism in general. As Alvin Gouldner has argued, Marxism should be considered what he called an 'ideal speech community', an intellectual terrain of dialogue rather than a body of consensually accepted theses. Analytical Marxists work on this terrain and share in this dialogue even if they transform many of the traditionally defended theses.

Finally, and perhaps most problematically given their political heterogeneity, Analytical Marxists broadly share the core normative orientation of Marxism in general. In varying degrees, their work is animated by a commitment to values of freedom, equality, and human dignity, and generally they are sympathetic to some conception of democratic socialism as the institutional vehicle for the realization of these values. While these values may be shared by many post- or non-Marxist radical intellectuals, the linkage between these values on the one hand and the theoretical agenda of questions and debate on the other systematically anchor Analytical Marxism in the Marxist tradition.

Explaining what it is about Analytical Marxism that makes it Marxist does not, of course, constitute an argument for why one should bother with such an arduous effort at reconstructing Marxism with the intellectual tools of modern social science. Quite apart from a general skepticism about the virtues of science, many radicals are even more skeptical about the virtues of Marxism. Putting the two together might seem a particularly diabolical medicine, more likely to poison than to invigorate radical thought. Why should a radical attempt to revitalize Marxism in this way?

I cannot, in this essay, provide anything approaching a systematic defense of Marxism as an intellectual tradition within which to produce radical theory. And, I should add, that not all the theorists who engage in Analytical Marxism would regard such a defense as particularly important. Some participants in the intellectual project of Analytical Marxism regard Marxism as simply one of a variety of sources of ideas, concepts, and tools. Indeed, they may not actually consider themselves to be 'Marxists' of even a weak persuasion. While they may find the intellectual task of analytically reconstructing Marxism to be a productive one, it is not out of any deep commitment to Marxism as such. It is thus possible to 'do' Marxism (make contributions to the reconstruction of Marxist theory) without 'being' a Marxist (having a general commitment, political and theoretical, to the Marxist tradition).

In these terms I am among the more intransigently Marxist of the Analytical Marxists. My defense of Marxism as a theoretical tradition, therefore, should not be taken as characteristic of Analytical Marxism as such.

There are two basic reasons why Marxism remains an essential theoretical framework for radical analysis: (1) The *questions* that are at the heart of

What is Analytical Marxism? 25

Marxism continue to be critical for any plausible political project for radical social change; (2) the *conceptual framework* for tackling those questions continues to produce new and insightful *answers*.

First, the questions. At the core of Marxism is the problem of explaining the development of forms of domination and exploitation that are rooted in the social organization of production, particularly in the historical epoch of capitalism, in order to understand the possibilities for the radical transformation of such systems of domination and exploitation. Marxist theory is preoccupied with understanding the potentials, constraints and dilemmas on radical social change imposed by the system of class relations. In the case of capitalism, this means that Marxism attempts to construct a scientific theory of the possibility of socialism, where socialism is understood as the central social form through which capitalist exploitation and domination can be transcended.

In these terms, Marxists have a distinctively *Marxist* interest in ideology, the state, culture, gender, race, etc., only in so far as these bear on the problem of understanding class relations and their potentials for radical transformation. Of course, the *people* who are Marxists may also be, for example, feminists, and thus have an interest in gender relations because of a desire to understand the development of gender oppression and the potentials for its transformation independently of the relevance of such concerns for class as such. But Marxism as a theoretical structure does not itself have anything *systematically Marxist* to say about this. Or, perhaps more precisely, once Marxism has been shorn of insupportable explanatory claims – such as the claim that male domination is to be entirely explained functionally by its role in reproducing class domination – then Marxism as such does not theorize the essential mechanisms that produce and reproduce gender relations. Marxism in this sense is 'sex-blind'. This, however, is not in my judgement a weakness of Marxism; it is a theoretical advance that there is now more precision in its range of theoretical relevance and explanatory capacities.[18] Of course, there may in the future be further scientific advances in which some more general theoretical structure is capable of fully integrating Marxist accounts of class mechanisms and feminist accounts of gender mechanisms into some more comprehensive theoretical system. But there is no necessary reason to believe that this will be possible, and in any case, until such theoretical synthesis occurs it is appropriate to consider class and gender to be distinct mechanisms, each requiring its own set of concepts and explanations.[19]

One might well ask why a person committed to understanding gender oppression or race oppression should care about the Marxist questions. If Marxism – or, at least, Analytical Marxism – no longer pretends to provide a comprehensive explanation of gender domination, why should feminists be interested in Marxism? I believe that a concern with class-based domination and exploitation should be central to the theoretical agenda of political radicals even if their commitments are more preoccupied with problems of race or gender or some other dimension of social life. In so far as projects of radical social change confront constraints embedded in the system of property relations – for example, day care costs money, the availability of these resources depends upon taxes, the tax base depends upon investment under the control of capitalists – then radicals in general need an understanding of class mechanisms. Marxism is still the theoretical tradition which, in my judgement, has most comprehensively explored those mechanisms.

It is not enough, of course, to defend the Marxist tradition for asking important questions. For Marxism as a theoretical perspective to be relevant today it is also important to defend the conceptual framework for producing answers to the questions it asks. Familiar Marxist concepts – class structure, exploitation, class struggle, class formation, mode of production, economic structure, the state, ideology – have come under systematic scrutiny in recent years, and as a result there has been considerable progress in specifying their explanatory potentials. As a result, while Marxists have generally narrowed their explanatory pretensions over the past decade or so, there has also been complementary deepening of the answers to the questions they pose using this repertoire of concepts.

The theoretical contributions by the participants in the 'Production and Democracy' series in *SR* amply illustrate this vitality of the Marxist tradition. Michael Burawoy's work on the labor process and factory regimes has significantly advanced our knowledge of the mechanisms through which cooperation is forged within production by showing how the adaptive strategies of workers and the responses of capitalists jointly shape a set of 'rules of the game' within which the interests of workers and capitalists are coordinated.[20] Sam Bowles' and Herb Gintis's work on the political nature of exchange relations in capitalism has given much more precision to our understanding of the role of power in a competitive economy by showing how control over assets inherently generates asymmetries of power within exchange (Bowles and Gintis 1990). Adam Przeworski's work on social democracy, discussed earlier, has powerfully illuminated the dilemmas posed to working-class politics in democratic capitalism by showing how democratic institutions force socialist parties to choose between an erosion of socialist ideals (if they seek class alliances to expand their electoral base) or permanent marginalization (if they remain faithful to radical visions of working-class interests). This body of work testifies to the continued capacity of research using Marxian conceptual tools to produce new answers to enduring questions.

THE RISKS AND REWARDS OF ANALYTICAL MARXISM

Analytical Marxism argues that to revitalize Marxism and reconstruct its theoretical power it must enthusiastically adopt the most sophisticated tools of contemporary social science. And, if Marxism hopes to play an active role inside of the academy in countering the ideological dominance of conservative and liberal currents of social research, it has to adopt the methodologically most powerful weapons available or risk permanent isolation and marginalization.

Has this strategy worked? What kind of real impact has Analytical Marxism had, either in the university or in the broader world of radical politics? Analytical Marxism is only about a decade old as a self-consciously constituted perspective, and thus it is probably premature to try to make a systematic assessment of its effects. Furthermore, as a partisan advocate of Analytical Marxism, it would in any case be hard for me to dispassionately weigh the evidence. Nevertheless, I think that there are at least some indications that this approach to Marxist theory has begun to have some impact beyond its immediate circle of supporters.

Despite the worldwide decline in Marxist scholarship, work by Analytical Marxists is increasingly appearing in publications around the world oriented towards progressive audiences outside of the academy. Analytical Marxist ideas are beginning to have an influence on public discussions on the left, and Analytical Marxist work has been translated into 13 languages. In more academic terms, a number of publications have appeared containing extended critiques of Analytical Marxism, which is also an indication that it is becoming more influential.[21] At a more institutional level, several of the central advocates of Analytical Marxism have gained positions of considerable importance within their universities.[22]

There are many radicals who will accuse this new breed of academic Marxists of careerism and opportunism.[23] It is certainly the case that assuming these kinds of institutional roles does pose risks and may both reflect and generate serious compromises of political commitments. The same can be said about the basic methodological strategy of Analytical Marxism: just as adopting the political weapons of capitalist democracy risks incorporating socialists into the normal regulative functions of the capitalist state, so adopting the scientific practices of conventional social science risks neutralizing the revolutionary aspirations of Marxism. Above all, there is the risk of narrowing the field of legitimate questions to those that are tractable with these sophisticated tools. Statistically rigorous data analysis tends to restrict investigations to problems that are easily quantifiable; rational choice theory tends to direct attention to those problems of strategic interaction that can be formally modeled within the repertoire of game-theory models.

These risks need to be acknowledged and resisted. But to respond to them by refusing to build enclaves of radical scholarship within leading universities robs Marxism of the capacity to play an effective role in the academy; and, to cope with these risks by rejecting these analytical and scientific methods altogether undermines the ability of Marxism to enhance its theoretical understandings of the world in ways which will enable it, once again, to play an effective role in politics.

NOTES

1. The term 'academic Marxism' is often used pejoratively, suggesting politically disengaged careerism and intellectual opportunism. While the expression does embody a certain irony, since Marxism is above all a social theory committed to transforming the world rather than simply reflecting on it from the ivory tower, I do not mean to impugn the motives of Marxists who work in the university by referring to them as 'academic Marxists'. Rather, this expression reflects the historical reality that in the present period, Marxism is most rigorously articulated and elaborated within academic disciplines rather than within revolutionary movements as such.
2. Some of the most important works published by this cast of characters would include: Cohen (1978); Roemer (1982a); Przeworski (1985a); Wright (1985); Brenner (1985); Elster (1985); van Parijs (1981); Bowles and Gintis (1986). Analytical Marxism is by no means restricted to the people who participate in the annual London meeting. Work by other scholars in the Analytical Marxist mode would include Levine (1984); Levine (1987); Miller (1984); Cohen and Rogers (1983).
3. The term itself seems to have been coined by Jon Elster in a seminar around 1980.
4. At one point in the history of the annual London meeting tensions generated by this political diversity sparked a serious disagreement over whether or not there should be any political-ideological criteria for 'membership' in the annual meeting. After considerable discussion of the matter it was decided that the essential principle of the group's cohesion was the possibility of

constructive dialogue among the participants rather than actual adherence to a set of political positions.

5. The issue of scientific realism, particularly of the sort advanced here, has not been explicitly discussed within the Analytical Marxist group. While I think that this perspective on the philosophy of science is quite consistent with the strategies of analysis one finds among Analytical Marxists, my arguments should not be viewed as being held by Analytical Marxists generally. The account of realism which I discuss here is based on the work of Bhaskar (1978) and Bhaskar (1979).

6. The argument that our theories shape what we choose to look at – by framing our questions and the choice of which facts to observe – does not imply that the actual observations we make *given these principles of selection* are necessarily 'biased' or distorted by our theories. 'Facts' can be 'objective' in the sense that anyone who used the same principles of selection would come up with the same facts.

7. Perhaps the strongest statement of this skepticism was made in the first chapter of Elster (1985), where he categorically denounces claims to a distinctive Marxian method as the unfortunate influence of Hegelian philosophy on Marx's work.

8. The meaning of contradiction preferred by Jon Elster. See Elster (1978) and Elster (1985) for discussions of this view of contradiction.

9. The scope and initial results of this project are briefly reviewed in Wright (1989).

10. For the revisions of Cohen's views on the theory of history, see Cohen (1989). Roemer's questioning of the relevance of exploitation can be found in Roemer (1985). The trajectory of my views on class structure is reviewed in the concluding chapter of Wright (1990).

11. The logical structure of these two conceptualizations is extensively discussed in the concluding chapter of Wright (1990).

12. Roemer (1982); Cohen (1978), Ch. 2; Cohen (1986); Elster (1985), Ch. 6.2; Cohen and Rogers (1983); Levine (1984).

13. See Przeworski (1985), and Przeworski and Sprague (1986); Cohen (1978).

14. A third dilemma occurs if a working-class socialist party were to get elected: should the party try to enact reforms within the constraints of capitalism, in which case it risks abandoning its socialist project; or should it try to initiate a transition to socialism, in which case it risks retaliation from capitalists and accompanying severe economic disruption which, in turn, would erode its electoral base?

15. Rational actor models of various sorts have played a particularly prominent role in the work of Jon Elster, John Roemer, and Adam Przeworski. See especially the defence of methodological individualism in the introduction to Elster (1985).

16. See, for example, Alan Carling, below, pp. 32–3, 70 n. 8.

17. See, in particular, Levine, Sober and Wright (1987). See also the exchange in *Socialist Review* between Adam Przeworksi and Michael Burawoy (below, pp. 136–99).

18. Feminists often criticize Marxism for being sex-blind, whereas I think that the sex-blindness of Marxism may actually enhance its usefulness for feminists. Marxism should not be a variety of feminism, attempting to somehow

subsume the specificity of gender oppression within its concepts. Various attempts to treat male domination as a species of class domination have largely obscured rather than clarified the relationship between gender and class. Marx*ists* may be sex-blind in the sense of not recognizing the importance of gender mechanisms in answering the questions which they ask; but it does not follow from this that Marxist *concepts* should be systematically gendered.

19. This argument endorses a variety of what is sometimes called a 'dual systems' approach to the relation of class and gender, although I would prefer to call it a 'dual mechanisms' approach, since I do not want to insist that class relations and gender relations are each fully integrated into some encompassing 'system'.

20. Burawoy (1985). Burawoy has at times distanced his own work from Analytical Marxism, first because he doubts the usefulness of formal rational actor models, and second because he is skeptical about the hard claims to 'science' made by Analytical Marxists. In spite of these disclaimers, I believe that his work does satisfy the four criteria for Analytical Marxism which I laid out at the outset of this essay.

21. Two issues of the journal *Politics and Society* have been devoted to discussions of Analytical Marxist work, one in 1985 on John Roemer's analysis of class and exploitation, and one in 1990 on Samuel Bowles' and Herbert Gintis's work on contested exchange. *Critical Sociology*, the *Berkeley Journal of Sociology* and *Theory and Society* have each contained symposia on problems of Analytical Marxism, while an entire issue of the *Canadian Journal of Philosophy* was devoted to Analytical Marxism in 1989. *Socialist Review* published a series of essays from within this perspective in 1989 (see below, 136–99). Examples and critiques of Analytical Marxism have appeared in *New Left Review* (see below, 31–135), *Philosophy and Public Affairs*, the *Review of Radical Economics*, and other journals. Examples of books containing extended critiques of Analytical Marxism include Carchedi (1987), Kamolnick (1988), Resnick and Wolff (1987).

22. Examples include Robert Brenner, the director of the Center for Comparative History and Social Theory at UCLA; John Roemer, the head of the Program in Economics, Justice and Society at the University of California, Davis: and myself, Director of the A. E. Havens Center for the Study of Social Structure and Social Change at the University of Wisconsin. While none of these centers can be considered 'Institutes of Analytical Marxism' – they all try to serve a relatively broad progressive community in their universities – they do represent a higher level of institutional support for this kind of theoretical exercise than existed in the past.

23. Russel Jacoby, in *The Last Intellectuals* (New York: Basic Books, 1987) makes this kind of accusation in a particularly strident and unsympathetic way.

3 Rational Choice Marxism[1]
Alan Carling

In 1977 and 1978, Paul Hirst and Barry Hindess published with their collaborators the two volumes of *Marx's 'Capital' and Capitalism Today*. In the latter year Gerald Cohen published *Karl Marx's Theory of History: A Defence*. In retrospect, it is possible to see in these events a turning-point for Anglophone Marxist theory, and the latest evidence of the remarkable capacity of Western Marxism to renew itself, despite everything. Hirst and Hindess, who had been for almost a decade the most influential English exponents of Althusserian Marxism, seemed to announce in 1977 their utter despair at systematic social thought in general and Marxist theory in particular. It appeared that the Althusserian project, initially promising nothing less than a total reconstruction of history and politics on a new basis of social science, had lapsed and crumbled into dust.[2] The virtues of Cohen's work only served to throw this denouement into sharper relief. It might be said tendentiously that while Althusserians talked a great deal about rigour, Cohen actually practised it. His argument was careful, painstaking: chock-a-block with nice distinctions other people hadn't dreamt were there.[3] It proceeded step by step, analytically. It was no longer a case of gathering Marxism into one great mouthful to be swallowed whole or not at all. Instead, Marxism was to be sorted into a list of distinct claims: each one deserving its own interrogation for meaning, coherence, plausibility and truth. The logical relation between claims was an explicit topic of the theory, so that it became more open to judgement which parts of a complex Marxist corpus stood and fell together.

A CUMULATIVE SHIFT

Despite the peculiar authority of his own work, Cohen was never alone in making the analytical move. It is now possible to see a range of other writers – especially John Roemer and Jon Elster, but also Norman Geras, Allen Wood, Adam Przeworski, Phillipe van Parijs, Erik Olin Wright Mark-II, Robert Brenner and all those of us who have bobbed about in the wake of Michio Morishima and Ian Steedman – as contributing in different fields to a cumulative shift in the accents of Marxist theory. Something of a parallel is apparent in the development of a 'critical human geography' by Doreen Massey and her collaborators, and also in the work of anarchist inspiration produced by the inimitable Michael Taylor.[4]

Inevitably, it is easier to detect that a decisive shift has taken place than to say in what exactly it consists. Precisely because the shift is analytical in the sense suggested above, one would not expect to find a new consensus of opinion across the whole spectrum of concerns brought into a new focus: historical materialism, the labour theory of value, class structure and exploitation, the relation between the individual and the social, conceptions of reason and human nature, the historical reference and general relevance of moral judgements, and much else besides. If complex topics like these are to be picked apart and probed and worried as a deliberate − almost obsessive − policy of method, it is not surprising that a range of competing views quickly becomes evident. This sense of variety will only be enhanced by an accompanying determination to face rather than evade the legacy of awkward questions that the history of the twentieth century has bequeathed Marxist theory − above all, the painful failure of revolution in the West and the almost equally painful success of revolution in the East.[5]

It is, of course, perfectly true (and important) that the attempt to assimilate this history has distinguished Western Marxism as a whole, but the ways in which this has worked itself out have often been rather oblique.[6] Sometimes it has paid homage to canonical texts with an extravagance disclosing the real distance travelled from them. At other times, it has moved into fields which, though very important in their own right, are set apart from the main interests of classical Marxist social and political theory: fields such as epistemology and metaphysics, literary and cultural theory, theories of ideology and aesthetics, the encounter between Marxism and psychoanalysis, and so on. Given the displacements making up this intellectual history, the analytical turn may be represented both as a continuation of the concerns of Western Marxism by other means and a *critical return to the classical agenda*.[7]

This sense of a return with fresh eyes is equally evident in Cohen's defence of a newly sophisticated version of technological determinism, in Steedman's and Roemer's critiques of the labour theory of value, in Geras's reflections on the *Theses on Feuerbach*, in Elster's presentation of Marx as a pioneer in the theory of collective action, and in Wood's persistence in that deceptive classical question: 'What's wrong with capitalism?'. This line of thought might suggest 'neo-classical Marxism' as an appropriate title for the new tendency. Other suggestions already in the field include 'Analytical Marxism', 'Game-theoretic Marxism', and − stretching a point – Post-post-classical Marxism. To the extent that a name is important, I would prefer the term *Rational Choice Marxism* to collect the new work under a single heading, and to suggest why a single heading may be appropriate. For if there is one distinctive presupposition of the intended body of work, it must be the view that societies are composed of human individuals who, being endowed with resources of various kinds, attempt to choose rationally between various courses of action.[8]

So much is a commonplace of that broad sweep of conventional economics and philosophy conducted in the liberal tradition. What makes the difference (and it is a dramatic one) is the joining of this presupposition with the classical agenda of Marxist theory. In the most schematic terms, the result is the subversion of a received dichotomy between social pattern and individual choice. That is, fundamental social pattern comes to be represented as the (usually unintended) outcome of choices made by deliberating agents. This approach is liable to prove as unsettling for those Marxists who have come close to the denial of individual choice as it will be for those anti-Marxists (or Marxist anti-theorists!) who have come close to the denial of fundamental social pattern. It has often seemed, in other words, as if there is one box, marked 'agentless structure', in which one peers to find modes of production, grand historical designs, epochal social change, ideological hegemony, sociological analysis, determinism and constraint, while one looks to another, marked 'structureless agency', to find the individual, volition and choice, moral judgement, politics-as-it-is-lived and history-as-it-is-experienced. If these options were the only two on offer, Marxists would indeed face a cruel dilemma, since their basic mental equipment ought to alert them equally to the existence of structured inequality, the efficacy of political action and the importance of the concrete historical process.

At least in specific domains of theory, rational choice Marxism opens up the third, transcendent box. It becomes possible to grant individual autonomy without thereby abandoning structured inequality (Roemer) or historical pattern (Cohen). No longer does the choice lie between agentless structure and structureless agency: the structure is now a structure of human agency.[9] It thus seems possible to sum up this whole change of perspective in one phrase: the reinstatement of the subject.

COHEN ON HISTORY AND SOCIAL STRUCTURE

In *Karl Marx's Theory of History* Cohen committed Marx once again to the view that history has a pattern, and that the pattern results from human deliberation in the face of scarcity. Accordingly, human rationality joined with historical scarcity creates a pressure to improve productive technique (to raise the level of the forces of production) which is ultimately unstoppable. Rationality works directly in the development and choice of productive technique and indirectly in the choice of social relations most suited to the further development of productive technique from its existing level. This latter gloss of Cohen's is intended to bypass the standing counter-example to straightforward technological determinism – namely, the effect that the relations of production undoubtedly have on the development of the forces of production (never more so than under capitalism). If one goes on to assume as an empirical premise that any given set of (pre-communist) relations of production will be unable to cope with forces of production developed beyond a certain level, a periodic choice of new economic structures is almost certain to occur.[10] Such revolutionary transitions divide historical epochs. The pattern of history is given in the corresponding sequence of economic structures, culminating in that high, unfettered regime of productive technique that communism is, or is supposed to be.

This bald view (very badly stated here) has been subjected to considerable refinement and amendment in the debates since 1978. It has been said by Wright and Levine that Cohen's reconstruction still relies on too individualist and trans-historical a concept of human rationality. Cohen has entered doubts himself concerning Marx's 'one-sided anthropology' and about the simple-minded view of 'fettering' that the earlier theory seems to involve. Elster has called for much closer specification of the mechanism through which the choice of new relations of production is registered in history, contributing thereby to the important and wide-ranging debate on the possibility of functional explanation in the social sciences which Cohen's treatment has inspired. Van Parijs has advanced a solution of the 'primacy puzzle' in terms of a 'slow dynamics' (of forces of production) 'embedded in a fast dynamics' of changing relations of production when the latter are in contradiction with the former. Both Elster and Wright and Levine introduce in different ways the role of political organization and timing in enhancing or frustrating the revolutionary transitions basic to the theory – and thereby bring into the new theoretical context all the old questions revolving around the distinction between class-in-itself and class-for-itself. Brenner has gone further in suggesting that the logic of the situation of the pre-capitalist peasantry often inclines it directly against the development of the forces of production.[11]

For present purposes, however, I wish to focus on Cohen's enduring reorientation of the 'theoretical object' in the chapters preceding his original statement of the theory itself. First, Cohen emphasized the distinction between the *material* and the *social* as basic to Marx's thought. This contrast introduces non-standard connotations of both terms, such that 'material' loses its ordinary contrast with 'mental'. The motive for this change is that knowledge (a mental phenomenon) is clearly central to the development of forces of production.[12] If the definition of the latter excludes knowledge, then Marx's theory of history cannot be materialist, whatever else it may be. Further, productively useful knowledge must be conceptually distinct from relations of production (from the 'social') in order for the theory to gain any empirical leverage. This does not, of course, mean that the creation, dissemination and utilization of productively useful knowledge are independent of relations of production. Quite the contrary, the theory is at bottom *about* the interdependence of social relations of production with the creation, dissemination and utilization of productively useful knowledge (in order to overcome scarcity).

If 'material' loses its ordinary contrast with 'mental', then 'social' loses its ordinary contrast with 'individual'. In Cohen's view, Marx uses the term 'social' in a special, power-denoting sense. Taking people and things people need (use-values) as its basic elements, Marx's theory centres on the relationships obtaining among people and use-values as they evolve through history. These relationships do not, however, set 'the individual' over against 'society': rather, the 'social' denotes these people, things and relationships under power-laden descriptions, while the 'material' denotes them under power-neutral descriptions.[13] The ordinary-language distinction between the 'social' and the 'individual' breaks down because individuals (or things) are importantly described by their relational properties, which may include social relational properties. That is, the same physical individual may be described in material terms as a computer operator (which is not purely 'physical' since it has reference to mental qualities – 'skill') or in social terms as a wage-earner. The person is evidently no less an individual under the second kind of description than she is under the first.[14]

These points would not be so important for the subsequent development of rational choice Marxism were it not for the general redirection of the sociological imagination that they entail. Visually, the effect is to *set societies back on the level*.[15] In other words, the reinstatement of societies as sets of relationships among individuals (and things) undermines the deeply ingrained habit of seeing societies in terms of hierarchies, pyramids, diamonds, heaps, layer cakes, jellies, blancmanges and other party pieces of social stratification.[16] Where it has not shared directly in this impression that people go around standing on each other's shoulders, recent Marxist theory has still used a metaphor of levels powerful enough to tear people apart and distribute them to the four ends of the social earth – to the political, the economic, the ideological and (for the favoured few) the theoretical. There would appear to be three ways in which the base–superstructure metaphor has been used misleadingly. With regard to its familiar role as an explanatory paradigm, Cohen's original work, and the subsequent debate with Elster and others, have done a great deal to clarify the issues at stake. The second and third abuses are concerned more with the strategic impression of a society which the metaphor has helped to sustain.

In Althusserian hands, the model of levels and instances was used both to banish 'the individual' as any kind of integral actor from a base–superstructure complex which was thought to constitute the whole object of social enquiry (apart from that residual patch allowed to the benighted followers of Edward Thompson – the 'conjuncture'), and at the same time to introduce into this object a division between the upper (political and ideological) and the lower (economic) reaches. By his decisive – almost triumphant – 'refutation of the legend' that Marx denied the existence of human nature, Norman Geras is able to rescind the second abuse. He reestablishes with full classical credentials the integrity of the human actor as an animal of a particular kind: an animal with unique and elastic powers, whose uniqueness resides in the elasticity which its natural powers provide. This human animal is restored to the centre of the social stage, so that 'historical materialism itself, this whole distinctive approach to society that originates with Marx, rests squarely upon the idea of a human nature.'[17]

It remains to rebut the third abuse of the base–superstructure metaphor, since the reintegrated individuals might still be thought to dwell at different levels of the social structure, rather like the inhabitants of a tower block, whose floors might be marked in ascending order: economy, family, party and – in the penthouse suite, no doubt – philosophy. As far as the pedigree of any such thought in Marx is concerned, it should be enough to point out that the social structures of *Capital* are sets of relationships between whole individuals exchanging, buying, selling, owning, producing and consuming use-values. In the topography of *Capital*, there are no vertical levels, but only horizontally disposed sites – market, factory, home – between which people move in conducting their characteristic business.[18] In these commutations, people are not moving between base and superstructure, as if they were stuck in the lift between floors or as if at one moment they concentrated on their feet and at the next had their heads in the clouds. To put it another way: the State, say, lies in the *background,* just over the horizon of the capitalist economy; it does not hover above it. It was said before that rational choice Marxism involves a *critical return* to classical views. In the matter of social structure, there is a return to views cured of the stratification fever caught from twentieth-century sociology.

FROM THE THEORY OF HISTORY TO THE ANALYSIS OF CAPITAL

In Marx there is a rich – seemingly inexhaustible – vein of theoretical insight, but there are only two theories. One of these, hardly more than a sketch, implies a long-range theory of history of the kind elucidated by Cohen. It might be called the general theory of historical materialism. In addition, there is the special theory of historical materialism, adumbrated in *Capital,* which refers to the capitalist regime of production alone.[19] It is true that the two theories are supposed to be related, since the laws of motion of capitalism ought to exemplify the principles of the general theory, and the transition from capitalism to socialism ought to stand in a (shortish) line of similar transitions from previous historical epochs. But it is also true that the general and special theories have theoretical presuppositions which generate different 'fixed points'.

In the case of the general theory, which claims to be an overall theory of historical change, the fixed point will necessarily be transhistorical. Anyone who thinks it is the first rule of Marxist science that history disqualifies fixed points would do well to abandon the search for a general theory right here. In Cohen's reading, however, the fixed point is supplied by human rationality facing a somewhat stable schedule of (largely physical) needs and goals across the long run of history. This reading can survive the objection that human capacity and motivation are influenced, rather than formed altogether, by social and historical circumstance, if it is plausible to think that a certain kind of technological rationality is sufficiently widespread, sufficiently urgent and insufficiently hampered or blocked for the forces of production to progress in every kind of society (or perhaps in at least one kind of society in each epoch!).[20] This assumption is not utterly outlandish, but it is nevertheless a large and controversial one – as any assumption sustaining a general theory of history is bound to be.

With the special theory, the situation is considerably easier. In Marx's version, the fixed point of the theory is the set of social relations constituting capitalism – strictly, the circuit of industrial capital. Given this fixed point, it is perfectly plausible to assume that the kind of human motivation obtaining is the one that the general theory also happens to presuppose. Indeed, the social relations of capitalism seem peculiarly adapted to foster the spirit of technological rationality, and to include the interests of those who already hold resources in favour of technological development. This correspondence is so striking as to raise the possibility that the presumed general theory may be an illicit projection from the special theory backward into history.[21] In any case, the problem in Marx's work is that the presupposition of the special theory – the class relation of capital – is left largely ungrounded in the general theory. There is of course an account of the historical genesis of the class relation – primitive accumulation – and a historical-cum-logical reprise of the development of the forms of value leading up to capital, but no systematic theoretical link is forged between the class action portrayed in *Capital* and the trans-historical action envisaged in the general theory. It is not shown why capitalism had to emerge when it did from a long-run environment structured minimally in terms of productive technique and human capacity.

Marx's special theory itself proceeds by offering a complex answer to the following question: How is it that a regime of class division and exploitation can arise from the interplay of market transactions freely conducted under norms of equality?.[22] There are two possible responses, leading theory and politics in somewhat different directions. First, it may be allowed that capitalism involves a measure of freedom (and equality) and reasons may be sought for the transformation of these qualities into the opposite experiences (domination and exclusion) in the lives of most people who live under capitalism. Roemer's work in particular belongs in this line of thought, and its great merit is to sharpen considerably the answer Marx was able to give in this direction. Here, classes emerge precisely from the conditions of freedom that market institutions promote.

Alternatively, criticism may proceed essentially through a denial of the description of market transactions contained in the question. This is to look for the source of the problem in the misrepresentation of itself offered by capitalism. It may be suggested, for example, that what passes for freedom under capitalism is a covert form of oppression because of the manipulation of tastes, the promulgation of false needs, or the generally illusory character of the choices on offer. The heavy artillery of ideology is often wheeled on at this point to depict a realm of mystified surface appearance radically at odds with the deeper and grimmer reality of capitalist class relations. Now, while it would be foolish to deny that manipulations and distortions of preferences occur under capitalism, and that their extent offers grounds for criticizing it, the most important question is the weight to be assigned to these processes in the overall indictment of capitalism. The judgement is important because the first line of attack points towards a theory of macroscopic properties which aspires to be true of capitalism, and in that sense scientific, while the second line of attack implies a more philosophical and literary critique of received ideological forms. The two lines of attack are further related to distinct recommendations for socialism, since, broadly speaking, if capitalism is recognized as in part genuinely free and equal, we want more of the very things capitalism now provides; while if the freedom and equality of capitalism are entirely chimerical, we want none of the things that capitalism now provides, since we want the reality and not the mere semblance of freedom and equality, and the endorsement of the appearance is likely to take us further away from the achievement of the reality.

The matter is further complicated because Marx's critique of capitalism – his version of the special theory – pursues both lines of attack. He wants to tell it as it is and how it appears to be. The two lines are also frequently entangled in his work, in part because he adopts the methodological principle that science is achieved through the critique of ideology – in other words, that the critique of false (ideological) representation opens the path to true (scientific) representation. Since Marx finds systematic misperception due to capitalism in two main areas, it is important from both a theoretical and a political point of view to determine whether the elucidation of these misperceptions invalidates or partially validates the claims made by capitalist ideology concerning freedom and equality. This is particularly the case with regard to freedom, whose reality is inscribed in the basic assumptions of the rational choice approach.

THE SOURCES OF MISREPRESENTATION

Marx located the first area of systematic misrepresentation in the political economy of his day. His theory of value led to a new representation of capitalism as a system of exploitation rather than the thoroughgoing system of equal exchange that its apologists portrayed. But this part of Marx's critique, which specifically connects distortion to the realm of circulation (for this purpose: 'appearance') as distinct from production (alias 'reality'), does not rely on denial of the fact or significance of choice (hence freedom) in the realm of circulation. Instead it posits a confusion in one crucial case over the *object* of choice – over *what* is being exchanged in the labour contract. Nor does it deny that *commodity* exchange is equal exchange. Inequality arises because the relevant exchange is not a commodity exchange, given the confusion about what is and what is not a commodity. In capitalist ideology, the worker is liable to believe that what she is exchanging at its value (labour-power) is something else (labour) for which she is denied adequate compensation. The fraud on labour may be concealed by the fair trade in labour-power.[23]

The second source of systematic misperception was analyzed by Marx under the heading of 'fetishism'. Economic fetishism (which certainly exists under capitalism, but to an extent that Marx may have exaggerated) involves the false attribution of economic powers either to unaided bits of matter or to unaided commodity forms – especially the spectacular forms of money – in isolation from the networks of social and/or material relations which are in fact responsible for the economic powers they appear to enjoy.[24] Yet the powers in question do exist in the said networks, so that, as Cohen explains, the illusion of fetishism is not like that of a hallucination or the emperor's new clothes (in which the appearance disappears with knowledge of the illusion) but like that of a mirage in which knowledge of the source does not destroy the appearance that gives rise to it.[25] The misperception of economic (but not religious) fetishism is not that something exists when it doesn't, but that something which exists is other than it is.

What effect, then, will Marx's disclosure of the mirage-image have on those who inhabit capitalist relations? Will the knowledge that economic power actually resides in the ensemble of social and material relations restore to agents the freedom to use their part of the powers in unalienated fashion? It seems unlikely that a merely cognitive process could wreak such havoc with capitalism, if only because those who command resources have powers and interests other than the power and interest at the centre of Marx's critique of capitalism – each person's labour-power and its creative expression. Ruling classes might be quite happy to exploit the alienated labour-power of others in order to satisfy their material requirements, thereby releasing their own creative powers for expression in a non-economic domain called 'culture'.[26] This is not an implausible picture of the creative achievement of historic leisured classes, corrupted and confined as this is (in any Marxian view) by its continuing dependence on the exploitation that makes it possible.

If we now turn to the exploited group itself, whose material interests and creative powers are alike thwarted under capitalism, the diagnosis of the mirage looks like an indispensable part of any programme of social change designed to restore their economic powers to the rightful owners. Without awareness of the illusion, it is not clear how the requisite change could be conceivable, let alone conceived as desirable. Diagnosis of the mirage is a liberating act in its own right: those no longer in thrall to the mirage are freer than they were before – or at least they are certainly not less free. Reversing the direction of comparison, one can say that those still subject to the illusion are really (in truth, that is) more free than they think they are when they falsely attribute economic motive force to money and unaided bits of matter. But, in this case, Marx's diagnosis of economic fetishism offers the worst possible paradigm for the converse situation – frequently invoked by the critics of consumer capitalism – in which people think they are free when they are not really (in truth) free at all.[27]

I conclude that those who would entirely debunk the freedom enjoyed under capitalism will find no comfort in the classical critique of capitalist ideology. They will also have to confront the position, implicit in their claims about capitalism, that the freedom to which socialists aspire is somehow above and beyond the mundane variety we currently experience. On this account, socialist freedom is not to be equated in any way with the greater freedom we seem to enjoy in a North American than a British supermarket to buy not just milk, but milk with six levels of fat content and two styles of pasteurization, each offered in eight different flavours. Socialist proposals corresponding to the two lines of attack on Marx's question then involve the suggestion either that everyone, and not just the privileged minority, should be offered the choice between chocolate and strawberry milk, or on the contrary that the choice is not worth having since no one in their right mind would choose either, especially when wholesome, regular milk is there for the asking. The contradiction between these proposals has not prevented both from being entertained simultaneously, as an understandable hedging of bets. Or perhaps, if the first proposal is not viable under socialism (or is viable already under capitalism), resort must be made to the second – as a reserve proposal in a process that Elster would include under the heading of Sour Grapes.

I believe that socialists should be predisposed towards the first proposal, while the maximization of freedom should be subject on the one hand to the technological constraint and on the other to the version of egalitarianism which rejects exploitative social relations.[28] The second proposal seems to me dispirited because at one stroke it delivers the ordinary vocabulary of freedom and most experience of common sense to the enemy camp. By judging that capitalism is not right only where it is not as it seems to be, it risks the concession that nothing seems to be wrong with capitalism. Ironically, for an approach which starts out looking very radical indeed, much more is conceded to capitalism than in the classical argument that the rich get the pleasure and the poor get the blame, not because the freedom of capitalism is an illusion, but because it is real. More precisely, the market-place really is a free space: what is constitutionally unfree is the state-place, which upholds property, and the workplace, where those without property find it is in their best interest to labour for their daily bread. This is the consequence that Marx took for granted. Roemer seeks to prove it, assuming the state, private property and the market.

ROEMER ON CLASS AND EXPLOITATION

Roemer's work may be introduced by a slight adaptation of the model through which he chooses to make his central point concerning the relation between class and exploitation. Imagine there are two people whom, for the sake of vividness, we shall locate on different islands. One is called Woman Friday, the other Man Crusoe.[29] Both have the same subsistence need – say, one bushel of corn per week. Each is also rational and wishes to gain this subsistence with the minimum expenditure of effort. But there is one important difference between Friday and Crusoe, or, more precisely, between the island environments they inhabit. Friday only has available a labour-intensive technology (LI) which can be operated from scratch and involves no material input apart from labour, but which requires that she work six days a week to produce one bushel of corn. Crusoe, on the other hand, has access to a superior, capital-intensive technology (CI) which uses an amount of material input (seed corn) but requires only three days' work to produce one bushel of corn plus the quantity of seed corn necessary to get the process going. Let us further assume that Crusoe has on hand a stock of seed corn double the amount necessary to run the CI technology for a week. All the material parameters of the subsistence model have now been set. They constrain what is jointly possible for Friday and Crusoe. It is worth noting, first, that what distinguishes the two technologies is their respective productivities: the CI technology being exactly twice as productive as the LI technology. It is this difference which is critical to the subsequent argument, and it corresponds precisely to the fact that the level of development of the forces of production is higher (twice as high) on Crusoe's than on Friday's island (according to the classical definition of these terms in Friday's case and the only plausible extension of classical usage in Crusoe's).[30] Second, the pictures of the production process on the two islands – one without constant capital and one with it – correspond to the Volume 1 and Volume 3 models of *Capital*. It follows that Roemer's results lie beyond the scope of Marx's Volume 1 analysis, in which it is necessary to assume the class relation that Roemer is able to deduce.[31]

We must now ask what Crusoe and Friday make of their respective situations. So long as they exist in isolation from each other, Crusoe simply works three days a week and Friday is stuck with working six. This is the limit of Robinson Crusoe economics, in Marx's pejorative use of the term. Once their mutual isolation is breached, a number of new possibilities open up. These possibilities involve the social relations that might be established in the given material environment.[32] Recall that Crusoe has more seed corn than he needs for his own subsistence. He could double his weekly output by working six days instead of three, but since his needs are satisfied after three days he would merely be stockpiling useless corn. (Trade in produced commodities cannot occur in a one-sector model.) So a generous, public-spirited Crusoe might simply give his extra stock of seed corn to Friday, who could then switch to the CI technique. Both islands would have three-day economies, and the net benefit of the two people would be equalized. In this egalitarian (petty-bourgeois or socialist) outcome the gains of productivity (and of the initial capital stock) are equally distributed between the two parties. Notice that once the initial endowment of capital is made, the two economies can reproduce themselves independently and indefinitely, since Friday will have sufficient surplus above subsistence after the first week to start production in the second.

Now suppose that instead of offering Friday what she needs, Crusoe proposes a deal whereby she receives pay of one bushel, in return for working with Robinson Crusoe's stock of seed corn and the CI technology. The crucial question is how long Friday will have to work, and therefore how much she will produce. If both parties are rational, and we assume that the transaction is a voluntary one, there must be incentives for both parties to make the agreement. Crusoe's incentive is obvious enough. He will certainly not make a deal involving less than three days' work by Friday, since this would not even reproduce the wage he pays and he would find his capital stock running down (though he could easily afford it to be run down to half its original level, in a drip-drip rather than one-shot gift to Friday). Nor will he be interested in making a deal beyond six days, since Friday can produce enough for both parties using the CI technology in this time, and we have assumed that Crusoe has no interest in surplus for its own sake. But if Friday works for any length of time between three and six days, the number of days above three will be the amount by which Crusoe can reduce his own working time and still end up with his net subsistence for the week. This is a clear incentive. But does Friday have an incentive to enter employment under such terms? She does, and this is the key moment of class reproduction according to Roemer's brilliant insight. As things stand, Friday is working six days for her subsistence, so that she has an incentive to work any time less than six days for a subsistence wage. It follows that both parties, *given their respective situations*, will benefit from a deal struck anywhere between three and six days. In the most extreme case, if Crusoe is able to maintain a 'take it or leave it' attitude to Friday's predicament – or, as Roemer assumes in his original presentation of the example, if there is an industrial reserve army in the labour market and no countervailing pressure on Crusoe to use the half of his capital stock which is surplus to his own requirements – then Friday will be bid down to six days' working and Crusoe will be a pure capitalist whose subsistence comes entirely from the work of other people.[33]

In terms of class formation, then, Friday is always a pure proletarian if she accepts any deal which yields a wage covering her subsistence. But we can see Crusoe moving monotonically from self-employment (from petty-bourgeois or peasant proprietor or any other independent status) to an employing, capitalist status which becomes progressively more complete as Friday works beyond three days up to the maximum of six. At any point in this interval, the gains in productivity available from CI technology are distributed unequally. We know that the collective gain – which is also the true gain – is a doubling of productivity. But if one looks at productivity narrowly, as an answer to the question each individual might pose: 'how much corn does *my* labour yield?', then in the extreme case Friday's productivity appears not to have increased at all (since she is still working six days to bring home one bushel), whereas Crusoe's productivity has apparently increased to infinity (since he manages to bring home one bushel without working at all). No doubt Crusoe will be inclined to fetishize this magical result, attributing it to the extraordinary properties of his seed corn, his skill in negotiation, his gender, his national origin or whatever was responsible for his having an extra supply of capital – virtue and judgement, in any case, rather than luck. But it is evident that these sterling qualities will avail him nothing unless he is able to induce Friday to accept his offer.

THE CLASSICAL CONSTRUAL

We now retell the story in the language of the classical theory of value, pointing up the conformity between Roemer's theory and the classical critique. The value of labour-power is defined to equal the value of the use-values required to reproduce the labourer, whose (material) measure is always one bushel of corn for both Friday and Crusoe in this example.

But the value of this material basket of goods alters. Under the LI technology, the value of labour-power is evidently six days whereas under the CI technology it is three days, made up of just less than three days working to produce a net output of one bushel, together with the balance of three days necessary to reproduce the constant capital required to operate the CI technology. These are the direct and indirect labour components of the value of labour-power in the CI regime. (In the LI regime, there is no indirect labour.) Under the LI regime, the value of labour-power completely exhausts the total value added by Friday (six days), whereas in the CI technology there is some remainder, depending upon the amount of time beyond three days that Friday works. This is surplus value, corresponding to the value of the net output above one bushel that Friday is able to produce in working beyond three days. In the extreme case of pure capitalism, surplus value represents three days' work: the total value (still six days of Friday's working) is split equally between the value of labour-power and surplus-value, and a transfer of value (three days' worth) has occurred between Friday and Crusoe. This is classically construed exploitation. The rate of exploitation is here 100 per cent, since each hour of Friday's net labour provides half-an-hour's worth of wages for Friday and half-an-hour's worth of profit for Crusoe. To put it another way, three days' labour (by both parties) is the socially necessary labour time under the CI technology – it is the amount each person would have to work on their own – and Friday is working more than is socially necessary while Crusoe is working less then is socially necessary. The person who is working more is the seller (of labour-power) while the person who is working less is the hirer (of labour power). In this correlation we have encountered for the first time Roemer's startling Class Exploitation Correspondence Principle (hereafter CECP) in its most classical form (the transfer of surplus value through the labour contract).

We have also followed classical usage by introducing the word 'exploitation' to characterize the unequal relation between Friday and Crusoe. If Crusoe is exploiting Friday we need to establish precisely what it is, in the circumstances portrayed by the example, that Crusoe is exploiting. First, and in a relatively non-evaluative connotation, both parties are making use of one or both of the technologies, hence exploiting whatever features of the natural world are responsible for the productivities that the technologies possess. But the use of the term 'exploitation' in the Marxian context also implies injustice, and it is unclear (to me, at least) what are the just claims of the non-human on the human world.[34]

If we restrict the discussion to the social relations established between Friday and Crusoe, the most obvious, and traditional, suggestion is that

Crusoe is exploiting Friday's labour. The problem, however, is that Friday's labour for Crusoe only exists after the deal between them has been concluded; it is a corollary of the deal, so it cannot be something of which Crusoe makes use in order to clinch the deal. Either the deal is exploitative, but it is not Friday's labour that is exploited, or the exploitation of Friday's labour is a consequence of a deal which is not exploitative (at least not exploitative of Friday's labour). I take it that the second possibility strains the credibility of the Marxian indictment. The same argument applies, *a fortiori*, to the suggestion that Crusoe is exploiting the product of Friday's labour, despite the fact that Crusoe makes use of this product by eating it. (Does Crusoe exploit the corn by eating it when it is already in his hand?) It is nearer the mark, and in line with the classical emphasis on the distinction between labour and labour-power, to say that Crusoe is exploiting Friday's labour-power, since this is something which exists prior to the deal. It is part of the environment from which exploitation is said to emerge. But, it is worth distinguishing between two aspects of labour-power: creativity, and the sheer ability to slog. Exploitation of the creativity of the majority – a fundamental feature of the Marxian critique of capitalism – is excluded by the terms of this example, since it depends on the alternative uses to which Friday might put her creativity, and the only activities allowed here are corniculture and leisure (or culture *tout court*). There is thus no evidence that Friday would prefer to do something other than grow corn, and if her creativity is engaged in that activity, the basic pay-off structures change, since Friday will want to follow her natural bent for as many days as possible, contrary to the behavioural assumptions of the example. Crusoe and Friday will in fact compete to reward each other for access to any means of expression held by the other! We are therefore returned for the answer to the slogging aspect of labour-power, which Friday will experience as a disutility when it goes into action, and try to avoid putting into action as much as possible. But we also have to ask what enables Crusoe to make use of this aspect of Friday's labour-power, since Friday assigns it voluntarily to Crusoe. We know from the example that this has to do with their differential access to the LI and CI technologies. Is Crusoe, then, exploiting his own access to the CI technology? The answer is basically no, since it is not clear in general that a person can exploit anything that lies in their environment alone (can I exploit myself?), and it is clear from this example that if Friday had access to the CI technology (e.g. via the 'egalitarian outcome'), Crusoe would have no means of inducing Friday voluntarily to enter terms of employment deemed exploitative. What Crusoe is therefore exploiting is the lack of access Friday has to the CI technology. And so we conclude that B exploits A when B takes unfair advantage of a situation in which A is placed by lack of access to resources.[35]

PRIVATE PROPERTY AND THE STATE

We can now make more explicit the cause of the lack suffered by Friday as a result of which it is in her best interest to be exploited. This was presented above in terms of a moral contrast, in which a generous, altruistic and socialist Crusoe would give Friday that access to resources which a mean, egotistical and capitalist Crusoe would deny. But the more fundamental source of exploitation will be found in the social institutions sustaining the exclusion from resources. In this case, it is the institution of private property that lurks behind the market, and the institution of the state that lurks behind private property. This institutional complex, one might say, allows Crusoe the opportunity to be generous or mean, and a rational if unreasonable Crusoe will be mean. So the source of exploitation has been traced to a situation of differential exclusion (from the means of production in this case) fortified by the institutions of private property and the state.

In what ways, and by what moral principle, is this outcome unfair, and thus finally an exploitation rather than simply an unequal exchange? Exploitation has been defined as taking unfair advantage of the situation of another person. The charge of unfairness cannot arise from the principle that everyone has a claim on the undiminished proceeds of their labour, since although the principle would deliver the required result in this case, there is a long list of classically honoured counter-examples, from the requirements of the young, the old, the sick and the handicapped to the requirements of investment, which tell against the application of the general principle to an adult, fit or present self. The principle must therefore be the negative one, that property ownership yields no valid claim on the proceeds of the labour of others. Respecting Cohen's distinction between productive and producing activities, we can say that capitalists as capitalists have no valid claim on any part of the product, even if their property ownership was in part responsible for the fact that the product was produced. In the language of the social and the material, no return is owed to a purely social contribution.[36]

There is a further element in the evaluation. Exploitation is an unfair use of a situation of exclusion, but the situation which is exploited may be fair or unfair in itself. It seems appropriate to call a situation of unfair exclusion by the term *oppression*. It is then easy to show via general counter-examples that oppression is neither necessary nor sufficient for exploitation, so that the issue of whether capitalism is oppressive must be approached independently of whether it is exploitative.[37]

In terms of the present example, the question to ask is evidently whether Friday's initial exclusion from the CI technology was fair. The answer will turn on the story that is told about Crusoe's acquisition. On some accounts such as one in which Crusoe's extra stock results from his extraordinary exertions in the previous week, the acquisition is not conclusively unfair. (Nor is it conclusively fair, according to the negative evaluative principle which is the only one so far allowed, and which only excludes title derived from property ownership of the means of production, saying nothing about title in the proceeds of my own, or anyone else's, labour.) The fairness of Crusoe's acquisition, and therefore Friday's initial situation, is thus far indeterminate, corresponding to the possibility of a 'clean path' of capitalist development. Suppose, then, that Crusoe's acquisition was clean and just by some unspecified principle. During the first week of production Friday is not oppressed, but she is still exploited since the justice of Crusoe's acquisition does not extend to his use of what he has acquired – otherwise justly appointed judges could pass any sentences they liked.[38] But there is constant, non-fixed capital in this example, so that the whole of Crusoe's justly acquired asset in seed corn is used up in the first week of working. If Crusoe is a pure capitalist, the whole of the constant capital for the next week's working will have been derived from Friday's surplus product of the previous week, acquired by Crusoe through his (just) ownership of the means of production in that period. But it now follows from the negative principle that Crusoe's title to means of production at the start of the second week is invalid: Friday's situation is unfair by Monday, and she is oppressed. Once capitalism gets into its stride, it is oppressive as well as exploitative by a single principle of (un)just distribution. This is the heart of the Marxian indictment of capitalism, and its statement will serve to conclude this exposition of Roemer's theory.

POWER AND EXPLOITATION

We should now sketch some implications of Roemer's basic approach for the special theory of historical materialism. Discussion will focus on the question of power in Friday's and Crusoe's two-island world, and then, very briefly, on Roemer's findings for models of capitalism beyond these two islands. The homily of the previous section omitted reference to power because the first task was to show how class division could come about through voluntary transactions. But what is commonly termed 'power' is still around here somewhere, and the relation of power to the example requires careful analysis. This question is generally important because rational choice Marxism is a theory with an 'economic' and utilitarian pedigree, whereas the concept of 'power' draws on an alternative tradition of sociology and political science which has often been divorced from economic theory. Posing the question hints at a reconciliation between the two traditions.

Let us start by attributing power to Friday and Crusoe over their respective forces of production: Friday has power over her labour-power and Crusoe over his means of production (seed corn) and labour-power. We note first that power over a force of production is a social relation of production, and a mode of production in conventional Marxist usage is a set of social relations of production.[39] But Crusoe has (monopoly) power over means of production and Friday only has power over her own labour-power, so that the attribution of these powers sets up the capitalist mode of production as the power structure of this example. Roemer's results may then be interpreted as showing that the existence of the capitalist mode of production implies the existence of the capitalist class structure, given rational behaviour.

What is meant, precisely, by the power that individuals are said to enjoy over forces of production? It is fairly clear that the relevant power is the capacity I enjoy to exclude you from access to my force of production against your will. This is power in the sense of real ownership – effective control.[40] On this view, Friday and Crusoe are alike in having power, but differ in having power over different resources. Interaction between Friday and Crusoe arises because each party requires the resources of the other to reach an outcome preferable to their initial situation. The initial situation now figures twice in the analysis. It remains the starting point but is also a permanent resort for either party. The distribution of power specifies the *current withdrawal options* of the actors, and the definition of their powers allows each to withdraw without suffering consequences apart from those entailed by the withdrawal itself. But this means that both parties enjoy power *over* the other since, if each respects the powers of the other, either can deploy their resource to affect the pay-offs available to the other.

We now illustrate how the *extent* of the power (colloquially – the power) I enjoy over you depends on: (i) the needs and preferences (the interests) of us both; (ii) your power; (iii) my alternative to interaction with you. It will be useful first to define the extent of the power each enjoys over the other by the *maximum damage* each could do to (the interests of) the other, should they so wish. Interestingly, this is three days' labour in each case, since Friday can penalize Crusoe by three days' work with respect to Crusoe's best option if Friday should withdraw, and Crusoe can penalize Friday by three days' work with respect to Friday's best option if Crusoe should withdraw. These penalties evidently depend on the interests represented by the pay-off structure (point i). The limits of the power of each over the other are therefore given by the *ultimate sanctions* each can bring to bear on the other, using the powers which define their position within the relations of production.[41] The threat of these sanctions appears in the example at two points. First, in a real case the implied threat may help to determine the point at which the agreement is concluded between three and six days' working. This point is indeterminate as far as economic theory is concerned unless there is competition in the labour market, when Friday is bid down to six days' working or unless Friday has access to seed corn from a source other than Crusoe, in which case she will work the minimum of three days. But these possibilities envisage other actors, or other resources of a kind which render the sanctions available to each party against the other ineffective. Both continue to enjoy power over resources, but they can no longer translate this into power over each other (point iii). In the case of a competitive labour market, Friday loses her power over Crusoe, and in the case of superabundant seed corn (cf. the 'open frontier') Crusoe loses his power over Friday. This also establishes the general relation between the power of B over A and the *dependence* of A on the resource of B. If alternative possibilities are excluded and there is interdependence, it must be assumed that Friday and Crusoe reach some compromise agreement between three and six days' working.[42]

THE ENFORCEMENT PROBLEM

Now the question arises whether the agreement will be honoured. If Friday is guaranteed a subsistence wage at the end of the week, she has no incentive to perform any work, since it is no longer her business where her corn wage is going to come from. Conversely, if Crusoe is guaranteed the work, he has no incentive to pay the wage (or to pay it in unadulterated corn). Given these incentives to default, can the agreement be enforced? Friday's enforcement problem has been solved historically by the abolition of the truck system, and the opening of alternative sources of supply through the money wage and competitive consumer markets (although a form of the problem reappears with inflation). Crusoe's problem has been solved historically by the factory system, and the domination of Friday within the labour process. In the tradition of Marxist sociology of which Braverman and the early Olin Wright are recent standard-bearers, exploitation is rooted in this domination of the worker, and the corresponding proposals for the socialist alternative emphasize the importance of industrial democracy. Without questioning in the least the significance of coercion at the point of production in the life of the worker, or the desirability of the countervailing socialist demand, Roemer's approach tends to make this form of coercion secondary to the powers already contained in the relations of production. The capitalist's problem is that, unlike other commodities, labour-power remains attached to the person of the labourer, and although the labourer has assigned it to the capitalist as an act of will, the use of labour-power in the interest of the capitalist requires the continuous, and not just once-for-all, cooperation of the labourer. This might suggest that power in the workplace is supplementary to the powers defining the relations of production, so that the two loci of power demand two independent critiques. But the worst that either party can do (the most damaging sanction either party can bring to bear) for non-performance of the agreement that constitutes the class relation is the threat of breaking the relation – the strike by Friday, the sack or the lock-out by Crusoe. And these ultimate sanctions coincide with the extent of the powers defining the relations of production. In particular, the sanctions available to Crusoe which would normally be considered under the heading of 'factory discipline' all fall within the scope of the powers defining his ownership of the means of production.[43]

This point can be clarified by supposing that the powers are infringed, so that the current withdrawal options are no longer available. Suppose, for example, that an accumulation-minded feudal Crusoe (more plausibly an accumulation-minded Crusoe with a feudal ally) were to impose corvée labour on Friday in the LI technology. Friday would have no reason to consent to the arrangement, which infringes her effective control over her labour-power and decreases her utility. But such an infringement would also render it in her interest to work longer than six days for a subsistence wage. The attribution of effective control of (power over) labour-power therefore sets the upper limit of exploitation. But now suppose that a socialist Friday expropriated half of Crusoe's seed corn, infringing the ownership of the latter. The effect is, of course, the same as in the previous case in which Crusoe lost *monopoly* power because Friday had an alternative source of seed corn. In either case, there is no way Crusoe can induce Friday to be exploited, so long as Crusoe is unable to expropriate the seed corn back – that is, so long as Friday enjoys power over the seed corn she has expropriated or otherwise acquired. This illustrates point (ii) – that the extent of your power over me depends on my power. Also, and significantly, the attribution of powers (the claim that a particular mode of production exists) bounds the outcome of interaction in a precise sense – between three and six days' working in this case – just as it bounds the sanctions available to the interactors. Vary the distribution of powers, and the outcomes range from Friday working for Crusoe as much as is compatible with physical reproduction of Friday and the converse outcome in which Crusoe works to the limit for Friday (if Friday expropriates all the seed corn and becomes a capitalist). These extreme distributions of utility over outcomes are set by material parameters, and not by social power. In summary, the power structure sets inner bounds to the outcome of interaction, whose outer bound is set by material constraints. The arena of interaction is circumscribed by material possibilities, and then, more narrowly, by the power structure. I believe that this result accords well with our general intuitions about 'power', and conforms in theoretical practice to the distinction between macrosociological analyses which focus on the power structure at the expense of the interaction, and economic analyses which focus on the interaction at the expense of the power structure.

For the sociological analysis, an important further question will then arise: what secures the power structure? In virtue of what are the powers properly attributed to Friday and Crusoe? The general Marxian answer has already been given: because a state exists. It is a defining characteristic of a *capitalist* state that it will intervene with the resources over which it has power to prevent the infringement of the powers which define the capitalist relations of production. It is this intervention which will confound a feudal Crusoe or a socialist Friday, although it must be said that, in this respect, actually existing capitalist states have been more punctilious with regard to Crusoe's than to Friday's powers.[44] The institution that so intervenes is a *state* because of the range of resources – unique in a given society – over which it has control (finance, real estate, labour-power, legal enactment, means of representation, armed forces), and especially because of the extent of its legal use of the last resource on the list.[45] To attribute powers to Friday and Crusoe is therefore to make implicit reference both to a third party (the state) and to other resources (especially armed force) which are excluded from analysis of the interaction which gives rise to classes under capitalism.[46] This is a perfectly reasonable procedure for a special theory, which respects the contours of power existing in a given social formation. It will not be so reasonable for a general theory of history, in which there is no longer a struggle on the basis of power but a struggle *for* power – a struggle to redefine the contours of power in a given social formation, generating a new distribution of freedoms and rights for the actors in the social formation. If this idea will guide the criticism of Roemer's attempt to interpret the general theory of historical materialism in terms of an equally general theory of exploitation, it remains to indicate what reservations about the special theory of exploitation lead Roemer himself to adopt the generalization he does.

ROEMER'S COMPLEX MODELS

Up to now, the classically inspired special theory has been presented in an impossibly restricted setting: a particular two-person, one-sector subsistence model. The reader will want to know: does surplus-value exploitation only and always arise in such a model? What happens to the basic results (especially the CECP) in a more complex theoretical universe? In order to answer these questions Roemer introduces a veritable battery of n-person, m-sector linear models whose parameters vary in the following three ways:

(i) *Behavioural Assumptions.* In the *subsistence models*, rationality implies minimization of effort (labour-time) to obtain a fixed bundle of consumption goods from given endowments (Friday/Crusoe). In the *accumulation models*, rationality implies maximization of revenue (through production and exchange) from given endowments. In classical notation, this is the difference between the C–M–C and the M–C–M chains of commodity production and exchange.[47]

(ii) *Behavioural Options.* Actors always have the option of self-employment and trade in produced commodities (means of production and consumption goods). In addition, they may be given access to a labour market or a credit market. In the Friday/Crusoe world, there was an embryonic labour market, but no credit. (Trade was excluded by attenuation to a single produced commodity: corn).

(iii) *Technology Employed.* This is either the Leontief technology familiar from neo-Ricardian price theory or the more general activity analysis or convex cone technology.[48] They all involve constant returns to scale.

In all cases, agents in the economy are alike in being rational, but differ in their initial endowments. Endowments (and therefore agents) are ranked by wealth, measured as the market value of agents' physical stocks at prices corresponding to the reproducible competitive equilibrium for the economy in question. (Crusoe had wealth in seed corn, and Friday none, though there were no prices in the one-sector model.) An equilibrium represents an individual optimum for each agent. Agents are further distinguished (and ranked) by the amount of time they work at equilibrium, and by their class position. The latter is a qualitative (set-theoretic) notion depending on whether agents at equilibrium are self-employed, employed by others, or employing others. These possibilities are not mutually exclusive and Roemer shows that in general agents sort themselves into a fivefold class decomposition: big capitalists (pure employers); small capitalists (employers self-employed), petty bourgeoisie (purely self-employed); semi-proletarians (self-employed employed); proletarians (purely employed). We encountered all these class positions in the Friday–Crusoe example, except the semi-proletarian, which would have occurred if Friday had some wealth in seed corn, but not enough to run the CI technology for three days.

A CECP arises when there is a correlation between wealth and class position (the resource rich optimize consistently at class positions made 'higher' by the correlation) and a further correlation between wealth and exploitation status. The latter is measured by the balance between the labour performed and the labour content of subsistence goods in the subsistence models, and by the balance between the labour performed and the labour the agent could command by purchasing goods out of revenue in the accumulation models. A favourable balance defines an exploiting and an adverse balance an exploited status. In the accumulation models, the 'model' definition of the balance implies that a 'grey area' of agents may exist who are neither exploited nor exploiting.[49] The general logic of derivation for a CECP is this: unequal wealth in resources plus common orientation as rational actors imply differential class position with covariant exploitation status. It is worth noting that this derivation reverses the sequence found in Althusserian sociology: here, individuals carve out class positions; there, individuals are carved out for class positions.

It now transpires that so long as the definitions of labour value (hence exploitation) are suitably adapted to the requirements of the successive models, the CECP is essentially preserved (strictly, a different CECP is provable for each model). The Friday/Crusoe case is no *ad hoc* construction. This is good news for the classical intuition. Indeed, it is an astonishing tribute to Marx's genius. (It doesn't reflect badly on Roemer, either.)

The bad news comes in three large doses. First, some orthodox positions on the labour theory of value must be sacrificed in order to preserve the CECP. In particular, values depend on prices for the most general linear technology.[50] Second, it is impossible to make classical sense of the notion of exploitation if labour is radically heterogeneous. This is because it is impossible to rank actors by their labour contributions at equilibrium and an alternative attempt to rank actors according to equilibrium wage-rates results in loss of the essential correlation between wealth and class position. The problem of skill cannot be handled within this framework.[51] Third, the classical focus on the labour market is logically misplaced, because the transfer of surplus labour through the labour market is neither necessary nor sufficient for surplus-value exploitation. It is not necessary because the transfer of value can take place either through product markets alone or credit and product markets together. Roemer uses the first case to examine unequal exchange and a corresponding 'world division of labour' brought about by free trade between self-employing national economies – Imperialism without Empire.[52] In the second case, isomorphism theorems connect the decomposition into credit classes I – I, with the decomposition into employment classes found when labour markets exist.[53] The sufficiency of labour-market labour extraction for exploitation fails in view of a special three-person counter-example according to which surplus labour is performed by one employed actor when the initial wealth, and subsequent welfare, of all three actors are identical, and so the question of exploitation cannot arise.[54] It is partly in the hope of resolving difficulties such as these that Roemer proposes his second, general theory of exploitation.

HISTORY AND EXPLOITATION

The avowed purpose of Roemer's major work is to provide a general taxonomy of exploitation: to escape from capitalism into history, socialism and beyond. This programme brings the general theory of exploitation which he proposes into close relation with the general theory of historical materialism. It offers a frame of reference for interpreting the past and, perhaps, for changing the future. To this end, Roemer proposes the following deceptively simple definition of exploitation: 'A coalition S, in a larger society N, is exploited ... only if: (1) There is an alternative, which we may conceive of as hypothetically feasible, in which S would be better off than in its present situation. (2) Under this alternative, the complement of S, the coalition N – S = S', would be worse off than at present.'[55]

The references to 'better off' and 'worse off' generalize the form of inequality essential to the intuition of exploitation – in principle extending the scope of the theory to cover any dimension of social life for which a criterion of rankable benefit is plausible. The conjunction of (1) and (2) is intended to capture the interactive element in the intuition: the sense in which the welfare of the exploiting coalition S' depends upon the poor fare of the exploited coalition S.[56] This way of identifying the inequality together with its presumptive source evidently relies upon a comparison between the status quo and the 'hypothetically feasible alternative', which is, in the first instance, a construction of thought experiment. Usually, Roemer takes the alternative to involve new social arrangements pertaining after the resources available in the status quo have been redistributed in some fashion. Two dimensions of generality then open: it is possible to extend the list of types of resources investigated under the definition, and to imagine different rules for redistributing the same kind of resource. At this point, the general theory connects directly with politics, because a political movement might be concerned with the consequences of maldistribution of a particular kind of resource in the status quo, and its programme of action might be informed by the attempt to achieve the redistribution of that resource specified by an appropriate rule. Any such redistribution rule will define a withdrawal option for the exploited coalition S. The pay-offs under the 'hypothetically feasible' alternative assume that the exploited coalition will be able to get out from under: that is, to escape that status quo with some portion of some variety of resources it doesn't enjoy at present, and to organize itself independently on this basis. It is then possible to speak in the plural of forms of exploitation under the status quo, each one wired to a different escape route for potentially distinct coalitions of people exploited in different respects within the status quo. It follows that when different observers return different answers to the question: which are the exploited coalitions in the society?, or the question: is a given coalition exploited?, there may be disagreement not about what exploitation is, but about the particular alternative to the status quo the observers have in mind.[57] On the other hand, each withdrawal option is liable to be associated with some differences of ethical standpoint, since withdrawal under terms set by the redistribution rule promises to overcome the injustice (the specific form of unfairness) which makes the comparative distribution of benefits and burdens in the status quo exploitative. The general theory might finally connect with a delineation of needs (of human nature), since it may be the resources required to satisfy a particular order of needs whose maldistribution leads to a particular form of exploitation in the status quo, and whose frustration the alternative regime promises to overcome.

If the horizons of the general theory are thus potentially as broad as the utilitarian tradition of social thinking, it is necessary to show in what sense it remains distinctively Marxist. It does so largely because the surplus-value theory of exploitation occurs within it as a special case, wherever the restrictive assumptions of the classical theory are allowed (above all, the homogeneous labour assumption). To confirm this it is necessary to show that a CECP will typically satisfy the two conditions in the general definition. But this is already clear from the correspondence principles: if wealth is equally endowed to all, there is no decomposition into distinct classes, and agents will all work socially necessary labour time at equilibrium. So, comparing the pay-offs in the equilibrium under equal endowment with the equilibrium in an unequal endowment status quo, the exploited would work less and the exploiters would work more in the alternative regime, satisfying the general definition. The redistribution rule involves withdrawal of the exploited coalition, with its proportional (usually per capita) share of the available social assets. Since this entails a redistribution of property rights, the general theory is also called the property-relations approach to exploitation. In the classical case at issue here the relevant property is property in what Roemer calls alienable assets (especially means of production). This rule serves to define *capitalist exploitation* in the general theory. If the general theory and the classical theory coincide for the central case, the general theory is not limited to surplus extraction through the labour-market, since we have seen that a CECP applies where there is trade and credit and a Wealth Exploitation Correspondence Principle where there is trade in produced commodities. Moreover, the general theory renders the appropriate verdict ('No exploitation') for the counter-example to the sufficiency of surplus extraction for exploitation, and the general theory can go on to accommodate cases in which the labour-value approach is ill defined.[58]

FORMS OF EXPLOITATION

The most important of these involves skill, and the extension of the resource list to include non-alienable alongside alienable assets. To model this case, Roemer assumes not that different kinds of labour are offered, but that absence of skill restricts the technology that can be worked by a given agent. This restriction in the status quo may lead the unskilled to do worse and the skilled to do better than either would do if the knowledge required to work the whole matrix of technology were equally available to all. For example, if Crusoe gave Friday the seed corn, but not the knowledge required to plant it, Friday would be in the same predicament as before, but out of a different variety of exclusion from productive assets. Roemer calls this case *socialist exploitation*, since it is a form of exploitation consistent with equal distribution of capital, and possibly characteristic of actually existing socialism. To complete the list of exploitation types, there is *feudal exploitation*, most conveniently thought to result from an unequal distribution of labour-power: serfs are deprived by feudal obligations of the ability to trade or otherwise to optimize the output from a part of their personal unit of homogeneous labour-power. (Slaves are similarly deprived of the whole unit)[59]. In addition, there is *status exploitation*, derived from differential returns to a bureaucratic position independent of any genuine expertise the bureaucrat may possess. (If bureaucrats have such expertise, they are not let off the book, since they may then become guilty of socialist exploitation).[60] Finally, there is *needs exploitation*, resulting from the differential welfare of the needy when income is equalized in respect of every other difference between agents. The redistribution rules which make these cases exploitative under the general definition involve restoring every serf (or slave) to the enjoyment of a full unit of their labour power, eliminating bureaucratic differentials and distributing handicaps from the needy to the less needy respectively.

As the terminology implies, these forms of exploitation may be viewed in a sequence corresponding to the sequence of regimes of production given by the theory of history and a progressive sociology of knowledge in which the forms are reflected successively in thought (capitalist ideology attacks feudal exploitation, socialist ideology attacks capitalist exploitation, communist ideology attacks socialist and ultimately needs-exploitation...). But the succession of forms of exploitation may also be held to settle the long-distance political agenda, according to which the historical task of each epoch is to eliminate one form of exploitation before moving on to confront the next. In Roemer's view, historical process resembles an onion, in which the removal of each skin reveals the next, deeper skin. The end of progressive politics is the elimination of the onion. If one cannot tame Tawney's tiger stripe by stripe, one has to tackle his onion layer by layer, and you cannot peel an onion from the inside out.[61] This is how the historical process selects time-bound 'historical tasks' of emancipation for the progressive social movements. In this way, Roemer snatches orthodoxy from the jaws of heresy.

It should be made clear at once that the general theory of exploitation is offered here only as an *interpretation* of the Marxist theory of history. It is parasitic on the latter rather than a substitute for it, unlike Roemer's special theory of exploitation (itself now embedded in the general theory) which is a full substitute for the classical labour theory of value. It is thus not surprising to discover that the difficulties of Roemer's interpretation revolve around the two concepts at the heart of current debates on the theory of history itself: power and rationality. I have argued above that it is possible to connect the special theory for each mode of production to a definition of each mode which attributes power to actors over resources and thereby specifies the *current withdrawal options* of the actors. These options may be used as threats in current bargaining situations. We have seen that the general theory also specifies a withdrawal option, but this time it is a *counterfactual withdrawal option*, and the facts to which it runs counter are above all the facts of power. The redistribution of power over resources envisaged under the 'hypothetically feasible alternative' lies the other side of an immense social revolution. It is the difference between Friday's threat to strike and her threat to expropriate Crusoe.

This distinction is connected to rationality, because there is a corresponding distinction to be made between proximate rationality (optimization given power) and long-distance rationality (optimization over the distribution of power). In order to achieve the latter optimization, exploited agents will have to be convinced that there are long-distance benefits and then to overcome the free-rider problem of collective political action in order to dislodge those in power before claiming the presumed benefits. In different ways, and in different historical contexts, Elster, Przeworski, Brenner and Taylor all raise the challenge that long-distance rationality may not be rational at all, or that it is so only under certain special circumstances which make proximate and long-distance rationality coincide.[62] Subject to these challenges, a Cohenesque version of the theory of history is considerably weakened, and with it the historical attachment and political implications of Roemer's general theory of exploitation.

Apart from these reservations, there is plenty of evidence internal to Roemer's discussion of this element of his theory – and one massive piece of evidence from outside – that it is inappropriate to consider forms of exploitation as sequential rather than pertaining to options of social organization which remain significantly open in principle. The great merit of the general theory of exploitation is to place these options on the same table. The effect of close attachment to the general theory of history is to sweep some of them under the carpet again.

To be more specific: the three most important forms of exploitation in Roemer's account are capitalist exploitation, socialist exploitation and status exploitation. The forms of social organization corresponding more or less clearly to these kinds of exploitation are the market, a regime of decentralized workers' cooperatives, and a centralized planning mechanism. If you eliminate the market and therefore capitalist exploitation, you may run into incentive problems, or problems of technical innovation which reduce the projected pay-offs of those exploited under the market regime. If you allow a regime of workers' cooperatives free rein, then those cooperatives which develop special skills and knowledge may pull ahead of the rest and become socialist exploiters. If the cooperatives are joined by extensive free-market relations, and can capitalize their advantages, there might be a return to capitalist exploitation.[63] But if you redistribute their surplus through a mechanism of central planning, you may just be substituting status exploitation for socialist or capitalist exploitation. Or consider the international context: the relations among the three worlds are very likely characterized by differential access to skills and to capital; their logic unfolds via the terms of trade and the international credit and labour markets, compounded by more or less direct forms of political domination. This suggests that a rich mixture of capitalist, socialist and status exploitation exists between the First and Third Worlds, with the Second perhaps poised somewhere in between. It would take a brave commentator to assert an unequivocal trend in the development of those relations.[64]

One might suppose that feudal exploitation at least had been left behind for good and all, but there is more than a passing family likeness between feudal and status exploitation. The exploiters in both cases owe their position to 'extra-economic' resources, despite the fact that personal advancement in one system is the result of birth and warfare, while in the other it may be due more to political reliability (to the extent that it is independent of true expertise). Loyalty and respect for hierarchy – with the odd stab in the back to keep everyone on their toes – seem important principles of co-ordination in both cases.[65] And if this family likeness between feudalism and bureaucracy offers some clues about the ability of Russian society to abridge the capitalist stage, then what are we to make of the Japanese transition from feudal forms to highly advanced capitalist ones? In any case, the modern capitalist corporation is a monument of rewards to position, alongside ownership and skill.[66] In short, the historical process may resemble an onion less than a balloon: exploitation is suppressed in one place only to pop up somewhere else. Roemer's application gives too much away to an unreconstructed classical vision of progress.

If these points are largely internal to Roemer's own discussion, massive evidence against the linear chronological conception is supplied by the example of gender. Here, 'we need a historical understanding of the ways in which gender and class have become so intertwined in capitalist society. ... Recognition of the different origins of class and gender oppression need not blind us either to the gendered character of class under capitalism or to the importance of struggling for a socialism that has been redefined in the light of feminism.'[67] This point is evidently of universal historical relevance.

Part of what needs redefining by its light is John Roemer's *General Theory of Exploitation and Class*.

LET SEVERAL FLOWERS BLOOM

I have introduced rational choice Marxism not as an assortment of remote specialist interests, but as a fully-fledged paradigm, which deserves to take its place beside the two other constellations of theory currently discernible within the broad spectrum of progressive social thought – namely, post-structuralism and critical theory. Rational choice Marxism qualifies as a paradigm because of the scope of its interests, and the elements of a common approach identifiable across these interests. Indeed, it is now only within the rational choice context that some of the leading items on the classical agenda of Marxist theory – historical explanation and the delineation of social form, the collective dynamics of class struggle, the evolution and evaluation of capitalism – can be fruitfully discussed. In these areas, rational choice Marxism has inherited the mantle of Althusserian structuralism. But it is not the linear descendant of Althusserianism, since it seems to have developed in wholesale reaction against, rather than critical engagement with, the Althusserian legacy. I take post-structuralism to be precisely the linear descendant of Althusser – at least in regard to the characteristic cluster of problems associated with the concept of ideology. The third paradigm – critical theory – has rejuvenated itself in the work of Habermas, on a route of intellectual history that has bypassed Paris via the Rhine, rather than via Oslo Fjord and the North Atlantic.

With all this variety and vitality of intellectual culture, and with the example of Althusserianism itself before us (or behind us), it would be wrong to make overweening claims for any one paradigm. We should therefore conclude by exploring certain limitations of rational choice theory, of Marxism, and – it must be said – of some rational choice Marxists. First, because rational choice explanation offers a particular kind of bridge for outcomes to a background distribution of values, beliefs, interests and resources, it is always possible that extra-rational motivations such as habit (if habit is a motivation) or emotion may render the bridge defective. It is also true that the background distribution itself remains unexplained, as in the case of the distribution of power and the historical process. In addition, rational choice explanation is inherently vulnerable to its own form of microscopic teleology, in which the behaviour leading to the outcome is treated as the principal evidence for the beliefs and values which would have made the behaviour rational. This is rationalization of action rather than rational explanation. But those who would write off the rational choice approach on this account should first consider the analyses of preference formation within a rational choice framework made by Elster in *Ulysses and the Sirens* and *Sour Grapes*,[68] and then reflect on the consequences for Marxism of abandoning the bridge between property distribution and class position constructed by Roemer.

GENDER DIFFERENCE

A second objection is more specific, perhaps symptomatic: namely, the sensitivity of the paradigm, as developed so far, to questions of gender division. The initial issue is one of language. The three leading lights of rational choice Marxism continue to use the masculine forms in generic contexts. This includes reference both to the true generic set (humankind) and, often, to a proper subset. For Cohen, for example: 'If an artist creates a beautiful object out of something which was less beautiful, then we would find it *natural* to say that he creates beauty.' (Wouldn't it be more natural to say that he or she creates beauty – or indeed that she or he creates beauty?)[69] Elster also has one or two asides and examples which I find slightly obtuse, to put it no stronger.[70] Altugh I have not searched out every last quotation, the usage is as far as I know unacknowledged and unexplained except in the bizarre case in which Cohen speaks of the 'sexist personification of humanity which Marxists have not always avoided', and then goes on not avoiding it.[71] It is true that rational choice Marxism has an intellectual background in philosophy and economics, which are the two backwoods disciplines in these respects. So it may be unfair to tax individuals with a collective fault. But the longer it goes on, the less the usage looks like adherence to a discredited convention and the more it looks like some kind of political statement. Where have these great men been for the last fifteen years?

Alongside these commissions, there is a remarkable – seemingly total – omission of reference either to feminist theory or to the general topic of sexual difference.[72] It is true that no one (not even three ones) can be expected to say something about everything. It is also hazardous, as Althusser discovered, to infer presences from absences. The case nevertheless seems to move from pardonable silence to purblind paralysis at the point when the discussion is led to the very brink of an illuminating connection with another (I thought, roughly adjacent) body of thought – and nothing is said. Let us examine two spectacular examples. In the course of

'Reconsidering Historical Materialism', Cohen describes as follows a human need to which 'Marxist observation is commonly blind': 'A person does not only need to develop and enjoy his powers. He needs to know who he is, and how his identity connects him with particular others .... [This is] a need to be able to say not what I can do but who I am, satisfaction of which has historically been found in identification with others in a shared culture based on nationality, or race, or religion, or some slice or amalgam thereof.'[73]

But not gender? Is it not beyond question that gender is a rather early and significant point of reference for 'who I am'? Do I not share a culture with people of my gender as well as, and probably before, I share one with people in my slice of the amalgamated union of nationality, race and religion? I have in mind's eye a snapshot of my son being chased terrified down a Bradford street, escaping, in the company of a muslim boy friend, from three girls: one muslim, one sikh and one a christian, his sister. And like nationality, race and religion, don't gender identifications 'generate, or at least sustain ... bonds whose strength Marxists systematically undervalue', not in this case 'because they neglect', but in spite of not neglecting, 'the need for self-identity underlying them'? Here, perhaps, we see the theoretical consequences of that widespread elision between the male and the species whose more innocent expression is the use of the generic pronoun.

The second example involves Roemer's concept of *status exploitation*. Here, at last, one might think, is the recognition that the existence of exploitation is an open question for every dimension of social division. In it lies the promise of a generalization adequate to the complexity of the real social world. But is this how Roemer intends the theory of 'status exploitation' to be taken? Not a bit of it. We have seen 'status' interpreted in an excessively literal – one might almost say, official – sense: to cover the exploitation of a bureaucratic position, independently of the alienable and non-alienable resources the status-holder may also command. So the only status that can be exploited is one of formal occupational position, as if there were no other dimensions of status generally recognized across the entire range of social interaction: tending to seal the fate of individuals within it.[74] Of these, the most important are surely gender, ethnicity and age. In the case of gender, it is difficult to miss the parallel between classical Marxism and second-wave feminism. Recall that the theory of value sets out with a group – the proletariat – and an intuition that their lot is not as just and happy as the official doctrine prescribes. The theory then recasts the distribution of benefits and burdens, representing the capitalists as doing less and getting more than they claim, while the workers are doing more and getting less than they are told to believe. It is characteristic that the current situation of the putative disadvantaged group is represented as worse than the disadvantaged group may currently think that it is. This is the radical politics of the long face. But the classical theory of value also holds out the alternative of a better world in which the current situation of apparent balance and real imbalance will be converted into a real balance.

What else has feminist theory set out to do? It has derided some of the activities and functions dear to the self-importance of men, and represented a range of other activities in which women are heavily engaged as workers, carers, nurturers and supporters as both more important and more burdensome than conventional wisdom allows.[75] Feminist theory has also held out the alternative of a better world in which there are no men as we commonly understand male behaviour – just as socialism envisages a world without capitalists, as we commonly understand capitalist behaviour. In the terminology of the general theory, we will have to say that women are *oppressed* as women so long as they are unfairly excluded from opportunities of satisfaction because of their gender (and there is a strong presumption that the exclusion will be unjust whenever it is caused in this way). They are *exploited* if they unfairly assume disproportionate burdens to the benefit of men as a result of the exclusion. Their counterfactual withdrawal option involves the elimination of the status differential – including the sexist practices defined as such by the maldistribution of resources or benefits which they entail.[76] Of course, we are not yet out of the woods, because it is true that women can be oppressed or exploited without being oppressed or exploited as a result of gender division (Friday was such a case). But this truth does not imply the converse proposition too easily taken for granted by Marxists: that whenever women are oppressed or exploited they are not oppressed or exploited by gender, but rather as members of a social class. The possibilities for two bases of social division, X and Y, are as follows: individuals are neither X nor Y oppressed or exploited; X but not Y; Y but not X; or both X and Y oppressed or exploited. These possibilities range independently over a potentially extensive list of resources, needs and criteria of benefit in the context of a variety of social institutions. In addition, there is the opaque but hopefully not impenetrable screen established by representation and ideology, in that an individual may be X while appearing to be Y oppressed or exploited (and all the other possible combinations of X, Y appearance with X, Y reality).

ETHNICITY AND EXPLOITATION

We can illustrate these points from the qualification that Cohen immediately enters to the perspective opened up by his assertion that Marxists ought to recognize the independent basis of the need for social identification: 'I agree with Frank Parkin that what I would call divisions or identity are as deep as those of class, and that they cannot be explained in the usual Marxist way. But I think he is wrong to suppose that this weakness in Marxism casts doubt on its treatment of domination and exploitation as centring on class conflict.... For racial exploitation and class exploitation are not two species of one genus. Racial exploitation is (largely) relegation to an exploited class because of race. And if, as Parkin thinks, Protestants exploit Catholics in Northern Ireland, then the exploitation is economic, and not in a comparable sense religious. Catholics are denied access to material values, not religious ones ...'.[77]

Let us take up the example of Northern Ireland. The use of the phrase 'relegation to an exploited class' suggests the opposite possibility, 'promotion'. Promotion to what? To a non-exploited or exploiting class, presumably. So the phrase seems to suggest at first sight that if a person were not a Catholic, they would not be in an exploited class. This might happen either because being a non-Catholic was, in itself, a sufficient condition for not being in an exploited class, or perhaps, that being a non-Catholic was a sufficient condition for owning some productive asset, with the consequence (endorsed by Roemer's work) that such a person could not be in an exploited class. But being Catholic or not seems to be the more fundamental feature of a person's situation either way, because in the first case the property variable has completely dropped out of the picture, and in the second it functions as an intermediate variable with no independent effect. If there is any exploitation, it is now an exploitation due to the ethnic rather than the ownership status of a person, and this was plainly not the conclusion motivating the choice of the phrase, or corresponding to the common Marxian thought about the kind of historical situation the conclusion was supposed to illuminate.

What is at issue here is obviously the relation between two features of an exploited person's situation – being Catholic and having no property (which are represented in theory under two descriptions of the same situation). Now, if not having property is independent of being a Catholic, we have the converse problem to the one considered just now that not having property is, in itself, a sufficient condition for being in an exploited class.

Contrary to the original claim, relegation has not occurred as a result of ethnic status. So what must be meant, and plausibly so in relation to the history of Northern Ireland, is that there is a distinction to be made between propertyless Protestants and Catholics, such that Catholics fare worse than Protestants (on average) and that they fare worse in this respect because they are Catholics. The opening claim is literally false, but can be amended to read with greater plausibility 'relegation to an especially exploited position within an exploited class because of race'. But now – and let us remember that there is only one person in one situation, described in two ways – to be Catholic and not to have property are both necessary conditions for the person's situation, but neither is sufficient on its own (i.e. we are not dealing with a case of overdetermination in which neither is necessary because either is sufficient). It is worth remarking that this irreducibility of the ethnic (likewise the gender) component in material exploitation will be obscured by any tendency to see the distribution of class positions as pre-given in a social formation: positions to which different kinds of people are subsequently hailed and nailed. Once class positions are seen with Roemer as the outcome of interaction, there is little reason to refuse the suggestion that the overall distribution of class positions and their correlative material values might reflect processes of status discrimination working directly in the workplace or indirectly through the distribution of productive assets and the mechanisms of the market.[78]

But what of 'religious values', and Cohen's denial of their denial in Northern Ireland? It may not be possible to deny people ultimate access to religious values, but their means of collective expression can certainly be heavily restricted. It is difficult to believe that this has not been the case in the long history of Catholic relations with Protestants in Ireland. This restriction will be oppressive so long as there is a presumptive right to the expression of religious or cultural values more generally. But is there anything directly analogous to exploitation in the sphere of non-material values? An argument to this effect must link the Protestant identity with the Catholic identity in a constitutive way, so that the oppression of the Catholics arises from a dynamic of Protestant association and the related requirements of the Protestant sense of self. Here it is surely significant that the variety of Protestant consciousness which is fateful for the history of Ireland does not just register the better material circumstances Protestants enjoy, on average. It tends to read these advantages into a social myth according to which Protestant people are a higher form of life than Catholic people (but no longer on average, since the discourse of moral segregation rarely admits of shades of grey). As is the custom in such cases, the attribution of superior qualities to Protestants conveniently forgets that it is often action (and inaction) by Protestants which has established a situation in which Catholics suffer the disadvantages to which the Protestant cause adverts. But the very maintenance of the Protestant identity seems to depend upon this notion of inherent and not just contingent (historical and material) ascendancy. This is one reason why the Battle of the Boyne is still being fought in East Belfast.

Now, it is true that every form of communal identification is in competition with every other, so that, at the very least, one might expect such identifications to jostle each other at the edges. It is also common, although hopefully not inevitable, that people feel good about themselves only in conjunction with feeling bad about somebody else. But there is a difference between feeling superior (which I am not here condoning in any way) and having a feeling of superiority whose security depends on some derogatory exhibition recurrently directed against those to whom you feel superior. A useful test of the distinction is the presence of flaunting, taunting and vaunting rituals designed to display the alleged superiority in terms so graphic that their meaning cannot be mistaken by the allegedly inferior group.[79] Especially when these flaunting rituals are backed by state power, those at the receiving end are placed in an unusually invidious position. If they do not respond to the ritual, they may appear to give (and will certainly be taken by the other side to give) a tacit endorsement to the sense of superiority – hence to collude in public recognition of their inferior social status. But if they resist, and are beaten back by the forces ranged against them, they risk the same outcome as before, but at a higher level, so to speak (with greater loss of life and limb). This is the challenge which lies behind the provocation that a flaunting ritual involves.

I submit that this is precisely what has always been at stake in the Orange marches, and the tenacity with which many Protestants adhere to the rituals cannot be explained by the superior material circumstances they enjoy. Often these are not, in any case, obviously better than those of their Catholic neighbours. If the Protestants have been bought off, the purchase trades on their sense of self and not their balance at the bank. But then we are able to suggest that Protestants are exploiting the Catholic sense of communal identity – strictly, exploiting the fact that they do not (cannot) share the Protestant identity. Catholics are placed in a situation in which their best option – probably, almost every option – confers a benefit on the Protestants, even if it redounds to the Protestants' distorted sense of self-esteem, and nothing material (apart from missiles) passes between the exploiter and the exploited. The Catholics are trapped and made use of in their being, just as surely as the proletarians are trapped and made use of in their doing. There is thus a politics of communal association which is irreducible to, and yet shows certain features in common with, the politics of material distribution.

OUT OF THE WOODS FOR THE TREES

Suppose it is right to insist on the self-seeking character of human behaviour: both in the sense of seeking a sense of self and in the sense of seeking satisfactions for the sought self. Then concern with the character of social identification is not only a concession to social phenomena which have proved intractable to Marxist theory in the past, but is intrinsic to the socialist project in the present and the future.

Imagine a group of people who have struggled together for as long as they can remember through a trackless and inhospitable forest, suddenly disgorged onto a vast, fertile plain transparent to their gaze. They break up and fan out across the new space. They expand somewhat, and no doubt relax a little. But after the first burst of enthusiasm, they look about them and take stock. Their material circumstances have eased, to the full extent, if you will, that the realm of necessity lies entirely behind them. They are free and human, so they look for ways of expressing their essential creativity and meeting all their other needs. We have assumed that some of these (and no doubt many more than at present) depend on the provision of resources immediately to hand, and have no repercussions for the activities of other people, save perhaps to supplement the goods which others can enjoy. But some kinds of expression (and probably not the least important of these) still depend on the provision of public goods, and the co-operation of other people.

How do we know in advance that the provision of these public goods spontaneously corresponds to the newly released impulses of all the people concerned? How do we know that the supply according to ability matches the demand according to need? We cannot be sure, and so long as there is a potential dispute about the provision of public goods, there is a potential problem of social order, because the individuals, being human, are rational and will be tempted to consume the public goods they need, whether or not the provision of all those goods was part of their first, unhindered action.

Let us suppose that they appreciate this, and they remember from their time in the forest that it will be foolish to nominate some of their number to be holders of state power, because it will be foolish to believe that any one among them is conspicuously immune from the corruptions of great power and high rank. So they will resort to a sense of collective identity, upon which the sanctions will bear which are necessary to resolve the problem of social order in the absence of a state.[80] All those who would take unfair advantage of the provision of collective goods by others will be admonished with respect to this sense of what the group is, and what it is about. We expect that the admonishment will be mild, by historical standards, since it is not undertaken in conditions of great scarcity and it is undertaken for reasons which everyone can approve. Nevertheless, it is necessary to guard against the renewed exploitation of some by others. The sense of identity must itself be non-exploitative – it must not make the sense of self-esteem enjoyed by some depend on the parade of superiority over others – since this is just one aspect of what the sense of collective identity is introduced to avoid. But then the socialist is indeed like Ulysses. She has entered a formative commitment, according to which she will develop a sense of self, binding her in the future against the temptation to satisfy her human needs unfairly at the expense of the needs of others.[81]

NOTES

1. I should like to thank Perry Anderson and Norman Geras for comments on an earlier version without which this essay would be even less balanced than it is.
2. Two full-dress retrospectives on Althusser are available: Benton (1984) and Callinicos (1976).
3. For an illustration of Cohen's style see his argument – a personal favourite of mine – that structure-preserving changes in an economy are conceivable in Cohen (1978), p. 36.
4. The major works after Cohen (1978) include Wood (1981), Roemer (1982a), Elster (1985), Przeworksi (1985a), Wright (1985).
5. The intention of the present essay is to provide not a comprehensive assessment but some preliminary bearings in the intellectual territory opened up by these writers. I will concentrate mainly on Cohen's and Roemer's contributions, which seem to me central to this purpose. A fuller assessment, inevitably displaying a greater variety of views, would deal in much greater detail with the controversy surrounding methodological individualism, and questions of explanation, recent work in the labour theory of value, the debate on 'Marx and Justice', the question of collective action and the political ramifications of the new approach.
6. For the definition of Western Marxism, and the most erudite expositions of its development, see the periodic Dean's reports issued by Perry Anderson

in Anderson (1976), (1980) and (1983). The verdict is nearly always 'promising, but could do better'.
7. Can it be a coincidence that this is happening at a time when capitalism itself has reverted to type? Although one approaches with some trepidation any work in which the words 'ludic' and 'veridical' may be found in the same sentence, Perry Anderson in Anderson (1983) does not go far to explain the remarkable shift he highlights in the centre of gravity of Marxist theoretical culture from Latin Europe to northern Europe and North America (Cohen is a Canadian in Oxford via London, Elster is a Norwegian in Chicago after an apparently rather uncongenial stay in Paris, Roemer is in California, of all the unlikely places for socialist innovation – although I suppose it had to happen eventually). True to former inspirations, and former paradigms, Anderson is more concerned to theorise the absence in Paris than the presence in LA. This geo-intellectual context of revival is another issue given inadequate coverage below.
8. 'Analytical Marxism' is the title that appears to have been chosen by the leading exponents themselves. 'Game-theoretic Marxism' occurs in Lash and Urry (1984). 'Post-classical Marxism' is taken from Anderson's discussion of Western European Marxism from 1918 to 1968 in Anderson (1983), p. 15. Of these terms, 'Game-theoretic Marxism' is too narrow because only part of the novelty of the approach is captured by it and only some of the findings of the theory are illuminatingly expressed in the technical vocabulary of game theory; neo-classical Marxism is too pretentious and post-post-classical Marxism is too clumsy. Roemer's introduction of the term 'Analytical Marxism' in Roemer (1986), pp. 1–7, stresses a common concern for 'logic, mathematics and model building' and an accompanying 'search for foundations'. The problem is that the non-economists only occasionally resort to formal mathematical models, and while the standards of logical exposition set by Cohen are indeed high, it would be presumptuous to regard them as distinctive. Equally, it is not the search for foundations, but the kind of foundation that is distinctive. (Althusser also searched for foundations.) I think the salience of the rationality assumption in the search deserves headline recognition, and it is significant that Roemer does adopt the term '"rational choice" Marxism' for his contribution to the edited collection Roemer (1986). There is nevertheless a spectrum of adherence to the rational choice paradigm: Roemer and the economists, Przeworski, Elster and van Parijs are at one end; Brenner, Wright, and Cohen are influenced but less clearly committed, followed by Geras (whose disavowal of the label I should record here; and Allen Wood is firmly situated at the opposite end of the spectrum, as the clearest example of a writer who is an 'analytical' without being a 'rational choice' Marxist. But it is worth emphasising that Wood is sharply at odds with nearly all the writers mentioned on a range of fundamental issues (e.g. the normative foundations of Marxism, sympathy with the Hegelian side of Marx). It is also fitting that, so far as I know, the patent on the term 'rational choice Marxism' belongs to Barry Hindess in Hindess (1984), and that Hindess has begun a counter-attack on its assumptions; see also Hindess (1985) and (1986).
9. The intuition underlying the remark is this: a structure is a set of relations between the members of a set of elements. At the highest level of description,

the elements of social structure are at most people, things and ideas (at most, depending on one's ontology). But these are also the elements which enter the description of action, so that actions seem to be structures with the same basis as the social structures allegedly distinct from actions.

10. I say 'almost certain' since it would be logically possible for productive forces to increase their level indefinitely but asymptotically to some level that stays within the compass of given relations of production.

11. See Brenner (1986), Cohen (1983a), Cohen (1983b), Elster (1980), Elster (1982a), Elster (1982b), Elster (1984), Levine and Wright (1980), Parijs (1981), Parijs (1984).

12. For Cohen's decisive argument on this point, see Cohen (1978), pp. 41–2.

13. 'A description is social if and only if it entails an ascription to persons – specified or unspecified – of rights or powers *vis-à-vis* other men' (Cohen 1978, p. 94). But not 'other people'? – a usage to which I will return.

14. 'The fact that we need the social point of view to discern the capitalist status of means of production or the slave status of a man does not mean that the means of production are not capital or the man not a slave. Each standpoint of a thing reveals a distinct set of properties, but the thing has all of them' (Cohen 1978, p. 91).

15. Doreen Massey says of her programme that 'the aim . . . is to link two discussions – the one concerning production and social class, and the other concerning spatial organization. In relation to much previous analysis within geography, the argument is that what has been seen simply as the spatial distribution of employment is underlain by, and can be approached through, analysis of the geographical organization of the relations of production. In relation to the substantive social sciences the argument is that the social structure of the economy, the social relations of production, necessarily develop spatially and in a variety of forms. These forms we shall call *spatial structures of production*' (Massey 1984, p. 68). Cohen prefigured the connection between the new critical geography and rational choice Marxism in a brilliant, fleeting paragraph (Cohen 1978, p. 97).

16. The alternative habit used to be most marked in Erik Olin Wright, whose oft-cited characterization of social classes in Wright (1978) mapped the organization chart of the average US corporation onto society as a whole – the larger pyramid imitating the smaller. Wright is one of the few theorists to have negotiated the transition from Althusserian to rational choice Marxism. Initially very sceptical, though appreciative, of Cohen's work, he seems to have fallen more into line after catching sight of Tony Giddens. Now he has made his peace with John Roemer's theory of class, but not before mounting a stout rearguard action on behalf of the old 'political' approach (power in the workplace) against the new 'economic' one (ownership relations and markets). See Levine and Wright (1980), Wright (1982), Wright (1983), Wright (1985).

17. Geras (1983), p. 107. For a succinct statement of Geras's position, see Geras (1983), p. 68. For Cohen's statement of a position very similar to the one later elaborated by Geras, see Cohen (1978), p. 151.

18. See Carling (1986).

19. This division, and part of the terminology, bear the authority of Engels; see, for example, his 'Speech at the Graveside of Karl Marx', in R. C. Tucker

(ed.), *The Marx–Engels Reader*, 2nd edn (New York and London: W. W. Norton), p. 681. Cohen has said that 'Marx produced at least these four sets of ideas: a philosophical anthropology, a theory of history, an economics, and a vision of the society of the future'. I think that 'an economics' is a downgrading description of the special theory (only the theory of history counts as a proper theory); see Cohen (1983a), p. 232. It is symptomatic of the underestimation of the status of the special theory which is, I believe, the greatest weakness in Cohen's overall treatment of Marx.

20. This comment has in mind Elster's 'torch relay model of development' among a number of nations; see Elster (1984), p. 38.
21. This is the burden of Brenner's view of the transition to capitalism: it is *only* capitalist relations of production which have a systematic tendency to raise the level of development of the forces of production, so 'it becomes just about impossible to see how the sort of argument Cohen makes for the primacy of the productive forces can be sustained'; Brenner (1986), p. 47, n. 13.
22. 'How does production on the basis of exchange-value solely determined by labour-time lead to the result that the exchange-value of labour is less than the exchange-value of its product?' (Marx, *A Contribution to the Critique of Political Economy*, quoted in Cohen 1978, p. 43; cf. Roemer 1986, p. 185). Notice how the very form of this question makes it the grandparent of all attempts to understand how non-straightforward structure arises from straightforward agency, that is, how the particular puzzle which capitalism presented to Marx requires the sort of theory rational choice Marxism aspires to provide.
23. '[Labour power] and not labour, is what the proletarian sells to the capitalist, who pays less for it than the value of what he is able to make it produce' (Cohen 1978, p. 43; see also Roemer 1985, p. 31, repr. in Roemer 1986, p. 261).
24. 'To make a fetish of something, or fetishize it, is to invest it with powers it does not in itself have' (Cohen 1978, p. 115). 'In commodity-producing societies there is a tendency to overlook the implicitly relational character of certain monadic predicates' (Elster 1985, p. 96). On Marx's 'exaggeration': 'Economic agents do not invest commodities and instruments of production with the full panoply of mysterious powers that Marx describes in such detail. Money is indeed a mysterious entity, but only in part for the reasons brought out by Marx' (Elster 1985, p. 99).
25. See Cohen (1978), p. 115 and App. 1.
26. This comment trades on the existence of two orders of human need – for creativity and subsistence – and the two corresponding conceptions of labour which are distinguished in Cohen (1983a).
27. A recent example is Jeremy Seabrook's *Landscapes of Poverty* (Oxford: Blackwell, 1985), which combines a brilliantly observed evocation of contemporary life in Britain with an argument that the experience of poverty has shifted decisively from the external to the internalized landscapes of capitalism. If this is Orwell plus ideology, the contrast is overdrawn.
28. The argument in the closing section is intended to show that these are independent criteria, that is, that egalitarianism cannot be seen merely as a historically conditioned response to scarcity. On the issues of whether Marx held values, what they were, and their importance for his theory, the range

of positions may be represented by Elster (1985), esp. Ch. 4, and Wood (1986), with the most comprehensive appraisal of the debate given in Geras (1985). I will adopt the 'pro' side of the debate in what follows without further ado.

29. Roemer adopts Friday and Crusoe in Roemer (1982b), p. 299.
30. I assume that the level of development of the forces of production is always measured by (labour) productivity, but there are various possible definitions of productivity in the presence of constant capital, let alone other complications. The best procedure is to define productivity always as the inverse of unit value, so that productivity is well-defined whenever value is. In general, productivity will then be a vector quantity, which raises problems about the meaning of its 'level' for a multi-product economy. For relevant discussion (though not in quite these terms), see Cohen (1978), pp. 55–62.
31. It is, however, highly significant that the circuits of commodity production and exchange which are the qualitative basis of the discussion in *Capital* involve transaction sequences coinciding with those given by the equilibrium outcomes of Roemer's models. Marx's sequences are examined in Carling (1986).
32. The vocabulary of the social and the material is properly inserted here, since the outcomes bear a direct relation to the distribution of power. The relations are not social only by contrast with the initial situations of individual isolation on the two islands.
33. The 'slight adaptation' of Roemer's opening statement of the two-person case in Roemer (1982a) is the provision of enough seedcorn to employ the whole population (two people) in the CI technology. Roemer makes the supply 'limited', in order to focus on the competitive outcome of extreme capitalism. It is also worth noting that Roemer consistently describes the models discussed in Part 1 of Roemer (1982a) as relating to a 'pre-capitalist, subsistence economy' (p. 109). This is fair enough if the capitalist 'mode of production' is defined via the capitalist impulse for capital accumulation (cf. Cohen 1978, p. 81). It may be misleading if capitalism is considered sociologically in terms of its characteristic class structure and mode of exploitation, which do appear in the subsistence models of Part 1 of Roemer (1982a). I have used the term 'capitalist' freely in the account of the subsistence model above with the latter consideration in mind (see also n. 39 below).
34. There are two routes to the greening of socialism from this point. One route concentrates directly on relations between the human and non-human worlds, and is out of sympathy with the classical emphasis on the 'mastery of nature'. The other looks at the non-human world as mediating human relations, especially between current and future generations. To say that current generations must not oppress the future by depriving the planet of non-renewable resources is fully consistent with the classical spirit, as I understand it.
35. Cf. Cohen's 'rough idea of exploitation, as a certain kind of lack of reciprocity' such that it is [unjust] exploitation to obtain something from someone without giving him anything in return' (Cohen 1981, p. 343). Elster's more refined dictionary definition is 'the asymmetrical notion of "taking unfair advantage of someone"' (Elster, 1983b, p. 278).

36. If this sounds odd, recall the special definition of the social and translate: 'no return is owed to an exercise of power alone' or 'might is not right'. For Cohen's distinction, see Cohen (1981), p. 219.
37. For the examples and further discussion, see Carling (1987). Wright uses the term 'oppression' in a similar sense in preference to Roemer's cumbersome 'Marxian unfairly treated', but Wright (1985), pp. 74–7, implies that oppression is necessary for exploitation.
38. This point seems to mitigate the impact Nozick's celebrated Wilt Chamberlain argument has for the debate about Marxian exploitation. Chamberlain may be entitled to his wealth. He may not be entitled to use it in ways connected with capitalist market relations.
39. This is a mode of production in the sense of Cohen's 'economic structure' and not his mode of production in the sense of 'way of producing' (Cohen 1978, Ch. 3). I have also used the term 'regime of production' as a synonym for the conventional 'mode of production'.
40. Cf. 'The proletarian may do anything he wishes with his labour power, short of violating the general laws of society, and nothing may be done with it without his contractual consent' (Cohen 1978, p. 66).
41. This reciprocal character of power will be difficult to 'think' in the social stratification paradigm, since the vertical metaphor tends to imply that 'power over' is an asymmetrical (unidirectional) relation. This is clear from Parkin (1979) in which the resistance offered by groups excluded from property is called 'usurpationary'. But there is no usurpation of bourgeois power when workers attempt to use the powers which define their own place in capitalist society relations: powers which run parallel with or exist on the same level as powers over means of production. A similar point applies to Althusserian notions of 'dominance'.
42. Given the agreement, it follows from the definition that each person has sacrificed some degree of power, since the maximum damage they might inflict has been reduced. Interestingly, the longer Friday works, the less power Crusoe enjoys over Friday, since Friday has a diminishing incentive to be exploited in the CI technology. It is natural to say that Crusoe does not have an interest in making use of his power to the full. This point may have wider application to the strategies of ruling classes.
43. This is the gist of an early exchange between Roemer and Wright, in which I have followed the Roemer line. For Wright's position, see Wright (1982), but note his frank retraction in Wright (1985): 'I now think Roemer is correct on this point.'
44. I have in mind the tendency of capitalist states to grant the formal 'right to strike' but to hedge this right around with such restrictions as to make the exercise of the right practically ineffective, above all, by maintaining capitalist access to an alternative labour supply. At some degree of restriction, probably surpassed in fascist regimes, the state would cease to be capitalist on this definition. A converse point would apply to restrictions on property rights.
45. 'Extent' rather than 'monopoly' in recognition of Gidden's amendment to Weber (Giddens 1985, p. 20).
46. This point illustrates why the use of the term 'power' is often indexical, making reference to actors or resources excluded from some analysis of current concern.

47. Marx used this transition in *Capital*, Vol. 1, to distinguish simple commodity production from capitalism, with respect both to class structure and motivational structure (the drive for accumulation). Roemer's basic model shows that the two aspects of the transition were inappropriately elided, since it has capitalist class structure and subsistence motivations. I missed this point in Carling (1986).
48. The Friday/Crusoe technology is strictly speaking non-Leontief, since there are two techniques for producing corn. But this will stand for a distinction between products made using LI and CI techniques in the multi-product model.
49. 'In [the modal] definition, we do not consider an agent to be exploited if he *happens* to purchase a bundle of goods which embodies less labour time than he worked; he is only exploited if he could not feasibly have purchased a bundle of goods embodying as much labour time as he worked' (Roemer 1982a, p. 135). A converse definition applies to an exploiter. Applications of the definition depend on an 'assumption of a large economy', since the supply of 'high-value' and 'low-value' goods must be large enough to absorb the revenues of any individual agent. The grey area always embraces the petty bourgeoisie (that is, those who optimize at self-employment). This conforms nicely with one of the traditional Marxist intuitions about their intermediate character. Elster, in Elster (1985), p. 173, gives the modal conception of class pride of place in his appreciation of Roemer's theory; cf. Cohen's modal workers: 'a proletarian must sell his labour-power in order to obtain his means of life' (Cohen 1978, p. 72).
50. The reason is that a CECP only holds if labour value is defined with respect to the profit-maximizing technologies rather than the whole technology set. But prices must be known before it can be ascertained which the profit-maximizing technologies are.
51. Roemer (1982a), Ch. 6.
52. There is no class decomposition in this case, because the actors (conceived as nations) are restricted to self-employment. But there is nevertheless a Wealth Exploitation Correspondence Principle – see Roemer (1982a), App. 1.1, and Roemer (1983). This extension of the theory also motivates the nomination of Friday and Crusoe as the actors in the basic theory.
53. The 'credit classes' are pure lenders, mixed lenders, petty bourgeoisie, mixed borrowers and pure borrowers respectively (Roemer 1982a, Ch. 3).
54. The counter-example occurs in Roemer (1982a), pp. 234–5, and recurs more prominently with different numbers as Examples 1 and 2 in Roemer (1982b), pp. 287ff. The latter paper gives a résumé of all the important cases. Example 2b is Credit Market Island; 3 is the Friday/Crusoe case and 9 exhibits unequal exchange through trade.
55. Roemer (1982a), pp. 194–5; 'if and' is deleted from the definition, together with a third 'dominance' condition, which Roemer includes in order to rule out a series of counter-examples involving the claims of the non-able-bodied on the social product. The difficulty is that the dominance condition is not precisely stated. Roemer gives two interpretations of its meaning (Roemer 1982a, pp. 195, 237), the second of which would imply that Crusoe does not exploit Friday and the first of which raises the general question of power in a way that I have tried to follow through in the previous section, but again without discriminating example from counter-

example. In my view, the solution to this difficulty lies with the moral conditions for exploitation: it may be possible to represent the claims of the non-able-bodied in terms of an unequal exchange with the able-bodied, but even if so, the exchange is not unfair.

56. Elster has provided an example in which the two major conditions are satisfied, but there is no interaction between the exploiter and exploited (Elster 1982c, p. 367). To meet this case and subsequent to Roemer (1982a), Roemer substituted for the dominance condition another one designed to capture the interaction more precisely ('Definition PR', condition 3 in Roemer 1982b, p. 285 (the dominance condition is banished to n. 12)). Elster replies that no set of counter-factual conditionals, however long, can ever capture the causal element in the intuition of exploitation. The story will run and run. . . . but not here.

57. An example is Roemer's 'non-subtle disagreement' between neo-classical proponents and Marxist opponents of capitalism (Roemer 1982a, p. 206).

58. Roemer uses the term 'Marxian exploitation' to distinguish cases of surplus-value transfer which do not constitute capitalist exploitation under the general definition. In Elster's view the problem with the value approach is that it adopts too microscopic a perspective (Elster 1985, pp. 175ff.). Parkin, in Parkin (1979), p. 53, also had a sense of this point.

59. This point is made by Wright in Wright (1985), pp. 77–8. The proposal has the additional merit of conforming to Cohen's definitions of the economic structures of feudalism and slavery (see Cohen 1978, p. 65).

60. See Roemer (1982a), p. 243. Throughout his book, Roemer defines socialism via the nationalization of alienable assets, and develops a strong case against any alternative, and less operational, definition (see Roemer 1982a, pp. 2–6). Both socialist exploitation and status exploitation exist in current socialist societies and 'are uncritically accepted' (Roemer 1982a, p. 249). Although he thinks one or both forms may be socially necessary at the current historical stage, Roemer's openness in calling the relevant inequalities exploitative is an important example of the healthy directness with which Marxists of this persuasion are prepared to approach the societies of actually existing socialism without abandoning their sympathy for them.

61. I am grateful to P. Jowers at Bristol Polytechnic for alerting me to Tawney's onion.

62. Elster's major contribution to rational choice Marxism lies in his treatment of the paradoxes and contradictions of collective rational action, applied to a wide variety of historical contexts (see esp. Elster 1985, Chs 6–8). Przeworski has surveyed the valley that workers' organization must cross in the pursuit of socialism (Przeworski 1985, Przeworski 1986). Brenner and Taylor deal with the peasantry in the context of the transition to capitalism and modern revolutionary movements, respectively. For both writers, the strength of pre-existing peasant community is the crucial background variable of rational choice, inhibiting capitalist development (Brenner) or facilitating revolutionary mobilization (Taylor) (Brenner 1986, Taylor 1988).

63. This may be so even in the absence of socialist exploitation when 'socialistically legitimate returns to differential skills can become embodied as differential ownership of capital' (Roemer 1982a, p. 261).

64. Cf. Pranab Bardhan's comment on the multiplicity of development paths in Roemer (1982a), p. 73.
65. Roemer 'note[s] a parallel' in which feudal and status exploitation are opposed to capitalist exploitation, because in the former examples property is derived from status, whereas capitalist status is derived from property (Roemer 1982a, p. 243).
66. This is the approach adopted in Wright (1985), although it should be said that his credential assets (educational qualifications) and organization assets (formal position) are not quite Roemer's non-alienable assets and status, since credentials may involve a pure status ('cultural capital') component and formal position may include a skills component (knowledge of how to organize).
67. See Barrett (1985), p. 146.
68. See Elster (1979) and Elster (1983c).
69. Cohen (1981), pp. 206, 223. Cohen also has the endearing and revealing habit of sometimes starting a sentence in resolutely non-sexist fashion and then sliding into the masculine by the end; see, for example, Cohen (1983a), p. 236: 'Why should a man or woman not find fulfilment in his or her work as a painter, conceived as his contribution to the society to which he belongs. . .'.
70. The most serious case is the following illustration indispensable for the account in Elster (1982c), p. 365, of the distinction between exploitation and extortion: 'women are exploited by their employers if they get more rapid promotion by sexual favours, but are victims of extortion if they have to give these favours to obtain even the normal promotion'. This example is criticized at length in Carling (1987), but I should also record my impression that sexist usage is on the decline among all those I complain of here.
71. See Cohen (1983a), p. 232.
72. Such an omission from the otherwise encyclopaedic ambitions of Elster (1985) is also striking.
73. See Cohen (1983a), pp. 234-5, from which the preceding quotations are also taken. Cohen has acknowledged this point gracefully in Cohen (1989).
74. The distinction between socialist and status exploitation has already taken Roemer outside historical materialism, since status, as distinct from non-alienable assets, is not a force of production whose level of development might be registered by the key theses of historical materialism.
75. It is also worth emphasizing that the analytical distinction between 'sex' and 'gender' which was a basic achievement of second-wave feminist theory is parallel to Cohen's distinction between the 'material' and the 'social', and the feminist statement preceded the Marxist one.
76. I take it that the defining characteristic of radical feminism is the completeness of the break with men thought necessary to bring this about. Wright discusses the counter-factual withdrawal options available to women, and expresses doubts whether women's labour in the home is exploited according to such a test, but his test explicitly leaves discrimination in the labour market in place! The empirical significance of the limitation may be judged from Wright (1985), p. 129, n. 77.
77. Cohen (1983a), p. 248, n. 10. I should like to acknowledge the rejoinder made by Cohen, in the source material in n. 73, that my criticism of this

quotation 'ride[s] roughshod over nuances' in its expression. In particular, I am not sure that anything offered in the rest of the chapter is incompatible with Cohen's statement that 'racial exploitation is (largely) relegation to an exploited class because of race'. In soccer, the result between notes 73 and 77 would be score draw.

78. Wright's data on income distributions is interesting in this respect. The differential of mean incomes between his 'agreed upon' middle and working classes in each gender category is around 1.9. The differential between men and women in each class category is around 1.7 (see Wright 1985, Table 5.15, p. 179). If, as Wright tends to do, one infers exploitation directly from income distributions (the inference may be incautious), it looks as if gender exploitation is just about as serious as asset exploitation for the situation of individuals in the United States today.

79. I assume that rituals of this kind are especially characteristic of the behaviour of men: towards women and towards other men. What is said here is intended to generalize beyond Northern Ireland, and beyond ethnic relationships.

80. This endorses the main argument of Taylor (1982). Cf. Taylor (1976), Ch. 7. Taylor's work seems to deserve the title 'rational choice anarchism'.

81. I owe the term and the concept 'formative commitment' to my friend and colleague David West's PhD thesis, 'Nature, Society and the Will', University of Bradford (1983).

4 Rational Choice Marxism: Is the Game Worth the Candle?[1]
Ellen Meiksins Wood

Some time ago, in the pages of the *New Left Review*, a claim was made on behalf of 'rational choice Marxism' as 'a fully fledged paradigm, which deserves to take its place beside the two other constellations of theory currently discernible within the broad spectrum of progressive social thought – namely, post-structuralism and critical theory' (see above, pp. 61–2). More than that: 'it is now only within the rational choice context that some of the leading items on the classical agenda of Marxist theory – historical explanation and delineation of social form, the collective dynamics of class struggle, the evolution and evaluation of capitalism – can be fruitfully discussed.' These are very large claims, and if this new 'paradigm' can even partially live up to them, it deserves the vogue it is now enjoying in the Anglo-American academy. A theoretical advance in any one of the 'leading items on the classical agenda of Marxist theory' would be a worthy accomplishment; but it would indeed be a remarkable achievement if, even without driving any likely competitors from the field, this body of thought could be shown to merit the status of a 'fully fledged paradigm', a comprehensive theoretical 'constellation' with the explanatory range of classical Marxism.

WHAT IS RATIONAL CHOICE MARXISM?

There is a difficulty at the outset in evaluating the claims of RCM. What are to be our criteria of inclusion? Alan Carling tells us that 'if there is one distinctive presupposition of the intended body of work, it must be the view that societies are composed of human individuals who, being endowed with resources of various kinds, attempt to choose rationally between various courses of action (see above, pp. 32–3). On the face of it, this 'distinction' places RCM in the company of a dauntingly large and heterogeneous collection of writers – only part of which is exhausted by Carling's own admission that this same 'distinctive presupposition' is 'a commonplace of that broad sweep of conventional economics and philosophy conducted in the liberal tradition.' The further specification that the 'dramatic' difference lies in RCM's 'joining of this presupposition with the classical agenda of Marxist theory' only complicates matters. To guarantee the comprehensiveness of this paradigm, its full coverage of the classical Marxist agenda, Carling is obliged to collect under its rubric a wide and disparate range of writers, at least some of whom would contest their own inclusion (he specifically acknowledges Norman Geras's disavowal of the RCM label though without apparently accepting this self-exclusion). It is not enough to include figures like John Roemer or Jon Elster, those who would most readily accept a 'rational choice' designation which carries the associations of game theory and methodological individualism. To make good his claims for RCM in the areas of historical explanation in general and the evolution of capitalism in particular – themes which on any conventional reckoning are central to the Marxist agenda – Carling must recruit into the RCM school writers who evince a very different attitude to methodological individualism – notably Robert Brenner and G. A. Cohen.

In other words, the 'distinctive presupposition' must remain very broadly defined indeed (so broadly, in fact, that it is difficult to see why that most 'classical' of Marxists, Friedrich Engels – who, after all, had something to say about the formation of social patterns from the unintended consequences of individual human actions – could not be taken on board). To say that this paradigm is also distinctively characterized by an 'analytic' mode of presentation (the term 'analytic Marxism' is sometimes taken to be synonymous with rational choice Marxism) hardly advances matters, since the 'analytic' style of argumentation is in principle compatible with any set of substantive propositions. Alternatively, if the 'distinctive presupposition' is further specified, if RCM is distinguished by its game-theoretic methodological individualism, then the most distinctive characteristic of this paradigm – the formal abstraction and the static, ahistorical individualism of the rational choice model – is the one which is least congenial to those central items of the Marxist agenda: social change and historical process, and in particular, the 'laws of motion' specific to various modes of production, their characteristic crises, the specific principles of motion in transition from one mode to another.

Carling himself seems aware of the difficulty when he acknowledges that Roemer's theory of exploitation provides no substitute of its own for the 'classic' Marxist theory of history but remains 'parasitic' on that general theory (as interpreted by G. A. Cohen) (see above, pp. 58–9).

Indeed, Roemer makes no pretence that his distinctive rational choice paradigm, which he offers as a substitute for the classical theory of exploitation based on the labour theory of value, can generate its own theory of historical process. What he offers us instead is a hybrid. As Carling puts it in his recent review of Roemer's latest book *Free to Lose* ('the textbook of contemporary Marxist theory'),[2] Roemer's 'standard contemporary Marxism' is 'Cohen on history plus Roemer on class and exploitation'.

A sensible way to proceed, then, might be to begin with a specific definition of RCM, which recognizes the distinctiveness of its game-theoretic models and their methodological individualism, but without prejudging the capacity of this paradigm to enter into a fruitful alliance with a theory of social change and historical process from outside its distinctive methodological boundaries. This leaves us, in the first instance, with three obvious major candidates for inclusion: John Roemer, Jon Elster, and (lately) Adam Przeworski. The latter is included with some hesitation, because, although he sometimes carries the rational choice model to extremes not envisaged even by Roemer, he is the least consistent of the three in his adherence to the paradigm, having done important political analysis which does not rely on the game-theoretic paradigm and which is, if anything, undermined by the model's theoretical demands. In what follows, the focus will be mainly on Roemer, who has provided the clearest and most comprehensive account of the RCM paradigm, with excursions into Elster and Przeworski when they help to clarify some important point or explicitly depart from Roemer in some significant way. Erik Olin Wright will be excluded from consideration simply on the grounds that his theoretical formation appears to be in a critical stage of transition: his recent book *Classes*, which constructed a theory of class on foundations of Roemer's theory of exploitation, was almost immediately followed by an article co-authored with Andrew Levine and Elliott Sober which deflates the explanatory pretensions of methodological individualism practically to the vanishing point.[3] The connection of Brenner and Cohen to this core group remains to be established and will be explored when we come to the question of RCM's treatment of history.

Roemer has written that 'methodological individualism', specifically in its 'game-theoretic' mode, is essential to the explication of historical materialism and its 'key propositions': 'the 'key questions of historical materialism,' he maintains, 'require reference to the specific forms of class struggle, and ... an understanding of such struggles is elucidated by game theory; ... class analysis requires microfoundations at the level of the individual to explain why and when classes are the relevant unit of analysis' (Roemer 1982c, p. 513). Let us say, then, that the *differentia specifica* of

RCM is a theory of exploitation and class in which various modes of exploitation and classes are logically generated according to the principles of game-theoretic analysis. This by no means reduces RCM to a purely methodological strategy. On the contrary, as we shall see, the *form* of the RCM theory is to a large extent its *substance*, and in its game-theoretic assumptions are secreted vital substantive theses about the social world.

The Roots of Rational Choice

The elusiveness of RCM's distinctive identity may have something to do with a certain lack of critical self-awareness among its practitioners. They are remarkably insensitive to the history and context of ideas in general, and their own ideas in particular; and they are generally inclined to remain within a very narrow universe of debate. RCMists, to judge by the extent of their mutually self-confirming footnoting and the restricted range of controversy encompassed by their writings, seem to talk largely to each other.

Despite its characteristic ahistoricism, the provenance of the paradigm is clear enough. The roots of this game-theoretic rational choice approach to social theory are to be found in conventional neo-classical economics and its extension to the other 'social sciences' in the work of such writers as James Buchanan, Anthony Downs, Mancur Olson and Gary Becker. In other words, the 'rational choice' paradigm has its origins in the rebirth of right-wing thought. This is not to say that the theoretical associations of the paradigm must inevitably propel its adherents to the political right, but since this filiation is never consciously and critically confronted, the resistance of RCM's politics impulses to attractions from the right is seriously weakened.

There are also, however, other intellectual contexts, less alien to Marxism, which might help to explain the emergence of RCM. The dominant school of Marxism during the period of RCM gestation was undoubtedly Althusserian structuralism. It is perhaps against the background of this Althusserian hegemony, and the excesses of its attacks on conceptions of human agency in favour of structural explanations from which the human subject was 'rigorously' expelled, that the attractions of the methodological individualism proposed by Roemer and Elster can be most sympathetically understood – though, as we shall see, there have been some unexpected points of convergence between these two apparently antithetical paradigms.

One more intellectual co-ordinate is worth mentioning: the analytic, formalistic mode of academic political philosophy, both liberal and conservative, which has evolved especially in the United States, as exemplified in particular by John Rawls and Robert Nozick. It is possible that RCM can most positively be conceived as an attempt to construct a *normative* socialist theory to counter the conservative philosophy of writers like Nozick. To say this, however, may be to circumscribe the claims which RCM makes for itself, to limit its application far more strictly than any of its exponents have yet been willing to do. Although Roemer in particular maintains that a principal benefit of the rational choice paradigm is that it reveals, as conventional Marxist theory cannot do, the ethical basis of Marxism, the claims for RCM as a superior *explanatory* model have been equally vigorous.

THE RCM THEORY OF EXPLOITATION AND CLASS

The *locus classicus* of the RCM theory of class is John Roemer's 'general theory' of exploitation. Jon Elster has described Roemer's methodological individualism as 'generating class relations and the capital relationship from exchanges between differently endowed individuals in a competitive setting' (Elster 1985, p. 7). More generally, Roemer's approach is an attempt to identify the 'key moment' in class exploitation by taking as his point of departure nothing more than individuals possessed of different endowments and showing how unequal distribution of the relevant assets necessarily produces unfair results, especially in the distribution of income, even without a direct transfer of labour from exploiter to exploited.

Beginning with a 'game-theoretic' model which classifies exploitative systems according to the various resources or assets that are respectively salient in each one, he concludes that people are *exploited* when they would be better off if the relevant asset were (according to his 'withdrawal' criterion)[4] differently allocated, and that they are *exploiters* when a reallocation of the relevant asset would leave them worse off. This definition, in accordance with the principles of game theory, requires that each mode of exploitation be defined in terms of a 'hypothetically feasible' alternative, establishing the criterion against which the status of exploiter and exploited can be assessed. So, for example, feudal exploitation entails 'differential access to freedom from bondage'; that is, 'feudal exploitation is that inequality which arises as a consequence of ties of bondage which prevent producers from freely engaging in trade, with their own assets (Roemer 1982a, pp. 20–1). Here, the 'hypothetical alternative' is capitalism; and the test of feudal exploitation 'is to calculate whether a person would be better off under the distribution where no feudal property exists but capitalist property still exists' (Roemer 1988, p. 136).

The essential feature of this theory is its focus on what Roemer calls property relations. What he means by 'property relations' is the distribution of assets or endowments, not the social relations of production and appropriation as Marxism commonly understands them. Indeed, it is the object of this focus on 'property relations' to shift the criterion of exploitation away from the direct relations between producers and appropriators and locate it in distributional factors. Thus the traditional Marxist concept of *surplus extraction* is rejected, while the relations and processes it entails are displaced by what might be called the static and indirect 'relations' of relative advantage.

The purpose of this reconceptualization is, in particular, to explain capitalist exploitation without resorting to the labour theory of value and the concept of surplus value, which Roemer judges to be inadequate as a measure of exploitation. But he does not stop here, with the special theory of capitalism. In order to provide a general theory under which the special theory of capitalism can be subsumed and which can also encompass socialism, he jettisons not only the concept of surplus value specific to capitalism but the whole notion of exploitation as the extraction of surplus labour. Unequal distribution of assets, rather than the relations between direct producers and the appropriators of their surplus labour, becomes the central focus.

This distributional theory of exploitation marks a critical departure from 'classic' Marxism. For conventional Marxism, *inequality* has no theoretical purchase except insofar as it entails a system of social relations between appropriators and producers. In those relations, and not in inequality as such, lies the dynamic principle, the contradictions and conflicts, which account for social and historical processes. The project of RCM, in direct opposition to traditional Marxism, is to construct a conception of exploitation which does not require reference to such relations. Where there is a direct link, a *class* relation, between exploiter and exploited – and not just a 'relation' of relative advantage – it is established by 'rational choice'.

Roemer's principal claim for his theory and its advantages over classical Marxism is that it can finesse all the criticisms of Marxian exploitation which can be made because of its reliance on the labour theory of value (Roemer 1982a, p. 20). In particular, he maintains that his 'game-theoretic formulation is superior in that it makes explicit what ethical presumption lies behind the Marxian theory of exploitation', by taking as its point of departure the alternative distribution of relevant assets against which relative advantages and disadvantages can be measured. It is, in fact, largely for the purpose of moral argumentation that he adopts his characteristic paradigm, and it is perhaps here, in its contribution to ethical arguments about exploitation, that RCM claims have their greatest validity. But since Roemer has sought to reconstruct the whole of Marxist thought on the basis of his game-theoretic theory of exploitation, we need to consider first the explanatory implications of the initial decision to displace the relations of surplus extraction from their central position in the theory of exploitation.

The Explanatory Consequences

Let us assume, for the sake of argument, that Roemer has succeeded on his own terms in constructing a foolproof demonstration that capitalism is exploitative and unjust, without resorting to the labour theory of value.[5] How does this procedure affect the larger project of reconstructing Marxist theory? Here it is important to keep in mind that the idea of surplus labour is not principally (or probably at all) intended to provide the kind of mathematical measure which Roemer demands for his moral indictment of exploitation in general and capitalism in particular. In any case, whatever the weaknesses of the concept as a mathematical device or even as a moral standard, they are not relevant to the one fundamental insight encased in this controversial idea: that at the foundation of social life and historical processes lie the conditions in which people have access to the means of subsistence and reproduction, and that a decisive historical break occurs when the prevailing conditions systematically compel some people to transfer part of their labour or its product to someone else. The critical datum in explaining social processes is not the quantitative measure of the 'surplus' but rather the very fact of the relationship between producers and appropriators, and the conditions in which it occurs; and this critical fact can be established without mathematical proof. Indeed, Roemer himself must begin with a tacit recognition of this fact, in order to have something to measure.

Capitalism undoubtedly represents a special case, because capitalist appropriation is not a distinctly visible act – like, say, the serf's payment of dues to the lord – which constitutes a separate act of appropriation, after the fact of the serf's labour and in the context of a visible relation between appropriator and producer. In contrast, there is no immediately obvious way of separating the act of capitalist appropriation from the process of production or from the process of commodity exchange through which capital realizes its gains. The concept of surplus *value* is meant to convey this complex relation between production, realization in commodity exchange, and capitalist appropriation.

There has been no shortage of critics, including Marxist economists, who are keen to point out the difficulties of expressing these relations in quantitative terms – that is, of measuring 'value' and 'surplus', or of relating 'value' to 'price'. But Roemer has done more than simply jettison an imperfect standard of measurement. He has elaborated a theory of capitalist exploitation which displaces the relevant social relations themselves from the centre of Marxist analysis. This may or may not be necessary to a persuasive moral argument against capitalism, but in either case, it remains to be seen whether the explanatory price is worth paying.

What, then, are the consequences of conceiving class exploitation as a 'relation' of relative advantage, or at best a 'rational' exchange between individuals, a conception in which the analytic starting point is *inequality* or the 'unequal distribution of assets', instead of a (historically constituted) *social relation* between appropriators and producers?

First, the individual and his/her 'endowments': the purpose of the RCM exercise is to break down 'macroprocesses' into their 'micro-foundations', the actions of individuals. But it turns out that RCM can achieve its objective of 'beginning' with the individual only by a sleight of hand; while the only direct relation overtly admitted by the theory is the 'rationally chosen' exchange between individuals – whole sets of relations or structures must be covertly secreted in the 'differential endowments' which constitute the individuals in question.

For example, in Roemer's definition of feudal exploitation, 'bondage' – with all the relations of power, domination and juridical dependence between lords and peasants which it entails – is treated as an attribute of individuals, what has been described as a 'relational property'. How, after all, can 'bondage' or freedom' be conceived as an *individual* attribute, in abstraction from relations with others? Hidden within the individual peasant's 'assets' are not only his possessions, but all the structural relations which render those possessions relevant which, in other words, constitute them – or *some* of them – as 'assets' at all; the communal organization that maintains peasant possession in their means of subsistence; and so on. Similarly, the lord's 'assets' encompass, among other things, his location in a structure of relations which make him capable of exerting extra-economic coercion; a community of lords, a state-formation, etc. In fact, it would be impossible to characterize the relevant 'assets' without first specifying the whole system of social relations that constitute them as assets in the first place for any given individual.

Analogous problems arise in dealing with capitalism. Methodological individualism requires that the behaviour of capitalists be reducible to their individual assets and motivations, on the basis of information visible to them. (Jon Elster, the most stringent critic of Marx for his so-called 'methodological collectivism', attacks Marx's value theory, for example, on the grounds that 'individual behaviour can never be explained by reference to values, which, being invisible, have no place in the purposive explanation of action.')[6] Yet the compulsions of capital accumulation cannot be derived simply from the 'optimizing strategies' of a rational individual with capital 'assets'. Those compulsions cannot be explained without reference to the competitive pressures of the capitalist market, indeed the whole historically constituted social structure which has made individuals in capitalist society uniquely dependent on the market for the conditions of their self-reproduction, and hence subject to the imperatives of competition and accumulation.

Having repudiated the conceptual apparatus by means of which 'classic' Marxism seeks to explain these systemic imperatives, RCM is obliged to take as given the compulsions of capitalism, and to impute them to the preferences and motivations of individual capitalists. It is no longer simply a matter of beginning with certain general assumptions about human nature; we must now take as our starting point the specific attributes of the *capitalist* nature. Indeed, it is difficult to see how the RCM model can escape a complete circularity, according to which individuals accumulate capital because they are capital accumulators. The impulse to accumulate capital itself cannot be further reduced to individual properties independent of social structures. Instead, the properties of capitalism as a social system, its systemic compulsion to accumulate, and arguably even the theory of value itself – everything that Marx sought to *explain* rather than assume – must be simply incorporated, taken for granted and not explained, into the individual 'properties' of the capitalist. And even then, since the individual capitalist cannot accommodate among his/her personal attributes all the complex transactions of capitalism which make accumulation possible as well as necessary, nor all the conditions which consistently upset the assumptions on which accumulation is based, the explanatory power of the RCM model is rather limited – without the constant intrusion of unexplained assumptions, or constant assistance from conventional Marxism. Whatever capacity the model has to clarify the issues of capital accumulation – by explicating the motivations of capitalists only on the basis of the information which is visible to them – depends on assuming first what most needs to be explained: the logic of the capitalist system which imposes the compulsion of accumulation.

At best, this means that all the important work must be done in advance of applying the RCM model, and entirely without its help. All the historical analysis which yields the structures that are to be smuggled into the attributes of the relevant individuals must be done first, very likely with the tools of conventional historical materialism; or, more precisely, the RCM model must take as given precisely what needs to be explained. Indeed, the individual 'properties' which motivate the 'rational choice' must in effect be deduced from the 'macro-processes' which are to be explained. The RCM model can 'explain' structures or 'macroprocesses' only in terms of individual motivations whose very presence must be deduced from the structures themselves.

There is no way of getting from individual choice to historical processes without inserting all these 'structural' factors, either by reading them into the individual psyche or, in a 'weaker' methodological individualism, as part of the data on the basis of which the individual's choices are made. If the model serves any useful purpose at all, it can only be in the *presentation*, but not in the construction, of an explanation.

The Game of Class Relations

But let us accept, for a moment, the vast array of social relations and structures that are already secreted within the 'assets' and 'endowments' with which individuals enter the 'game' of class. What of the 'game' itself? At this point, the individual, however richly endowed with historical and structural presuppositions, must enter into relations with other individuals and make strategic choices. This is when unequal individual endowments and 'relations' of relative advantage need to be supplemented by 'rational choice'. Class position, according to Roemer, has to do with whether individuals work for themselves, work for others, or employ the labour of others. These positions are described as 'chosen' by people as they adopt 'optimizing' strategies which, given their respective endowments, may lead them to work for themselves, work for others, or employ the labour of others or some combination of these options.

The notion that classes are 'chosen' immediately raises questions about the RCM model of choice. However much RCMists may appreciate that individual choices are never made in a social vacuum, there is little room in the model itself for the *social construction* of choice, for the many ways in which individual choices are structured not only by the social conditions of self-preservation and self-reproduction, by the determinate range of viable options made available within any system of social relations, but also by the complex mechanisms which operate to reproduce the system itself, including its cultural and ideological supports and their effects in the shaping of preferences. And the RCM model must begin anew with every isolated individual. It cannot accommodate the simple proposition that choices available to any single individual, or to a limited number, may not be available to all, even *with* the relevant preferences and the necessary 'assets', as the 'choice' of any particular 'optimizing strategy' by some individuals may make it less readily available to others or less economically viable in a competitive market. The reproduction of social relations cannot be explained within the strict requirements of this model except as the product of individual preferences; and even this individualistic focus is skewed by an exceptionally limited and crude psychology which must assume a strong, stable and unchanging ego (not to mention perfect knowledge), influenced neither by its cultural and ideological environment nor by its own less conscious impulses.

But let us, for the sake of argument, take for granted the complex mechanisms of social reproduction and remain on the narrow terrain of 'rational choice'. What are the implications of the proposition that classes are constituted by choices in pursuit of 'optimizing' strategies? The consequences are, in the first instance, obscured by Roemer's emphasis on the *necessity*, even the *automaticity*, of the choices, which follow from the original unequal distribution of assets. It is even possible that for him the stage of 'rational choice' is an afterthought, into which he has been forced by his non-relational conception of exploitation. Some of his more enthusiastic disciples, however, have eagerly followed the path of 'rational choice' to its logical conclusions, dispensing with Roemer's assumption of automaticity and thereby starkly exposing the major weaknesses in the RCM concept of 'choice'.

A notable example is Adam Przeworski, whose work is significant particularly because he, more explicitly and systematically than other RCM notables, has used this approach to theorize a *political* stance. Przeworski proposes to counter the conventional Marxist notion which, as he describes it, takes 'class positions as a given from which to begin the analysis', and to replace it with a view which acknowledges that 'individuals face choices, and one choice might be to become a worker and another choice might be to cooperate with other workers' (Przeworski 1985a, p. 97). The object of this is to understand the connection between social structure and individual behaviour, especially the connection between class conflict and politics, avoiding the assumption that certain class positions will automatically produce certain behaviours or political commitments.

It is undoubtedly wise not to assume that class positions will automatically produce certain behaviours, notably certain political commitments and actions. But there is more at stake here than a sensible injunction against simple-minded determinism. Przeworski is not content to argue that there is no necessary connection between class positions and political preferences. Instead, he asks us to treat class itself as an object or 'choice', analogous to other 'optimizing' choices, such as political preferences. Classes are 'contingent', dependent upon a 'structure of choices', not simply a reflex of production relations alone (Przeworski 1985a, p. 96). In fact, entering a class – e.g. becoming a worker – is treated here as analytically equivalent to joining a trade union organization or a socialist party; both constitute ' choices' – and any qualitative difference between the two kinds of 'choice' is elided.

The example constructed by Przeworski to illustrate his point reveals the presuppositions and consequences of the proposition that people choose classes as they select other 'optimizing' strategies. The exemplary worker is a certain Mrs Jones who for reasons of her own sells her labour power for a wage. Conventional Marxism (which, Przeworski argues, takes as given Mrs Jones's class position as a 'ready-made' worker and deduces from it how she should behave) cannot, he says, answer the critical question: *why* is Mrs Jones a worker? We cannot assume that she has no choice. 'After all, she owns some land, which she can perhaps sell; she is married to a machinist, who can perhaps work overtime; and she has, or will have, an accountant son, who might help her set up a resale shop' (Prezeworski 1985a, p. 97). She chooses to become a worker because, given her objectives and resources, this is her optimizing option.

To begin with, the necessity of explaining *why* the exceptional landowning Mrs Jones is a worker is not at all clear, nor is the explanatory power of an answer to this question. It might tell us something about Mrs Jones; but what would it tell us about other workers or about the operation of capitalism – or, indeed, about the process of 'choosing' classes? Could a landless Mr Smith be said to 'choose' his class position in the same sense as the lucky Mrs Jones? For that matter, what will we learn from this example even about the most mundanely practical conditions of class organization or politics? Of course we should not assume that Mrs Jones's political preferences will be unaffected by the fact that she is a woman, white and Catholic, as well as a worker. But why does this oblige us to obscure the difference between 'choosing' to enter a class and joining a political party? What can we learn from such procedures that would not be far more misleading than any conclusions we might draw from the traditional Marxist assumption that the logic of capitalism compels people, separated from the means of production, to sell their labour-power in order to gain access to the means of subsistence? Is it really more informative to proceed as if people entered classes in order to earn pin-money?

What *is* clear is that Przeworski has loaded the dice, and he has done so because his model of class formation requires it. He seems aware of how absurd this example is ('I do not cherish being an object of ridicule'),[7] but he is apparently unconcerned about the extent to which the whole model depends upon the analytic centrality of exceptional cases. Possibilities which could conceivably be available to any one individual, no matter how exceptional, are here given the analytic weight of choices available to *all* individuals in order to characterize class formation as the result of 'optimizing' choices. It is not only the fortunate Mrs Jones who 'chooses' her class position. The RCM model of class formation in general is constructed on the assumptions of this privileged condition.

Choosing Classes

Przeworski here reveals what Roemer conceals. With his Mrs Jones, he may have taken the RCM model to lengths unforeseen by Roemer, but he has not fundamentally traduced his mentor's theory of class. It is in itself significant that there *are* two stages in Roemer's theory of class — first the assets, then the rational choice — and that class *relations* belong to the second stage: people find themselves with assets (of mysterious origin), and then they choose to enter a class relation — i.e. to be exploited. This formulation cannot be dismissed as simply a rhetorical or heuristic device; for however much Roemer may recognize the necessity of the 'choice', the conceptualization of class in this way has substantial consequences. A great deal follows from the premise that class *relations* are secondary and contingent, entered into — or not — by choice. Above all, in order to permit a characterization of class relations in terms which do not endanger the model of *choice* and a free exchange between individuals with different endowments, there must be a redefinition of what is at stake in the relation between classes.

According to the RCM model, the operative principle in class relations is relative advantage — not whether one party is compelled by coercion to transfer surplus labour to another, or obliged to do so in order to gain access to the means of survival and reproduction, but rather whether and to what extent each party can 'optimize' by entering the relationship. Even Roemer, who is most emphatic about the necessity of these choices, cannot avoid this voluntaristic language. The 'rational choice' model of class formation *requires* that the relevant issues be presented as having to do with 'optimization' or relative advantage rather than with compulsion or the necessities of existence itself – and herein lies perhaps the most substantial modification of 'classical' Marxism, as well as a radical weakening of its explanatory power.

For 'classical' Marxism *compulsion* is the essence of exploitative relations. In cases where direct producers – like feudal peasants – remain in possession of the means of production, the transfer of surplus is determined by direct coercion, by virtue of the appropriator's superior force. In capitalism, the compulsion is of a different kind. The producer's obligation to forfeit surplus is a precondition for access to the means of production, the means of sustaining human life itself. What compels direct producers to produce more than they will themselves consume, and to transfer the surplus to someone else, is the 'economic' necessity which makes their own subsistence inseparable fom that transfer of surplus labour. Thus, wage-labourers in capitalism, lacking the means to carry on their own labour, only acquire them by entering into an exploitative relation with capital. This need not, of course, mean that those who are obliged to transfer surplus labour will get *only* the barest necessities; it simply means that the transfer is the necessary condition for their access to the means of survival and reproduction – and whatever they can acquire above and beyond that with those means. Such relations can be shown to exist even in the absence of any means of quantifying a 'surplus' or measuring the relative gains of producers and appropriators. We need only acknowledge that the producer's reproduction has among its necessary conditions a relation to an appropriator who claims some part of his/her labour or product.

In defining exploitation, then, the limiting case for Marxism has to be one in which the relations between appropriator and producer are determined by the latter's compulsion to transfer surplus labour, either because of subjection to a superior force or in order to secure access to the conditions of existence. The limiting case for RCM cannot be of this kind without making complete nonsense of the element of 'choice'. Roemer himself sets up his model in the way he does, not in order to deny the compulsions which constitute exploitative relations, but rather to demonstrate that given unequal distribution of assets there can be exploitation even when everyone owns the means of production to guarantee their subsistence and even without a direct exchange of labour. But the model thereby acquires imperatives of its own – and one of its demands is the assumption that people are free not to enter the relationship at all.

The example cited by Carling in his explication of Roemer's model is instructive. In this example, both Man Crusoe and Woman Friday begin with direct access to the means of securing material existence, though

Friday possesses only a labour-intensive technology, while Crusoe enjoys a superior capital-intensive technology. Given their different 'endowments', they enter into a relationship, each one seeking to guarantee subsistence with the least effort. Although their assets are unequal, there is no suggestion that C has the power to coerce F into forfeiting surplus labour or to deprive her of the conditions of existence. The issue between them is simply the extent to which F's labour will be to the relative advantage of C, in the sense that F (though better off than before entering into a relationship with C) does not get the full benefit of her labours, part of which accrues to C. The 'equality' between C and F – their 'equality as rational actors' – which the model demands, requires minimally that both (though not equally endowed) have direct and sufficient access to the means of subsistence. What is at stake is never more than 'optimizing' or 'maximizing'. Carling then proceeds to characterize the *power* relations between C and F in terms of the 'maximum damage' or 'ultimate sanctions' each party can bring to bear on the other (pp. 49–50). Here, he truly gives the game away. The ultimate penalty is measured simply in days of work: the number of days' work over and above F's 'best option' which C can impose on F by withdrawing from the 'game', and the number of days' work which F's withdrawal would substract from C's 'best option'.

The model thus begins – indeed depends upon – removing both forms of compulsion which have historically operated in class exploitation: the 'economic' necessities of capitalism and the 'extra-economic' coercions of pre-capitalist formations. Combining the best of both worlds, Carling offers us two 'free and equal' individuals, neither one subject to the superior force of the other, yet both in possession of the means of production. The transfer of surplus is not determined by direct coercion, nor is it a condition of access to the means of self-reproduction. The assumptions of this benign – and completely imaginary – condition are then transposed to real capitalism, where one of the parties begins with no access to the means of production and has only labour-power to sell. The issue between worker and capitalist is still presented on the principles of Carling's limiting case, as if the issue were still just 'optimization'. Even survival itself is effectively treated as simply a specific instance of 'optimization' only quantitatively different from any other good.

Lowering the Stakes

RCMists may argue that the choice to live or die is not the analytically relevant one in questions of class. Sometimes this means simply that, at least in principle, for any given individual (like Przeworski's Mrs Jones) there may be other options than selling labour-power to a capitalist – options such as begging, street-vending, busking, living on welfare, relying on family support, or even leaving the working class to become self-employed. This is not a serious objection to regarding survival as the ultimate stake in capitalist class relations. From the point of view of explaining social and historical patterns, it makes a critical difference how widely available such options are; and a society in which, say, street-vending were as available an option as wage-labour would be structurally very different from one in which it is only an exceptional possibility. The other argument for weakening the compulsion involved in class relations is to say that selling labour-power is not the only option but the only *acceptable* one (perhaps coupled with Elster's observation that a choice made out of necessity is still a choice).[8] It is probably safe to say that all RCMists, and not just Roemer, recognize what is finally at stake. The important point, however, is that their model so absolutely requires that the stakes be relatively low and non-coercive that they must give a preponderant analytic weight to exceptional contingencies and marginal possibilities.

But even if we grant the premise that there are in principle other ways to survive, there still remains a critical difference between choosing ways of surviving and simply 'optimizing', in the sense of choosing to be 'better off'. The RCM model depends on blurring this distinction too. Finally, the model requires us to ignore the ways in which even the means of escaping the necessity of transferring surplus labour are themselves determined by the dominant conditions of acquiring access to the means of production in any given class regime. So, for example, the welfare system and unemployment benefits in a capitalist system are determined by the logic of capitalist exploitation and its roots in the complete separation of the worker from the means of production. It is precisely because the logic of the capital relation for the worker means that s/he must sell his/her labour power or starve, that institutional means of preventing starvation had to be created – but only to the extent that they did not completely undermine the logic of the capital relation itself (for instance, by making such options too widely available).

There may be certain situations in which the stress on choice rather than on compulsion in relations of exploitation has rhetorical advantages; but on the whole, the costs of this focus far exceed the benefits. The effect is to make this theory of class finally indistinguishable from conventional stratification theories (common to both bourgeois social science and liberal ideology), in which the location of class divisions is more or less arbitrary because there is no qualitative break in the distributional continuum and no focal point of class antagonisms or conflicts of interest. In fact, in the final analysis Roemer (and indeed, Erik Olin Wright in his elaboration of Roemer's theory of class) can give no consistent account of class which goes beyond identifying *income differentials* as the essential criterion.[9] If the principal criterion of exploitation is an indirect relation of relative advantage, and especially when the issue for both parties in such 'relations of comparison' is simply 'optimization' – in contrast to the Marxist theory of class exploitation which emphasizes the coercive relation between those who are compelled to transfer surplus and those who appropriate it – the unequal distribution of 'assets' can have no significance apart from its merely distributional consequences, its effects in producing inequalities of income.

Elster: A 'One-Sided' View?

Elster here departs in some significant ways from Roemer. He is aware of many of the difficulties in Roemer's non-relational theory of exploitation and its extension to class, noting in particular its inadequacy in *causal* explanation (for example, in accounting for social conflict),[10] which requires, among other things, a more systematic acknowledgement of *power* relations. The same strictures would apply to Roemer's theory as those Elster levels against 'stratification' theories which focus on 'relations of comparison' as distinct from 'relations of interaction'. Yet Elster's 'relations of interaction' are themselves constricted, and limited in their explanatory value, by a similar view of what is at stake in the relation between classes, a view which is demanded by the imperatives of the rational choice model.

In his own account of rational choice models, and 'intentional' models in general, Elster makes reference to some passages from Marx in order to demonstrate that there are times when Marx himself adopts intentional explanations, though inconsistently and in contradiction to many of his basic assumptions. Elster's interpretation of these passages is revealing. It is not the object here to deny Marx's emphasis on human agency, choice and purpose, but rather to demonstrate how Elster's interpretation of Marx is distorted by his own understanding of the issues at stake in the relation between classes. Elster cites the following passages from the *Grundrisse* as an example of Marx's emphasis on choice:

> [The worker] is neither bound to particular objects, nor to a particular manner of satisfaction. The sphere of his consumption is not qualitatively restricted, only quantitatively. This distinguishes him from the

slave, serf, etc. Consumption certainly reacts on production itself, but this reaction concerns the worker in his exchange as little as it does any other seller of a commodity. ... [The] relative restriction on the sphere of the workers' consumption (which is only quantitative, not qualitative, or rather only qualitative as posited through the quantitative) gives them as consumers ... an entirely different importance as agents of production from that which they possessed e.g. in Antiquity or in the Middle Ages, or now possess in Asia (Elster 1985, p. 12, Marx 1973, p. 283).

Elster's purpose is to demonstrate a contradiction (he is generally more interested in seeking out inconsistencies in Marx's theory than in working out its fruitful insights) between this emphasis on the worker's consumer choice and passages in which 'Marx comes close to suggesting that the consumption of the worker is uniquely determined by his need to reproduce his labour-power' (Elster 1985, p. 11). Marx, argues Elster, 'had strong theoretical reasons for wanting to keep workers' consumption fixed, since otherwise the labour value of goods might depend on preferences.'

Without engaging in a dispute about the labour theory of value, we should note the confusion of issues in Elster's interpretation. In the 'non-choice' passages, Marx is seeking to explain the conditions in which the worker under capitalism gains access to the means of subsistence through the exchange of labour-power for a wage. In the *Grundrisse* passage cited by Elster as an example of Marx in his RCM mode, he is analyzing the exchange between labour and capital first in a 'one-sided' way, that is, simply in the 'sphere of circulation'. Marx makes it clear, in words elided from Elster's quotation, that he is for the moment examining the capitalist relation incompletely, 'as regards mere circulation'. At this level of analysis, the freedom of choice may be relevant, as is the 'equality' between capital and labour as parties to the exchange. Marx is here also alluding to a unique relation between consumption and production which characterizes capitalism. But he goes on to emphasize that the worker's equality and liberty as a party to the exchange (as well as his/her freedom as a consumer) has as its presupposition 'an economically different relation – outside that of exchange',[11] a relation which is indeed masked by the exchange. It may appear to the worker, and 'to a certain degree on the other side', that the object of the exchange is (*on both sides*) to obtain 'exchange value' or wealth (with the possibility of such an illusion being specific to capitalism). But, Marx continues:

what is essential is that the purpose of the exchange for him (the worker) is the satisfaction of his need. The object of his exchange is a direct object of need, not exchange value as such. He does obtain money, it is true, but only in its role as coin; i.e. only as a self-suspending and vanishing mediation. What he obtains from the exchange is therefore not exchange value, not wealth, but a means of subsistence, objects for the preservation of his life, the satisfaction of his needs in general, physical, social etc. It is a specific equivalent in means of subsistence, in objectified labour, measured by the cost of production of his labour.

The last sentence, of course, suggests that Marx is even here adhering to precisely the view which this passage, according to Elster, is supposed to contradict. This should have been enough to put Elster on his guard against facile accusations of inconsistency. But the critical point is that, while at one level of analysis – that which relates to the one-sided sphere of circulation – the worker's consumer choice may be relevant, at the other – in the account of the fundamental relation between capital and labour which is 'presupposed' by the exchange between them – what is essential is the *necessity* of the exchange as a means for the worker to secure the conditions of survival and reproduction. The fact that workers are not constrained by their relation to the means of production to choose any specific food, for example, is not what determines their position as exploited producers. The important factor here is that, since people are not in any meaningful sense free to choose *not* to eat, their situation is determined by the conditions in which they may gain access to food at all.

It is significant that the issue for Elster is an alleged contradiction in Marx between two different accounts of the worker as *consumer*. He has a tendency in general to depict class struggle as the 'maximization' of 'consumer bundles', and shows a fondness for Weber's characterization of class systems in terms of different kinds of 'market' relations. Among the theories of development he attributes to Marx, he seems happiest with a periodization (of his own construction) in which the 'dynamic element' is trade (Elster 1985, pp. 310–17, 180 ff). Elster, in short, generally stops at the 'one-sided' analysis which remains in the 'sphere of circulation', indeed seems wholeheartedly to adopt the *illusion* fostered by capitalism concerning what is at issue in the capital relation, without unmasking the other relation which is the 'presupposition' of the exchange between capital and labour.

Elster does, after all, have what he would call 'strong theoretical reasons' for characterizing the relation between capital and labour in this one-sided way, since it is only as an exchange 'as regards mere circulation' that the rational choice model makes any sense at all. The model is not much use – and the notion of 'choice' has not much meaning – in explaining the *'presuppositions'* of the exchange between capital and labour. Or, to be more precise, the model can deal with those presuppositions only by transposing to them assumptions derived from the 'sphere of circulation'.

In fact, the RCM model in general seems to depend upon a resolute adherence to the 'sphere of circulation', in the manner of bourgeois ideology. More than that, the premises on which the whole model is based, even as it is applied to non-capitalist societies, represent a generalization of assumptions specific to capitalism – the assumptions of 'freedom', 'equality', and market-rationality – and to capitalism only as viewed in a 'one-sided' way.

Cost and Benefits

If the object of Rational Choice Marxism is to improve on classical Marxist explanation by breaking down 'macrostructures' into 'microfoundations', it seems not to have got us very far. At best, this procedure yields very modest results. Just how modest the pay-off really is has been persuasively illustrated by Levine, Sober and Wright in their discussion of Elster's attempt to subject the problem of class formation to the rigours of his methodological individualism. The results produced by their attempt to rescue some explanatory power for Elster's methodological individualism, while in some respects uncontentious and sensible, are on the whole predictable and uninteresting. 'Class formation' here has nothing to do with the historical processes which produce class relations. Instead, it refers to the process of *organization* 'by which classes are constituted as collective actors in class struggles'[12] – and even this in a very limited sense. At this level of analysis, the problems of 'class formation' are simply the problems faced by organizations in the attempt to mobilize support within their potential class constituencies. We learn, for example, that, since individuals are more likely to engage in action if they have some assurance that they will not be left holding the bag, organization and leadership are needed to provide an 'indirect communication network' which will convince them 'that they will not be "suckers" in collective struggles' (Levine *et al.* 1987, p. 82). This is, to be sure, a useful axiom of political organization, but it is scarcely a startling revelation (or one that requires RCM theory); and if this is the depth of insight offered by RCM, it hardly seems worth the trouble.

Besides, there are costs to offset even these modest benefits. The adjustment of the stakes in the game of class to meet the needs of the RCM model illustrates the extent to which the (purely 'heuristic'?) *form* of the game-theoretic method has been allowed to dictate the *substance* of RCM theory. This may mean, among other things, that there is a closer connection between the substantive theses of Marxism and its methods or 'tools' than RCM allows, making it rather more difficult to carry out the RCM proponents' often stated project of separating the two in order to defend the substance of Marxism by conventional analytic methods or 'the standard tools of microeconomic analysis' (Roemer 1988, p. 172). There is precious little left of historical materialism by the time RCM has finished begging all its questions and trivializing the stakes in the game. By returning to a distributional model of capitalism and severing the connection between the various 'moments' of the capitalist process, the RCM theory of exploitation has overturned every one of the central principles which Marx laboured so long to establish in his critique of political economy. If this reconceptualization had produced a paradigm with a superior explanatory power, such departures from classical Marxism could only be welcomed. As it is, we seem to have moved backward to a pre-Marxist understanding instead of forward beyond Marxism.

And one more curious result: this approach, for which Alan Carling has claimed the distinction of solving the old conundrum of structure and subject by 'the reinstatement of societies as sets of relationships among individuals[13] (what, then, are social relations for 'classical' Marxists like Marx himself?), has instead produced exactly the opposite effect. Laden with 'endowments' in the form of a whole system of social relations and structural necessities, the 'individual' turns out to be an embodied structure; and when the moment of 'choice' arrives, there is nothing important left to do. In the end, the principal function of 'choice' in the model is not to reinstate the subject but to render class contingent and ineffectual as a historical and political force.

IS THERE AN RCM THEORY OF HISTORY?

We need to be reminded why Marxism ascribes a determinative primacy to class struggle. It is not because class is the only form of oppression or even the most frequent, consistent, or violent source of social conflict, but rather because its terrain is the social organization of production which creates the material conditions of existence itself. The first principle of historical materialism is not class or class struggle, but the organization of material life and social reproduction. *Class* enters the picture when access to the conditions of existence and to the means of appropriation are organized in class ways, that is, when some people are systematically compelled by differential access to the means of production or appropriation to transfer surplus labour to others.

It is no doubt possible to identify transfers of surplus labour which are not determined by such coercive imperatives (e.g. gifts, the fulfilment of kinship obligations), but these are not the kind to which the concept of class specifically refers. It is also important to acknowledge that class may not always entail direct relationships, in the sense of face-to-face confrontations, between exploiter and exploited, and that in the absence of such confrontations, class relations may not generate conflict as readily as other, more direct non-class antagonisms may do (see Elster 1985, pp. 338 ff.). But class conflict has a particular historical resonance because it implicates the social organization of production, the very basis of material existence. Class struggle has a distinctive potential as a transformative force because, whatever the immediate motivations of any particular class conflict, the terrain of struggle is strategically situated at the heart of social existence. A trivialization of the issue between classes cannot but deprive the concept of class of its explanatory power. There can be no denying that it is difficult to imagine epochal transformations generated by games in which the stakes are relative advantages in access to 'consumer bundles'.

Given these limitations, what kinds of claims can be made for RCM in the explanation of history? It is not altogether clear how much Roemer *et al.* want to claim for themselves. Carling, as we have seen, appears to concede that on the question of historical transformations – from one system of exploitation, one regime of property, one distribution of endowments, one mode of production, to another – RCM theory must remain 'parasitic' on some other general theory of history. Roemer *sometimes* (though not always)[14] appears to share this modest view, generally refraining from any claim to provide a dynamic model of transformation, as distinct from a kind of 'comparative statics' – even a theory of capitalist accumulation or crisis, let alone a theory of epochal transformations. This does not, however, prevent him from associating his own theory of exploitation and class with the theory of historical materialism as interpreted by G. A. Cohen. In general, Carling has struck more or less the right note by drawing a line between RCM's efforts to construct a theory of exploitation and class, and its attempts to establish a connection with a theory of history borrowed from elsewhere.

In his review of *Free to Lose*, Carling addresses himself more specifically to Roemer's ventures into history. One of the major reservations in this otherwise respectful review concerns Roemer's treatment of the theory of history. The objection is that Roemer fails to resolve what appears to be a fundamental contradiction between the two principal accounts of history on which he draws: Cohen's theory of history, and

Robert Brenner's historiography, the latter being 'the most systematic presentation of the evidence in the case (the development of capitalism) which is the acid test for the truth of the whole theory.'[15] The problem, Carling suggests, is the inconsistency between Cohen's attribution of primacy to the forces of production and Brenner's to class struggle; and he questions the force of Roemer's facile response that Brenner's evidence concerning the emergence of capitalism in the historically specific conditions of England does not contradict Cohen's reading of historical materialism, with its general law of technological determinism, because a difference of 'a few centuries' in the development of capitalism in different parts of Europe hardly matters (Carling 1988, p. 95; Roemer 1988, pp. 123–4).

The question for Carling is which of the two accounts of history is a more suitable match for Roemer's theory of class and exploitation. Roemer, he says, seems to be offering us '"Cohen on history plus Roemer on class and exploitation" as standard contemporary Marxism'; but, suggests Carling, given Cohen's use of functional explanation, as distinct from what he takes to be Brenner's rational choice explanation, it might be more methodologically consistent to propose 'Brenner on history plus Roemer on class and exploitation' – even though this option would be taken 'at the cost of depriving Marxism of the support it traditionally thought it enjoyed from the theory of history'(Carling 1988, p. 95).

There are several points to be made about this judgement, even before we attempt to choose between 'Cohen plus Roemer' and 'Brenner plus Roemer'. Posing the question in this way – Roemer plus what?– reaffirms the discontinuity between RCM and the theory of history. The implication is that the theory of exploitation and class, for which the rational choice model is supposed to be well adapted, cannot generate its own theory of history and may indeed be incompatible with any *theory* of history at all. This unhappy conclusion is based not only on a clear-sighted recognition of RCM's undynamic character, but also on a particular view of what counts as a theory of history. Like other RCMists, not least Roemer himself, Carling has no doubt that a theory of history (as distinct from, say, a 'special' theory of capitalism) must be a super-general, indeed *trans*historical, account which posits some universal law of historical change in a determinate direction – not even just some common mechanism (such as class struggle, the outcome of which is variable and indeterminate and which has its own historically specific rules and conditions in every particular social form), but rather a general law, a 'deep cause', that transcends all historical particularities. Thus Cohen has a theory while Brenner has only historiography.

An attempt to resolve the Cohen-plus-Roemer v. Brenner-plus-Roemer issue may tell us as much as we need to know about RCM and its relation to the theory of history. Let us first try to reconstruct Roemer's argument. One thing is clear: Roemer, despite some reservations, still associates himself with historical materialism as a theory of history, and for him this means (evidently without question) Cohen's technological determinism (Roemer 1988, p. 108). It remains to be seen whether he is wrong to think – as Carling suggests he may – that his own theory of exploitation and class can be consistently coupled with Cohen's theory of history, and whether Carling is right to propose that Brenner would make Roemer a more suitable match.

Roemer on History

History, according to Roemer, takes the form of an evolution in property relations, in which 'progressively fewer kinds of production factors remain acceptable as property' (Roemer 1988, p. 126). For example, property in persons is eliminated as slave society passes into feudalism, leaving some property rights in the labour of others and property in alienable means of production. The transition from feudalism to capitalism eliminates property rights in the labour of others while still allowing property in the alienable means of production, and so on. This 'progressive socialization of property' occurs for reasons 'related to efficiency', that is, the advancement of the forces of production. 'The mechanism that brings about this evolution is class struggle', but the reason such an evolution occurs lies somewhere deeper: evolution occurs because *the level of development of the technology outgrows the particular form of the social organization, which comes to constrain and fetter it.*[16]

The connection between the mechanism (class struggle) and the deep cause (technological determinism) can be explained in the following way. Class struggle serves as a 'facilitator' in the transition from one social form to another, when the 'dissonance' between the level of development of productive forces and the old economic structure reaches a crisis point. So, for example, Roemer asks us to 'imagine' (his word) 'a feudal system, with lords and serfs, but one in which a nascent capitalist economy is emerging alongside' the feudal system (Roemer 1988, p. 115). 'Now there is an option: capitalists and feudal lords can compete for control of the working population. If the technology or forces of production that the capitalists are using enables them to pay higher real wages than serfs can earn, then there is an economic advantage to the liberation from serfdom that did not formerly exist.' Serfs can become independent peasants, taking advantage of the trade opened up by the capitalists, or they can become artisans or proletarians in the towns. 'The competition between feudalism and capitalism now enables class struggle against feudalism to be successful even though formerly it was not.'

We now have three levels of explanation: (1) the deep cause (technological determinism); (2) the historical process (the successive elimination of forms of exploitation or the progressive socialization of property); (3) the 'facilitator' (class struggle – though this only 'facilitates' a process that was 'bound to come sooner or later').[17] It is not entirely clear at what level the rational choice model should be introduced. The most obvious place is in class struggle, which implies that change occurs when (if not because) people are in a position to choose the available option of the next, more progressive mode of production. At the same time, there appears to be an overarching rational choice, at the level of the deep cause, having to do with 'the ceaseless effort of rational human beings to alleviate their conditions of scarcity'[18] – though they do not actually choose the next available economic structure *because* it is conducive to technological progress. In either case, the necessary link between the rational choice model and the theory of history is the presupposition that there is a direct correspondence between the self-interested actions of individual rational actors and the requirements of technical progress and economic growth.

This three-layered structure raises rather more questions than it answers, not least about the connections among its three levels. Are rational individuals, insofar as they are the makers of history (but are they?), motivated by the desire to alleviate scarcity through technological improvement or by the wish to escape exploitation – or neither? Is class struggle necessary or not; and if not, what is the mechanism of historical change? Or does the deep cause somehow make mechanisms and facilitators redundant, since change is somehow 'bound to come sooner or later' anyway, behind the backs of rational individuals? And where, in any case, is the *struggle* in class struggle? We have lords and capitalists competing to give more attractive terms to producers, to serfs who might want to become proletarians; and we have serfs escaping from lords – apparently without constraints, and willingly giving up their rights of possession – as soon as a more attractive option comes along; but *struggle* ....? What, indeed, is the 'economic advantage' which would impel serfs to prefer a wage which, by some sophisticated statistical measure, was higher than their 'earnings' as serfs, at the cost of losing their rights of possession, giving up the land which provides them with full and direct access to the means of subsistence in exchange for the uncertainties of the proletarian condition? For that matter, even if serfs choose this option, how do they manage to achieve it? If the lords' property 'rights' in the labour of others have anything to do with the 'control' – i.e. the power – that they exercise over the serfs, what is the nature of that 'control', and how is it that when the critical moment of transition comes, serfs can simply choose to escape the lord's 'control' just because a more eligible option has presented itself? Has feudalism no self-sustaining logic and resources of its own to resist this easy transition?

All this is quite apart from the fact that the whole edifice is constructed without benefit of evidence. Roemer has chosen his words carefully when he asks us to 'imagine'. We can hardly do anything else. ('Imagine' and 'suppose' are the basic vocabulary of this game-theoretic discourse.) We are not (or not always) being asked to believe that this is how things actually happened, or even that it was historically possible for them to happen in this way, only that it is logically conceivable that they did (though it is never made clear why we should be interested in such imaginary logical possibilities). Indeed, it is very unlikely that Roemer himself believes his own imaginary account of the transition to feudalism; and it is a measure of the price exacted by his game-theoretic model that it obliges him to set aside everything he undoubtedly knows about the power relations between lords and serfs, the dispossession of small producers and the concentration of landlordly property which were the conditions of the transition; everything, that is, about coercion, compulsion, imperatives, or indeed about the *social relations* of exploitation. This process of transition which Roemer asks us to 'imagine' evidently has little to do with history, and it would serve no purpose to counter this imaginary story with evidence. History is, apparently, a subject about which we can say anything we like.

Begging the Question

There is one thing that Roemer asks us to 'imagine' which is inescapably critical to his argument, an assumption upon which the whole shaky edifice rests and which goes to the very heart of RCM and its relation to history. We *must* accept that capitalism already exists as an 'option', that a 'nascent capitalist economy is emerging alongside' the feudal system. We must also never ask how this came to be so, though for Roemer this evidently presents no problem:

> According to historical materialism, feudal, capitalist, and socialist exploitation all exist under feudalism. At some point feudal relations become a fetter on the development of the productive forces, and they are eliminated by the bourgeois revolution. . . . Historical materialism,

in summary, claims that history progresses by the successive elimination of forms of exploitation which are socially unnecessary in the dynamic sense (Roemer 1982a, pp. 270–1).

He goes on to characterize this interpretation as 'a translation of the technological determinist aspect of historical materialist theory into the language of the theory of exploitation'. According to this interpretation of historical materialism, all successive forms of exploitation are already contained in the preceding ones (his account of the progress from slave society to capitalism suggests that this retrospective analysis goes back beyond feudalism), so that all forms of exploitation which have emerged in the course of history have apparently been present since the beginning; and history proceeds by the process of elimination.

A similar conflation has, of course, already occurred at the elemental level of Roemer's rational choice model, in the very foundations of his general theory of exploitation, where every mode of exploitation is defined in terms of its alternative, the successor mode which is already (or rather, still) present in the existing one. Remember, for example, the 'test' for feudal exploitation in terms of its 'hypothetically feasible alternative': 'to calculate whether a person would be better off under the distribution where no feudal property exists but capitalist property still exists' (Roemer 1988, p. 136). In Roemer's account of history, the 'hypothetical' alternative turns out to be an actually existing one, indeed the very next historical stage which happens to be already present in embryo.

It has been a favourite ploy of theorists who have trouble with *process* to beg the question of history by assuming that all historical stages – and especially capitalism – have in effect existed, at least as recessive traits, since the beginning. The perennial quality of capitalism has been a staple of bourgeois ideology, and also a common assumption of influential historians like Henri Pirenne. The usual approach in those Marxisms that go in for this kind of thing – the most recent and well-developed example is Althusserian structuralism – is to conjure up images of aspirant modes of production lurking in the interstices of previous ones, waiting only for the opportunity to establish their 'dominance' when certain obstacles are removed. The Althusserian concept of 'social formation', in which any and all modes of production can coexist without any need to explain their emergence, has done yeoman service in this regard. But Roemer has truly perfected this strategy, with his theory of elimination (it seems so much easier somehow to account for the demise of what already exists than to explain its coming into being). There can be no doubt that this kind of conceptual conjuring has far too often served in place of a Marxist theory of history; and, no doubt, Marx's more formulaic aphorisms about the stages of history and successive modes of production could be read as invitations to evade the issue of historical processes in this way. It was Marx, after all, who first spoke of 'fetters' and 'interstices'. But there is much more in Marx which demands that we look for the key to historical change in the dynamic logic of existing social relations without assuming the very thing that needs to be explained.

Brenner plus Roemer?

This is the point at which we can best judge the compatibility of Roemer's RCM with Robert Brenner's approach to history, for Brenner's primary purpose has been precisely to break the prevailing habit of begging the central historical question, the practice of assuming the existence of the very thing whose emergence needs to be explained. He distinguishes between two kinds of historical theories in Marx's own work, the first still heavily reliant on the mechanical materialism and economic determinism of the eighteenth-century Enlightenment, the second emerging out of Marx's mature critique of classical political economy. The first is characterized precisely by its begging of the question, invoking the self-development of productive forces via the division of labour which evolves in response to expanding markets, a 'nascent' capitalism in the womb of feudal society.

> The paradoxical character of this theory is thus immediately evident ... there really is no *transition* to accomplish: since the model starts with bourgeois society in the towns, foresees its evolution as taking place via bourgeois mechanisms (i.e. change and competition leading to the adoption of the most advanced techniques and to concomitant changes in the social organization of production. EMW), and has feudalism transcend itself in consequence of its exposure to trade, the problem of how one type of society is transformed into another is simply assumed away and never posed (Brenner 1989, p. 280).

Later, Marx was to pose the question very differently. He substantially revised his views on property relations in general and pre-capitalist property relations in particular: 'In the *Grundrisse* and *Capital*, Marx defines property relations as, in the first instance, the relationships of the direct producers to the means of production and to one another *which allow them to reproduce themselves as they were*. By this account, what distinguishes pre-capitalist property relations ... is that they provided the direct producers with the full means of reproduction'. The condition for maintaining this possession was the peasant community, and its consequence was that the lords required 'extra-economic' means of taking a surplus, which in turn demanded the reproduction of their own communities. The structure of these property relations was thus reproduced 'by communities of rulers and cultivators which made possible the economic reproduction of their individual members' (Brenner 1989, p. 287). Given these property relations, reproduced by communities of rulers and direct producers in conflict, the individual lords and individual peasants adopted the economic strategies that would best maintain and improve their situation – what Brenner calls their rules of reproduction. The aggregate result of these strategies was the characteristic feudal pattern of development. The transition to a new society with new developmental patterns thus entailed not simply a shift from one mode of production to another alternative mode, but a *transformation* of existing property relations, from feudal rules of reproduction to new, capitalist rules. Under these, the separation of direct producers from the means of production, and the end of 'extra-economic' modes of extraction would leave both appropriators and producers subject to competition, and able to move in response to the requirements of profitability under competitive pressures. This inevitably raised a new and different question about the transition from feudalism to capitalism: 'it was the problem of accounting for the transformation of pre-capitalist property relations into capitalist property relations via the action of pre-capitalist society itself' (Brenner 1989, p. 293).

This is the challenge which Brenner has taken up: to offer an explanation of the transition to capitalism which relies entirely on the dynamics of feudal relations, and its conditions of *reproduction*, without reading capitalism back into its predecessor or presenting it as an available option.[19] This project also requires an acknowledgement that pre-capitalist property relations have a logic and tenacity of their own, which cannot be conjured away by the convenient assumption that people are driven by an urge to take the next available (capitalist) option, an urge that existing structures cannot resist. This is something which Roemer's model is systematically unable to take into account. In this respect, Roemer's model reproduces those of Adam Smith, the early Marx, Henri Pirenne, and Paul Sweezy, which Brenner has consistently criticised. They too, he argues, tend to assume the existence of capitalism in order to explain its coming into being. Roemer would be subject to the same criticisms levelled by Brenner against what he calls 'Smithian Marxists', because, on the rational choice reasoning to which Roemer is committed, he simply cannot get from feudalism to capitalism without already assuming capitalist structures and capitalist motivations. The relations of capitalism and the associated compulsions of capital accumulation, the specific logic of capitalism and its systemic imperatives, can in no way be deduced simply from the unequal distribution of 'alienable assets' which for Roemer constitutes the kernel of capitalism already existing in feudalism. (Here, the inadequacy of Roemer's model of exploitation – defined in terms of inequality or relative advantage – becomes most starkly obvious, since whatever value it may have in explicating the injustices of exploitation, it is completely incapable of apprehending capitalism as a particular system of social production, appropriation and accumulation.) Nor can the relations and imperatives of capitalism be deduced from the mere existence of towns, on the assumption – unwarranted both logically and historically – that towns are by nature capitalist.

Brenner's approach represents a challenge to the RCM model at every level of analysis, from the most specifically empirical to the abstractly theoretical. Empirically, Brenner's history of capitalist development puts in question nearly every point in Roemer's imaginary scenario. Capitalism does not, in his account, simply exist, miraculously, 'alongside' the feudal economy, nor is it here a product of mercantile interests in the towns competing with feudal interests in the countryside. Direct producers do not join the capitalist economy by fleeing the countryside to become artisans or proletarians. The development of capitalism is rather a process set in train by the transformation of agrarian relations themselves, in particular conditions which have little to do with some exogenous expansion of trade. Indeed, this account (like others in the famous 'Transition debate'[20] begins by casting doubt on the inherent antagonism of markets and trade to the feudal order. It is not capitalism or the market as an 'option' or *opportunity* which Brenner seeks to explain, but the emergence of capitalism and the capitalist market as an *imperative*. His is a history of the very special conditions in which direct producers in the countryside were subjected to market imperatives, rather than the emergence of 'options' for direct producers, opportunities offered them by trading interests in the towns.

More generally, the facts of the case as presented by Brenner run counter to Roemer's 'deep cause' (and Cohen's technological determinism) – as Roemer himself is apparently aware – by indicating that there is no historical necessity for less productive 'economic structures' to be followed by more productive ones and by stressing the historical specificity of the conditions in which the process of 'self-sustaining' growth was first established. Roemer's response to this challenge, readers may recall, is simply that capitalism did eventually spread to other parts of Europe, even if it first emerged in England, so that Brenner's evidence does not contradict

Cohen's version of historical materialism, with its universal law of technological determinism. This response depends on a cavalier treatment of historical time (who cares about 'a few centuries'?), as Carling has observed, and a similar treatment of geographical space (who cares about the world beyond Europe – or indeed beyond western Europe?). More fundamentally, it depends on treating the historically specific process of capitalist expansion, *a priori*, as a transhistorical law of nature.

When Roemer invokes the universality of capitalist development, at least its eventual spread to other parts of Europe, this is no reply to Brenner. It is, again, a begging of the question. The whole point of Brenner's argument is to avoid simply taking for granted the universal development of capitalism by subsuming it under some universal law of historical change, and instead to explain how historically specific conditions produced capitalism's unique drive and its unique capacity for expansion and universalization, from historically specific origins. The very least that can be said about the inadequacy of Roemer's response is that the universality of capitalism can be deployed as evidence for Brenner's account just as easily as for Cohen's. Brenner's has the advantage of resting on a wealth of historical evidence and of not assuming the very thing that needs to be explained.

What Is a Theory of History?

What is at stake here is not, however, only Brenner's empirical challenge to Roemer-Cohen's theory of history. Brenner's explanation of capitalist development as emerging out of feudal relations themselves, instead of 'alongside' them, plays havoc with the very foundations of the RCM model. Historical change is generated in his account by processes within existing social relations, and not by the 'choice' of some other, exogenous or co-existing, 'option'. Certainly lords and peasants make 'rational choices' (what serious historian would deny this?), but those choices occur within the existing relations. Indeed, they are aimed not at attaining the next, more attractive, historical stage (which the parties involved cannot, in any case, anticipate) but at the *reproduction* of existing conditions.

Such an account implies something more than individuals with (fixed and static) 'resources' or 'endowments' plus 'rationality' (with magically available options). It implies a whole historically constituted and dynamic network of structured relations – between lord and peasant, between each and his community, between class and state – always in process; and it cannot beg the question of historical origins. Brenner's contribution to 'analytic Marxism' (explicitly stated in the volume of that name edited by

Roemer) is to break the link which ties the game-theoretic model to the theory of history: he undermines the presupposition that there is a direct correspondence between the self-interested actions of rational economic actors and the requirements of technical progress or economic growth. If there is anything distinctive in RCM, if it is more than just an 'analytic' mode of presentation or even a very general acknowledgement that people make history by making choices which have unintended consequences (if, for example, RCM is serious about constructing its game-theoretic universe out of just individual resources plus rationality) then Brenner's history represents a challenge to its very first methodological premises.

It should already be evident that Brenner's approach also challenges the whole notion of historical theory as a general account of universal laws which move in a pre-determined direction. Not only does he question the historical-materialist credentials of such a theory by attributing it to an undeveloped phase of Marx's work, still uncritically bound to classical bourgeois thought; but his whole historical project testifies to a view that a theory of history subsuming the entire developmental process from classical antiquity to capitalism (let alone the whole of world history) under one universal and essentially unidirectional law of motion, would need to be so general as to be vacuous. How useful, after all, is a 'theory' of technological progress which claims to be equally compatible with moments of rapid technical improvement and long epochs of stagnation or 'petrification'?[21]

To say this is not to accept Carling's view that Brenner has empirical evidence but not a theory of history. It is instead to suggest that there may be other conceptions of theory, and indeed that the most distinctive feature of historical materialism – that which distinguishes it most radically, in form as well as substance, from conventional bourgeois theories of progress – is not its adherence to a general law of technological determinism. It is, rather, a focus (such as that which characterizes the most complete and systematic of Marx's own works, his actual practice in the critique of political economy and the analyses of capitalism) on the specificity of every mode of production, its endogenous logic of process, its own 'laws of motion', its characteristic crises – to use Brenner's formula, its own rules of reproduction.

This is not simply a matter of distinguishing, as Carling does, between a 'general theory' of history and a 'special' theory of capitalism. It is rather a different (and general) theory of history of which the theory of capitalism, with its specific laws of motion, is the prime example. While Cohen's 'general theory' takes the form of retrospective or even teleological predictions, with the benefit of hindsight, with such a degree of generality that no empirical evidence could possibly falsify it, Brenner's theory demands empirical specification which does not assume a predetermined outcome. But if the mark of a theory is the existence of 'fixed points' which remain constant throughout its specific applications, there are more than enough fixed points in Brenner's account – in particular, the principle that at the foundation of every social form there are property relations whose conditions of reproduction structure social and historical processes.

Cohen plus Roemer?

Does this mean that 'Cohen plus Roemer' works better? There are, of course, problems here too, not the least of which is that Cohen's account of technological determinism, with its emphasis on 'functional explanation', seems to run counter to all the RCM strictures against 'methodological collectivism'. And yet, on second thoughts, the attraction which Cohen exerts upon Roemer and other RCMists may be understandable and not at all inconsistent, or at least it is entirely consistent with the irreducible contradiction at the heart of RCM.

RCM requires that, if functional explanations are invoked, a mechanism must be found to account for how the 'functional' effect is produced. Cohen's functional explanation of the development of productive forces rests on a particular theory of human nature which purports to supply the necessary mechanism: given a rationality which involves a disposition to seize the means of satisfying compelling wants, and a kind and degree of intelligence which permits them to improve their situation, in conditions of scarcity, human beings will generally seek and/or adopt whatever means are available to curtail labour, which is inherently unpleasant to them (never mind evidence to the contrary, such as that provided by Brenner). It is this transhistorical rationality, and the impulse to improve productive forces which it entails, that underlie the functional argument for the primacy of productive forces.

Because of RCM's own static model of 'property relations', the first requirement in an RCM-compatible theory of history is that the 'motor' must come from outside any given system of property or exploitation. In other words, it is in the nature of the RCM model that, in order to account for historical process, it requires a *deus ex machina*. Traditionally the most popular 'external' forces have been trade (markets enlarging and contracting, with trade routes opening and closing) and/or technical progress, both conceived as exogenous to the systems being transformed either in the sense that they are determined by alien intrusions such as barbarian invasions, or in the sense that they operate according to some universal natural law (progress, the natural development of the human mind, or perhaps, more scientifically, demographic cycles ...). RCM, however, has the special requirement that the explanation must be reduced to motivations which can be attributed to the rationality of individual human beings. A particular kind of transhistorical rationality, which can serve as the common denominator among all the various systems of property and exploitation, and can supply the mechanism for moving from one to the next, in effect containing the whole of history within it, seems tailor-made for the purpose. To put it another way, if historical motion can be explained only by presupposing each successive historical stage as an option or motivation already available in the preceding one, then it helps to have some exogenous cause for its availability. An RCM-compatible theory of history requires also that the 'rational choice' model of exploitation be left intact, and this means that production *relations*, which are not so much the *conditions* of rational choice as its product, can play no immediate part in setting off the dynamic of change. What is needed is a theory of history which, as it were, runs parallel to the analytic model without impinging upon or challenging its constitutive analytic fiction, which presents the exploitative 'relation' as an agreement between rational agents.

Cohen, unlike Brenner, permits RCM to maintain its static model and does not place upon it the intolerable strain of motivating historical change from within specific property relations, without the aid of exogenous forces or 'feasible alternatives' which appear by spontaneous generation, in the form of already existing options, motivations or 'assets'. Thus RCM, a theory ostensibly devoted to rescuing human agency from structural determinisms, is forced to readmit a fairly old-fashioned historical determinism through the back door, while retaining the fiction of 'rational choice' at another, ahistorical level of analysis.

On balance, Roemer appears to be right in thinking that an alliance with Cohen is a safer bet than collaboration with Brenner. At the same time, since neither match is unproblematic, it might be more precise to say that Roemer's theory of class and exploitation is uncongenial to *any* explanation of history. Anyone who believes that a vacuously general theory is little better than no theory at all in historical explanation, might be inclined to think that it is just here, in its fundamentally ahistorical character and in its hostility to historical specificity, that RCM has most in common with Cohen's technological determinism.

Elster on Marx and History

Elster's approach to technological determinism presents problems of its own. He is more inclined than Roemer to demand from Cohen a specific account – in methodological-individualist terms – of the mechanisms by which the long-term 'functional' effect of technological progress is achieved, and in this sense significantly qualifies his adherence to the 'general theory' and its reliance on functional explanation. He also questions the extent to which Marx himself consistently adhered to the general theory. On this point, Elster's principal concern is to demonstrate that Marx's theory of history is inherently inconsistent; and his argument centres on one important insight, namely that in Marx's own accounts of historical transitions, the development of productive forces plays little role as the primary motor.

This observation is both true and significant. Although the 'general theory' appears in various (though not many) aphoristic formulae in Marx's work, it is not generally deployed in his systematic attempts at historical explanation. So, for example, his most comprehensive accounts of pre-capitalist societies in the *Grundrisse* and of the historical transition to capitalism – especially in the section on 'Primitive Accumulation' in *Capital* – do not invoke the development of productive forces as the motivating impulse of historical change, and indeed are based on the premise that what needs to be explained is precisely the *origin* of capitalism's distinctive drive to improve the forces of production. Here, in the critique of political economy which formed the core of his life's work, Marx laid the foundation for a different kind of 'general' theory – the foundation on which Brenner, for instance, has constructed his own account of history. But Elster is not interested in this theoretical alternative, if he even recognizes it as such (as distinct from a 'special' theory of capitalism). He is interested only in demonstrating the incompatibility between Marx's adherence to the primacy of productive forces and his analysis of capitalism, a contradiction between the general theory of history as the development of productive forces and the view that the maximization of technological development is specific to capitalism.

There is no doubt that Marx never bothered to resolve the inconsistencies between his aphorisms about the forces of production and his insistence on the specificity of capitalism. It needs to be said, however, that even in the context of the 'general theory' (if such it is), there is room for a specifically capitalist dynamic. The critical issue for Marx was always the *specific compulsion* of capitalism to revolutionize the forces of production, which differs from any more general tendency to improve productive forces that may be ascribed to history as a whole. In that sense, it was possible for him consistently to hold both the view that history displays a general tendency to improve the forces of production and the view that capitalism had a special need and capacity to revolutionize productive forces. Beginning early in his career, Marx never deviated from the view that the capitalist drive is specific and unprecedented and that, whatever progressive tendencies may be generally observable in history, the specific logic of capitalism and its specific compulsion to improve the productivity of labour by technical means are not reducible to these general tendencies. They require a specific explanation. He also made it very clear that the capitalist impulse to improve the productivity of labour is quite distinct from, and often in opposition to, any general human inclination to curtail labour. The capitalist impulse is to *increase the portion of unpaid labour*. He devoted much of his life's work to explaining this specifically capitalist dynamic.

Marx's critique of political economy, the core of his mature work, proceeds precisely by way of differentiating himself from those who take for granted and universalize the logic and dynamic of capitalism without acknowledging the historical specificity of its 'laws' or seeking to uncover what produces them. Marx, unlike the classical political economists, and indeed a host of other ideologues of 'progress' and 'commercial society', did not assume that the 'progress' embodied in modern society was simply the outcome of a drive inherent in human nature or natural law, but insisted on the specificity of the capitalist demand for productivity and the need to find an explanation for it. It was Marx's identification of that specific dynamic which made it possible even to raise the question of the 'transition' to capitalism, to seek an explanation of how that dynamic was set in train, something which remained impossible as long as people assumed the very forces that needed to be explained. Marx himself never produced a systematic account of the historical process of transition, and his discussions of pre-capitalist modes of production were never more than retrospective analyses, part of a strategy to explicate the workings of capitalism and emphasize the historicity of its laws and categories. But he took the qualitative leap that was required to make an explanation of the transition possible, and he thereby established a basis for a general theory of history which would also treat other modes of production on their own specific terms.

History or Teleology?

It is especially ironic that the strategy adopted by Marx to highlight the specificity of capitalism is mistaken by Elster for a *teleological* account of history. This misunderstanding by itself tells us something important about Elster's conception of what counts as a theory of history and its essential affinity to 'Roemer-plus-Cohen'. In a particularly significant passage,

Elster cites Marx's famous aphorism that 'Human anatomy contains a key to the anatomy of the ape', from the *Grundrisse*, as a statement of his 'teleological stance' – which is, according to Elster, 'closely related to the propensity for functional explanation ...' (Elster 1985, p. 54). Elster compounds the misunderstanding by interpreting this aphorism to apply to the 'teleological' relationship between communism and capitalism, as it does to the relationship between capitalist and pre-capitalist modes of production. Although capitalism can, of course, be analysed from the standpoint of socialism – that is, by identifying the potentiality within capitalism for a socialist transformation – the analogy suggested by Elster is an imperfect one. Capitalism can provide the 'key' to pre-capitalist society, in the sense here intended, only because it actually exists and because it has given rise to its own historically constituted categories, whose historical specificity Marx is trying to demonstrate by *critically* applying them to pre-capitalist forms. That is precisely the meaning of his *critique* of political economy. The point is not that capitalism is *prefigured* in pre-capitalist forms but on the contrary that capitalism represents a historically specific *transformation*. Marx adopts this paradoxical strategy precisely in order to counter 'those economists who smudge over all historical differences and see bourgeois relations in all forms of society'[22] – that is, precisely against what might be called the teleological tendencies of classical political economy, for which 'bourgeois relations' are the natural and universal order of things, the destination of progress already present in all earlier stages of history. To the extent that Marx's point of departure is a refusal to incorporate capitalism into the historical process which produced it, and especially with a theory of history in which every mode of production is propelled by its own distinctive laws of motion, his characteristic procedure is exactly the reverse of teleological or even functional explanation.

Although a teleological account of history represents the most serious violation of methodological individualism, RCM has a tendency to incorporate the destination of history into its very beginnings – a teleological procedure if ever there was one. On the one hand, RCM can give no account of history but must begin afresh with every social form, an already given and static 'property relation' represented in the person of the rational individual whose 'endowments' and 'relational properties' come from nowhere and are going nowhere; on the other hand, it is drawn to theories of history in which the end is already given in the beginning – as forms of exploitation coexisting until they successively fall away, or as a transhistorical drive for technological development, requiring only 'elimination' or the removal of impediments to come to the fore. In both cases, the question of *historical process* is begged. Perhaps, then, it is simply the idea of *process* that sticks in the RCM throat, and the problem — for someone like Elster — is not that conventional Marxism is *teleological* but that it is *historical*, a distinction which may not be altogether clear in the RCM framework.

At worst, then, the RCM model as a guide to history is positively misleading. At best, it can add little to what Marxism can achieve by other less precious and circuitous means. And since the context in which 'rational choices' are made must always be specified first (and the model cannot help us to arrive at that specification), if the model is to be used at all in the explanation of social and historical processes, then all the real work — the historical and structural analysis — needs to be done before the model can be inserted. In such a case, the model is, again, largely rhetorical or persuasive. If that is so, we really have to ask whether the game is worth the candle. What rational being would choose RCM if the pay-off is so incommensurate with the effort?

THE MORAL ARGUMENT

We are left with claims of RCM as a mode of moral argumentation. If it can make good Roemer's claim that 'the game-theoretic formulation is superior [to conventional Marxism and its "surplus labour" theory — EMW] in that it makes explicit what ethical presumption lies behind the Marxian theory of exploitation', if it can thereby enhance the ideological arsenal of socialism by securing the case for its moral superiority to capitalism, then a useful purpose will no doubt have been served. And if this is RCM's principal project, we may be inclined to conclude that its explanatory weakness is not such a serious shortcoming after all. It would certainly fill a gap in socialist thought which, among other things, has put Marxism on the defensive against the charge that the explicit disavowal of ethical considerations in the interest of 'scientific socialism' has disarmed it in the face of deformations such as Stalinism. This vacuum in Marxist argumentation has been more acutely felt as growing disappointment with revolutions in the East and their absence in the West have sapped an older confidence in the historical tendency toward, if not the inevitability of, socialism, which as a historical necessity could, apparently, dispense with an ethical justification.

It is, however, unlikely that such considerations have weighed very heavily with Rational Choice Marxists. They have generally shown little interest in socialist history, in its international dimension, and have been almost exclusively preoccupied with interlocutors on the academic Right.

What seems to have concentrated their minds on ethical questions is the rise, since the 1970s, of an increasingly aggressive and confident intellectual Right. For the first time in recent memory, the Right has marshalled its intellectual forces, inside and outside the academy, to demonstrate that capitalism is materially and morally better than socialism, both more efficient and more free.

But if RCM is principally designed to meet the philosophical challenge from the academic-intellectual Right, it has entered the battle with (at least) one hand tied behind its back. This paradigm is singularly ill-designed to give us a sense of capitalist accumulation as a ruthless world process which inevitably generates economic catastrophes outside the privileged North, as well as regular crises within it, not to mention the threat of nuclear or ecological destruction for the world altogether. Indeed, the RCM corpus generally leaves the impression of a very limited mental universe, confined within an opulent Northern capitalism, and even there constricted by a remarkable insensitivity to the irrationalities and destructive effects of capitalist accumulation. The RCM case for socialism is generally predicated on a relatively benign capitalism – a capitalism which is particularly effective in satisfying material interests (always narrowly conceived in terms of 'consumer bundles'). Even Roemer, who is committed to the view that capitalism is in principle anarchic and inefficient, is constrained by his overriding methodological commitment to the abstract models of conventional economics. He presents his indictment of capitalist inefficiency not by exposing the realities of its wasteful destructiveness but, indirectly, by mildly acknowledging, in very general and abstract terms, that some of the assumptions of equilibrium theory (a theory which he nevertheless regards as 'one of the great contributions to social scientific method of the past century') may not apply in real capitalist economies.[23] Other RCMists are evidently not prepared to concede even this much to the critique of capitalism, suggesting at best that the superior efficiency of capitalism may have to be sacrificed in the interests of some higher commitment – perhaps to democracy and collective decision-making (Przeworski 1985a, pp. 237–8). Such a restricted analysis of capitalism not only deprives the socialist project of any historical foundation but weakens the moral case against capitalism.

RCM leaves little ground for socialist struggle against capitalism, nor does it seem to matter very much. On the one hand, there being little historical or material foundation for the socialist project as an outcome of real conflicts and struggles generated by capitalism, that project has been reduced to a largely academic moral disputation, a rhetorical exercise designed to *persuade*. On the other hand, the terrain of moral contest has itself been severely restricted by a sanguine view of capitalism that narrows the ground on which socialism can claim superiority. It is, in any case, a simple matter of preference, and the choice appears to be of little moment.

It is not surprising, given the contingency and inconsequentiality of the choice between capitalism and socialism, that RCM tends to be obsessed with mathematical formulae and narrowly formalistic questions which have little connection with the real and urgent moral-political problems confronting humanity and the socialist movement today. Its constricted conception of the issues, and its casuistic formalism shaped to the narrow standards of a very particular specialized audience, are unlikely to produce anything particularly useful or politically effective. Still, it is perhaps early days and something more substantial may yet emerge from RCM efforts to construct a normative socialist theory. For the moment, if we are not simply to dismiss the moral argument out of hand as largely irrelevant to the realities of contemporary capitalism and the conditions of socialist struggle, we need at least to be persuaded that the moral theory, which in its most developed Roemerian form purports to reveal the exploitative foundations of capitalism, adds something to our understanding of capitalist exploitation, or rather, that it adds more than it subtracts.

Moral Argument v. Explanation?

Let us for the sake of argument accept that Roemer has indeed successfully revealed the moral principle on the basis of which capitalism stands condemned (Carling's gloss on Roemer on pp. 48–50 of his article above may be taken as the most sympathetic account of the argument); and we can overlook the doubts cast by Elster on the usefulness of the concept of exploitation as a tool 'for a more fine-grained investigation into moral theory' (Elster 1985, p. 229). The concern here will be with the consequences of the theory when it is given the benefit of the doubt. Here, Elster makes a striking point. He suggests that the very conceptual devices which constitute RCM as a moral-rhetorical strategy disable it as a mode of explanation.

> The importance of exploitation in Marxism is twofold. First, the presence of exploitation in a society provides the outside observer with a ground for normative criticism. Exploitation is wrong; exploiters are morally condemnable; a society that tolerates or generates exploitation ought to be abolished. Secondly, exploitation can provide the exploited with a ground

for taking individual or collective action against the system, and hence enters into the explanation of such action. When constructing a more elaborate theory of exploitation, one may face the problem that the normatively relevant concept is one that does not have much explanatory significance (Elster 1985, p. 166).

Elaborating on this point later in the book, Elster writes:

> the immediate transfer of surplus-value is not an important notion from the moral point of view .... Hence the moral and the explanatory aspects of Marxism diverge rather sharply at this point. It would have been theoretically satisfactory to argue that the grounds on which capitalism is to be condemned are also those that will motivate the struggle to abolish it. Marx, however, does not succeed in showing that this connection holds (Elster 1985, p. 340).

Elster's principal concern has to do with the role of class struggle in the socialist project: if the moral evil of capitalism lies in its unequal distribution of the relevant 'resources', while conflict and struggle are generated by a transfer of surplus which has no place in the moral argument, then the moral condemnation of capitalism has little to do with the motivations for struggles against it.

It needs to be said, first, that 'classical' Marxism never did make this kind of connection, in the form suggested by Elster. Certainly it is a distinctive characteristic of Marxism to insist on an organic connection between theory and practice; but this does not take the form of claiming that the 'scientific' analysis of capitalism can also yield a moral judgement which will motivate the revolutionary transformation. The argument is rather that the explanatory theory which exposes the workings of capitalism also expresses the self-emancipatory project of the working class by revealing the convergence of its interests and capacities with the conditions of a socialist transformation made possible by capitalism. This is not to deny Marx's moral condemnation of capitalism; but it is precisely because he deliberately avoided the kind of connection suggested by Elster that there has been so much controversy about the very existence of a moral dimension in Marx's account of capitalism.[24]

The force of Elster's argument, however, does not derive from the claim that Roemer has broken a link on which the coherence of classical Marxism depended. It lies rather in the suggestion that Roemer's moral argument itself has no explanatory power, and even that there is a contradiction between the requirements of the moral argument and the explanatory capacity of Marxist theory. Elster diverges from Roemer in a way which reveals an important truth about the Roemerian theory and about RCM generally, a truth which Roemer often hides from himself by stressing the automaticity of the links connecting the unequal distribution of assets (the moment of exploitation) to the generation of classes and in turn to the necessity of the struggle for socialism. Elster recognises that the connections have been severed – not just modified in their degree of necessity but cleanly severed – by the exclusion of the transfer of surplus labour from the theory of exploitation. This affects not only our understanding of the revolutionary agency which will bring about socialism but also the whole Marxist explanation of history.

Elster's answer, however, is not to reintroduce the transfer of surplus labour into the original account of exploitation, but rather to isolate the definition of exploitation as a normative concept while displacing the transfer of surplus labour to a different, explanatory plane. He suggests that without the 'surplus labour theory' there is much that Roemer cannot explain – in particular, about social conflict; but the conclusion he draws from this is simply that a theory of exploitation which might serve to establish a normative concept must be essentially devoid of explanatory power.

By itself, the separation of normative and explanatory arguments need not be disabling. It can be a legitimate exercise to construct a moral argument at an angle different from that required by, say, historical explanation. But problems do arise when there are outright contradictions, or when the premises of the moral argument require us to believe things which flout historical evidence or cloud our historical vision. The problems here do not flow simply from the decoupling of the moral and explanatory aspects of Marxism. The real difficulties lie in the *explanatory* implications of the moral argument itself – or rather, the explanatory weakness of RCM is traceable to the very first step in its moral argument, the point at which the moment of surplus-transfer was detached from the unequal distribution of assets. For Roemer, the requirements of the moral theory were not – yet – visibly distinct from those of the explanatory model because both the moral and the causal aspects of exploitation had their origins in inequality and the apparent automaticity of its consequences. For Elster, the necessary consequence of the moral argument, which required isolating the moment of injustice by situating it in the original unequal distribution, is that moral and explanatory theories had to diverge.

But from then on – and this is the critical point – the separation remains in place not only for the analytic purpose of isolating the normative moment but as an intrinsic element in the explanatory model. In order to make this moral argument about exploitation without resorting to the labour theory of value, Roemer jettisons the whole apparatus which renders explanation possible, and thereafter seeks to reconstruct Marxist theory upon this hollow foundation. His vacuous account of history is the most notable result. Whether the fateful step was taken in order to meet the needs of an analytic theory of justice, or in order to satisfy the requirements of a game-theoretic explanatory model, or both together, the effects are the same. Either way, the theory of exploitation entails breaking the connections among the various 'moments' of capital – production, distribution, exchange, consumption – and destroying any conception of capitalism as a *process*, in which these analytically distinct moments are dynamically united. In other words, there has been a complete reversal of the theoretical advances which Marx so painstakingly laboured to establish in his critique of political economy. That this represents progress in our understanding of capitalism, and not a regression to the worst simplifications of pre-Marxist political economy, remains to be demonstrated.

Przeworski on Roemer: Exploitation and Class Struggle

Przeworski too recognizes the problem in Roemer's argument – yet it is in his own attempt to find a solution that the weaknesses in the RCM paradigm are most starkly revealed. Roemer's definition of exploitation, writes Przeworski, is superior to the 'surplus value' definition 'not because it provides a better causal explanation' but because it 'makes clear "the ethical imperatives" of Marxian theory' (Przeworski 1985a, p. 226). Indeed, he argues, the explanatory power of Roemer's theory is so weak that it 'does not establish any logical correspondence between exploitation and class struggle, that no such correspondence is here to establish, and that his historical assertions [about the necessity of the connections between inequality and exploitation, and between exploitation and class struggle – EMW] are entirely rhetorical (Przeworski 1985a, p. 227). There is, for Przeworski, no 'tight correspondence' of the kind proposed by Roemer between the original distribution of assets and its consequences in the inequality of income. The connection between the two is mediated and variable, subject, for example, to struggles between capital and labour at the point of production. Roemer simply factors out such mediations and thereby assumes out of existence 'the problem of extracting labour out of labour-power (Przeworski 1985a, p. 229). (Przeworski might have added that the RCM model in general does not accommodate the *open-endedness*, the *incompleteness* of the capitalist labour contract but proceeds as if the exchange between capital and labour were between two known quantities, a wage in exchange for a given service or product.) The automaticity of Roemer's equation, Przeworski argues, does not allow, among other things, for the possibility that people will work more intensively for themselves than for others, and that the income of capitalists will depend on their success in extracting surplus labour from their reluctant workers. The problem, suggests Przeworski, is that Roemer has simply transported the assumptions of his original model of exploitation, where no exchange of labour takes place and where there is no problem of *extracting* labour, to an exploitative relation where there *is* a labour exchange and where the original assumptions are therefore no longer appropriate.

The rigid necessity of the connections in Roemer's formula, between the distribution of assets and the distribution of income, leaves no logical place, argues Przeworski, for class struggle *within* a mode of production but only in the transition from one mode to another. This arbitrary automaticity allows Roemer to assume that no significant redistribution of wealth is possible under capitalism, given its original distribution of assets, and that workers are obliged to struggle for socialism if they want to improve their material conditions. Przeworski sets out to correct Roemer's formulation in order to make room for class struggle within capitalism, to reconnect exploitation with class struggle and the process of capital accumulation, and above all to lay the foundation of an argument for socialism which does not depend on its presumed superiority in satisfying workers' material interests.

There are some perceptive and telling arguments here, but it turns out that Przeworski is himself handicapped from the start by his own adherence to the RCM model. Indeed, he adheres to it in some respects more rigidly than does Roemer. The trouble with Roemer, apparently is that he is not *enough* of a game-theorist, and that he has not introduced enough choice or contingency into the connection between exploitation and class struggle. But Przeworski's faithfulness to the game-theoretical model leaves him with problems of his own. To Roemer's rigid necessities, he can reply only with almost unlimited contingencies. Since for the purposes of the rational choice model capitalism exists only as a 'game' between consenting adults, a game in which the stakes are no more compelling than a desire for 'optimization', there is no 'logical place' in his argument for capitalism as a compulsive and coercive system, a ruthless logic of process.

There is little room, first, for the compulsions which operate on capital, the *imperatives* of accumulation and self-expansion. We no longer have any notion of how to explain the relation between the 'distribution of assets' and the *need* for accumulation, the *necessity* of extracting surplus at the point of production and the contradictions and conflicts this necessarily occasions. All we have is a game in which capitalists have 'assets' which, if they wish, they can use to increase their wealth by extracting surplus from workers, as long as they succeed in overcoming whatever power of resistance the workers may have.

Second, there is little room for the fundamental coercion imposed on the worker from the beginning, before the 'moment' of labour-extraction and independent of the balance of power between any particular capitalist and any particular group of workers. This is the compulsion inherent in the initial disposition of property relations which systematically obliges some people to forfeit surplus labour to others simply in order to gain access to the means of labour itself.

If Roemer's model is inadequate because of its failure to acknowledge the problem of extracting labour from labour-power, Przeworski's is inadequate because of its failure to appreciate the coercive presuppositions of surplus extraction. If Roemer's paradigm suffers from an inability to allow that people may work harder for themselves than for others, Przeworski's is weakened by an inability to acknowledge the strength of the compulsion to intensify labour in cases where the obligation to labour for others is the pre-condition of access to the means of labour. If Roemer transports assumptions from one model to another where they do not apply, from an exploitative relation without a labour exchange to one in which there is such an exchange, an analogous transportation of assumptions occurs in Przeworski's model: exploitative relations where access to the means of survival is conditional on the transfer of surplus labour are here analyzed on the assumptions of a model where no such condition exists. If the explanatory weakness of Roemer's model lies in its presumption of necessity, Przeworski's fails because of its insistence on contingency.

In the guise of establishing connections between exploitation, class struggle and capital accumulation (connections which he says are missing in Marx as well as Roemer), Przeworski has effectively dissolved the systemic connections and compulsions long ago demonstrated by Marx. Capitalism appears at best as an inert 'constraint' on individual choices, and the constraint seems very weak, very permissive in the latitude of choices it allows. Przeworski's argument is, in fact, based in large part on the assumption that a 'major redistribution of wealth endowments' is 'feasible' under capitalism, that class struggle can not only accelerate or retard accumulation but 'transform' it altogether while leaving the original distribution intact. This highly abstract proposition evinces an attitude on historical fact even more off-hand than Roemer's.[25] It is perhaps a measure of the imperatives imposed by the rational choice model that Przeworski ends by contradicting the very convictions concerning the implacability of capitalism, and the limited scope it permits to reform, upon which he bases his critique of social democracy.

In the end, Roemer's compulsive paradigm may be less misleading about the coercive realities of capitalism than is Przeworski's permissive model – though the latter is more logically consistent with RCM premises, its conception of choice and the weak compulsion of 'optimizing strategies'. Yet, though the consequences of Roemer's procedure are masked in his own work by his insistence on the absolute necessity of everything that follows from unequal distribution, it cannot be said that his RCM critics are wrong to claim that the tight connections in Roemer's equation are largely arbitrary and rhetorical; for once having made the first move in detaching the moments of capital, once having undermined the power of his theory to explain the coercive dynamic of capitalism, Roemer leaves no barrier to the conclusions drawn by Elster and Przeworski about the permissiveness of capitalism or the contingency of the relation between exploitation and class struggle.

The Pay-Off

If the moral theory of RCM is weak on its own terms, as a moral theory, because it lacks any purchase on the major moral and political issues of our time, it is doubly weak because it further undermines the power of the model to *explain* the conditions in which those issues must be contested. If RCM is to make good its claims as an improvement on conventional Marxism on *any* grounds, we have a right to expect a moral argument much more powerful than anything produced so far, not only to fill the gaps in the existing moral theory but to compensate for the explanatory sacrifices made on its behalf. The prospects, however, do not seem promising, for reasons that are inherent in the model itself. It seems unlikely that a moral theory capable of coming to grips with the realities of contemporary capitalism will come out of the constricted conception of the world and human experience contained in the RCM model. That model tends to be simplistically 'economistic' in its theoretical focus. Whatever their individual convictions about the complexity of human motivation, RCMists remain trapped in a theoretical paradigm which is blind to any motivating forces that cannot be reduced to the narrow terms of 'market-rationality', the calculation of 'utilities'. It often seems that RCM, like the crudest Benthamite utilitarianism, can acknowledge only those emotions or beliefs which can be rendered in potentially quantifiable or economic terms – so that, for example, Elster can write of guilt or shame as 'a utility fine', and something like parental care for children might appear as a 'transfer of utility'. The model is, after all, designed according to the specifications of bourgeois economics. In this respect, the RCM image of human nature has more in common with the 'economic man' of liberalism than with historical materialism. It is difficult to imagine that any profound moral insights will emerge from this banal and shrivelled *homo economicus*.

It is a telling comment on the weakness of Roemer's claim to provide the essential moral critique of capitalism that Przeworski, the most explicitly political of the three RCMists, feels compelled in the end to step outside the paradigm to justify a preference for socialism. Capitalism, he argues, can meet any challenge on the economic terrain marked out by Roemer. If socialism is preferable at all, it must be because it permits 'society as a whole to choose in a democratic way' how to allocate its resources (Przeworski 1985a, p. 238). The decisive moral criterion is not, then, equality but something like autonomy, or perhaps collective responsibility and community. Nothing in the RCM theory of exploitation has prepared us for this new moral standard.

But there is an even more curious anomaly. Roemer tells us that, according to historical materialism as he understands it, transformations of property relations are not caused by ideas about injustice and exploitation but by material conditions.[26] He does not dissociate himself from this proposition. Indeed, his adherence to technological determinism suggests a particularly deterministic interpretation of Marxism. What, then, is the point of reconstructing the whole of Marxist theory to satisfy the needs of an abstract moral argument? Why should RCM proceed as if moral persuasion were the principal agency of revolutionary change?

WHAT IS THE POLITICS OF RCM?

The intellectual pay-off of Rational Choice Marxism appears to be strictly limited, and the costs may be far greater than the benefits. There remains the question of its political charge. A certain caution is required in the attempt to extract political implications from a theoretical tendency as abstract and formalistic as this. Its political significance may, in fact, lie precisely in a political amorphousness which makes it vulnerable to the vagaries of political fashion. One or two things can, however, be suggested about the political direction in which we are pointed by the theoretical assumptions of RCM.

If one were simply to list the principal features of the RCM model, the result would be something very like a caricature of Anglo-American liberalism as it has evolved since the seventeenth century: methodological individualism; 'analytic' method; ahistoricism (which is not necessarily incompatible with technological determinism or its functional equivalent and frequent corollary, a conception of history as the triumph of 'commercial society'); class conceived as income stratification; a preoccupation with market relations as distinct from production relations; an 'economic' model of human nature. This theoretical constellation could represent a rough sketch of the Anglophone liberal mind-set with its typical symbiosis of liberal ideology and British empiricism, in which a reductionist focus on human nature has been associated with a formalistic tradition of analytic philosophy. The striking resemblance between RCM and this liberal-empiricist ideal-type does not, of course, guarantee that all, or any, RCMists must subscribe to the relevant political doctrines; but the analogy is at least suggestive.

At the same time, there is another, at first glance opposing, tradition to which RCM has certain striking affinities – utopian socialism: a detachment of the ethical ideal of socialism from the historical conditions of its realization; a distributional theory of exploitation which locates the moment of injustice in the sphere of circulation and exchange; a 'one-sided' presentation of capitalism which abstracts the 'free' (if 'unfair') exchange between capital and labour from its 'pre-suppositions', thereby conjuring away the barriers between capitalism and socialism by implicitly constructing a continuum from capitalist to socialist 'freedom and equality'. This is a tradition about which Marx had a great deal to say, much of it uncannily prophetic of RCM, culminating in the following assessment:

> It is forgotten, on the one side, that the *presupposition* of exchange value, as the objective basis of the whole of the system of production, already in itself implies compulsion over the individual, since his immediate product is not a product for him, but only *becomes* such in the social process, and since it *must* take on this general but nevertheless external form; and that the individual has an existence only as a producer of exchange value, hence that the whole negation of his natural existence is already implied, that he is therefore entirely determined by society; that this further presupposes a division of labour etc., in which the individual is already posited in relations other than that of mere *exchanger*, etc. That therefore this presupposition by no means arises either out of the individual's will or out of the immediate nature of the

individual, but that it is, rather, *historical*, and posits the individual as already *determined* by society. It is forgotten, on the other side, that these higher forms, in which exchange, or the relations of production which realize themselves in it, are now posited, do not by any means stand still in this simple form where the highest distinction which occurs is a formal and hence irrelevant one. What is overlooked, finally, is that already the simple forms of exchange value and of money latently contain the opposition between labour and capital etc. Thus, what all this wisdom comes down to is the attempt to stick fast at the simplest economic relations, which, conceived by themselves, are pure abstractions: but these relationships are, in reality, mediated by the deepest antithesis, and represent only one side, in which the full expression of the antithesis is obscured. (Marx 1973, pp. 247–8).

This is Marx's account of the capital relation as it appears to those 'foolish' French socialists 'who want to depict socialism as the realization of the ideals of *bourgeois* society'. And here perhaps is the crux of the matter. If the theoretical apparatus of RCM has any specific political implications, they too may lie in the *conflation of capitalism and socialism* which inheres in the very structure of the argument and which would account for its joint affinities to Anglo-American liberalism and French utopian socialism.

Conflating Capitalism and Socialism

Carling's text on Rational Choice Marxism illustrates how the theoretical imperatives of RCM, and its rhetorical or ethical requirements in particular, exert a political pressure of their own. The essence of his argument has to do with how and why it might be *philosophically* legitimate to regard capitalism as *exploitative*, and hence unjust, despite the freedom and equality inherent in it. At first, this procedure appears to be a rhetorical strategy designed to meet defenders of capitalism on their own terrain. Carling suggests, however, that these rhetorical devices contain an important truth and that we should – as he would argue Roemer does – take seriously the claims to freedom and equality contained in their account of capitalist relations.

The extent to which Carling's argument here depends upon a 'onesided' view of capitalism is nowhere more strikingly illustrated than in his suggestion that 'the market-place really is a free space: what is constitutionally unfree is the State-place, which upholds property, and the workplace, where those without property find it is in their best interest to labour for their daily bread.'[27] (Note the rather coy formulation according to which propertyless workers 'find it is in their best interest' to labour for capital). Carling thus completely misses the essence of capitalist unfreedom on two principal counts – by masking the necessity of the 'choice' between exploitation and survival rooted in the structure of capitalist social-property relations, *and* the ultimate compulsion of the capitalist market, the universal subjection of all human beings to its sovereignty summed up in Marx's 'fetishism of commodities'. He thereby evacuates the ground for any adequate statement of the socialist project. What he concludes from his analysis of capitalist freedom and equality is simply that we should regard socialism not as something qualitatively different from capitalism but rather as more of the same, more of the freedom and equality already inherent in capitalism.

In Carling's account of RCM there appears to be an explicit warrant for drawing political-strategic conclusions from the rhetorical merger of capitalism and socialism. But even short of that, the tendency to conflate capitalism and socialism, which is inherent in the RCM project, has political implications. If socialism is simply a quantitative improvement, an extension of capitalist freedom and equality, the passage from one to the other is likely to be relatively smooth and non-antagonistic – with all the implications this perception has for the marginalization of class politics. But even if the conflation is merely a rhetorical device, then at the very least it guarantees the vacuity of RCM as a guide to the strategy, because its moral-rhetorical value depends precisely on ignoring the critical barriers – such as class antagonisms – standing in the way of a smooth transition from one social form to the other.

There is, however, a significant paradox here – a paradox that belongs to the essence of every utopian socialism. On the one hand, the conflation of capitalism and socialism appears to suggest that the latter will grow directly, and more or less smoothly, out of the former. On the other hand, that same conflation is accompanied by, and indeed has as its principal corollary, a detachment of the socialist project from any historical foundation in the actual conditions of capitalism. Socialism grows out of capitalism not in the sense that the one creates the structural and historical conditions which make the other possible, the contradictions which place socialism on the historical agenda, and the agencies capable of carrying out the socialist project, but rather in the sense that socialism is a 'realization of capitalist ideals'. This juxtaposition of apparently contradictory ideas helps to account for the curious blend of optimism and pessimism which so often characterizes this kind of socialism: the transition to socialism will come about smoothly, without radical breaks or antagonistic encounters, but it is a very long way off – so long that it has receded into invisibility; hence the task of socialists is to 'humanize' capitalism. It may also help to explain the ambivalent quietism, even cynicism, of an Adam Przeworski, in which a hard-headed scepticism about the prospects of socialism exists in uneasy tandem with a trenchant critique of social democracy.

The RCM analysis of capitalism – its detachment of the 'moments' of capital, its theoretical annihilation of the capitalist *system* and capitalist *process*, the effects of these procedures in dissociating class and class struggle from the logic of the capitalist process and rendering them contingent – severs the socialist project from its historical and political roots in the conditions of capitalism. The feasibility of the socialist project, and the possibility of mobilizing forces to carry it out, are no longer historical and political questions but simply rhetorical ones, having to do with the discursive conditions for persuading 'free and rational' individuals to 'choose' socialism – conditions that have little to do with the processes by which political movements are actually formed.

The 'tough-minded' scepticism about the feasibility of socialism expressed by RCMists like Adam Przeworski, in other words, has less to do with a hard-headed assessment of capitalist realities than with an abdication of the ground on which any such assessment could be made. If there is a difference between RCM and utopian socialism in these respects, it is not that the former provides a more effective analysis of the historical conditions for the realization of socialist ideals but rather that it offers a less effective, because more constricted and less passionate, moral vision.

The Convergence of Post-Marxist Theories

There is, it is true, a range of political positions among exponents of the RCM 'paradigm', from Elster and (now) Przeworski on the right to Roemer further left. But if the political logic of the theoretical model is too weak to produce any single political outcome – apart from an inevitable strategic vacuity – the developmental trajectory of the trend as a whole is instructive. There has been a visible shift from RCM's original efforts to set Marxism on a more rigorous analytic footing, against attacks from the right, to what Elster has described as an 'unstated consensus' among its practitioners that leaves 'probably not a single tenet of classical Marxism' intact (Elster 1985, p. xiv). As 'classical Marxism' has given way to neoclassical economics, game theory, methodological individualism, and neocontractarian philosophy, as RCM has set itself the task of 'making sense' (in Elster's phrase) of Marxist nonsense, so too the political commitment to socialist values has been tempered by a new 'realism' about the prospects of socialism. The cynical quietism evinced in the latest work of Adam Przeworski suggests the direction in which the logic of the trend is moving.

In some respects, this trajectory has much in common with another major theoretical tendency in contemporary Marxism, from Althusserianism to 'post-Marxism', which also began as an effort to reestablish 'rigour' in Marxist theory and has ended for many in a general repudiation of Marxism in theory and practice. In the latter case, the theoretical evolution of the trend is traceable to immediate historical coordinates and especially to the life-cycle of the European Communist movement, or one of its significant off-shoots, as it wound its tortuous way from flirtations with Maoism through Eurocommunism and its current fatal disarray. RCM has not been similarly anchored to a political movement of this – or any other – kind, though it has been shaped by the general move to the right in its own geo-political backyard. But if its academic detachment has acted as a safeguard against some varieties of dogma, the absence of roots in the labour movement has also made it more susceptible to other dangers – not the least of which are the pressures of the academy, the attractions of current academic fashion, the professional requirements of an academic career, standards of judgment and a sense of proportion deriving not from the political arena but from the senior common room (or its American and/or Scandinavian equivalent), where the principal adversary is likely to be a professional neo-classical economist.

We may now be observing a curious convergence between two apparently antithetical tendencies, the super-rationalism of Rational Choice Marxism and post-structuralist irrationalism (see below, pp. 301–19). RCM's abstractions, so typical of analytic philosophies which pride themselves on their empyreal detachment from the uncertain flux of historical process, paradoxically come together here with the irrationalist dissolution of history from the opposite direction. Both are impelled toward a politics detached from the anchor of history, as game-theoretic choices join postmodern contingency in a contradictory amalgam of political voluntarism, where rhetoric and discourse are the agencies of social change, and a cynical defeatism, where every radical programme of change is doomed to failure.

POSTSCRIPT 1994

On rereading this piece in preparation for its inclusion in this volume, I was struck (not for the first time) by an unresolved tension in my account of RCM, which presents that body of thought as both a kind of voluntarism and a kind of determinism. This tension is very much present in RCM itself, as I suggested at various points; but I should have confronted it more directly than I did.

On the one hand, RCM proceeds *as if* the constitutive social relations of any social form, specifically the relations of class, were a matter of choice. So, for example, we have Adam Przeworski's workers 'choosing' to belong to the working class in much the same way that they might choose to join a political party. On the other hand, I argued, by the time RCM finishes loading the individual with all kinds of presuppositions, 'endowments' or 'resources' (which really represent social relations and structural necessities), he/she turns out to be an embodied structure with very little scope for choice. Similarly, in accounting for historical movement from one mode of production to another, RCM tends to offer us another contradictory amalgam: feudal people, for example, 'choose' capitalism, while a fairly old-fashioned technological determinism *really* accounts for historical change. The end result of this paradoxical procedure is, I suggested, a political mixture of voluntarism and defeatism, not unlike the curious combination, arrived at from the opposite direction, that can be found in various post-structuralist and post-modernist currents.

When I first wrote this piece, I don't think I was quite sure which, if any, side in the polarity of determinism and voluntarism played a greater role in RCM theory. My first second-thought was that, despite its insistence on the language of choice, RCM is above all a kind of determinism, and that it might better be called RDM, since rationality does little more in this theory than act as a medium of determination. In any given situation, there really is no choice. There really is only one 'rational' option. What looks like choice is simply a proliferation of determinants.

More recently, it has occurred to me that, while this account of RCM as a disguised determinism still seems generally right, there may be a better way of describing its paradoxical mixture of determinism and indeterminacy. One of the striking things about other currents in modern Marxism, notably Althusserianism, was their dependence on a sharp dualism between theory and empirical reality. Theory was the sphere of rigid determinism, while empirical reality, history in particular, was a realm of pure contingency. So, in the theoretical sphere, there were modes of production, fixed totalities with rigid internal connections, while in the empirical realm there were 'social formations', bits of various modes of production combined in any old way. Theory could be reconciled with empirical analysis only by proliferating theoretically generated taxonomic categories, multiplied to embrace any possible empirical specificity, so that what purported to be a theoretically informed *explanation* was merely a disguised *description*.

A similar dualism may operate in RCM, a dualism in which determinism is paired not so much with voluntarism as with contingency. RCM's theoretical starting point appears to be directly antithetical to that of Althusserianism – subject and agency rather than structure; but in fact it proceeds in much the same way. Since RCM's choosing subject is little more than an embodied structure, an all-but-absolute determinism – rendered here in the idiom of 'choice' – prevails in the theoretical sphere. But on the empirical plane, what purports to be theoretically informed explanation here too is little more than disguised description, accomplished simply by proliferating the conditions of 'choice'. So, as I suggested in my later reply to Alan Carling (Wood 1990; see also Carling 1990), what explanatory power RCM has in its application to any empirical occurrence depends not on the rational choice model itself but on a detailed description of the context in which 'choices' are made, an empirical multiplication of the factors which, through the mechanism of 'rationality', determine how individuals act. If determination (through the mechanism of rationality) dominates the theoretical sphere, in the empirical domain something like contingency prevails. Both these (fundamentally ahistorical) varieties of Marxism display their explanatory weakness in similar ways, notably in their inability to explain the transformation of one social form into another without assuming, in circular fashion, the pre-existence of the form whose emergence is being explained.

Althusserian Marxism, with its unstable combination of absolute determinism and (almost) absolute contingency seems to have been a mid-point between a very deterministic reading of Marx and a post-Marxist flip of the coin, in which contingency ended on top. The transition from there to post-modernist currents has been relatively quick and easy. But if contingency is now in the ascendant, the coin's other side is always present. The post-modern world of fragments and 'difference' has no systemic unity and is not susceptible to 'totalizing' knowledges. Yet if the world is, in theory, now a bricolage of fragments and plural identities, in practice a triumphant capitalism apparently confronts the 'decentred' subject as total, universal, and inevitable. Post-modern capitalism is a world where emancipatory struggles are fragmented and only the most local and particularistic resistances are possible. This capitalism is no longer a *historical* product, accessible to human knowledge and agency, but an unfathomable and irresistible natural force. It cannot be contested from a standpoint outside it, in theory or practice. So in theory, there is no *critique* of capitalism; in practice, there is only (more or less) room for manoeuvre within its interstices. Agency is effectively disabled, choice and/or contingency turn into their opposite. *Ergo* determinism and the end of History.

Is this very far from where RCM has ended? At least for some of its leading exponents, there is apparently no choice but capitalism, and capitalist rationality is a transhistorical law. What we really need now is a theoretical standpoint from which a *critique* of capitalism is once again possible, and that means a truly *historical* historical materialism in which history is not alternatively swallowed up in determinism and contingency.

NOTES

1. I am very grateful to Perry Anderson, Robert Brenner, Diane Elson, Norman Geras and Neal Wood for their comments and suggestions.
2. Carling (1988), p. 95.
3. See Levine *et al.*, (1987). For a more recent version of Wright's theory of class, see Wright (1989).
4. According to this criterion, a 'coalition of agents' is exploited if it would be better off withdrawing from, rather than remaining within, the 'game' with its per capita share of whatever assets are relevant to the mode of exploitation in question.
5. This is certainly not to deny that Roemer's theory of exploitation is open to criticism even on its own economic terms. See, for example, Kieve (1986), esp. pp. 558–65. My own argument has more to do with evaluating the utility of this theory even if it succeeds on its own terms.
6. Elster (1985), p. 515.
7. Przeworski (1985a), p. 97.
8. Elster (1985), p. 13.
9. For a discussion of this point, see Peter F. Meiksins, 'A Critique of Wright's Theory of Contradictory Class Locations', in Wright (1989), pp. 173–83.
10. Elster (1985), pp. 203, 335–42.
11. Marx (1973), p. 284.
12. Levine *et al.* (1987), p. 80.
13. See above, pp. 35–6.
14. In Roemer (1982c), for example, Roemer seems to be arguing that methodological individualism of the type advocated by Elster is essential to the explanation of historical transformations and superior to conventional Marxism in this respect.
15. Carling (1988), p. 95. See Cohen (1978); Brenner (1986), Brenner (1977), and Aston *et al.* (1985).
16. Roemer (1988), p. 6; emphasis in the original. Given RCM's need to lower the stakes in the game of class, it may be significant that Roemer chooses to emphasize the progressive socialization of property as the *elimination* of exploitative forms, in contrast to Marx's focus on history as the progressive

separation of direct producers from the conditions of their labour (this is, for example, the basic premise of the *Grundrisse*).
17. Roemer (1988), p. 124.
18. Roemer (1988), p. 123.
19. Brenner's contribution to Roemer (1986), which presents his account of the transition in a schematic form, argues that the conventional explanation of the development of capitalism, based largely on Adam Smith, assumes precisely the extraordinary phenomenon that needs to be explained: that property relations must be understood as 'relations of reproduction'; that pre-capitalist economies have their own logic and 'solidity', which are in effect denied by the conventional view; that capitalist development is a more historically limited and specific occurrence than is allowed by theories which attribute it to some universal law of technical progress; and that the history of the transition cannot be explained by assuming that there is a necessary correspondence between the self-interested actions of individual actors and the requirements of economic growth. In these respects, his argument runs directly counter to Roemer's basic assumptions, and to Cohen's technological determinism. It is worth adding that his schematic argument in this volume, in contrast to the contributions of Rational Choice Marxists, is grounded in historical work and is based on the premise that the work of historical *explanation* needed to be done in advance of the analytical *presentation*.
20. Hilton (1976). See also Hilton (1985).
21. It was Marx himself who insisted that capitalism is unique in its drive to revolutionise productive forces, while other modes of production have tended to conserve existing forces, and that 'petrification' may have been the rule rather than the exception. See, for example, Marx (1986), pp. 616–17. A similar view appears even in the *Communist Manifesto*, which in other respects still adheres to the early, uncritical theory of history.

   I have criticized Cohen's technological determinism elsewhere, in Wood (1981), pp. 70–4, and in a more general discussion of technological determinism in Wood (1984).
22. Marx (1973), p. 105.
23. See, for example, Roemer (1988), p. 151. The weakness of the barrier erected by RCM against right-wing triumphalism is illustrated by John Gray's review of *Free to Lose* in *The Times Literary Supplement*, 24 February–2 March 1989. Roemer is here castigated for adopting the worst features of neo-classical economics, its complete abstraction and detachment from the real world of market processes – though in Gray's account, of course, the real world triumphantly vindicates capitalism and decisively demonstrates the inferiority of socialism. Nothing in Roemer's argument equips him to withstand this onslaught.
24. For an excellent account of the debate surrounding these issues, and a persuasive argument that Marx himself did, if involuntarily, have a concept of justice, see Geras (1985).
25. Przeworski (1985a), pp. 236–7. Przeworski here makes a truly extraordinary argument in support of his claims. To demonstrate that a 'major redistribution' within capitalism is historically no less feasible than socialism, he cites Henri Pirenne's suggestion that 'from the beginning of the Middle

Ages to our time ... for each period into which our economic history may be divided, there is a distinct and separate class of capitalists. In other words, the group of capitalists of a given epoch does not spring from the capitalist group of the preceding epoch. At every change of economic organisation we find a breach of continuity ... there are as many classes of capitalists as there are epochs in economic history' ('The Stages of the Social History of Capitalism', *American Historical Review* 19 (1914), pp. 494–5). Quite apart from the flippant attitude to history and historical evidence revealed by this perfunctory reference, one short, outdated, and highly debatable article, in order to support a very large historical claim, Przeworski's appeal to Pirenne on this point suggests a rather hazy understanding of capitalism. Pirenne is notoriously loose in his usage of 'capitalism' (though not uniquely so), and is generally inclined to imagine capitalism as already present in or coexisting with other social forms. The 'capitalist' is virtually anyone engaged in commerce for profit, any (urban) trader or merchant who, driven by the 'love of gain', uses moveable property to amass more wealth, usually simply by buying cheap and selling dear. By these standards, the Renaissance Florentine merchant is a capitalist, but the English 'improving' landlord, or the capitalist tenant-farmer of the famous English 'triad', extracting surplus value from a wage-labourer, is not. In the article in question, Pirenne simply outlines a series of different merchant types who, he argues, successively came to the fore in European economic history. What prevents him from pushing capitalism even further back in history, to ancient Greece or Rome, is not any conviction about the historical specificity of capitalism, but simply the fact that the evidence is insufficient. There is no sense in his argument of a specifically capitalist dynamic, a logic of accumulation essentially different from the age-old inclination to buy cheap and sell dear. It is, in any case, hard to see what support his argument lends to Przeworski's contention about the feasibility of a major redistribution within capitalism, since Pirenne's argument has nothing to do with a redistribution between exploiting and exploited classes.

26. Roemer (1988), p. 124. Roemer does not present this account of historical materialism as contradicting his view that 'it is perceptions and ideas about justice that are at the root of people's support for or opposition to an economic system' (p. 3), a view which is not inconsistent with a materialist account of historical transformations or even a materialist account of moral perceptions themselves.
27. See above, pp. 41–2.

5 Marxism without Micro-Foundations[1]
Michael Burawoy

> Empirical observation must in each separate instance bring out empirically, and without any mystification and speculation, the connection of the social and the political structure with production. The social structure and the state are continually evolving out of the life process of definite individuals, but of individuals, not as they may appear in their own or other people's imagination, but as they *really* are; i.e., as they operate, produce materially, and hence as they work under definite material limits, presuppositions and conditions independent of their will.
>
> –from Marx and Engels, *The German Ideology*

Two anomalies confront Marxism as its refutation: the durability of capitalism and the passivity of its working class. Successive encounters with these anomalies – encounters stimulated by different political and economic circumstances – have shaped many incarnations of Western Marxism. Classical Marxism, for example, which included such disparate thinkers as Kautsky, Luxemburg, Plekhanov, Jaurès, Adler, Bauer and Hilferding, emerged out of Marxism's golden age. Europe's historical circumstances between 1890 and 1920 could be interpreted as vindicating Marx's scientific investigations. During this period economic forces did appear to be propelling Europe toward a major international crisis and class struggle did appear to be escalating. The events warranted optimism and anomalies could be passed off as temporary aberrations.

The legacy of this golden age gone by is orthodox Marxism. Orthodox Marxism today could be characterized as classical Marxism in a period that no longer warrants optimism. Now, the veritable laws of motion of capitalism no longer point to the objective necessity – and inevitability – of socialism. In the quiescent 1980s, Marxism's contradictions cast a particularly long shadow, making orthodoxy even harder to sustain.

There have, of course, been many critiques of classical and then orthodox Marxism – from critical theory, which attacked both the possibility and the desirability of a Marxist science, to French structuralism, which sought to revive Marxist science as 'theoretical practice.' Symptomatic of the most recent times are two further trajectories of Marxism. The first is the move beyond Marxism to broaden its appeal: socialism becomes participatory democracy, the working class becomes one of a number of possible agents of transformation and the economic realm becomes one of a number of sites of oppression. From this mosaic of domination spring new social movements, potentially bound together by a common political discourse.[2]

The second response to orthodoxy – the one that concerns me here – restricts rather than expands its audience. Marxism is packaged for consumption in the academic world by equipping it with the perquisites of science. Preeminent in this domain is the self-defined school of *analytical Marxism*, whose core members include such established and brilliant philosophers and social scientists as Jon Elster, G. A. Cohen, John Roemer, Adam Przeworski and Erik Olin Wright. Their mission is to purge Marxism of its dogmatic elements by introducing the clear, rigorous thinking of analytical philosophy and the logico-deductive models of neoclassical economics. They seek to bring Marxism out of the nineteenth century by tackling its abiding theoretical problems with the sophisticated techniques of modern social science.

Analytical Marxists, therefore, seize on the logical flaws and unsubstantiated assertions of orthodox Marxism to justify its wholesale renovation. Their criticism runs as follows. Orthodoxy has devoted much energy to explaining away the gap between contemporary reality and what were two conclusions of classical Marxism: (1) capitalism's tendency toward crisis and collapse, and (2) the revolutionary potential of the working class. In the hands of orthodox Marxists these empirical conclusions become articles of faith, protected by auxiliary hypotheses. Theories of imperialism, for example, are proposed to explain how capitalism's tendency toward self-destruction is postponed through the 'exploitation' of third world countries. Theories of the state present it as an omnipotent body capable and willing to fill functional gaps in the economy, to negate crisis tendencies. Rather than arguing that capitalism is able to reproduce itself, orthodoxy preserves the postulate of collapse by proposing mechanisms which counteract its more fundamental tendency toward self-destruction.

A second set of auxiliary theories explain why the working class has not realized its revolutionary mission. Orthodoxy calls on the betrayal by working-class leaders, on the 'false consciousness' of the appointed revolutionaries, the corrosive effects of bourgeois ideology, repression of the state, the development of a labor aristocracy, the divisive forces of racism and sexism, and more. A common thread ties together these strategies to preserve orthodoxy: *teleology* and *functionalism*. The inevitable collapse of capitalism and the rise of the working class are taken as given – teleological premises – and countervailing forces are conjured up as functional for capitalism, seemingly by definition.

Analytical Marxism dispenses with all such teleology and functionalism as ungrounded metaphysics. For too long orthodox Marxism has protected itself from refutation by unrigorous, speculative and *ad hoc* hypotheses. Instead, analytical Marxists propose to build new scientific foundations for Marxism. The teleology of inevitable capitalist collapse and of inherent revolutionary potential of the working class should be rigorously justified or abandoned. The unfaltering 'functionality' for capitalism of the state, of imperialism, of ideology, and so on, must be proven. Analytical Marxists diagnose the problem of orthodoxy as the failure to base its conclusions on real social mechanisms that work through individuals. For instance, philosopher Jon Elster, a leading spokesman of analytical Marxism, finds of lasting importance Marx's use of methodological individualism: 'the doctrine that all social phenomena – their structure and their change – are in principle explicable in ways that only involve individuals – their properties, their goals, their beliefs and their actions' (Elster 1985, p. 5).

Social phenomena, whether they be macro tendencies of the economy or the role of the state, must be explained as the result of strategic action of individuals defined by their preferences and property endowments. This is what John Roemer, analytical Marxism's beacon economist, intends when he writes:

> Marxian analysis requires micro-foundations. What Marxists must provide are *mechanisms*, at the micro-level, for the phenomena they claim come about for teleological reasons....In seeking to provide micro-foundations for behavior which Marxists think are characteristic of capitalism, I think the tools *par excellence* are rational choice models: general equilibrium theory, game theory, and the arsenal of modelling techniques developed by neoclassical economics. (Roemer 1986, p. 192)

The purpose of this essay is to show how analytical Marxism's uncritical adoption of the scientific tools of neoclassical economics – tools which have become increasingly fashionable in all the social sciences – do *not* supply micro-foundations. Analytical Marxism's critique of orthodoxy can be turned against itself. The inadequacies of orthodoxy, that is its failure to ground its historical claims in micro-institutions, reappear in analytical Marxism.

PRZEWORSKI'S MARXISM: RECONSTRUCTION OR ABANDONMENT?

Of all the analytical Marxists Adam Przeworski stands out as going beyond programmatic statements to take up the challenge:

> Marxism was a theory of history without any theory about the actions of people who made this history....Statements about individuals and collectivities must be carefully distinguished: attributions of the status of collective actor to 'capital,' 'the working class,' or 'the state' must be subjected each time to critical scrutiny to see whether the collective action is consistent with individual rationalities. The challenge originating from the rational-choice framework is specific: a satisfactory theory is one that can explain history in terms of the actions of individuals who are goal oriented and rational. All theory of society must be based on such foundations: this is the challenge (Przeworski 1956, pp. 382–3).

Whereas Cohen, Roemer and Elster regard abstraction and clarity as an end in itself, Przeworski seeks to deploy his powerful theoretical apparatus to understand the world as we know it. He alone addresses the empirical world with models of strategic action to bring together new conceptions of class struggle, the dynamics of capitalism, the state as a strategic actor, and the transition to socialism. He captures the real dilemmas of socialist politics, giving a new sting to what it means to be a socialist in a capitalist world, to participate in a society one seeks to transcend. More generally he makes theoretical and empirical sense of what it means to make history under conditions not of one's choosing. Przeworski demonstrates how strategic action, whether it be socialist parties in electoral competition or workers forging class compromises, is limited but also makes a difference. He shows how past choices reappear as contemporary constraints, how the present might have been different if alternative paths had been followed in the past. In short, he suggests concretely how we might actually learn from history.

He confronts two shibboleths of orthodox Marxism: first, that workers and capitalists are in irreconcilable conflict. Taking the character of class conflict as non-zero sum (that is, the possibility that labor can, in a sustained way, advance its material interests within capitalism) as his point of departure, he develops a genuine political economy – a theory of the dynamics of capitalism in which class struggle and accumulation, state and economy are systematically connected. Second, he shows that struggles for those material gains, whether these take place through electoral politics or trade union struggles, are unlikely to lead beyond capitalism. Reforms are not cumulative – they are an improbable road to socialism. He draws the uncomfortable conclusion: 'The struggle for improving capitalism is as essential as ever before. But we should not confuse this struggle with the quest for socialism' (Przeworski 1985a, p. 48).

Forsaking the reformist road to socialism could be taken as a call for revolution. But Przeworski shows no inclination toward such a solution. For him, this is too closely associated with Leninism and the defects of Soviet societies. He provides no grounds for thinking that a revolutionary transition to socialism would be any more likely or successful than the electoral road. Given his pessimism, one might say counter-Marxist conclusions, what remains of Marxism in his work? Is Przeworski's work a reconstruction or an abandonment of Marxism? Let us see how *he* understands his work.

Class and Contradictions

Przeworski defines Marxism as 'an analysis of the consequences of forms of property for historical processes' (Przeworski 1985b, p. 380). Orthodox Marxism understands the link between property and history in two ways. First, it defines history as the interaction of the forces of production and relations of production. In particular, orthodoxy understands the dynamics of the capitalist mode of production as resulting from individuals pursuing interests given by relations they have to enter. The economy develops according to its own laws. Second, orthodoxy defines history as the history of class struggle. Class struggle takes place in and around the state between classes that have their basis in production. Class-in-itself, shaped in the economy, becomes a class-for-itself, a collective actor in the political arena. Przeworski's Marxism begins with a critique of the 'class-in-itself/class-for-itself' problematic and ends up introducing 'class struggle' into the analysis of the dynamics of the capitalist economy.

We begin then with orthodox Marxism's understanding of how a class-in-itself becomes a class-for-itself. The argument rests on two assumptions: that the tendency of capitalist class structure is toward the polarization between capital and labor, and that workers cannot realize their material interests within capitalism and therefore combine to struggle

Marxism without Micro-Foundations

for socialism. Within this framework corresponding sets of questions arise. First, what is the class position of those occupations — managers, professionals, and state workers — which don't fit the conventional categories of capital and labor, and of those adults who are outside production altogether — the unemployed, domestic workers, students, retired workers, and so on? Second, do economic positions give rise to specific interests, and, if so, what are those interests and how are they produced? Finally, under what circumstances are those interests realized?

One strategy of dealing with these questions is to create new class locations to which one imputes material interests. Foremost in pursuing this strategy is another analytical Marxist, Erik Wright. In the first incarnation of his scheme, Wright introduced three sets of contradictory class locations between the three major classes of advanced capitalism: capital, labor and petty bourgeoisie. More recently in his 1985 book, *Classes*, he defines three forms of exploitation: capitalist, organizational and skill. These determine the interests of different classes: capital, managers, professionals (Wright 1985).

Each class has an objective material interest in maximizing its own form of exploitation. The test of the adequacy of such models is their power to explain variations in class consciousness and class identity. The task is to create that theory of class which offers a map of class locations and corresponding material interests which best explains class action. In other words, the goal is to redefine the meaning of 'class-in-itself' to obtain the best fit to 'class-for-itself'.

Przeworski rejects this way of dealing with the problem. While Wright *assumes* there is a link between class position and class actors and in order to discover it he, as *scientist*, redefines the meaning of class location, Przeworski insists there is no necessary link between economic places and collective actors, and if there is a link it is *forged through struggle*. What defines a class location and class interest for Przeworski is not given *a priori*, but is the subject of struggle:

> The problem of the relation between objectively defined classes and classes qua historical actors will not be resolved by any classification, whether with two or many objective classes, with or without contradictory locations. The problem persists because such classifications, whether made in party headquarters or within the walls of academia, are constantly tested by life, or more precisely by political practice. Wright's 'contradictory class locations' are contradictory only in the sense that his assertions about the 'real interest in socialism' are not

borne out by the consciousness and the organization of those who are supposed to have this interest. On paper we can put people in any boxes one wishes (sic), but in political practice one encounters real people, with their interests and consciousness of these interests. And these interests whether or not they are 'real,' are not arbitrary; their consciousness is not arbitrary; and the very political practice that forges these interests is not arbitrary. (Przeworski 1985a, p. 66).

Instead of arguing that social relations define classes which then enter into struggles, Przeworski reverses the relationship and argues that classes are the effects of struggles which are in turn shaped by political and ideological as well as economic relations. Classes do not exist before class struggle, but are the result of class struggle. Or to put it another way: class struggle is first a struggle about the very meaning of class before it is a struggle between classes.

The analysis turns away from deciding how location in production defines class position and class interest and toward deciding how economic, political and ideological relations shape struggles. Here too Przeworski avoids any determinate relationship: 'The assertion that social relations structure class struggles must not be interpreted in a mechanical fashion. Social relations – economic, political, or ideological – are not something that people "act out" in ways reflecting places that they occupy, but are a structure of choices given at a particular moment of history' (Przeworski 1985a, p. 73).

Thus, Przeworski substitutes his own two projects for those of orthodox Marxism. His first project abandons the class-in-itself/class-for-itself problematic. Classes are no longer inherent but are shaped by struggles; they are the effect of struggles. Specifically, he focuses on how political and economic structures create the parameters within which political parties seek to maximize votes by redefining class. The result is an historically variable mapping between *location in production and class*. This is the project of *class formation*.

His second project criticizes the idea of a self-propelled economy, expanding according to determinate laws. Instead, he shows how property relations shape struggles, which in turn reshape those property relations, and incorporates struggles into the analysis of accumulation. In this project he takes class actors (capital and labor) as given and shows how they strategize under conditions shaped by the political order. The result is a historically variable mapping between *class and interest*. This is the project of *class compromise*.[3]

Analytical Abstractions

Przeworski's achievements add up to nothing less than the reconstruction of Marxism. Nevertheless, his theories are without micro-foundations. For all his programmatic commitment to 'methodological individualism', for all his rhetoric against Wright's 'arbitrary boxes' in the name of 'political practice' and 'real people, with their interests and consciousness of these interests', and for all his repeated insistence on dealing with 'lived experience', he consistently fails on each of these counts. Specifically, in his analysis of electoral politics voter preferences are implanted from outside so that workers become the dupes of macro-actors, in particular, of parties and trade unions. Instead of founding his analysis of politics on *real* individuals, he founds them on *mythological* individuals. His study of class compromises restores the centrality of social relations, but as *abstract* entities and not as they *concretely* exist in specific sites. Marxist micro-foundations cannot be created out of mythological individuals and abstracted relations but, I argue, must be constituted by the concrete relations that real people are compelled to enter. Absent from his analysis are the micro-institutions which, on the one hand, shape the interests and identities of individuals, and on the other, set limits on the form and effects of macro-forces.

Inasmuch as he ignores the lived experience generated by micro-institutions, his analysis is undoubtedly incomplete. But is it also wrong? Throughout, he reduces interests of workers under capitalism to material interests: 'Those needs that can be satisfied through the consumption or use of objectifications of socially organized activities of transformation of nature, which, under capitalism, are commodities' (Przeworski 1985a, p. 172). The relevant micro-foundations would be the micro-institutions of consumption – the dependency of all but the wealthy on obtaining a job, improving their standard of living, making ends meet within an uncertain economic environment. Were he to include such a micro-analysis of consumption and distribution his theory would be enriched, but in all likelihood, his conclusions would remain the same.

However, if there are other arenas of daily life around which non-material interests congeal, then introducing micro-institutions endangers his theory. Thus, theorists of new social movements focus on demands for the expansion of political rights. Rather than confining attention to who *gets* what, when and how, they shift attention to who *decides* what, when and how in a diverse set of arenas. They are concerned with democratization as an end in itself. That certainly is one challenge to Przeworski's analysis, but not the one I will be centrally concerned with here. Instead I draw attention to interests that congeal around who *does* what, when, and how, around the micro-processes of capitalist production underpinning distribution. The examination of class interest, class formation and class struggle, I argue, requires attention to production and the lived experience it generates.

This is an uncontroversial claim until one studies Przeworski's reconstruction of Marxist theory of class. His view of class as the effect of struggles removes class from any direct ties to production. His definition of politics – 'a process of establishing the priority of claims to the national product [as well as conflicts concerning] the direction of production and the organization of politics' – emphasizes the macro determination of who *gets* what, when and how and systematically ignores who *does* what, when and how. Here lies the challenge of Przeworski's analytical Marxism.[4]

Clearly, a conception of class and politics which ignores production is Marxism without micro-foundations. What do I mean? I do *not* mean ignoring production is by *definition* incompatible with Marxism. Rather, it is a substantive claim. In the following discussion, I propose to show three things: (1) that Przeworski cannot carry out either his class formation project or his class compromise project without micro-foundations, specifically those that include production and the lived experience it generates; (2) that the contradiction between his two projects – that in one class is problematic and in the other it is given – can only be resolved by introducing micro-foundations of production, and (3) that an account of class struggle, electoral politics, the organization of consent and the transition to socialism which *includes* an analysis of production arrives at conclusions different from his.

THE PROBLEM OF CLASS FORMATION

Social democracy, and here Przeworski takes Kautsky's writings as his point of departure, promised socialism through the ballot box. There was some question whether capitalists would allow their expropriation without a violent struggle, but there was no doubt that the working class would form the majority of the population and thus vote the socialist party into office. The defining problem of Przeworski and John Sprague's *Paper Stones* is why this didn't happen: why have socialist parties been so unsuccessful in acquiring office?

Their answer is as follows. Socialist parties initially define their constituency as 'manual wage earners employed in mining, manufacturing, construction, transport and agriculture, persons retired from such occupations, and inactive adult members of their households'. They discover that there aren't enough voters in this narrowly defined working class to gain office. So socialist parties seek out the support of 'allied classes', but in so doing they dilute the salience of class in their appeals and thus lose their ability to attract working-class support. They face a trade-off between increasing the vote of allied classes and instigating a decline in working-class votes, which varies between countries. It increases with the presence of communist parties or parties with particularistic (religious) appeals, which draw off votes when the socialist party dilutes its working-class program, and it falls with the presence of alternative national class organizations, such as strong and centralized trade unions, which maintain workers' allegiance to the socialist party even when it expands its support beyond the working class. In this way Przeworski and Sprague are able to explain the trajectory of support for socialist parties in terms of the strategy of parties, the trade-offs they encounter and the occupational structure. They are able to examine whether socialist parties are vote maximizers and whether their present strategies take into account future effects.

Sources of Identity

The theoretical assumptions that inform Przeworski and Sprague's analysis can best be appreciated by comparison with the conventional approaches they criticize. These attribute patterns of voting to preformed identities – race, religion, class, and so on – without ever explaining how those identities are first created and then become connected to parties. Przeworski and Sprague do away with preformed identities, arguing that 'individual voting behavior is an effect of the activities of political parties' (Przeworski 1985a, p. 100). 'Through a variety of means, ideological as well as organizational, conflicting political forces impose images of society on individuals, mold collective identities and mobilize commitments to specific projects for a shared future' (Przeworski and Sprague 1986, p. 143). Even more emphatically they write: 'To impose a cultural interpretation on our findings we would have to find aspects of working-class culture that are independent of the strategies pursued by parties and other organizations. We do not believe that such aspects exist' (Przeworski and Sprague 1986, p. 73).

This certainly is consistent with Przeworski's view that class is not inherent, but an effect of struggles – in this case party strategies – on *tabula rasa* individuals. Yet throughout *Paper Stones* alternative perspectives slip into their analysis, interpretations which do recognize the importance of lived experience generated independently of parties and unions. For example, in their discussion of the electoral strategy of the German Social Democratic Party they suggest that its leaders' impetus towards vote maximization was constrained by the rank and file (Przeworski and Sprague 1984, p. 119).[5] In explaining why socialist parties initially sought to organize all workers and only workers, Przeworski claims elsewhere that only a working-class party could offset the competitive individualism among workers and the integrative tendencies of the bourgeois ideology of universalism (Przeworski 1985a, pp. 20–1). Yet he writes in *Paper Stones* that workers 'were distrustful of any influences originating outside their class', that is to say they possessed a collective consciousness independently of socialist parties (Przeworski and Sprague 1986, p. 22). Indeed, Przeworski and Sprague note that workers resisted the message of socialism (Przeworski and Sprague 1986, p. 49). If they were to be successful, socialist parties had to cater to the more reformist inclinations of workers. Finally, at the end of their book they again observe that individuals, far from drifting in and out of parties according to party strategy, created their own grassroots institutions – cooperatives, councils and communes – which socialist parties devoted their energies to dismantling (Przeworski and Sprague 1986, p. 184). All these examples suggest that party leaders were forced to respond to class struggles they didn't organize.

Przeworski and Sprague might well reply that such class consciousness predated the absorption of political parties into electoral politics. Once mass political parties were established, then collective identities come to the working class from without. But even then they have *to assume* the causal efficacy of a lived experience that is generated independently of parties and trade unions. Take, for example, what they regard to be clinching evidence for their argument. They show that the effect of left-wing parties mobilizing white-collar workers was to dampen the working-class vote. 'Their problem was not only to convince white-collar employees that they are workers but also to persuade workers that white-collar employees are workers' (Przeworski and Sprague 1986, p. 179). They assume that manual workers regard white-collar employees as different, *independent* of party appeals. It is difficult to understand why this would be the case were it not for some lived experience of manual workers which places them in some unspecified opposition to white-collar employees, a lived experience that shapes the trade off facing party leaders.[6]

What is the source of their ambiguous treatment of individuals as, on the one hand, blank slates upon which parties and unions impress identities and, on the other, as having preformed identities shaped by lived experience? The answer seems to be as follows. When it comes to explaining *variations* in the trade-off they assume *tabula rasa* individuals whose identities are shaped by parties and trade unions. But to explain the very *existence* of a trade-off in all countries, Przeworski and Sprague place their bets on 'a hypothesis that the line of sharpest divisions, of interest and values, lies between narrowly defined manual workers and other wage earners' (Przeworski 1985a, p. 105). Here again is an unmistakable reference to the lived experience, presumably based in production, of a core working class.[7]

For anyone interested in the possibilities of a transition to socialism, the ubiquity of the trade-off is more fundamental than its variation. So why then do Przeworski and Sprague devote their attention to explaining variations? One doesn't have to look far for an answer. To explain the general phenomenon – why, for example, socialist parties have never won the support of more than half of those entitled to vote – they would have to examine the lived experience of different fractions of the working class and its allies. But they do not have the theoretical-apparatus, the 'micro-foundations', to accomplish this task.

When they do refer to the lived experience of workers, Przeworski and Sprague fall back on homilies from Marx about the individualizing effects of labor market competition: 'The interests which workers have in common place them in competition with one another, primarily as they bid down wages in search of employment. Individual workers and particularly workers of a specific firm or sector have powerful incentives to pursue their particularistic claims at the cost of other workers' (Przeworski and Sprague 1986, p. 53). Or they deny that workers can generate class identity without the help of macro actors: '[lived] experience [of workers] may be one of poverty, of compulsion, of inequality, of oppression. It may be one of similarity. But it is not an experience of class' (Przeworski and Sprague 1986, p. 8). Even if these claims were true, they only tell us that the spontaneous experience is *not* an experience of class; they don't tell us what it actually *is*. Above all, they don't explain why manual industrial workers might have different interests or values than state sector office workers. That would require a theory of production and the experience it generates – notably absent in Przeworski and Sprague's analysis.[8]

The Micro-Foundations of Electoral Politics

What would be the task of such a theory of production? It would have to explain how production structures the experiences of different groups of wage earners, thereby accounting for the very existence if not the variation of electoral trade-offs.

At this point I can only provide a schematic prolegomenon for such a theory. It begins by refusing the reduction of production to economic activity, to the labor process. Production has a political and ideological component as well as an economic one. It is not simply the production of things, but the production and reproduction of social relations as well as an experience of those relations. The reproduction of relations *of* production (property relations, who *gets* what) and of relations *in* production (the labor process, who *does* what) require what I call apparatuses or the regime of production – which in other conceptual schemes might be called forms of labor control or industrial relations. Different sectors of the working class are not only characterized by different occupations, but more importantly, are bound into different regimes of production, creating different experiences of class. Steel workers, garment workers, office workers in a welfare agency develop different visions of their employers through elaborate machinery of grievances, collective bargaining and seniority rights. Garment workers experienced more arbitrary, despotic and personalistic relations of domination, leaving them more vulnerable to the market. Office workers in a welfare bureaucracy have careers in the state, whose activities are circumscribed by politically negotiated rather than market constraints.

Over time the regime of production varies. For example, steelworkers now find their jobs in continual jeopardy, which elicits greater dependence and cooperation between unions and employers. More generally over the last fifty years, with state regulation of industrial relations and the rise of social insurance, employers have had to reorganize the balance of force and consent within production. Moreover, this has been accomplished in different ways in different advanced capitalist societies, in part reflecting the role of the state in supporting unemployment and constraining managerial practices. According to Przeworski and Sprague, a steelworker is a steelworker is a steelworker, and all that varies is the identity that is impressed upon him or her by political parties and unions. These are mythological steelworkers. Real steelworkers are bound up in different regimes of production which generate different experience of class.

But even if the lived experiences of workers were relatively homogeneous across advanced capitalist societies and over time (and therefore unable to explain *variations* in outcomes), they would still be important in setting limits on the trade-off and the class composition of party support. In Przeworski and Sprague's model the trade-off – that is, the rate at which socialist parties lose votes when they adopt supra-class strategies – decreases with the existence of powerful and centralized unions, which in turn intensifies class identity and increases with the strength of the communist or religious parties to which workers can gravitate. Constraints that derive from the immediate lived experience of workers become invisible in Przeworski and Sprague's analysis. But that doesn't mean they don't exist.

The same is true of the class composition of party support. Rather than argue that workers respond to their concrete experience and set limits on leaders' strategies for maximizing votes, they assert that leaders' 'quest for electoral support was circumscribed by an autonomous concern for class loyalty' (Przeworski and Sprague 1986, p. 80). But where does this 'autonomous concern' come from? Here Przeworski and Sprague require a theory of political parties and their leaders rather than a theory of voting, of how rank-and-file workers exercise or don't exercise their influence on party leadership, how and when party leaders decide to maximize votes. Why should party leaders be viewed as strategic actors while party followers are regarded as blank slates? They require, in other words, a micro-foundation of party organization as it affects both leaders and led. Przeworski and Sprague begin by attacking political sociology for failing to develop a theory of interests among voters, but they end up ignoring sociology's contribution to a theory of organization that would explain the conditions under which leaders choose, for example, between an autonomous class loyalty and maximizing their electoral support.

Nor do they take seriously enough their leitmotif from Gramsci – that 'the counting of votes is the final ceremony in a long process'. Parties discover the 'coefficients' that set limits on their strategy not only in elections but in the campaigns leading up to elections. It is here that they learn, sometimes wrongly, which appeals are going to work and which are not. Just as conventional studies reduce voting behavior to individual traits without explaining why those traits are important – *a theory of voters without a theory of voting* – so their own analysis reduces the outcome of elections to party strategies without examining how those strategies are shaped in response to the autonomous interests of voters – a theory of elections without a theory of electioneering.

Przeworski and Sprague do succeed in explaining variations in voting patterns by reference to parties and unions, but in so doing they conceal the premise of their argument: the existence of a core working class whose interests and values are different from other wage earners. This is why socialist parties lose worker votes when they try to attract the support of other classes and why the electoral road to socialism is doomed to failure. Their theory lacks micro-foundations at its most critical point. Furthermore, such micro-foundations would explain how production shapes experience, but once introduced they would lead to alternative interpretations of variations in voting patterns, interpretations that would give greater credence to the independence of the working class even in advanced capitalism. Przeworski and Sprague would be led back to a terrain they have abandoned – to production as the place where class is organized and disorganized. And this reversal would suggest that the obstacles to the transformation of capitalism are more fundamentally rooted in production than in electoral politics.

In concluding this section, I therefore propose two theses. The first is a *weak thesis*: an explanation of variations in voting behavior cannot ignore production as a micro-foundation. The second is my *strong thesis*: production and not electoral politics is decisive in explaining the failure of socialism in advanced capitalist countries. It doesn't matter how many workers there are – so long as consent is manufactured in production, socialist parties will not be able to forge an electoral road to socialism. I will extend these two propositions in my response to Przeworski's analysis of class compromise.

THE PROBLEM OF CLASS COMPROMISE

Przeworski's second project abruptly switches the focus from class *formation* to class *interests*. He abandons the first project before it becomes untenable, before classes become figments of party propaganda or evaporate in electoral discourse. What had been so problematic in the first project – the formation of classes – suddenly becomes unproblematic in the second project. Classes are now *given* as strategic actors, allowing Przeworski to ask how capitalist relations of production shape the interests of capital and labor.

As before, his point of departure is orthodoxy. Do the material interests of capital and labor place them in irreconcilable antagonism? Orthodoxy assumed that because the product of work is divided into profits for capital and wages for workers, what one class gains is at the expense of the other. Which is to say the relationship between capital and labor is of a zero sum, that is non-cooperative character. Przeworski shows how this is only a static picture. When dynamic considerations are introduced relations become non-zero sum. Labor has an interest in capital accumulation just as capital has an interest in eliciting 'consent' to exploitation through wage increases. In fact, workers can make material gains within capitalism on a relatively continuous and organized fashion without threatening capitalism.

Each side agrees to avoid striking the limits of the capitalist system: labor agrees not to demand wages that would be confiscatory (expropriate the expropriator) while capital assures labor minimum wages below which labor withdraws its 'consent' to exploitation. Within these limits labor is prepared to forgo wage increases now if it is assured that capital will invest a certain proportion of its profits which will be turned into future wage increases. Przeworksi shows that when labor is too militant – that is, when it demands a particularly high return to labor out of profits – short-term advantages give rise to longer-term losses as there is less capital to be turned into wage increases. When labor is too quiescent wage increases continue to be small relative to a more militant strategy. Although Przeworski develops a precise mathematical model, intuitively one can see that, given a particular time preference, and a particular rate of investment out of profits, there is an optimal level of militancy which will bring maximal wages within the specified time period.

Compromises: Between Whom and Where?

As a critique of the social-democratic road to power, his model is devastating, but as a theory of class interests it raises many questions that remain unexplored. The first question is: where does the class compromise take place? Przeworski's formulation of capital–labor relations is so general that it could take place at the level of the workshop, the firm, the enterprise, the economic sector, the economy as a whole or at the level of the state. For example, when speaking of the breakdown of consent in terms of its effect on the class compromise, Przeworski ranges from collective bargaining and countrywide collective agreements, to election results and changes in electoral representation (Przeworski 1985a, p. 163).

The capitalist economy is not simply an enterprise writ large. The interests of the individual capitalist do not coincide with the interests of the capitalist class. A centralized class compromise that increases wages, or more precisely, the labor share of value added, across the working class (as in Sweden and Austria) forces capitalists either to withdraw when they are inefficient or to invest at higher rates. In decentralized systems, such as the United States, firm-based or industry-based class compromises lead to a dual wage system with lower labor shares and lower rates of investment out of profits overall.[9]

Przeworski actually provides the conceptual tools for developing a distinction between different arenas of compromise when he extends the specific argument about the dependence of labor on capital to a wider characterization of capitalist society. The material interest of any group, not just labor, is dependent on the prior realization of the interests of capital. 'Capitalists are thus in a unique position in a capitalist system: they represent future universal interests while interests of all other groups appear as particularistic and hence inimical to future developments. The entire society is structurally dependent upon actions of capitalists' (Przeworski 1986, p. 139). The combination of capitalism and democracy is a compromise in which those who don't own the means of production consent to private property while those who do own the means of production consent to political institutions that organize an uncertain but limited redistribution of resources. Moreover, it is the possibility that different groups may make gains that draws them into participation in democratic politics and elicits their consent to capitalism. Although Przeworski does not make the distinction, there are in fact two compromises: a *class compromise* between capital and labor, and a *democratic compromise* between capitalism and all interest groups in society.

This immediately suggests two arenas of compromise: the economy and the state. As soon as one takes seriously the possibility of class compromise at the level of the enterprise then it is no longer possible to confine the analysis to the distribution of profits between wage increases, investment and capitalist consumption. It is not enough to examine why workers should consent to the appropriation and distribution of the product. We must proceed to the more basic question: why should workers actually produce the product? By remaining at the very general level of relations *of* production – property relations – Przeworski overlooks the relations *in* production, the relations of the labor process through which profit is produced. Moreover, not just the relations of production but also the relations in production have to be reproduced.

As soon as work and production are introduced, it is easy to see that Przeworski has misspecified the character of the class compromise. He stays at the level of distribution, which is premised on the private appropriation of the product, and he therefore emphasizes the dependence of labor on capital. But as soon as one introduces production it becomes clear that capital is also dependent on the spontaneous cooperation of labor. The decisive problem for managers is to *produce* greater value than workers receive in wages. It entails a conception of *production politics* that is as much concerned with who does what, when and how as it is with who gets what, when and how.

In the class compromise workers agree to cooperate in the pursuit of profit so long as capitalists agree to pay them a wage. The link between wage, production and profit varies according to the political regime of production. In a hegemonic regime, for example, workers are persuaded to cooperate by tying wages to profits and also to seniority. Political apparatuses of production, such as the internal labor market, the grievance machinery and the mechanism of collective bargaining, organize the concrete coordination of the material interests of workers and capital's interest in the production of profit through the expenditure of effort.

Consent or Legitimacy?

Undoubtedly one of Przeworski's greatest contributions is the sense he makes of Gramsci's concept of consent and the contrast he draws with legitimacy. Consent to an institution involves active pursuit of its goals:

> Social actors, individual and collective, do not march around filled with 'predispositions' which they simply execute. Social relations constitute structures of choices within which people perceive, evaluate and act. They *consent when they choose particular courses of action and when they follow these choices in their action.* Wage earners consent to capitalist organization of society when they act as if they could improve their material conditions within the confines of capitalism (Przeworski 1985a, p. 146).

Consent cannot be reduced to a state of consciousness, to the articulation of attitudes or beliefs which justify domination – that is, to legitimacy. Regimes may be legitimate or illegitimate, but their breakdown follows from the withdrawal of consent.

Legitimacy is an assessment of normative validity based on, but not constitutive of, lived experience. On the other hand, hegemony, in this case meaning consent to capitalism, has to be constituted in everyday life (Przeworski 1985a, p. 136). But the distributive decisions upon which Przeworski focuses are not part of workers' daily lives. Collective struggles against capital (often confined to trade unions or other forms of worker representation) or voting are ephemeral and infrequent. The class compromises that Przeworski describes provide the basis of the *legitimacy of* capitalism but not *consent to* capitalism. Consent is organized continuously in day-to-day life, particularly in the workplace, where specific political and ideological apparatuses of production lead individuals to bind themselves to the interests of the enterprise.

More specifically, Przeworski asserts (following his interpretation of Gramsci) that there is a wage below which workers withdraw their consent to capitalism. 'If it is true that reproduction of consent requires that profits be transformed in the course of time into improvements of material conditions of wage-earners, then given the past history of profits *there must exist at any time a level of wage increases which is minimally necessary to reproduce consent*' (Przeworski 1985a, p. 147). But what evidence is there for such a minimal wage increase?[10] Certainly in the last five years, US labor has had to make concession after concession. In many sectors real wages and benefits had declined steadily, contract negotiations now revolve around 'give-backs' from labor to capital. Yet there is no sign of workers withdrawing consent to capitalism. Quite the contrary: the absence of resistance or its lack of success lies not simply in higher levels of unemployment but in the character of the pre-existing hegemonic regimes of production that are still in place and still function to concretely coordinate the interests of labor and capital, so that workers will expend ever greater effort and accept a decline in material conditions to keep their enterprise alive.

Because it absorbs so much of daily life and because all realms of capitalist society are dependent on it, *production is the decisive arena for the organization of consent*, decisive in Gramsci's sense that it constitutes the final '"trenches" and the permanent fortifications of the front in the war of position' (Gramsci 1971, p. 243). The possibility that workers will receive increased future wages in return for what they forgo today, a distributive issue in which workers are rarely involved, is not the basis of consent but of legitimacy. When that legitimacy breaks down, the sturdy structure of the production regime is at once revealed.

The Democratic Compromise: State as Actor

These criticisms notwithstanding, Przeworski's insights into the potentially collaborative relationship between capital and labor are crucial for the analysis of the state. So long as Marxists assumed that the conflict between capital and labor was irreconcilable, that workers can advance their material interests only as individuals or by abolishing capitalism, the role of the state was clear – an instrument for maintaining capitalism against struggles aimed at its overthrow. It accomplished this function through repression, through ideological domination or through co-optation (Przeworski 1985a, pp. 200–1).

The functionalist conception of the state, whether of the 'autonomy' or 'instrumental' variety, derived then from the assumption of a zero-sum relationship between capital and labor. If this assumption is altered so that labor as a collective actor can advance materially within capitalism a very different conception of the state emerges. It becomes the expression or even instigator of class compromise. Are there limits on the class compromise that can be struck? In a more recent paper Przeworski and Wallerstein argue that by taxing the consumption of shareholders the state can redistribute income without a detrimental effect on investment: 'The conclusion is that when all wage earners are organized in one centralized union federation and the government is purely pro-labor it will choose a tax on capitalist consumption the effect of which will be to bring wage-earners' material welfare almost to the level they could obtain under socialism' (Przeworski and Wallerstein 1988, p. 19). This is true only in the static sense since, when capital gets wind of any such move, it will reduce the rate of investment or flee, that is to say the transition costs to such a situation could be prohibitive. Przeworski and Wallerstein present this as a subsidiary issue but in reality it is the heart of the matter. Capitalists can withdraw their consent to democracy and either instigate its overthrow or move elsewhere, but workers have no such alternatives except under unusual circumstances and therefore do not withdraw consent even if their wages are falling.

Przeworski successfully dispenses with the idea of the state as confined to an external agency preserving capitalism and calls for a true 'political economy' which will bring together 'Marxist economics' and a 'Marxist theory of the state' in a dynamic relationship:

> The most striking feature of the vigorous development of contemporary Marxism is that the world of 'economics' and of 'politics' have been hermetically sealed from each other. Since the state is 'autonomous,' politics is studied without any reference to economic dynamic. Since economic actors never organize collectively, economic dynamic can be studied without any reference to politics. Economic actors behave strategically but only as individuals seeking to maximize their wages or profits. Political actors are not actors at all: they are automata struggling with each other over ill-defined or completely conjured 'long-term' interests. (Przeworski 1985a, p. 232)

Przeworski unquestionably advances our understanding of the interrelationship of politics and the economy. Nevertheless, in his scheme, they are still external to each other. The economic arena has its own dynamics now linked to class struggle and class compromise while the political arena organizes and cements these and other compromises and struggles.

Przeworski overlooks the existence of political institutions *within* the economic arena, in particular, political and ideological regimes of production which link class relations to class action. Without such a politics he has no explanation of whether and under what circumstances workers will be optimally militant, or how their time preferences are determined. He cannot understand changes in work organization that give rise to different levels of accumulations. Nor can he explain actual rates of investment when the state taxes capitalist consumption. Economic relations should indeed be understood as a structure of choices, but without a theory of production regimes he cannot explain how those choices are perceived, the source of interests (preferences) that determine those choices, whether they will be made individually or collectively and so on. He can only produce models of abstract possibility rather than explanations of reality.

Just as Przeworski overlooks the political dimension of the economy, he also overlooks the productive dimension of the state. The absence of a 'politics of production' is complemented by an absence of a 'production of politics'. 'The state' is no more an actor than 'the economy', it is a 'mode of production' itself with its own hierarchical and horizontal divisions. Przeworski once more commits the sin of methodological collectivism, ignoring the divergence of individual and collective rationalities.[11] The state is a site of production in which so-called public goods take a privileged position and as a result struggles both between and within apparatuses assume a distinctive form. They take place primarily over the distribution of budgets rather than of profits. In advancing their claims, contestants appeal less to market forces than to public needs. Within the state, struggles between managers and workers assume different forms in different apparatuses, depending on, for example, their politically negotiated centrality within the state and their relationship to the public they serve.[12]

Here too there are class compromises which set limits on the provision of goods and services as well as intervention in the economy. In criticizing theories of accumulation that abstract from class struggle, Przeworski writes: 'abstractions from processes that affect predictions are bad abstractions' (Przeworski 1985a, p. 232). This applies no less to his own theory of the state which leaves no logical place for production or class struggle. Once more it is a theory without micro-foundations. We are now in a position to understand the riddle with which we began this part of the essay, namely the disjuncture between Przeworski's two projects. In his analysis of electoral politics class formation is problematic, whereas in his analysis of class compromise both class and state are given as collective actors. The only way to reconcile the two projects is to provide a politics of production which would link the dynamics of capitalism to class formation. Without such micro-foundations he has not transcended the duality of 'class-in-itself' and 'class-for-itself', but suspended half his work from one branch and half from the other. We must now examine Przeworski's conception of socialism and see whether it manages to reconcile these divergent perspectives on class.

SOCIALISM: UTOPIAN AND SCIENTIFIC

We saw earlier how Przeworski argued that the electoral route to socialism is self-defeating. If socialist parties are to gain office they have to dilute their working-class platform in order to attract votes from allied classes. Przeworski now digs even deeper into the premises of orthodox Marxism. He challenges the assumption that the transition to socialism is in the 'objective' (material) interests of workers. He asks: what are the conditions for workers to rationally opt for socialism out of their material interests? He answers: '...that socialism be more efficient in satisfying material needs than capitalism and that moving toward socialism would immediately and continually improve workers' materials conditions' (Przeworski 1985a, p. 174). Even if we assume that socialism is more efficient than capitalism, it may not be rational to opt for socialism because (1) workers can make material gains under capitalism and (2) the costs of transition will be very steep due to capital strike and capital flight.

Who Chooses What, Where and When?

While this premise may deal a devastating blow to the theory of social democracy, as a theory of the transition to socialism it is inadequate. Przeworski sets up a mythical problem embedded in the theory of social democracy but absent from the reality of capitalism. Only under exceptional conditions do workers choose between capitalism and socialism, and this is precisely because capitalism as a system of exploitation is absent from their lived experience. For the most part workers experience relations in production, but not relations of production. Przeworski is not strictly correct when he talks about the way capitalism organizes consent to exploitation, since exploitation is mystified. Instead, the object of consent is domination – the willingness to render up labor in exchange for a wage. The systemic character of capitalism is obscured so that workers only see individual enterprises operating in competitive relations with one another. Without experiencing capitalism, socialism is not a meaningful alternative and so the question of whether workers would rationally opt for socialism is moot.

This is true for capitalist workers, but not for workers under state socialism, whose lived experience is very different. There, society presents itself to workers as a totality, a system of exploitation. The state presents itself as an expropriator and seeks to legitimate itself as presenting the interest of all. State socialism is organized as an alternative to capitalism. Workers participate in rituals that celebrate its efficiency and justice – campaigns, production conferences, brigade competitions, and so on – while they live a reality that appears devoid of these qualities. However, here the choice is not between capitalism and socialism, but between existing state socialism and a society implicit in the rituals – a socialism of efficiency and justice, a workers' socialism.[13]

Yet, of course there are occasions even in capitalism where workers consider their options when the naturalness of everyday life is suspended. When class struggles accumulate momentum, leading to ever more intensive confrontations with the state as, for example, in the concept of the 'mass strike', then the choices open to workers can change significantly. The possibility of an emergent commitment to socialism through participation in struggles is marginalized by Przeworski's embrace of a neoclassical conception of strategic action: 'the power of neoclassical economics lies in being able to separate the analysis of action at a particular moment from everything that created the conditions under which this action occurs' (Przeworski 1985b, p. 385). Preferences are taken as given rather than made and remade through participation in the world. History teaches us a different lesson – what appears real, feasible and viable is molded and remolded by social movements as they unfold, whether these are struggles in nineteenth-century France and England, or after the first world war in Italy, Germany and Russia.

Przeworski reproduces social democracy's focus on the material interests of workers, on the distribution of wages and profits. He shows that workers can make material gains and thus capitalism has a durability unanticipated by Kautskyist orthodoxy. He justifies his analysis of material interest by arguing that capitalist democracy reduces all needs to material interests. But how true is this? Don't movements for peace, for protection of the environment, and for the extension of civil rights all contest the narrow economic logic of Przeworski's class compromise?

While I am not persuaded that these movements generate 'radical needs' that lead beyond capitalism, they nevertheless cannot be ignored in the analysis of contemporary capitalism, not least in the way they compel capitalists to introduce new technologies and new products.

Przeworski's Ethical Socialism

Przeworski's sober picture of capitalism is counterpoised to a correspondingly radiant picture of true socialism. As ever, Przeworski's critique of social democracy is illuminating. When socialists realized that reforms were not leading to socialism in the foreseeable future, he argues, they lowered their aspirations. They took advantage of Keynesian economic strategies to introduce social welfare measures, but now that Keynesianism is no longer viable they are bereft of any alternative program. Przeworski resuscitates the original ideals of socialism. Instead of full employment he proposes emancipation from labor; instead of spreading democracy from the political to the economic realm he proposes the reduction of mutual constraint and the liberation of free time. 'Socialist democracy is not something to be found in parliaments, factories, or families: it is not simply a democratization of capitalist institutions. Freedom means de-institutionalization; it means individual autonomy' (Przeworski 1985a, p. 247).

Once more production is eclipsed. The defining problem of socialism, as in capitalism, is distribution: 'The intrinsic feature of a socialist organization of society is the capacity of the society as a whole to choose in a democratic way the mix of needs to be satisfied in the allocation of resources' (Przeworski 1985a, p. 238). He proposes a society in which the labor time devoted to the production of necessities is negligible. He clings to the fantasy of automation, of machines replacing people. To be sure we would hope that socialism would bring with it a reduction of the working day, but production there will always be. Przeworski's conception of socialism resonates with his analysis of capitalism: they both avoid an examination of production and its regulation, and thus also the implications they have for distribution. I can only repeat: without production there is no distribution.

The Micro-Foundations of Class

Przeworski's socialism is doubly utopian: it has no basis for existence and there's no point of entry. It is time to return to socialism on earth and the conceptualization of class. Writing of 'rational choice Marxism', Przeworski, unintentionally perhaps, supplies his own auto-critique:

What is thus wrong with methodological individualism, I believe, is not the idea that collective actions must be explained by referring to individual rationality but the idea that society is a collection of undifferentiated and unrelated individuals. The appropriate view is neither one of two ready-to-act classes nor of abstract individuals, but of individuals who are embedded in different types of relations with other individuals within a multidimensionally described social structure (Przeworski 1985b, p. 393).

As I have tried to show, Przeworski is not true to his prescriptions. In the analysis of electoral socialism his individuals are abstract, in his analysis of capitalist dynamics he has two ready-to-act classes and a ready-to-act state, and finally, in his analysis of the transition to socialism, he shuttles between the two. He never describes or analyzes the concrete relations in which real individuals are embedded. It is now time to piece together our criticism of Przeworski and replace his theory of class with one that takes seriously the concrete relations of micro-institutions.

As point of departure, I take the two anomalies that drive Przeworski's work: the durability of capitalism and the passivity of its working class. He resolves these anomalies by reconstructing the concept of class. Because so many economic activities don't fall into conventional class categories and because class interests are not given by economic location, Przeworski dispenses with the idea of class as prior to struggle and instead proposes that class be considered as an effect of struggles. He begins by criticizing the idea that class interests are stamped onto workers by virtue of their position in production, but he ends up with another stamping of interests – this time by parties and trade unions. He finds himself in this contradictory position because he doesn't take seriously the lived experience of workers.

In making lived experience irrelevant, particularly the lived experience in production, Przeworski is led to absurd conclusions. In his scheme there is no obvious way to discriminate between class actors and non-class actors. There's no reason for workers and capitalists to be classes rather than men and women, or Catholics, Jews and Protestants. He doesn't even rule out the possibility of workers and capitalists combining to form a single class. Workers and capitalists may indeed form an alliance and come to act in a solitary way, as in wars, but that hardly warrants calling them a single class.

Viewed as an effect without roots in production makes nonsense of the concept of class, so it is hardly surprising that in the analysis of 'class compromise' Przeworski reappears as a methodological collectivist. The project of class formation is jettisoned and we are confronted with two ready-made classes, capital and labor. From being dupes of parties and unions, workers suddenly become active militants, forging class compromises as part of their daily life, as the basis of consent to capitalism. To whom is he referring? Whose daily life?

But, just as important, he doesn't care to tell us how capital and labor become actors. We don't care to ask him because we know that capitalism generates distinct class experiences, yes class experiences, in which those who own the means of production or their representatives periodically bargain with, but generally direct those who sell their labor power or their representatives. Workers and capitalists don't have to be told by parties and trade unions that they have distinct interests. That's why the idea of class compromise sounds so plausible.

How might we construct an alternative theory of class with real microfoundations? Instead of abandoning the concept of 'class-in-itself' in which class position is defined by relations to the means of production, I propose to give it more depth. Specifically, I introduce the idea of class experience which is rooted in production but entails more than economic interests. Typically, Marxists – and this includes theorists of the labor process as well as of class – argue for a one-to-one correspondence between economic position and the experience of the position. They overlook the importance of production as a site of political and ideological formation as well as of economic activity. Moreover, the political and ideological aspects can vary independently of the narrowly economic or labor process aspect of production.[14]

That is to say, if classes emerge at all as actors, they do so first under the combined influence of the economic, political and ideological moments of *production*. The character of production relations, the way they are reproduced and the experience generated thereby provide the ground for incumbents of particular places in the labor process to become a collective actor, a class-for-itself. Only on this basis can we talk about the role of parties and trade unions molding or reshaping class. Workers are neither more nor less the victims of the machinations of parties, trade unions, churches, or schools than are party leaders, general secretaries of unions, archbishops, teachers and even analytical Marxists. In each case interests and values are grounded in lived experience.

This leads once more to my *weak thesis*: the analysis of *variations* in class formation cannot ignore production and the lived experience it generates. According to my *strong thesis*, on the other hand, capitalist production and its hegemonic regimes give rise to the *common* attribute of advanced capitalist societies: the eclipse of working-class struggle for socialism. Specifically, I argue that a necessary but not sufficient condition for a class to struggle for socialism is its proletarianization – that is, separation from the means of production and incorporation into a socialized labor process. The requisite 'socialist' consciousness emerges only when proletarianization is combined with a specific regime of production – one that is found in state socialist societies. Here, workers become aware of their class interests and why they cannot be realized within the confines of state socialism. The character of the production regime leads them to an imminent critique of state socialism for failing to live up to its ideals. The absence of electoral competition between parties, of open public discourse or of a civil society does not prevent workers from developing a class understanding of their society. Quite the contrary: their class consciousness is more deeply embedded even though class mobilization is more difficult to organize.

Under advanced capitalism, the regime of production bottles up struggles within the enterprise by coordinating the relations of capital and labor. And, by obscuring exploitation, it obstructs the development of a radical class consciousness. The effective demobilization and deradicalization of the working class draws attention to social movements whose basis is an immanent critique of capitalist democracy. These movements are 'new' precisely because of the weakness of working-class participation. Theorizing the political and ideological apparatuses of production supplies the answer to why it is that socialist parties have disdained radical mobilization and succumbed to electoral politics.

NEOCLASSICAL MARXISM

Classical Marxism never thought to critically examine whether workers would in fact become the vast majority of the people, whether in fact socialist parties did represent the interest of workers or whether workers themselves had a material interest in socialism. Classical Marxism simply took these for granted. Przeworski counterpoises his own arguments: workers haven't, don't and won't form the vast majority of the population; in order to succeed in electoral competition socialist parties have sought support from allied classes, thereby diluting their commitment to the working class; and workers don't have a material interest in socialism because of the gains they can make under capitalism and because of the costs of transition. This critique is particularly damaging because it shows that by challenging just two assumptions – workers forming a majority and zero-sum character of capital–labor conflict – the entire edifice of classical Marxism crumbles.

But as a positive explanation for the durability of capitalism and the passivity of its working class, Przeworski's critique lacks precisely what orthodoxy lacks – micro-foundations. First, his analysis of electoral socialism misspecifies the causal forces at work. Identities, including class identity, are not forged by macro-actors alone but also by and through lived experience. Reflecting the regime of production, workers evolve their own identities, and parties and unions are compelled to take them into account. Second, his analysis of class compromises rests on a very abstract characterization of relations of production which obscures the distinction between micro- and macro-arenas and thereby misspecifies the actual dynamics within each arena. The class compromise at the level of the enterprise involves not just who gets what, when and how, but also who does what, when and how.

There may be an optimal militancy which maximizes the material interest of workers, but there is no evidence that real workers actually operate with such a conception. The same is true of his postulated minimum wage increase below which consent is withdrawn. In the final analysis he fails to accomplish his own stated goal: 'We will never understand the resilience of capitalism unless we seek the explanation in the interests and in the actions of workers themselves' (Przeworski 1985a, p. 3). Rather than discovering those actions and interests of workers, he either regards them as shaped by macro-actors or imputes to them a plausible but empirically unfounded rationality.

Przeworski effectively challenges two assumptions underlying the theory of social democracy, but fails to furnish it with micro-foundations. He replaces the assumption of polarization of class structure with the idea that class is produced as the effect of struggle and the assumption of irreconcilable class conflict with a non-zero sum conflict in which class compromises are possible. By themselves, however, these two new assumptions cannot provide the framework for an analysis of the history and future of capitalism. That would require micro-foundations grounded in production and the lived experience it generates. Przeworski knows this: throughout his writings he calls for the examination of such a lived experience. There is a fatal discrepancy here between intent and execution, between the programmatic defense of micro-foundations and their absence in practice. He begins by criticizing classical Marxism, but ends up reproducing precisely those aspects of orthodoxy which analytical Marxism claims to abandon.

For this reason alone his analytical Marxism may be more appropriately called 'neoclassical Marxism'. But there is another more fundamental reason for this relabeling. Analytical Marxism looks to neoclassical economics for mechanisms at the micro-level to explain phenomena at the macro-level. Now it is true, on occasion, that Przeworski has been critical of this enterprise. He reproaches methodological individualism for assuming 'undifferentiated, unchanging, and unrelated "individuals". Thus, while any theory of history must have micro-foundations, the theory of individual action must contain more contextual information than the present paradigm of rational choice admits' (Przeworski 1985b, p. 381). And while approving Roemer's use of game theory, Przeworski admonishes him for committing the same errors of neoclassical economics: separating economics from politics, looking upon the system of production as a 'self-operating automaton'. The problem with Marxism, says Przeworski, lies *not* in how it departs from but in what it shares with neoclassical economics (Przeworski 1985a, pp. 231–5).

Yet he carries into his own analysis the same neoclassical props: mythological rather than real individuals, abstracted rather than concrete relations, distribution rather than production. To be sure, Przeworski recognizes the limits posed by relations of production on distribution. But relations *in* production, the *lived* experience of class, completely eludes him. It is not just that things have to be produced before they are distributed. Equally important, production has its own political and ideological regime which shapes interests, identities and capacities, and thereby limits and underpins both class formation and class compromise.

NOTES

1. An early version of this chapter was delivered at a workshop on the Politics of Production held at the University of Chicago, 13–14 November 1987. I am grateful to Adam Przeworski, Erik Wright and Carol Hatch for reading and commenting on subsequent versions.
2. I examine one such post-Marxist solution in Burawoy 1989.
3. Sometimes Przeworski appears to veer towards a post-Marxism, similar to Ernesto Laclau and Chantal Mouffe's *Hegemony and Socialist Strategy* (London: Verso, 1985), which makes class a historically contingent actor. The tendency is greatest in his analysis of class formation where his 'subjects' have first to be constituted by struggle before they engage in struggle.

However, these subjects still turn out to be an alliance of classes or class fractions. By gesturing toward lived experience and Gramscian limits, Przeworski avoids being swept away in articulatory practices and suturing discourses. His second project, on the other hand, is the very antithesis of post-Marxism. Here the dynamics of capitalism set limits on 'class compromise'. Laclau and Mouffe would no doubt accuse him of 'classicism', 'essentialism', 'economism', 'reductionism' and countless other post-Marxist sins because he privileges the material base and treats capital and labour as preformed actors.

4. Interestingly, Przeworski criticises Roemer's neoclassical Marxism for ignoring the labour process. Roemer cannot assume out of existence the problem of extracting labour from labour power because it significantly affects his claimed correspondence of wealth and income (Przeworski 1985a, pp. 229–30). But in his own theory Przeworski ignores production not only from the standpoint of its economic effects but more importantly from the standpoint of its political and ideological effects.

5. Yet, only a few pages later, when they again confront the fact that party leaders don't pursue vote maximising strategies, they obfuscate the nature of constraints from below by asserting that party leaders maximise 'expected utility' (Przeworski and Sprague 1986, p. 124). They don't tell us what the utility function is or from where it comes. In this way they deny the importance of changes in working-class experiences brought about by its self-organisation, such as those that took place in Germany between 1900 and 1920.

6. Indeed, Przeworski himself elsewhere writes: 'No ideology, Marxism included, can perform its function of coordinating individual wills unless it is validated continually by daily life, by what Althusser calls "the lived experience". If an ideology is to orient people in their daily lives, it must express their interests and aspirations' (Przeworski 1985a, p. 136). Even more explicitly he writes: 'if any ideology is to be effective in instituting an image of social relations, if it is to achieve the effect of generating a collective project of social transformation, then it must correspond to the manner in which people experience their everyday life. Hence, the effectiveness of socialist ideology with regard to workers depends upon characteristics of their life situation that are secondary from the point of view of class membership, namely, size of revenue, life-style, position within relations of authority, work conditions, character of work – "misery", "poverty", "oppression"' (Przeworski 1985a, p. 76). This implies that an understanding of the constraints on party ideology requires a careful examination, indeed theorization of lived experience and its determinants. But this is imply absent in Przeworski's analysis.

7. It should be noted that this quote referring to an autonomous lived experience is from an early summary of the argument (although published for the first time in 1985). In Przeworski and Sprague (1986) the authors simply report that they couldn't find any such lived experience independent of parties and unions and so they assumed it didn't exist.

8. Gramsci, the inspiration behind Przeworski and Sprague's work, suffers from the same problem. To be sure, Gramsci insisted on the importance of lived experience as limiting political appeals: ideology is neither 'cold

utopia nor learned theorising', but has to galvanise the collective will by resonating with a lived experience (Gramsci 1971, p. 126). Elsewhere he has denied that parties can have autonomous ideologies: 'It is evident that this kind of mass creation cannot just happen "arbitrarily", around any ideology, simply because of the formally constructed will of a personality or a group which puts it forward solely on the basis of its own fanatical philosophical or religious convictions. Mass adhesion or non-adhesion to an ideology is the real critical test of the rationality and historicity of modes of thinking' (Gramsci 1971, p. 341). But for all his programmatic insistence on lived experience, Gramsci never tells us what it is or where it comes from. In the final analysis Gramsci, too, is without micro-foundations.

9. The data on the relationship between rates of investment and labour shares for different countries is taken from Przeworski, 'Capitalism, Democracy, Pacts: Revisited', unpublished manuscript (1988).

10. Przeworski here relies on Gramsci: 'the interests of the dominant group prevail, but only up to a certain point, i.e., stopping short of narrowly corporate interest' (Gramsci 1971, p. 162). Whether Gramsci intended all that Przeworski attributes to him is not important. More important is that an interpretation of Gramsci cannot be a substitute for empirical evidence. Przeworski does not provide evidence of a minimum wage below which workers withdraw their consent.

11. In their examination of the obstacles to popular sovereignty Przeworski and Wallerstein do open up the black box of the state, examining what states control, the locus of decision-making and the organization of production of services. They also discuss the potential autonomy of apparatuses as well as constraints on such autonomy. They conclude that: 'The cohesion of the state is always problematic for purely institutional reasons: the state is a complex system without a fixed center of cohesion' (Przeworski and Wallerstein 1986, p. 242). One wonders, then, how useful it is to assume the state to be a coherent actor.

12. I have been particularly influenced by Paul Johnston's work on the state as a distinctive 'mode of production' which examines the implications of the production of social goods and services for the organization of work, for the politics of state production and for the development of class struggles (Paul Johnston, 'The Politics of Public Work', unpublished PhD dissertation, University of California, Berkeley, 1988).

13. I have developed these ideas at length in Burawoy (1989).

14. This is where I part company with Wright. In trying to maximise the explanatory power of his map of class structure, Wright has shifted from an original but clearly Marxist model to one in which classes are defined not in relationship to one another through the appropriation of labor, but by the assets (capital, organisation and skill) they can mobilize. I am inclined to return to his original model but to seek explanations for the non-correspondence of class position and class consciousness or class identity in the political and ideological components of production.

6 Class, Production and Politics: A Reply to Burawoy
Adam Przeworski

Ours is perhaps the first time in two hundred years that is without blueprints of a radical social transformation. In particular, the socialist alternative that emerged around 1848 and became the guiding idea of mass movements around 1890 seems to have faded from the public scene. The countries which assumed the socialist appellation are desperately grasping for capitalist remedies to their economic and ideological breakdown, while political parties in capitalist societies that bear the socialist label have abandoned even the semblance of an alternative. The question guiding most of my work which received Michael Burawoy's scrutiny is why the left in democratic capitalist countries has failed to offer a politically, economically and ideologically viable alternative to capitalism.

This question concerns socialism as an historical phenomenon. The nineteenth century is a cemetery of movements that rejected capitalism – from anti-industrial communitarianism, mutualism, and diverse incarnations of anarchism, to religious millenarianism and non-Marxist socialism. Yet only one movement grew to lead victorious revolutions in some countries and to mobilize the masses, compete in elections and even govern in other countries: the movement which blended socialist objectives with the Marxist theory and a working-class base.

Marxist socialism of that hopeful period was a movement with a theory and a project: a theory of collective action and a project for the new society. According to this theory, wage-earners suffer material deprivation and are compelled to toil just in order to survive as a result of the private ownership of productive wealth. Each individual wants to improve his or her life conditions, so they combine with others facing similar conditions and struggle for their interests. But they soon discover that no improvement is possible under capitalism. Only if capitalism is abolished – if the instruments of production become public property – could they free themselves from misery and compulsion. Conversely, once capitalism is abolished other sources of deprivation would also disappear. Hence, struggles for individual material interests turn into one big struggle for socialism. This struggle would be victorious under democratic conditions because wage-earners would become an overwhelming majority of voters.

This theory of collective action has solid micro-foundations in the idea that individuals are motivated by their own material welfare, and it is the only micro-foundations it has. People do not like to perform unpleasant labor (toil) and they like to consume, in the broad sense of using objectifications of socially organized activities, for example, a canvas to paint beautiful pictures for everyone's enjoyment. They have many other wants, tastes and ambitions, and these may matter. But individual material interests were considered by Marxists as sufficient to conclude that history would bring about socialism as a consequence of a movement of workers.

My studies over the past twenty years have persuaded me that this theory is not valid and the political project associated with it is not viable. The method by which these conclusions are derived is analytical: my procedure was to accept Marxist premises and to examine whether the conclusions drawn by Marx and his followers follow in the light of contemporary social scientific knowledge. For those who like labels, this is 'analytical Marxism': I take Marxist assumptions and study whether the stipulated consequences follow, given what social scientists know today. The reference to 'social science' is important to me: I think, with Bernstein, that 'no -ism is a science', and that it is a responsibility of politically committed scholars to expurgate beliefs that cannot be supported in a scientific way, by logical inference and empirical evidence.

Marxism is for me not a *parti pris*, but a set of hypotheses, subject to routine scientific scrutiny. I realize that there is more than one ideal of 'science' and that every set of procedures can be criticized as being in some way naive, but I consider obscurantist any notion that Marxism has its own philosophy of science which exempts it from the criteria used to evaluate other theories. Moreover, any science that is to guide social practice must at least answer causal questions, such as, 'what are the possible, likely, or certain consequences of alternative courses of action?' Otherwise, it is politically impotent.

The conclusions at which I arrived using this approach are the following: (1) Wage-earners and other people can improve their material conditions within the confines of capitalism. (2) The state can make a difference in allocating resources and distributing incomes; hence, partisan control over the state does matter; hence, democracy has consequences for the welfare of particular groups under capitalism. (3) The opportunity inherent in democracy forces mass movements to orient their strategies toward short-run improvements and to de-emphasize class identities; movements which fail to do so vanish. (4) All major social transformations, including the 'transition to socialism', are costly and, if the only motivations for them are material interests, they will not be attempted by movements that are powerful under capitalism.

These conclusions do not constitute an apology for capitalism, which continues to generate mass poverty amidst affluence, unnecessary compulsion to toil, avoidable oppression in workplaces, schools and families, inequality of opportunity, accidental distributions of income, irrational allocations of resources and a number of other harmful consequences. Moreover, I believe that many of these consequences are avoidable and that they could be avoided given a different organization of the economy and the state. I do not think, therefore, that capitalism is an immutable form of societal organization. But the traditional notion of socialism conceived in terms of public ownership of the means of production is no longer credible and the juxtaposition of capitalism versus socialism no longer informs future alternatives.

Burawoy does not question any of these conclusions. He agrees that the durability of capitalism and the reformism of the working class have refuted Marxist theory. He questions neither the central hypothesis of *Paper Stones* – that socialist parties undermined class organization of workers in an inevitable pursuit of electoral victories – nor of Michael Wallerstein's and my work on class compromise – that organizations of workers consent to capitalism when this strategy is best for the material interests of their members. And when Burawoy discovers in Hungarian workers the agent of the socialist transformation neither of us found in the West, he puts socialism in quotation marks, probably because he is as unclear about the content of this possibility as all the rest of us.

Nor does Burawoy question the analytical method. His exchange of views with Erik Wright (Burawoy 1987, p. 23) may indicate that he is just being charitable, but he dresses his critique of my views under the guise of a methodologically internal critique: he chastises me for not adhering to my own methodological program in failing to specify micro-foundations of collective action.

Burawoy's fire is directed neither at the conclusions nor at the method, but on the assumptions from which these conclusions are derived. What he finds at fault is that I repeatedly ignore the importance of production as a determinant of collective identity of workers, as a terrain of politics and as a factor in global transformations of society. But if Burawoy disagrees neither with my conclusions nor with the method, then what is at stake in his argument for the importance of production? His main critique is that because I ignore production, I end up with a poor description, both of class formation and of class conflict. The analytical apparatus that abstracts from production, Burawoy insists, is descriptively misleading. In other words, even if my conclusions are valid, they are valid for wrong reasons. And ultimately I do pay the price: not having found prospects for socialism in the West, I stopped looking instead of discovering them in the East.

To anticipate what follows, I find Burawoy's critique of my view of class formation incisive and valid. All I can do is to explain why I think all approaches to this issue are incomplete and why differences of approach are likely to persist. However, Burawoy's emphasis on the primacy of production for class formation is unpersuasive and at times relies on ritualistic reductionism. The importance of production for questions of class conflict is more evident, but we still do not understand the role of unions in the labor process. Finally, I think that Burawoy's preoccupation with production causes him to misunderstand both the longevity of capitalism and the reasons the political alternatives we face appear so limited.

ON CLASS FORMATION

To judge competing approaches to class formation, we need to agree first what it is that theories of class formation explain. They answer two sets of questions: (1) At the individual level, why do individuals act on the basis of some specific interests, values, norms, instincts or motives or, alternatively, why are they vulnerable to particular appeals? (2) At the collective level, why do particular collectivities acquire a strategic capacity to act as unified actors, why do they become 'organizations' in Alessandro Pizzorno's apt definition of organization as a capacity for strategy?

As Mancur Olson has shown, Marxists have traditionally confounded these two questions when they reasoned that if workers have the same interests as individuals, then all workers will act collectively to promote these interests. This inference is fallacious because, as Marx in fact emphasized several times, being a worker puts individuals in competition with one another. It is in the collective interest of workers to have a minimum wage above the subsistence level, but it is in the interest of each individual looking for employment to work for less than the minimum wage. It is in the collective interest of all wage-earners to have compulsory retirement laws, but many individuals would prefer to work beyond the retirement age. Hence, workers act collectively only if they are organized – that is, only if some organization has the capacity to prevent individual workers from pursuing their interests. The power of unions is due to this capacity: the ability to persuade or coerce individual workers not to work for less even at the cost of unemployment and perhaps the ability to control the effort of individual workers in production. The power of political parties is less direct since they are less able to coerce: political parties work by shaping collective identities, the identities on the basis of which individuals act.

Traditional approaches to class formation reduce the answer to the second question to the first one. In the Marxist version of reductionism, individuals acquire class interests in production and they organize collectively on the basis of these and only these interests. Classify 'locations' in production, impute to them 'class consciousness' or 'class interest' and you have resolved all problems of collective action. If the observed patterns of collective action do not correspond to the classification, go back to production and reclassify. Explaining collective action is just a matter of a correct classification of places in production.

The Marxist reductionist approach, in all its versions, fails to meet elementary challenges imposed by the life around us: it fails to explain why the particular developed capitalist countries differ greatly in the way they experience and conceptualize class structures and it fails to explain why the politics in none of these countries can be reduced to class. Why is it that people who are neither workers nor capitalists constitute 'the middle class' in the United States, '*cadres*' in France, '*cetti medi*' in Italy, '*beamte und angestellte*' in Germany and 'intelligentsia' in other places? Similar questions can be posed with regard to those excluded from productive activities (and I posed both in my polemic with Wright (Przeworski and Wright 1977): for example, why is it that, in the United States, poverty has assumed a social form of a distinct underclass, while in France, which has a lower per capita income and an even more unequal income distribution, no such distinct group is apparent? Another difficulty is even more obvious: how can we explain, beginning with production, that Sweden or Austria have encompassing, centralized unions allied with electorally dominant social-democratic parties, while the United States and Italy have neither? Even worse, what can we do with those collective organizations that appear not to have any class roots – say, the French Socialist Party, the ecological movement, Young Women's Christian Association, or the Irish Republican Army?

But the emphasis on production does not exhaust reductionist possibilities. Political sociologists typically reduce the question about collective action to the question concerning individuals without relying on production: sociological theories of voting behavior normally do just that. Nation, religion, sex or language have been used as a basis for reduction as effectively as places in production, and I think with the same meager results.

In my 1977 article on class formation, and in *Paper Stones*, co-authored with John Sprague, I attacked this approach by claiming that individuals do not congeal into ready-made political actors, either in workplaces, markets, churches, or anywhere else, but collective identity – that identity on the basis of which people act in collective life – is continually generated, destroyed and molded anew in the course of conflicts.

In response to the vision of class formation in which individuals first acquire a collective identity within workplaces, nations, or churches, and only then go on to act politically, we juxtaposed a view in which parties, unions, churches, schools, newspapers, armies and corporations compete with each other to persuade and coerce individuals to act on the basis of particular interests or values. Instead of assuming that identity is given by 'positions', we developed a model in which this identity is continually molded by political parties. We applied this model to study why class has played such a different role as a determinant of individual voting behavior in seven Western European countries since the beginning of the century, and I continue to think that the results this model generated are impressive. In particular, we pulled off the feat that mattered most theoretically: we reproduced results of surveys conducted in each election since the 1950s on the basis of our understanding of a process that started decades earlier. We have shown that the way workers voted in France in 1973 or in Sweden in 1976 depends on the strategies followed by socialist parties in all the previous elections. Hence, we validated our central tenet: collective identity is a consequence of a long-term process in which political parties play a central role.

Yet Burawoy succeeded in turning tables. His basic claim is that our approach is also reductionist: *Paper Stones* only changed the direction of reduction, confusing the answer to the second question for a response to the first one. We treat individual behavior as an effect of activities of organizations, but we do not explain why individuals behave the way they do. We explain why a higher proportion of workers voted for left parties in Sweden than in France, but we cannot tell what distinguishes those who did from those who did not. Hence, in the end, *Paper Stones* has nothing to say about workers: they are just an abstract, homogeneous raw material from which parties do or do not produce socialist supporters.

This criticism is valid and devastating. The only question is to what extent the problem identified by Burawoy is inherent in the approach and to what extent it is limited to our misuse of it. Let me thus first sketch the approach in general terms and then explain how it was applied in *Paper Stones*.

COLLECTIVE IDENTITIES

The approach I proposed in 1977 can be schematically summarized as follows. At any moment there exist in any society several organizations that seek to realize goals that entail militancy, support, collaboration, or at least compliance of large numbers of individuals. As they pursue their goals, organizations compete to instill in individuals particular collective identities and to evoke from them particular behaviors. In France, the Socialist Party seeks to mold individuals who are machine operators, males, Catholics and small-town dwellers into workers; the Catholic Church tries to convert them into Catholics; the army seeks to forge them into Frenchmen; the Employers' Association strives to model them into self-interested individuals. Their strategies involve symbols and organization; persuasion and coercion. Hence, struggle about class precedes eventual struggle between classes. The result of this strategic interaction at every moment is some structure of identities on the basis of which individuals act in collective life, the structure of collective action. In turn, the effect of collective actions is a structure of identity. And so history marches on.

One way in which this structure can be characterized is by tracing collective identity to positions in the system of production. This analytical procedure serves to identify the class basis of collective action. 'Class formation' is thus but one aspect of a multi-faceted process of collective organization. In my 1977 essay I feared that this view was leading too far and I ended up arguing that forms of collective action that cannot be traced to class position can be still understood in terms of class since they emerge only if class does not become the dominant form of collective organization. But several commentators were correct to point out that there is no basis for any asymmetry in treating class and non-class roots.

Paper Stones also begins with this asymmetry, but for methodological rather than substantive reasons. To use the language of my neoclassical fellow travellers, *Paper Stones* is a partial equilibrium model. Our central hypothesis was that class does not emerge as the dominant form of collective action unless someone, specifically some political parties, appeal to class and organize on class basis. Hence, we looked at the entire process of class formation from the point of view of one actor facing a parametric environment. We assumed that each socialist party seeks to maximize class-based electoral support given two sets of constraints: the actions of other organized actors and those features of workers that are independent of the actions of all organizations.

This assumption meant that we did not have to examine the strategy of every possible actor relevant for the process of class formation. We did not have to study what was the response of the Catholic Church to the socialist support of public education or the response of unions to socialist entry into government. We could characterize the entire political environment of the socialist party – unions, other parties, churches and all – in terms of a few parameters that we considered constant during long periods. This assumption made it possible to analyze the process. Moreover, when we tried to interpret the observed cross-national differences in terms of national working-class cultures or other characteristics of workers, we did not get anywhere.

Focusing on other organizations turned out to be fruitful. We found, for example, that socialist parties which appeal to non-workers lose fewer votes of workers in those countries in which unions are strong and in which no parties make particularistic, religious or linguistic, appeals. Hence, we ended up attributing the observed patterns to the political environment of socialist parties rather than to any features of workers that might be autonomous from or at least prior to actions of organized actors.[1]

In retrospect, I think that the partial approach was a reasonable compromise. I also continue to be surprised that the statistical results we obtained made so much historical sense. But Burawoy correctly identifies what is wrong with our procedure: it is the failure to distinguish those constraints that confront the socialist party because it faces other organizations from the constraint faced jointly by all the organizations competing to forge collective identities, those constraints that are due to autonomous characteristics of workers. As a result, we did a much better job in explaining differences among the seven countries we studied than in answering the central question we posed: why is it that in all capitalist countries socialist parties lost votes of manual workers when they directed electoral appeals to other people? Indeed, in the epilogue to *Paper Stones* we were forced to speak of 'real conflicts of interests and values' which all political parties confront, but these interests and values were absent from the analysis. We did reduce questions about individuals to questions about organizations: a mirror image of what we criticized.

This reduction is costly because without an understanding of the structure of interests, values or norms that are autonomous from the activities of organized collective actors we fall into a radical indeterminism in which everything is possible and hence the success of political projects is exclusively a matter of will. This danger is best exemplified by Ernesto Laclau's and Chantal Mouffe's book, *Hegemony and Socialist Strategy*, which, in spite of its title, is incapable of even conceptualizing a notion of strategy, precisely because it argues that identity is exclusively a product of discourse. If I were to rewrite *Paper Stones* today, I would worry about what workers want and what they do independently of unions, parties and other political actors. I learned that to study class formation, one must study both the structure of interests of individuals and the strategies of collective actors.[2]

PRODUCTION AND CLASS

If we were to look for the micro-foundations of class, would we find it in production? As Burawoy notes, this is not a definitional question; a definitional question would be trivial. He makes two substantive assertions: that it is production that shapes experience of class and, most importantly, that it is because of whatever happens in production that workers consent to capitalism. He also rejects Marx's theory and he arrives at the same conclusions as I did but for a different reason: according to Burawoy, Marx thought that the experience of production would lead workers to organize as a class while in fact this experience has led them to consent to capitalism.

I think that Burawoy fails to provide reasonable support for either proposition and I believe that both are false. No one would dispute that 'production shapes experience', but the issue is whether wage-earners become or do not become collectively organized as a class because of what happens in production. And while most people perform unpleasant tasks in production against their liking, any inference to consent is fallacious. The secret of consent lies in the available alternatives and these must be organized beyond the world of production.

Note that in spite of his tone, Burawoy's assertions are not self-evident. While I maintain that consent is generated because organizations of workers get involved in struggles over allocations of resources and distributions of income, he argues that consent is manufactured in production. But we may be both wrong or only partially correct: what about Ira Katznelson's emphasis on the role of local communities in the United States; what about Pierre Bourdieu's and Jean-Claude Passeron's claim that in France consent is engendered in schools; what about E. P. Thompson's emphasis on the role of religion? Alternative hypotheses are many and the issue cannot be resolved without argument and evidence.

Burawoy could have advanced three kinds of support for his assertions: direct empirical evidence, a demonstration that production explains equally well or better the observed cross-national differences or arguments from some first principles. In fact, he presents no empirical evidence. He suggests how he would go about explaining the results of *Paper Stones*, but never goes beyond declarations. Instead, he insists that the truth of his propositions is obvious. As a result, his argument is mainly hortatory.

Burawoy's view of the role of production in class formation is novel and interesting: nothing I have said thus far is intended to undermine his superb understanding of what happens in production. The originality of his position lies in that he reduces class formation to production without reducing the question about collective action to the question about individuals. Class consciousness and class interests of individuals are not given in a unique way by their 'positions': Burawoy is careful to mark his distance from Erik Wright. To the contrary, they are generated via some process of complex interaction within what he calls 'production regimes'. Moreover, Burawoy offers a comparative morphology of such regimes, contrasting in particular developed capitalism with Eastern Europe. But in order to demonstrate that these production regimes explain the cross-national differences in class formation observed in *Paper Stones*, he would have to specify in what way the production regimes in Denmark, Norway and Sweden differed historically from those in Finland, France and Germany. He knows that this is the challenge he must meet and he approaches the task, but he does not get anywhere. And I doubt that the 'production regimes' of advanced capitalist countries are so different that they could explain the cross-national differences in collective identity and collective action.

Instead, several of Burawoy's arguments in favor of the importance of production are purely ritualistic. His favorite one is that 'without production there is no distribution', which I take to mean that when workers first arrive at the factory gates, they are famished and naked, since nothing had been distributed before producing. Questions about production are 'more basic' than other questions; without introducing production one 'cannot explain', and so on. Marx might have thought so and it may be true, but it must be shown, not just posited, to be true.

WHERE IS 'PRODUCTION'?

Why am I so hard to persuade? I do have a particular bias which I spelled out above: because individuals facing the same conditions are pitted in competition with one another, any collective action on their part requires some kind of a glue, whether persuasion – endogenous change of preferences resulting from a 'dialogue' described by Claus Offe and Helmuth Wiesenthal – or coercion. Without glue, class is a house of cards.

Burawoy maintains that if class is ever organized, it always happens 'in production'. But production is not a place: only factories and offices are. Either he means that classes are organized in workplaces or that they are organized because of what happens to individuals in production. Let me comment on the first interpretation; I discuss the second interpretation below.

Suppose that workers in a particular factory or office do organize: they overcome conflicts among them and acquire the capacity to act in the collective interest against interests of others and against the individual interests of workers. Organization is thus generated in production. Let me grant even more: suppose that workers in all factories and offices organize collectively. However, members of the particular collectivities still compete with one another: when workers in a highly-paid factory strike, workers in the less well-paid factories offer to replace them. When workers walk out of all the factories within which they are collectively organized, they do not yet make a class: I find myself repeating Marx's Inaugural Address to the First Workingmen's Association. The reason the issues of class and party have been so inextricably connected in the history of socialist thought is that there can be no class without 'party': some organizational device, from the full range of such devices that game theory finds appropriate depending on the structure of strategic interaction, that would enable workers from particular workplaces to act in pursuit of their collective interests.

Perhaps we are both overstating the difference between our views. Let me cite Burawoy and indicate what I do and what I do not find objectionable in his position. In his critique of my work, Burawoy writes:

> If classes emerge at all as actors, they do so first under the combined influence of the economic, political and ideological moments of *production*. The character of production relations, the way they are reproduced and the experience generated thereby provide the ground for incumbents of particular places in the labor process to become a collective actor, a class-for-itself. Only on this basis can we talk about the role of parties and trade unions molding or reshaping class (see above, p. 161).

Of this, I would agree to the following proposition: 'The character of production relations ... and the experience generated thereby constitute a constraint under which parties and trade unions mold and reshape classes.' Later, on p. 163 above, Burawoy makes in fact an almost identical statement: 'Reflecting the regime of production, workers evolve their own identities, and parties and unions are compelled to take them into account.' I agree, but then nothing is 'first' (whatever that means) about *production*, which does not even have to be underlined; and there are no 'grounds' and superstructures. Production is just one objective condition among others.

ORIGIN OF CONSENT

The central issue that does divide us concerns the origins of workers' consent to capitalism. Burawoy asserts that 'as long as consent is manufactured in production, socialist parties will not be able to forge an electoral road to socialism'. To translate it from our shared Gramscian jargon, I understand this to mean that as long as workers go to factories which they do not own and exert effort once there, they will not vote for socialism. In itself, this proposition is innocuous, but Burawoy seems to believe that it implies its converse: if consent was not manufactured in production, socialist parties could forge this road. And in my view the latter proposition is vacuous, since I believe that only if socialist parties were to organize a feasible alternative to capitalism, could consent *not* be manufactured in production.

Individual workers do not have a choice to consent or not to consent to capitalism. They can engage in struggles to improve work and life conditions under capitalism and they can even struggle for socialism, but they must go on selling their capacity to work for a wage; they must exert some, albeit variable, amount of effort; they must listen to their bosses and they must teach their children to do the same. Indeed, as a father of a fifteen-year-old daughter, I know that consent is manufactured long before she enters the world of production – by me, by her teachers and peers, by television, by the entire world around her. Consent *can* be withdrawn only when there exist feasible alternatives and these alternatives can be organized only outside the world of production. Unless socialist parties have feasible legislative proposals of nationalizing the means of production, unless unions have a realistic project for building a network of employee-owned enterprises, or at least someone has the means and the idea to form cooperatives, what is the choice workers have? Consent may be organized *in* production, but only because no alternatives to it are organized *beyond* production.

Yet production might still constitute 'the decisive arena for the organization of consent' if the collectively organized alternatives, offered by unions, movements and parties, concerned production. But historically they have not. Burawoy may not like it, but the socialist movement as we have known it never offered an alternative way of organizing production. Utopian or not, Marx's original vision was to emancipate workers from any form of labor that is just an instrument of survival. And short of this emancipation, the relation between forms of property and organization of production has been and continues to be fuzzy. Nationalization of the means of production – the centerpiece of the socialist revolutionary transformation – did not necessarily imply a transformation of the labor process: as Lenin observed once, 'Industry is necessary, democracy is not.' Also, while Sam Bowles and Herb Gintis have recently provided powerful arguments that a democratic labor process would be more efficient than a hierarchical one, 'industrial democracy' entered socialist discourse only when they could not nationalize anything and had no idea what else to do, during the 1920s and again recently. And the alternatives which parties and unions did organize concerned wages, employment, education, and material security. If I focus on wages and employment while studying strategies of working-class movements, it is because these movements were concerned with wages and employment. And is it not startling that all the movements of 'associated producers' – cooperatives, communes and councils – lost in competition for survival to electoral parties and negotiating unions, both oriented toward material security rather than production?

To conclude, consent is a matter of alternatives and these alternatives must be collectively organized. Hence, the key to the durability of capitalism lies in the strategies of organizations which found it better to concentrate on improvements in material conditions than on revolutionary transformations of production. This brings us to issues of class compromise, the state, and democracy.

PRODUCTION, CLASS CONFLICT AND THE STATE

In a number of articles, Michael Wallerstein and I examined two questions concerning the structure of class interests and the role of the state under capitalism. We asked whether it is inevitable, as Marx had thought, that if workers organize to pursue their material welfare they will always find it best to be maximally militant under capitalism and to opt for socialism. And we inquired whether constraints originating from the private ownership of capital are so binding that all governments under capitalism, regardless of their goals and their social bases, must avoid acting against the interest of capitalists. Specifically, we examined whether governments can distribute income to wage-earners without hurting private investment and hence economic growth.

We posed the study of class conflict in the following way: suppose that organizations of workers are as strong as they conceivably might be under capitalism, so strong that they unilaterally control the share of wages in net output, while capitalists control investment. Under these conditions, would unions choose to restrain their demands in exchange for investment? The answer is that, indeed, workers would be better off with a lower wage share and higher investment than with a higher wage share and lower investment. Unions would thus offer wage restraint as long as they had reasons to expect that workers would benefit in the future from the present sacrifice. In turn, capitalists are willing to invest as long as they are not afraid that unions would become militant in the future.

Our approach to the second question was similar: we assumed that firms control investment, unions control wages and governments tax and transfer incomes. We discovered that governments can tax consumption out of profits, transfer the revenue to wage-earners and not suffer a decline in investment, and that this is what pro-labor governments will want to do.[3] If pro-labor governments coexist with strong unions – again unions which unilaterally control the wage share – they will raise the material welfare of wage-earners to the same level that they would obtain if the means of production were publicly owned and wage-earners would make investment decisions.

Underlying both questions was a concern about the possibility and the role of democracy under capitalism. Marx had thought that democracy and capitalism could not coexist: wage-earners would use the political rights they enjoy under democracy – combination and suffrage – to abolish private property, while capitalists, faced with this threat, would seek protection under a dictatorship, as they had in France between 1848 and 1851.

Yet this prediction was too strong: while the relation between capitalism and democracy is fragile, democracy has been solidly entrenched for long periods of time in several capitalist countries. We argued that this was possible precisely when organizations of wage-earners choose strategies which allow capitalists to appropriate profits and to own instruments of production while firms invest, even though wage-earners struggle collectively for their interests. In this compromise, wage-earners consent to capitalism and capitalists to democracy – that is, they 'act in ways entailing [its] perpetuation'. And since governments can tax profits and transfer income without reducing investment and growth, the control over state offices does matter for the material welfare of particular groups. Hence, democracy is 'real' rather than 'formal': it offers a real opportunity for people who do not own capital to compensate for the effects of the system of property.

These conclusions are subject to a number of criticisms. Some logical links are far-fetched; alternative reasons for some results can be plausibly adduced; and the work in general has not been systematically confronted with empirical evidence. Indeed, several issues are still unclear to me. But I will limit the discussion to the two specific issues raised by Burawoy: our models neglect production at the cost of distribution and they do not specify who enters into compromises with whom and where.

Let me distinguish two ways in which production could be introduced. The first would be to assume that unions include some features of organization of production among their objectives. In some countries they have done so, at least in so far as unions cared about self-management councils and work conditions. But I feel quite confident that a systematic review of evidence would show that unions care much more about employment and wages, which Burawoy insists on calling 'distribution'. Anyway, the second way of introducing production is more interesting and potentially more consequential. In our analyses, we invariably assume that the same technology put into motion by the same quantity of labor power yields the same output. To introduce production into the model would require making output depend on the quantity of labor actually exerted, on effort, and specifying what determines effort.

The last issue is one of the most interesting problems around, as witnessed by a fascinating discussion between Michael Burawoy and Sam Bowles at the Workshop on Politics of Production, held at the University of Chicago in 1987. My understanding of this debate is the following. In a path-breaking article in the *American Economic Review* in 1985, and in a number of subsequent papers written with Herb Gintis, Bowles incorporated the classical Marxist problematic of squeezing labor out of labor power into the edifice of the neoclassical economic theory. He argued that individual workers exert effort if losing the job would be costly to them and if they would be likely to lose it when they did not work hard. How much effort they exert depends on the cost of job loss (what would happen to them if they lost this job) and its probability, where the latter depends on the extent of supervision. This model implies that worker's effort increases as his wage rises above the next best alternative or if he is more closely supervised: both options are costly to the firm.

The assumption that effort increases with wage rate and the degree of supervision could be introduced without major difficulties into our models of class compromise and the state. My guess is that we would find the room for class compromise expanded, since firms would not want wages to be too low, but our main conclusions would remain intact.[4]

Yet, educated by Burawoy's writings and his critique of Bowles in Chicago, I suspect that workers are not individually supervised in production and that they are not easily fired even if they are caught goofing off. Hence, it need not be true that effort increases with the cost of job loss. If I understand Burawoy's own view, he thinks that, in effect, the firm subcontracts a job to a group of workers who then develop among themselves informal rules about performance. This would imply that the role of unions is to assure the firm of some aggregate amount of effort, and that the union bargains not only about wage rates and employment, but also about effort. As Burawoy puts it, 'The class compromise at the level of the enterprise involves not just who gets what, when and how but also who does what, when and how.' Hence, effort should be considered in analyzing class conflict and I do not know how introducing effort would affect our conclusions. The one consequence I can see is that under these conditions governments would face the problem of structural dependence on labor: unions could threaten to decrease effort if a government taxes wages. Clearly, the field is wide open for both analytical and empirical work.

Burawoy's second critique of our work is best summarized when he asks, where do all these compromises take place? Answering this question requires a more complex conceptual apparatus than Wallerstein and I needed for our purposes. We were interested in the possibilities inherent in capitalism in any of its potential incarnations, not in the modalities of class relations, although we did at times confuse our model for a historical description. Since our work has been published, there has been a massive outpouring of writings on class conflict. I have no space to summarize them here: with minute attention to union structure and institutional details of industrial relations systems, they cover bargaining over employment, wage rates, benefits and investment at the level of the firm, particular economy and the international system, with or without government.[5]

The thorny problem is the power of unions. The anti-union offensive of the last ten years has shown that this power is brittle; at least, the monopoly power that unions were thought to exercise in the labor market proved to be largely illusory. Unions may be powerful because they organize a large proportion of the particular labor pool (although statistical studies show that density has no effect), because they are large, because they are centralized (which is statistically important), or because they are influential politically. But note that none of these sources of union power is derived from production. Here, Burawoy's emphasis on production may be of crucial importance. Indeed, we know that in the United States unionized plants are more productive, even though they are less profitable. We also know that the cooperation of unions in reorganizing plants and introducing new technologies is necessary for the success of modernization. Perhaps, then, the power of unions does consist of the control over the amount and the quality of effort exerted by workers in production. Note, however, that such power would depend on the minute details of each workplace; one could not characterize union power at the level of sectors, countries and even less so 'regimes of production'.

To answer Burawoy's question, class compromises may occur in different places and between differently organized actors. Depending on the forms of organization of wage-earners, institutional features of the collective bargaining system and partisan control over the government, union federations and smaller groups of workers may be more or less militant, more or less prone to compromise. And these compromises may include effort as well wages, employment and investment, they may be more or less favorable to workers and more or less efficient.

I do not think that more can be said at this point. In spite of the centrality of class conflict in Marxist theory, Marxists never developed a theory of such conflicts other than Marx's own static zero-sum model from which he drew mistaken dynamic consequences. The study of class conflict has begun only recently and there is much terrain to cover. Still, a few years ago, neoclassical economists had no place for any actors other than households and firms in their theories, while Marxists concerned with class conflict were unwilling to use neoclassical methods. Indeed, when Wallerstein and I were writing our article on class conflict in 1980, we could find only one earlier model extending beyond firm-level collective bargaining. Today, the literature is already enormous, but it is still fragmented between models of collective bargaining at the plant level, models of relations among union federations, models of union-government relations and analyses of class relations in the context of growth economies. And perhaps the weakest link is the shop floor: we need an understanding of the labor process which is both descriptively valid and formulated in terms that would relate it to other theories. Hence, Burawoy has an important contribution to make, as soon as he becomes a neoclassical Marxist. I have no doubt it is just a matter of time.

POLITICS AND PARADOXES

What then about the political implications of the conclusions presented at the beginning of this article? Let me begin on a personal note. Although Burawoy searches throughout his critique for a label under which he could file my views, I care not at all whether I reconstruct or abandon Marxism, whether my approach belongs to 'analytical Marxism', 'neoclassical Marxism' or simply neoclassical economics, not even whether my political opinions qualify me as a 'socialist'. However, I am deeply concerned that we are incapable of specifying an alternative project of society, unable to take off the quotation marks from our hesitant references to 'socialism' and, worse, even to explain why democracy is so anemic in the societies in which we live, why it is not capable of at least assuring material security for everyone.

The most succinct summary of my conclusions is this: where workers' organizations are strong under capitalism, they do not need a widespread nationalization of the means of production, because they can control the allocation of resources and the distribution of income via the power over the labor market and the influence over the state. Where these organizations are weak, they have much more to gain by being militant all the way to nationalizing productive wealth.

This conclusion appears paradoxical. The notion that strong unions would be less militant goes against the entire tradition according to which

'One Big Union' – the guiding slogan of the labor movement – was necessary for workers to strike effectively and to win wage increases. Yet this conclusion is strongly supported by many statistical studies which show that wage-earners strike less and restrain the exercise of their market power in those countries which have encompassing, centralized and politically influential union federations. The same studies conclude that these countries exhibit superior performance in terms of inflation and unemployment, growth and income equality and public provision of welfare services. Hence, although we have no direct evidence, these findings strongly suggest that wage-earners are better off in these countries. The quiescence of strong labor movements is not paradoxical.

Yet the paradox is that those working-class movements that may have the political muscle to bring about socialism by legislation have no incentives to do so, while those movements that have much to gain by nationalizing productive wealth have no power to do it. Hence socialism without quotation marks, socialism as the program of public ownership of productive wealth, is the political project of only those movements that cannot bring it about.

To understand why that is true, we need to remember that socialists wanted to nationalize productive wealth for two distinct reasons: justice and rationality, or, more narrowly, distribution and efficiency. Capitalism is unjust because some people take away the fruit of the work of others: this is exploitation. Hence, one appeal of nationalization is distributional: ownership of capital would no longer be a source of income, which would be distributed according to labor contributions, need, or some other criteria.

One way to see the distributional cost of capitalism to wage-earners, suggested a long time ago by Paul Samuelson, is to look at the proportion of net income consumed by owners of capital. The net output in any economy can be partitioned into consumption of wage-earners, investment, and consumption of capitalists. The last part is forever lost to wage-earners; it is the price they pay for the private ownership of productive wealth. And this price varies enormously among capitalist countries: for example, for every dollar of value added in manufacturing in 1985, consumption of capitalists ranged from about 10 cents in Austria and Norway to well under 40 cents in the United Kingdom and the United States to about 60 cents in Brazil and 70 in Argentina.

Hence, in purely distributional terms the Austrian and the Norwegian wage-earners have little to gain from nationalization. Since transition has some inevitable costs, they are best off relying on their market power and electoral influence. British and US workers have more to gain by squeezing profits or owning productive wealth directly: as a result, they end up striking more. In turn, the distributional effect of nationalization in Argentina and Brazil would be enormous since well over one-half of output is consumed by capitalists: in Brazil, one-tenth of households gets one-half of the national income. Hence, in Argentina and Brazil nationalization is attractive to wage-earners for purely distributional reasons.

Yet the injustice of capitalism was not the only traditional Marxist argument for public ownership (although I do think it was the most important). The central idea of socialism was the rational allocation of resources for human needs. Public ownership of productive wealth was necessary to produce things and services which people need rather than those they can pay for and to avoid the 'chaos', the 'anarchy', 'the waste' inherent in capitalism. Although central planning is an idea which the Soviet Union imitated from the German World War I experience, socialists invariably rejected the notion that collective rationality could be achieved by decentralized, self-interested actions until 1954. An additional argument for the rationality of nationalization was that public ownership would increase productivity. Working 'for themselves', the immediate producers would be willing to exert effort independently on material incentives. Hence, they would not have to be supervised and, if we are to believe Bowles and Gintis' estimates, that in itself would save astronomical amounts.

If these arguments for the superior rationality of public ownership are true, then the Norwegian and the Austrian workers have as much of a reason to want socialism as the Argentine and Brazilian ones. Yet, for better or worse, these arguments have fallen into disrepute. Hungary and Poland have recently passed laws giving equal legal status to all forms of property while China and the Soviet Union are on their way to do the same. In France during 1977, Socialists and Communists quarrelled over how many firms to nationalize, but neither side could adduce any reasons. After 1981, the Socialist government nationalized some, again for reasons that were not clear to anyone. The post-1985 right-wing government denationalized some of the firms nationalized by Socialists and by de Gaulle for equally hazy reasons. Finally, when Socialists came back in 1988, they decided to stop the match and leave things just as they happen to be. This is not to say that important issues are not discussed: economists continue to argue whether ownership or competition matter for an efficient allocation of resources, whether public ownership is the best solution to increasing returns to scale and externalities, whether worker-owned firms would underemploy and whether they would avoid new technologies, and whether employee-ownership has a positive impact on productivity. But the idea of making all productive wealth public by legislation seems to no longer attract theoretical support.

The reason public ownership is no longer seen as the embodiment of rationality is not just the collapse of centralized planning in the East or the pro-market ideological offensive in the West. The fact is that today we know only one practicable mechanism by which people can truthfully inform each other about their needs: the price mechanism. And the price mechanism seems to work only when individuals experience the consequences of their decisions in terms of their material welfare. A rational economic system must adequately perform three tasks: it must produce what people want, it must eliminate inefficient techniques of production and it must satisfy social welfare objectives. And while for some time there were good reasons to claim that the public-ownership economies are superior at least in terms of the third task, they failed miserably in performing all three.[6]

WHITHER SOCIALISM?

Without public ownership of the means of production, the term 'socialism' loses its original meaning. It becomes just a generic word for a better society, to be interpreted by each as we see fit. It signals an alternative but does not identify it. Indeed, the search for 'socialism' may be just a result of a habit acquired when we believed that nationalization is the one and only broom that would sweep away all the social ills. Having lost confidence in nationalization, we are nostalgically searching for another panacea. But, as the late Peruvian novelist Manuel Sforza observed in *La Danza Immovil*, so many things are wrong in our societies that no one revolution could possibly cure them; we need many revolutions. And perhaps the one that would make most difference in the lives of people today would be to stop the continuing genocide and the perpetual preparations for it. One can obviously go on, to issues concerning hunger, sexism, the environment, racism, and so on.

In fact, several concrete proposals have been elaborated during recent years within the walls of academia. The development of analytical methods in moral philosophy led to several debates, most importantly one concerning distributive justice, that proposed norms and even implementation schemes for a just society. The Bowles-Gintis program of industrial democracy focuses on another feature of a normatively desirable social order. John Roemer's current work on mechanisms that allocate resources in ways that are both efficient and egalitarian is a pioneering attempt to rationalize public ownership. The proposal for universal basic income, recently revived by Philippe van Parijs and Robert van der Veen, is already an objective of a political movement in Europe.[7] Distributive justice, industrial democracy, public ownership, basic income: all these are 'socialist' projects. But they no longer add up to socialism in singular.

What I thus find puzzling is not that socialism is no longer the unifying cry of the left, but that democracy is so ineffective in bringing about the particular measures that would improve life and work conditions of large numbers of people. I need not enter into the grim details, admirably depicted by Joshua Cohen and Joel Rogers in their book *On Democracy*, about mass poverty, inequality of opportunity, injustice, exclusion and oppression that are widespread under democratic capitalism. Nor do I need to reiterate that people who are most disadvantaged are also the ones least likely to act politically. Neither of these observations constitutes a puzzle for traditional Marxism, which maintains that democracy cannot be effective under capitalism and that workers are repressed by force, dominated ideologically or repeatedly betrayed by their leaders. But my work leads to the conclusion that if unions acquire market power and political influence, and if parties of wage-earners win elections, they can greatly improve welfare, at least to assure a minimum of material security for everyone. The economic constraints originating from the private ownership of capital are not so binding as to make democracy ineffective. Why then is democracy so anemic? Why is it that in most capitalist countries trade-unions are weak, political parties rarely mobilize poor people and attempts to form councils, cooperatives or communes almost never get off the ground? And why do democracies coexist with so much inequality and so much oppression?

Contrary to Burawoy, I do not think that answers to these questions are to be found 'in production'. I certainly do not believe that workers do not know what is best for them because they do not understand the mechanism of exploitation characteristic of the capitalist economy – something only we Marxist scholars understand and keep secret. What impedes collective action is not ignorance of our own interests, but conflicts among them. And these conflicts can be overcome only by collective organization which extends beyond the world of production, not only for all the reasons adduced above but for the simple fact that most poor people today do not produce. Yet if I criticize Burawoy for not giving a convincing answer, it is not because I have a better one. Indeed, as I look in retrospect, I am struck by how little I advanced in answering the questions that motivated my work. I learned that most standard reasons cited by the Marxist theory to explain poverty and oppression under capitalism are either faulty or insufficient. But, then, what are the reasons?

NOTES

1. In general I find that those approaches to working-class formation that start from the state, notably the work of Pierre Birnbaum, better explain the observed patterns than those that stick closer to society, including production.
2. This assertion does not imply that in order to study everything one must consider both individuals and collective actors. For example, when studying conflicts between unions and firms one need not each time worry about individual workers or stockbrokers; when studying the state one need not worry each time about individual bureaucrats and politicians. Organization, to return to Pizzorno, is the capacity for strategy, the capacity to act on behalf of individuals even if such actions go against their individual interests, those interests that pit individuals in competition with one another. Hence, there is no contradiction between being concerned about interests of individuals and problems of collective action when studying class formation and taking ready-made collective actors as the point of departure when studying class conflict. Burawoy does to me what he criticized Elster for having done to Marx; he takes assumptions for independent analyses and claims they are contradictory. Assumptions serve to hold some aspects of the world as given for the purpose of pursuing a particular question. In spite of the first principle of dialectics, which asserts that everything is related to everything else, all science is a partial equilibrium analysis: something, somewhere is taken as given.
3. We are not yet certain, however, how robust this finding is. Michael Wallerstein has discovered that, contrary to our initial conclusions, this result does hold even if capitalists anticipate tax changes and that it holds in an international economy with mobile capital. But it may not hold if both tax changes are anticipated and capital is internationally mobile; we are still studying this topic.
4. The same would be true, by the way, if we introduced demand and made investment rise with aggregate demand.
5. For a sample, see the special issue of *Scandinavian Journal of Economics* (1985). A brief summary of this literature can be found in Przeworski (1990a). In turn, the Bowles – Gintis approach, which promises to lead to many surprising and important consequences, would stress the conflict between employed workers and the unemployed.

6. Just one anecdote: in Czechoslovakia, the value of goods in the stores which no one wants at a zero price equals the growth of the economy in the last two years.
7. See the special issue of *Theory and Society* 15/5 (1986), and the bulletins of BIEN, a European political movement for this proposal.

7 Mythological Individualism – The Metaphysical Foundation of Analytical Marxism
Michael Burawoy

Social science stands at the cross-roads of the natural sciences and the historical sciences. It involves both explanation and understanding. As compared to the natural sciences its distinctiveness lies in the shared humanity of scientists and their subject matter. Its data exists preconstituted as meaningful action, and must therefore be decoded before explanation is possible. Because the meaning of action is dependent on context, actors have first to be located in their specific social situation. That goes for ourselves as social scientists just as it applies to the subjects of our study.

Analytical Marxism stands opposed to these premises of social science by insisting on methodological individualism. Here individuals are abstracted from the concrete context of their action and the meaning of their action is imputed rather than studied. Moreover, the imputation is speculative in that it does not take place through any dialogue with those it describes. If there is dialogue at all it is with fellow academics, often neo-classical economists and analytical philosophers from whom they borrow much. They regard themselves as free-floating scientists, prepared to ditch any hypothesis, any claim, any theory, any tradition if it does not measure up to their keen sense of rigor.

Therefore, their methodological individualism becomes mythological individualism in two senses. First, the objects they write about are snatched from any context that gives their action meaning. Second, as scientists, analytical Marxists regard themselves, like their subjects, as free from social determination, from commitments to theoretical traditions. Even their political commitments are divorced from their role as scientist. If they are Marxists it is because they are fond of dismantling the works of Marx, purging them of inconsistency, ambiguity and philosophy and then straightening them into the works of a mythological individualist.

So long as they make no effort to address the empirical world in any systematic fashion their mythological individualism remains triumphant. But what happens when they use their methodological principles to study real phenomena? In this respect the analytical Marxism of Adam Przeworski stands as a bold attempt to base his analysis on empirically rooted assumptions and to draw conclusions about the world in which we live. I will show how mythological individualism (1) underpins his view of class compromise and class formation and (2) how it informs his pursuit of science. In each instance I will offer an alternative perspective which restores both object of science and scientist to the social context of their work.

MYTHOLOGICAL SUBJECTS

In an earlier debate I argued that notwithstanding his repeated appeal to lived experience, to individual preferences and to methodological individualism, Przeworski's Marxism has no microfoundations. In his analysis of the history of electoral politics in Western Europe he traces out voting behavior as though individuals were the dupes of collective actors. Class formation becomes the effect of the strategies of political parties, trade unions in the context of a changing occupational and political structure. The lived experience of workers, in particular, is not given any autonomous place in his theory. In his reply Przeworski agrees he has no microfoundations but he is not convinced by the micro-foundations I supply which are based on experience in production. First, their inclusion doesn't give rise to conclusions different from his. Second, I don't demonstrate the primacy of productive experience over other micro arenas.

In this rejoinder I want to take up both challenges in connection with his theory of class compromise. Przeworski takes as his point of departure an assumption of classical Marxism, namely that there is an irreconcilable conflict between capital and labor. In a static model it is true that what capital gains in profits labor loses in wages but, in a dynamic model, future wage increases come out of present profits so that workers do have an interest in containing immediate wage demands. Przeworski shows that for a given time horizon there is an optimal level of militancy for which workers will maximize future income. Militancy greater than this optimum would appropriate too much profit, so limiting future wage increases, while militancy less than the optimum would deprive workers of future wage gains by allowing capital to appropriate too much. The terms of this class compromise are that workers agree not to expropriate capital in return for which capital agrees to redistribute a proportion of future profit in the form of wage increases. In short, labor makes gains within the framework of capitalism without challenging its foundations. Reform does not lead to revolution.

As a critique of the assumptions of classical Marxism Przeworski's model is very powerful but as an account of the tendency of wages it lacks any empirical referent. It is one thing to say there is an optimal militancy, it is quite another to say workers are able to achieve it. Przeworski operates at the level of an imputed class interest without links to actual class interests or to the class capacity that could enforce those interests.

My own explanation of the trajectory of wages also recognizes the possibility of class compromise but insists that these are shaped by what I call the regime of production or the political and ideological apparatuses of production. It is here that relations between capital and labor are concretely coordinated and that working-class capacity is determined. Hegemonic regimes of production forge a compromise whose terms are spontaneous consent to managerial interests in production in exchange for wage increases related to profits. The hegemonic regime, which is to be found in core sectors of the US economy, has two components: the regulation of class conflict through collective bargaining and the constitution of workers as industrial citizens with rights and obligations. Once established, the hegemonic regime demobilizes the working class, weakening its capacity to struggle for higher wages until, in the face of a capital offensive, it is not able to defend the hegemonic regime itself. It gives way to a more despotic order under pressure of global competition. Thus, I would anticipate that the consolidation of such 'hegemonic' regimes of production leads to an initial high rate of wage increase but its continued existence leads to smaller and smaller wage increases.

With this hypothesis in mind, David Weakliem has analyzed wage trends in the United States since World War II. He shows that indeed wages have moved together in those industries with similar regimes of production. Second, the effects of economic conditions, in particular levels of unemployment and inflation, are not constant but vary over the period 1947–87. Third, when variations in these effects are allowed for, the relative wage changes between sectors characterized by hegemonic and despotic regimes points to the curvilinear movement anticipated by the model. In short, not the strategic interests of workers in long-term maximization of wages but the class capacity of workers determined by regime of production determine the movement of wages. Incorporating production as micro-foundations for societal forces makes a difference and a right difference.

Weakliem's data analysis supports the thesis that wage movement is determined by production regime. Because his model has no theory of changes in class capacity, and because he assumes that the working class has unlimited capacity, Przeworski cannot anticipate actual wage movements. But Weakliem's analysis refers to the United States and Przeworski might well argue that his own model better applies to those countries, such as Sweden, where strong centralized trade union federations do pursue wages policy for the entire work force. There, perhaps, wages vary less with the consolidation of different factory regimes and more with strategies pursued by collective actors. Still, the condition of possibility of such strategies would rest on production regimes that organized class struggle at the level of the enterprise. Central trade union organization depends on regime of production whatever their relative importance in determining the trajectory of wages.

I am not defending exclusive determinism by production regime but rather propose the operation of two logics: that of the lived experience of workers rooted in an albeit distorted communicative interaction which provides the microfoundations of a second logic, the strategic action of collective actors. Both logics operate in the formation of classes as well as of class compromises.

MYTHOLOGICAL SCIENTISTS

There is a close correspondence in the way Przeworski constitutes the workers he studies and the way he sees himself as scientist. Just as he divorced workers from the concrete social relations which gave meaning to their action so he now divorces himself from the social context which gives meaning to his science. In his guise as a scientist he presents himself as liberated from intellectual tradition and political commitment: 'Marxism is for me not a *parti pris*, but a set of hypotheses, subject to routine scientific inquiry' (above, p. 168).

But this doesn't answer what you do when you discover that Marxism's hypotheses are wrong. Przeworski never poses this question. By his silence, I can only assume that when the hypotheses of Marxism are found wanting, then he would say off with its head. But this is a very naive view of science, one in which hypotheses are tested, refuted and abandoned, then to be replaced by new hypotheses. If this were really the scientific method then no science would have got off the ground as it would have drowned in a sea of refutations. A certain dogmatism is necessary for the growth of science.

Marx himself would certainly not have written *Capital* if he had accepted refutations as a reason to abandon his project. Subsequently Marxism thrived on refutations of its hypotheses: Luxemburg's analysis of the negative as well as the positive moments of capitalist democracy sprang from the unexpected reformist tendencies of the German socialist movement, Trotsky's theory of combined and uneven development of capitalism demonstrated why revolution would come first to a backward rather than an advanced country, Lenin's theory of imperialism sought to explain how competitive capitalism transformed itself into monopoly capitalism rather than giving way to socialism, his theory of the dictatorship of the proletariat anticipated the degeneration of the Soviet revolution, Gramsci's theory of superstructures explained the failure of revolution in the West and pointed to new political strategies. And so on.

Marxism has developed into a powerful tradition because Marxists have stuck to the basic principles of Marxism, taking up anomalies as a challenge. Rather than abandoning Marxism in the face of refutations they chose to refute the refutations by developing remarkable new theories. Marxism has developed because Marxists were committed to the core postulates of historical materialism. And that commitment was fuelled not just by its explanatory power but also by a political allegiance to the desirability if not the realization of an emancipated society.

In these respects Marxism is no different from any other expanding science. Based on a critical dialogue with positivist and post-positivist philosophers of science Imre Lakatos developed his methodology of scientific research programs. Scientists are embedded in research programs defined by a negative heuristic which stipulates that a set of core postulates be defended at all costs and a positive heuristic which lays out the models and exemplars for the development of new theories. In a *progressive* research program successive theories not only save core postulates by normalizing anomalies but also make predictions, some of which come true. *Degenerating* research programs save core postulates by patching them up with *ad hoc* hypotheses which if they make predictions at all, prove to be wrong. Lakatos argues, with precious little evidence, that progressive research programs replace degenerating ones.

Przeworski insists on the separation of science from politics: 'I think, with Bernstein,"no -ism is a science," and that it is a responsibility of politically committed scholars to expurgate beliefs that cannot be supported in a scientific way, by logical inference and empirical evidence' (above, p. 168). Despite his lofty rhetoric, however, Przeworski developed his theories of class formation and class compromise in order to save Marxism from a particular anomaly – the failure of revolution in the West.

I presume he chose to save Marxism rather than neoclassical economics because, at least in part, of the attractiveness of Marxism's political aspirations. Just as we had to restore mythological workers to their productive context, so now we have to restore Przeworski to his intellectual moorings.

WORKING WITHIN THE MARXISM RESEARCH PROGRAM?

If indeed both Przeworski and I are working within a Marxist research program then we can begin to compare our different perspectives from the standpoint of its growth. Both of us are interested in the way capitalism successfully incorporates the working class. Przeworski argues that the possibility of wage earners improving their material conditions means that the state is not merely an instrument of oppression but also of organizing the redistribution of resources. Political parties, therefore, under penalty of death, seek electoral victory to secure short-term gains for their constituencies. Because workers do not form a majority of the population, this leads parties to de-emphasize class identity.

I, on the other hand, argue that the incorporation of the working class already is organized through the regime of production which orchestrates a class compromise based on returns to spontaneous cooperation of workers and partial redistribution of profit by capital. Class compromise and individualization is organized in production before parties even enter the picture. Przeworski responds, 'Consent may be organized *in* production, but only because no alternatives to it [capitalist enterprise] are organized *beyond* production' (above, p. 179). Przeworski adopts Lenin's theory that (a) workers can only achieve trade union consciousness and (b) socialist consciousness comes only from without through a political party. I, on the other hand, don't believe that socialist parties can engineer a socialist consciousness so long as there is a *hegemonic* regime of production. While neither of us denies that consent is organized both in production and beyond production, each asserts the primacy of our own realm but without demonstrating that primacy.

We have to take another tack. What are our respective contributions to the Marxist research program? Do our theories address the central anomalies of Marxism: the success of capitalism and the failure of state socialism? Do they generate new predictions? Przeworski uses his account of the dynamics of politics to explain variations in the success of socialist parties in electoral competition. But this hardly explains why they all fail: 'As a result, we did a much better job in explaining differences among the seven countries we studied than in answering the central question we posed: why is it that in all capitalist countries socialist parties lost votes of manual workers when they directed appeals to other people' (above, pp. 174–5). Przeworski has a brilliant answer to the 'wrong' question – wrong from the point of view of the Marxist research program.

My own analysis of regimes of production concentrates on the common impediment to challenges to advanced capitalism but fails to explain variations in class formation. (Although others have tried to explain such variations.) Instead of comparing the effects of regimes of production in different capitalist societies I chose to compare the effects of regimes of production in capitalist and state socialist societies. I argued that the emergence of bureaucratic despotic regimes in Eastern Europe and the Soviet Union engendered not only dissent to the existing order but 'socialist' dissent. The central appropriation and redistribution of surplus because it is transparent and not mystified (as under capitalism) requires ideological legitimation, namely that it is undertaken in the interests of all, that it is just and efficient. This ideology is embedded in rituals affirming the virtues of state socialism and thereby becomes the basis for working-class critique of state socialism for failing to live up to its ideals. Based on the development of Solidarity I argued that state socialism generates a working class committed to the democratization of state socialism. I anticipated that the break-up of state socialism would lead to working-class mobilization toward democratic socialism.

I was wrong but that's par for the course. The collapse of state socialism came not through popular revolt (except in the case of Rumania where, interestingly, members of the old regime were voted back into office) but the disintegration of the party bureaucracy. The working class may indeed have developed a socialist class-consciousness but its class capacity was very weak. The bureaucratic despotic regime of production had effectively demobilized and atomized the working class. At the same time the ruling class lost its self-confidence to govern in the name of socialism. It finally abandoned all efforts at bridging the gap between ideology and reality through repression and reform. Instead of trying to bring reality into conformity with ideology the ruling class jettisoned socialist ideology in favor of the ideology of the marketplace and free enterprise.

WHY MARXISM MATTERS

The point of this excursus is not to suggest the superiority of one or other set of answers but to underline the importance of working within a research program. Przeworski is only irritated by the issue: 'I care not at all whether I reconstruct or abandon Marxism, whether my approach belongs to "analytical Marxism", "neoclassical Marxism" or simply neoclassical economics' (above, p. 184). He does not want to be bound by any package of assumptions, questions, and exemplars. Przeworski prefers to shift allegiances while giving the impression of consistency. On the one hand anomalies of Marxism did lead him to study class compromise and class formation. His theories make an important contribution to the Marxist research program. On the other hand, carried away by his discovery of the dynamics of class compromise, this now becomes the basis of a new research program whose defining puzzles are the existence of poverty and oppression on the one side and the fragility of democracy on the other. Embracing Adam Smith's theory that the capitalist division of labor should deliver universal opulence he is puzzled by immiseration. Starting from such a trickle-down theory of class compromise, he is further puzzled by the instability of democracy. His theories become the hard core of a research program which combines neoclassical economics and political science in the language of class. Within this framework, however, his theory of class compromise becomes banal.

Not surprisingly, therefore, but with precious little argument, Przeworski concludes: 'most standard reasons cited by the Marxist theory to explain poverty and oppression under capitalism are either faulty or insufficient' (above, p. 189). This is indeed a curious rendition of Marxism. For, if Marxism has been able to accomplish anything it has been the explanation of immiseration and democratic instability – and it has been so successful precisely because it has insisted on production as its micro-foundations. If Marxism has taught us anything it is that the reproduction of capitalist relations of production sets limits on redistribution and therefore the effectiveness of democratic politics. Przeworski can only find these phenomena puzzling, from the standpoint of assumptions that are alien to Marxism.

The point about working within a research program is not that it should provide an answer to all questions. To the contrary, it defines a hard core of assumptions and theory, delimits anomalies and creates specific conceptual tools with which to tackle those anomalies. It provides the focus, discipline and continuity necessary for scientific growth. As long as it has some successes, its failures are what drive it forward. Analytical Marxists, however, don't want to be encumbered by the legacy of Marxism. In repressing the historical development of Marxism, they hope to project their own achievements onto a universal plane. They set out by mythologizing those they study and end up mythologizing themselves. Separating themselves from politics, from those they write about, and from an evolving intellectual tradition, they easily succumb to the reigning orthodoxies of the academy.

So why is commitment to Marxism important? First, in times of capitalist triumphalism, it is indeed appropriate to focus on continued poverty and oppression but from the standpoint of capitalism's inherent irrationality. In this regard Marxism has no equal. Second, as Przeworski underlines, it is important to construct models of socialist alternatives. Again Marxism is the obvious point of departure. Third, Marxism has survived profound challenges to its principles before – the break-up of the Second International and support for national war, the defeat of revolutionary movements after World War I, Stalinism. Placing oneself in the Marxist tradition offers the resources and perspectives to maintain commitment to radical critique in times when it is increasingly out of fashion. Finally, conceived of as an historical phenomenon, Marxism seeks to understand its own social determination. It heightens self-consciousness of the limits and pretensions of intellectual production.

8 Social Democracy and Rational Choice Marxism
Desmond King and Mark Wickham-Jones

INTRODUCTION

During the twentieth century many socialist parties in Western societies have embraced a social-democratic strategy based on electoral, instead of revolutionary, means to achieve their aims.[1] Three features are commonly held to define this social-democratic approach: first, an attachment to the existing institutions of capitalist society (notably parliament); second, an attempt to seek electoral support from a coalition of classes and not from workers alone; and last, a commitment to the introduction of gradual reforms rather than to an immediate transformation of society (Esping-Andersen 1984, p. 10, and Przeworski 1985, p. 3). (Some supporters claim that reforms can cumulatively lead to a transformation.)

Despite its widespread adoption, questions remain about the viability of social democracy, either to implement limited reforms or to transform society (even over a long period). Its electoral orientation and economic strategy have been controversial. Differences developed over many matters including the tactics social democrats should adopt, the support that the objectives of social democracy can sustain and its ability to manage a capitalist economy. Some sympathetic scholars, often called 'labour movement theorists', have argued that a social democratic strategy is the basis potentially for a progression of measures which will amount eventually to the dissolution of capitalist society (Esping-Andersen 1984; Korpi 1983; Stephens 1979). Others are more pessimistic: they regard social democracy as a compromised approach which cannot meet even the more limited objectives of its advocates.

An influential critic of social democracy is Adam Przeworski. Three themes stand out in his work, especially in his book *Capitalism and Social Democracy* and in several papers co-authored with Michael Wallerstein (Przeworski 1980; Przeworski 1985a; Przeworski and Wallerstein 1982a; Przeworski and Wallerstein 1982b). First, Przeworski argues that social democratic parties are unlikely to win sufficient votes to gain office. In *Paper Stones*, co-authored with John Sprague, he develops this argument and claims that, while electoral moderation may result in social democrats gaining some votes, such a strategy alienates many workers who transfer their allegiance elsewhere (Przeworski and Sprague 1986). Not only does such strategic modification mean that social democratic parties have diluted their socialist aims, it fails to win over enough net votes to gain power. Second, Przeworski suggests that workers have strong reasons for not supporting the social democratic project, namely that capitalism provides a better means of meeting their immediate material needs. Last, he contends that social democratic governments will be unable to introduce economic reforms because of the constraints of a capitalist economy. Social democracy lacks the tools to manage a capitalist economy in a reformist manner. These last two themes are often combined and termed 'structural dependence theory' referring to the dependence of workers and the state upon capitalists.

Much of Przeworski's analysis is presented in formal language, a style now referred to as 'rational choice' or 'analytical' Marxism (see Cohen 1978; Elster 1985; Roemer 1982a; and Roemer 1986). Much of the work within rational choice Marxism is concerned with abstract and theoretical issues rather than empirical ones. What distinguishes Przeworski's work is the application of the tools of rational choice to the dilemmas of social democracy. The behavioural postulates of rational choice theory underpin his analysis of the principal actors in capitalist systems (Przeworski 1985, p. 5; and Przeworski 1990b). The actions of capitalists, workers, voters and social democratic politicians follow from their objectives and the choices they confront (to which they respond rationally). From these assumptions Przeworski deduces firm conclusions. He is able, he claims, to 'demonstrate' rather than assert his pessimistic judgements about social democracy (Przeworski 1985, p. 239; Przeworski and Sprague 1986, p. 181). Others have reached similar conclusions but they have not stated their arguments as precisely and directly as Przeworski (see, for example, Coates 1975, pp. 154–61). He uses his assumptions to reach straightforward and unambiguous conclusions. If his verdicts are correct the implications for social democracy are far-reaching. However, it is possible to query the assumptions made about the objectives that actors hold and the choices they make. Modifications to the assumptions and to the interaction of the relevant actors produce different conclusions while retaining the rational choice framework.

In this chapter two tasks are undertaken. First, the three propositions at the centre of Przeworski's opus are summarised and discussed. These three propositions are drawn from Przeworski's books *Capitalism and Social Democracy* and *Paper Stones*. Second, the usefulness of these propositions for illuminating the trajectory of social democracy within the UK is considered. We do not test Przeworski's general model with the British case; rather we assess its value for an analysis of salient British trends. The propositions discussed are not the only ones of importance in Przeworski's repertoire but they are pivotal to his critique of social democracy.[2]

SOCIAL DEMOCRACY AND THE ELECTORAL DILEMMA

When socialists first contested elections with mass electorates, including working-class voters, many believed that participation was a straightforward means to electing a socialist government (Przeworski and Sprague 1986, pp. 22–8). Social democratic parties would receive the support of the mass of workers and so win office. Yet electoral success did not prove to be as simple a process as social democrats had anticipated. Even if a socialist party received the votes of all the workers, it could not win power. As Przeworski and Sprague note, 'workers never were and never would become a numerical majority in their respective societies' (Przeworski and Sprague 1986, p. 31, see also pp. 31–40). To win elections, socialist parties needed to attract the support of voters other than workers.[3] The need to secure wider support became one of the defining features of social democracy. Electoral socialists were not concerned unduly about this strategy: allies would be added to working-class voters and the objective of the party would remain, as before, to bring about a peaceful and evolutionary transition to socialism through the enactment of gradual reforms (Esping-Andersen 1984). Allies would endorse, they claimed, radical goals while proving the necessary support to win elections. Labour movement theorists continue to argue that social democrats can widen their appeal without diluting the socialist reformism that they advocate (Fulcher 1987, and King 1987).

Such an appeal to middle-class voters, as well as workers, has, Przeworski and Spraque suggest, major consequences.[4] The core identity of the socialist party is modified. The party becomes more responsible and constitutionally orientated in order to win middle-class voters. It depreciates extra-parliamentary activities. Diluted reforms and moderate aims come to dominate the party at the expense of radical goals. To capture votes, the social-democratic party abandons the socialist aspirations that were initially its very rationale. Unlike more optimistic writers within the social-democratic tradition, Przeworski and Sprague argue that electoral moderation alters the ideology and the objectives of the party: there is a trade-off between holding socialist principles and widening the party's electoral basis.

The perception of a contradiction between left-wing principles and power is common. Many commentators have charged that social-democratic parties can only win office by abandoning their socialist objectives. Such arguments are to be found in the 'Revisionist' debate within German Social Democracy at the turn of the twentieth century (Gay 1970). They are also found in deliberations within the British Labour Party during the 1950s. The British Revisionists claimed, like their German forerunners, that social democrats would not win office on a radical platform of socialist measures. The leading exponent of this view, Anthony Crosland, concluded that much of Labour's ideological past had to be jettisoned if the Party was to reverse electoral decline (Crosland 1960). At the same time Anthony Downs's median voter model of party competition provided a rational choice foundation for this approach (Downs 1957). Downs suggested that, in order to win a majority, socialist parties were driven to the centre ground. It was assumed that the party's more radical supporters, at the fringes of the Downsian Spectrum of the electorate, were trapped into voting for the now moderate party. Dissatisfied as they might be, there was no other party they could turn to with any prospect of winning. The logic of electoral competition forced parties to compromise and move to moderate positions.

Przeworski and Sprague add a new element to this argument. They claim that the desire to attract middle-class votes is problematic not just for the party's objectives but also for the ability of the party to maintain its support among working-class voters (Przeworski and Sprague 1986, pp. 50–62). The adoption of moderate reformism alienates workers so that some, at least, desert the social-democratic party. Przeworski and Sprague conclude that social-democratic parties 'cannot remain a party of workers alone, and yet they cannot broaden their appeal without undermining their own support among workers' (Przeworski and Sprague 1986, pp. 55–6). The main impact of electoral moderation is on workers entering the electorate for the first time. They would support a radical class-based socialist party but instead they are given a choice of a more moderate social-democratic body. Many do not endorse it.

Working-class voters, according to Przeworski and Sprague, are less likely to support a socialist party which is no longer predominantly class-based. They may abstain or choose other left-wing parties when voting (Przeworski and Sprague 1986, p. 61). They may cease to regard themselves primarily as members of the working class and come to vote on other grounds than class such as religious affiliation. The policy and organizational changes wrought by the logic of social democratic moderation mean that for every hundred votes a party wins from allies, it will lose some from workers which it would otherwise have won (Przeworski and Sprague 1986, p. 68). The rate of this loss will vary, but where there are alternative left-wing parties or weak corporatist structures the rate may be high. The alienation of working-class voters from social- democratic parties means that such parties cannot win office. The ebb of working-class votes is likely to be too great, no matter how many middle-class votes are gained.

Social democratic parties are rooted in this impasse. If they remain a class-orientated workers' party, they can be socialist but they will not attract sufficient support to win office. They are condemned to permanent opposition. Yet if the parties broaden their support, they will lose votes at a rate which still precludes attaining power. The prospects of electoral reformism are illusory:

> social democrats appear condemned to minority status when they are a class party, and they seem equally relegated when they seek to be the party of the masses, of the entire nation. As a pure party of workers they cannot win the mandate of socialism, but as a party of the entire nation they have not won it either (Przeworski 1985, p. 27).

Although most parties have opted for broad, rather than class-based support, neither approach is successful in the long term.

AN ASSESSMENT OF THE ELECTORAL DILEMMA

The upshot of Przeworski and Sprague's argument is that the era of electoral socialism has failed and may now be over (Przeworski and Sprague 1986, p. 185). This conclusion is supported by a theoretical model of parties' voting strategies and the class shares which make up the support for social democracy. Statistical tests confirm the thesis, although there is considerable variation in the results, with evidence from a variety of European countries: social democratic parties will confront, over the long term, a threshold above which their vote will not rise.

Parsimonious and persuasive though the model may be, it neglects important qualitative factors. The theoretical relationships upon which it rests remain, somewhat curiously, undeveloped. Przeworski and Sprague's central claim is that 'the voting behaviour of individuals is an effect of the activities of political parties' (Przeworski and Sprague 1986, p. 9). Yet they offer little by way of theoretical underpinning or detailed reasoning to sustain this argument. It is never explained in any detail why a voter's choice depends upon party strategy. Most importantly, it is never established exactly why moderation by socialist parties must alienate its working-class voters (Kitschelt 1993). Przeworski and Sprague touch briefly on two points. First, they suggest that moderate policies antagonise workers (Przeworski and Sprague 1986, pp. 52–3). Second, they state that the basis for working-class organisation is fractured so that workers cease to conceive of themselves in class terms (Przeworski and Sprague 1986, p. 54). Neither of these arguments is explained in depth or justified. Instead Przeworski and Sprague argue that moderation must result in a zero-sum trade-off in policy terms at the same time that it erodes the class basis of politics. These claims remain unconfirmed assertions: the potential ability of a party either to offer catch-all policies or to organise workers and allies successfully in a cross-class alliance is not examined.[5]

Further confusion is caused by the actions of the voters who abandon social democratic parties. On occasion those who choose not to support a reformist party continue to vote on the basis of class. For example, they may endorse communist candidates. On other occasions, potential voters desert not only the moderate party but also class as the basis of their political affiliation. They may vote for a religious or an ethnic party. These choices represent different trajectories: in one, class remains central to voting, in another it is forsaken. Przeworski and Sprague argue that, where they are viable, voters are likely to turn to communist parties (Przeworski and Sprague 1986, p. 61). As will be seen, this explanation is incomplete: voters in the UK confronted with socialist moderation did not turn to communist or other radical parties. The processes at the core of *Paper Stones* remain ambiguous: why does socialist moderation cause some voters to look to communists and some voters to cease voting on a class basis altogether?

The lack of a theoretical underpinning in *Paper Stones* is all the more surprising given that Przeworski and Sprague reverse the causality at the heart of most standard rational choice accounts of voting behaviour. As Przeworski has noted elsewhere in a critical survey, in these theories 'support maximizing candidates offer policies collectively preferred by citizens and they pursue these policies once in office' (Przeworski 1990a, pp. 4–5). It is the preferences of voters which determine the policies adopted by parties and the strategies for office that politicians employ.

In fact, few rational choice accounts adopt such a stark formulation of party strategy following from the exogenous and unyielding preferences of voters. Indeed Downs himself notes that 'in forming policy, parties try to follow the wishes of voters, but once their policy is formed, they endeavour to lead all voters to accept it as desirable' (Downs 1957, p. 84). Many rational choice analysts of voting accept that preferences are malleable and liable to shift (see, for example, Dunleavy 1991; Miller *et al.* 1991; Popkin 1991; and the survey in Miller 1990). They conclude that parties will be able to manipulate voters' choice – alongside many other influences on the electorate's preferences such as the media and actions of state actors. But these accounts do not go as far as Przeworski and Sprague. Not only do the authors of *Paper Stones* invert the causality of voter–party relations: they place considerable stress on party strategy as the key determinant of voter choice.

This emphasis on party strategy as the determinant of voter choice is puzzling given Przeworski's claims about class formation. In *Capitalism and Social Democracy* Przeworski outlines an individualist-orientated theory of class which emphasises the subjective decision of the agent. He states 'if Mrs Jones becomes a worker, it is not because she was directed to do so by an internalised norm, nor because she has no choice; she becomes a worker because she *chooses* to become a worker' (Przeworski 1985, p. 95). In *Paper Stones* an individual's choices are seemingly determined by party strategy alone. Elsewhere Przeworski denies that there is a contradiction: party strategy determines preference formation while individuals act on those preferences (Przeworski 1990b, p. 70). This denial is unconvincing: it is not apparent that Przeworski's emphasis on class choice in *Capitalism and Social Democracy* can be reconciled with the theory within *Paper Stones* which claims preference formation to be so much the result of factors external to the relevant individual.[6]

In other work Przeworski has been critical of theories which downplay or deny the role of individual choice: 'workers never appear within this framework as subjects: they are either victims of repression, dupes of ideological domination or casualties of betrayal by leaders' (Przeworski 1990a, p. 97). A similar point might be made of *Paper Stones*: that voters never appear as subjects but as the dupes of party strategy whose decisions are determined by their external circumstances.[7]

There is a further contrast concerning class. In *Paper Stones* Przeworski and Sprague appear to see class as a construct of party strategy. They write: 'when parties do not seek to organise workers as a class, class ideology is altogether absent from political life and other principles or organisations and identification come to fore' (Przeworski and Sprague 1986, p. 60). At other points they retreat from such a claim: for example, stating that 'parties which appeal to the masses continue to represent interests of workers' (Przeworski and Sprague 1986, p. 54). Nevertheless, it is not apparent how the argument that class depends upon the strategy adopted by socialist parties can be reconciled to the choice-orientated account of *Capitalism and Social Democracy*.

Ultimately Przeworski and Sprague present a theory of voting which lacks micro-foundations. The absence of micro-foundations precludes an understanding of the reasons for the alleged trade-off between allies and working-class voters. There is no sustained analysis of why winning middle-class votes must cost working-class ones. Przeworski and Sprague focus theoretically on the behaviour of parties trying (vainly) to win office and not on the reasons workers (and allies) give for their electoral choice. Analysis of the reasons for voting could strengthen the argument by establishing exactly why the problems of social democratic parties are so severe. Just as logical reasoning could explain why workers desert social-democratic parties which build cross-class support, so qualitative evidence and survey data could demonstrate that this pattern was actually the case.

The electoral problems of social democracy can be illuminated by an analysis of the British Labour Party. If Przeworski and Sprague are correct in their hypothesis of a trade-off, what evidence would be anticipated? First, it would be expected that the Labour Party would have chosen either a class-based strategy or one directed at attracting allies. Second, the trade-off in class votes between allies and workers would be observable. Third, any survey evidence should demonstrate that the chosen strategy alienated that group of voters at which it was not directed (allies in the case of the class-based approach, workers in that of the moderate programme). Last, evidence should confirm that voters were making their choices as a result of party strategy.

Since 1951 Labour has steadily and consistently moderated its electoral platform, with the exception of a period between 1970 and 1983. For most of the postwar period Labour's electoral strategy has been targeted at attracting the votes of allies. What is less apparent is that this approach (or Labour's brief shift leftwards between 1970 and 1983) has been in some way 'pure' or inconsistent with sustaining a broad base of support. At the same time that Labour leaders have moderated many of their policy proposals, they have offered specific measures aimed at workers (a perennial in the 1950s and early 1960s was steel nationalisation) as well as rhetorical catch-all policies designed to attract the support of wide sections of the electorate, workers and non-workers alike. Take, for example, Harold Wilson's emphasis in 1963 on a 'new Britain', one 'forged in the white heat of this [technological] revolution' (quoted by Pimlott 1992, p. 304). In the mid-1980s Neil Kinnock attempted to construct a similar positive-sum strategy which would yield benefits to all (Kinnock 1986).

Since 1918 Labour leaders have maintained that the party can organise allies and workers at the same time. Individual membership is open to those who want to participate actively, while workplace involvement through the unions who affiliate to the party provides the bulk of the party's members. Labour attempts to package policies for workers and allies together in the same programme may have failed. Nevertheless Labour leaders did not perceive their strategic choice about electoral platforms in the way that Przeworski and Sprague suggest: they did not accept that they had to follow a strategy designed almost exclusively for either workers or allies.

A second area for analysis concerns trends in class voting. Table 8.1 shows the increasing dependence of the Labour party on non-manual voters between 1959 and 1979 – a period in which the party's electoral strategy was predominantly moderate. Table 8.2 shows the share of manual and non-manual social classes voting Labour in the same period. It indicates that between 1959 and 1979 Labour's share of working-class votes declined. But this decline was not matched by an increase in Labour's share of non-manual votes: it remained at around 22 per cent of the electorate – a figure confirmed by other studies (Robertson 1984, p. 28). There was no substantial rise in the proportion of middle-class voters attracted to the party. If Labour leaders were pursuing an electoral strategy based on increasing the party's allies, it does not seem to have been successful.

Superimposed on these voting trends is the numerical decline of the working class as a percentage of the electorate which has inevitably made the Labour party more dependent upon middle-class voters. It might be charged that this process has meant that Labour has had to increase its

Table 8.1 Percentage of Labour vote drawn from non-manual and manual sections of the electorate

	Non-manual	Manual
1959	19	81
1964	18	82
1970	23	77
1974 (Feb)	25	75
1979	27	73

Source: Sarlvik and Crewe 1983, p. 90.

Table 8.2 Percentage of social class voting Labour

		Non-manual		Manual	
1959		22		62	
1964		22		64	
1970		25		58	
1974 (Feb)		22		57	
1979		23		50	
		ABC1	C2		DE
1979		22	42		49
1983		16	32		41
1987		18	36		41
	AB	C1	C2		DE
1992	19	25	40		49

Sources: For 1959–79, Sarlvik and Crewe 1983. For 1979–92, Butler and Kavanagh 1980; Butler and Kavanagh 1984; Butler and Kavanagh 1988; and Butler and Kavanagh 1992.

non-manual base and that its party leaders choose their electoral strategy accordingly. While Labour has had little success in increasing its share of non-manual voters, a strategy which sustained the support of allies at a constant rate might have been optimal if the share of electorate taken by allies was growing at a fast enough rate.

The decline in Labour's working-class support needs careful study. If Labour's decline among working-class voters from 64 per cent in 1964 to 50 per cent in 1979 was the result of a trade-off for middle-class votes, Labour actually lost twice as many workers' votes as it won by sustaining its share of the moderate electorate.[8] The trends in class voting are inconclusive but it appears that not only was Labour's moderation unsuccessful in increasing the party's share of the non-manual electorate, it was an irrational strategy for the leadership to pursue. They would have done better to concentrate on sustaining Labour's working-class base, rather than its middle-class support, even allowing for the decline in numbers of manual voters. If Przeworski and Sprague are correct about the trade-off in votes, it is puzzling that over several elections Labour leaders did not realise their errors and revert to a class-based strategy. An alternative explanation would suggest that working-class voters left Labour for a myriad of reasons, in spite of and not because of the party's moderation.

After 1979 Labour followed a more left-wing strategy (which some members of the party had advocated since 1970). Alongside radical policies, a series of constitutional reforms were implemented which strengthened the left within the party. While this left-wing electoral strategy might appear to have alienated middle-class voters at the 1983 election, there is no evidence that it succeeded in attracting back the support of workers previously disaffected by the party's moderation. Labour's support among workers fell at the 1983 election to its lowest postwar level. Since 1983, Labour's leadership has attempted to pursue a moderate trajectory aimed at attracting the support of workers and non-workers alike. As Table 8.2 shows, Labour has succeeded in rebuilding support among workers and allies at the same time, although electoral victory remains elusive.

The claim that workers have been alienated by social-democratic moderation is weakened by an analysis of those manual voters who continue to endorse Labour. It is the older working-class voters who have been most loyal to Labour in the postwar period. This group, made up of council-house tenants, members of unions and public-sector workers, stayed with the party during the 1970s and 1980s (Crewe 1983; Crewe 1987a; Butler and Kavanagh 1988, pp. 275–6; and Dunleavy and Husbands 1985). Yet it is this very cohort of voters which, according to Przeworski and Sprague's analysis, should be alienated from Labour. This group is diminishing as the changing class structure fragments the electorate and many new working-class voters are hostile to Labour. Such voters are likely to work in the private sector and non-unionised employment, live in the South of England and own their own homes. For a variety of reasons they are unlikely to vote Labour, but the party's moderation is of no concern to them.

What would working-class voters, alienated by Labour Party strategy, do? According to Przeworski and Sprague they have three options: abstain, endorse another class-based party or cease to vote on class terms. There is little evidence of workers either abstaining in protest or supporting more radical class-based parties. For example, there has been no increase in support for the Communist Party throughout the postwar period. Nor have British workers opted for religious or ethnic parties. Instead they have voted for more moderate parties, usually the Conservatives. It is unlikely that such a choice has been motivated by the belief that Labour has become too moderate or respectable. Workers, like allies, have abandoned Labour for reasons other than the party's moderation. One important factor has been their financial self-interest – ironically a point that Przeworski has discussed at length elsewhere (Przeworski 1985, pp. 136–44; see also Crewe 1987b; and Sanders 1992).

To establish that a trade-off between allies and workers is taking place, qualitative evidence is needed – the third area for consideration here. What grounds are there for concluding that workers have been alienated by Labour's moderation during the postwar period? Survey evidence of the attitudes of potential Labour voters is hard to come by and problematic in its status. The authors of one famous study, *Must Labour Lose?*, reached the opposite conclusion to *Paper Stones* (Abrams and Rose 1960). They claimed that Labour was antagonising workers, especially the young, by its failure to modernise. In a series of surveys at the same time it was surmised that electoral moderation was essential to rebuild the support of manual and non-manual voters alike (see Butler and King 1965, pp. 66–71). These surveys were contested but opponents did not adopt the kind of categoric arguments at the core of *Paper Stones*. In the 1980s there is evidence that voters were concerned by Labour's drift leftwards (Webb and Wybrow 1981; Webb and Wybrow 1982; and *Gallup Political Index* monthly). Such concerns were not confined to middle-class voters but extended to workers. Moreover, voters saw neither a shift from the party's class base nor a return to it as decisive factors in electoral alignments. Far more emphasis was placed by the electorate on Labour's divisions as a cause of the party's poor performance than on its ideological stance.

A last point for analysis concerns the voting decision itself. What evidence is there that voting decisions in the UK have been the result of party strategy? The theoretical literature and empirical research on this subject are extensive and unsurprisingly the conclusions are varied (Denver and Hands 1992). None adopt the stark version of the Przeworski and Sprague hypothesis that party strategy is the key cause of the voting decision. Labour leaders appear to have rejected decisively such a notion: between 1987 and 1992 they went to extreme lengths to mould the party's policy platform to the apparent desires of the median voter. The British case, at any rate, does not substantiate *Paper Stones*.

Britain may be a rogue case. It is not part of the statistical analysis in *Paper Stones*. The reason for this exclusion is technical and not substantive. Although the problems of Britain will be different, it seems unlikely that other European social democratic parties do not face some of the same difficulties. It is doubtful whether their problem is a narrow class trade-off, when those of the British Labour party are so wide. A contextual examination of the motivation of voters is required in addition to the statistical analysis upon which Przeworski and Sprague rely.

Paper Stones does not explain all the problems confronting social-democratic parties. Ironically, Przeworski has highlighted one of them elsewhere: the unpopularity and costs of socialism, discussed below. Although it receives no attention in *Paper Stones*, this problem is central to a consideration of the fortunes of social-democratic parties. In

Capitalism and Social Democracy Przeworski asserts that a major reason for the weakness of social democracy is the popularity of capitalism among workers. This theme – that the success of capitalism is the reason for social-democratic parties' problems – contradicts the stress in *Paper Stones* on the impasse of the class trade-off in votes.

In *Paper Stones*, the strategy of forming cross-class alliances by social-democratic parties costs these parties working-class votes. In *Capitalism and Social Democracy* workers' rational interests encourage them to grant consent to capitalism as a better way of satisfying their needs than is offered by a transition to socialism. It is not explained why workers do not rationally build cross-class alliances as the basis for constructing social-democratic governments to pursue gradualist reform policies with transformative outcomes. It appears that workers are rational economically (when looking to the future and accordingly form a compromise with capitalists) but not rational electorally (where they become quickly alienated by any attempt to widen the basis of support that a party requires in order to win elections). Since such support is needed for the party to win office (which was its initial attraction for workers) workers appear irrational. Why does rationality operate in one pursuit but not the other? Indeed, might not the history of Swedish social democracy indicate that worker rationality regarding cross-class alliances need not cost these parties working-class votes but in fact constitutes the basis for social-democratic success (Esping-Andersen 1984)? Furthermore, why do substantial numbers of workers continue to vote for socialist parties if they cannot deliver socialism? If Przeworski is correct about rational behaviour and about socialism then social democratic parties should do much worse electorally then their record indicates.

Przeworski and Sprague set a tough criterion for social democratic party success. The target of 51 per cent of the vote cast is a difficult one for any political party to obtain. The electoral system and constitutional order influence parties' behaviour and partly structure the success or failure of their electoral participation. In Britain no government since the Second World War has obtained a majority of the votes cast – in October 1974 Labour won a majority of seats with only 29 per cent of the electorate's votes. Social-democratic parties do not require 51 per cent of the vote to form governments: the recent history of the French, Spanish, Jamaican and Swedish parties confirms this conclusion. From a study of Swedish policies, Lewin argues that parties can hold office without an electoral majority through strategic log-rolling (Lewin 1988). Such possibilities release parties from the single-minded search for electoral dominance.

Przeworski's pessimism about the impasse of electoral social democracy is overstated. With regard to Britain, he is correct to suggest that social-democratic parties must be cross-class-based and reasonably moderate. But the argument that this strategic choice must cost working-class votes is unconfirmed. There is little evidence that parties have followed strategies which have alienated sections of the electorate at the expense of others. There is a paradox here: the problems of social-democratic parties are more numerous than Przeworski suggest, but they are not as severe as the one contradiction highlighted in *Paper Stones*.

CAPITALISM AND THE MATERIAL BASES OF CONSENT

The second theme from Przeworski's work to be addressed concerns the material bases of consent to capitalism (Przeworski 1985a, pp. 7–46, 133–204, 239–48). Many socialist writers, including Marx, considered winning the support of workers for a transition to socialism as unproblematic. Capitalism is exploitative: workers are not paid the full product of what they produce because surplus value is extracted from their labour which capitalists take as profits. Workers, aware of this exploitation, do all they reasonably can to change these arrangements, including promoting socialism. In this view the outcome of capitalist economic relations is class conflict as rational workers follow their objective interest (Przeworski 1985a, pp. 133–4, 171).

Przeworski disputes this analysis: far from it, he argues, many workers endorse capitalism, not socialism. He claims that the continued legitimacy of any society depends on its ability to meet basic material needs. The endurance of capitalism is founded neither on 'false consciousness' nor on coercion (Przeworski 1985a, p. 3). It is based on capitalists' ability to meet the material needs of workers. Przeworski concludes that workers rationally support capitalism because of the material benefits it provides.

Workers want high material incomes, not just in the present but also in the future. They are therefore rational to discount some present income if such forfeits lead to higher future returns. But, Przeworski suggests, higher future incomes depend, in a capitalist economy, upon present investment: 'development cannot take place in the long run unless a part of the product is withheld from immediate consumption and allocated to increase productivity' (Przeworski 1985, p. 138). The two crucial variables in his model of the economy are: first, the share of national income that workers receive as wages; and second, the rate at which capitalists choose to invest after they have received the remainder of national income. Przeworski suggests that workers have the ability to determine the former variable, while capitalists choose the latter. Accordingly workers have a powerful reason for wage moderation: the lower the share of national income that they take in immediate wages, the more capital available for investment. The higher the share of potential investment that capitalists plough back, the higher future national product will be. The higher national product is in the future, then the higher wages will be.

This straightforward relationship between wages and investment sustains a class compromise between workers and employers. Workers agree to low wages because they will benefit from higher future incomes. The share of national product taken by wages will remain stable but higher growth means that workers' incomes will rise. Capitalists will sustain investment because they too benefit from growth in the form of future profits. Przeworski's model is similar to a neoclassical model of the economy where capitalists and workers can cooperate in a market economy to everyone's benefit.

Economic growth depends on three factors: the level of profits in national income, the rate of investment and the capital–output ratio (the productivity of capital).[9] Przeworski is unconcerned with the latter: it is implicitly seen as a function of the other two variables. As a result growth in a capitalist economy 'varies proportionately to the rate of profit and the rate of saving out of profit' (Przeworski 1985, p. 179). Accordingly, to maximise future wages, workers should not strike or erode profit levels but allow capitalists to make high returns: 'if wages are to increase in the future, a part of the societal product and the associated authority to organise production must pass out of the control of immediate producers' (Przeworski 1985, p. 139). In this model class conflict is neither inevitable nor rational. Indeed, militancy does not benefit workers. If they either strike or make threats of further action, they may be able to increase their wages in the short term. But higher wages mean lower profits and less investment. Less investment means slower growth and less product to be distributed in the future. Wages will fall.

Under the class compromise, capitalists are dominant. They control investment through profits and through their ownership of the means of production. By making the crucial decisions regarding the rate of investment, they control the future well-being of society and assume general rather than particularistic interests. Moreover, because of their stocks of wealth, capitalists can, unlike workers, withstand economic crises. This set of relationships means that 'the entire society is structurally dependent upon the actions of capitalists' (Przeworski 1985, p. 139). The powerful position of capitalists and the control they hold over investment and future growth influence workers to compromise and to accept profit as a legitimate return to employers.

Any class compromise can break down. If wages or profits fall, either workers or employers may cease to cooperate. They may also cease to participate if they are suspicious of the motives and likely future action of the others. Such a situation will precipitate an economic crisis which will further endanger the compromise. Przeworski states: 'if wages fall below the minimal level and/or profits are not sufficient to reproduce consent and to allow future profits, a crisis must ensue' (Przeworski 1985, p. 157). Rational workers are aware of the costs of economic crisis and this knowledge will influence any assessment of the compromise. Not only do workers benefit materially from the compromise, they want to ensure the future, free from economic crisis: such crises 'are a threat to wage-earners since capitalism is a system in which economic crises must inevitably fall on their shoulders' (Przeworski 1985, p. 43).

Workers will opt rationally for capitalism over socialism for a further reason. Socialism involves redistribution, at the very least, from employers to workers, more probably the loss of power by capitalists. Socialist policies are therefore a threat and capitalists will counter by disinvesting, an action which will precipitate economic crisis. Przeworski notes 'a transition to socialism must therefore generate an economic crisis. Investment falls sharply, prices increase, nominal wage gains become eroded and eventually output falls, demand slackens, unemployment reappears as a major problem' (Przeworski 1985a, p. 46). Even if socialism is potentially better for workers' welfare in the long run, they may not opt for it because the material costs in realising it are prohibitive: 'if the transition to socialism involves a deterioration of workers' welfare and if workers have an option of improving their material conditions by cooperating with capitalists, then the socialist orientation cannot be deduced from the material interests of workers' (Przeworski 1985a, p. 177).

AN ASSESSMENT OF THE MATERIAL BASES OF CONSENT

Several questions arise from Przeworski's account of the class compromise (Freeman 1989). First, do workers perceive wage negotiations and approach them in the way that Przeworski's model suggests? Second, are workers in a position to moderate their wage demands? And third, are capitalists so sensitive to wage levels when they make decisions about investment? Does disinvestment occur in the way Przeworski claims? Central to these issues is the question of the class compromise itself. Przeworski treats workers and capitalists as single actors able to act collectively.

Przeworski claims that workers, realising wage moderation is in their long-term interest, will restrain their wage demands. This argument assumes that workers and capitalists are able to reach broad agreement over the appropriate division of national income between wages and profits. However, the distribution of national income has proved contentious, the subject of considerable antagonism between workers and their employers. In postwar Britain, workers have doubted that higher wages would damage investment and maintained that incomes could rise considerably without harming future growth. They have repeatedly claimed to be underpaid and exploited: As one trade unionist put it at the 1977 TUC Congress 'I believe that I have the right to expect the sort of wages so that I, too, can pay my rent, support a family, and enjoy all the pleasures of ordinary life' (TUC 1977, p. 476). Workers have also disagreed with employers over the suitable level of investment. At the same Congress one union leader, Ken Gill, stated:

> we gave them [capitalists] high profits .... but what did they do with them? The rich beneficiaries of our recent policies did not oblige us. They conformed to their normal patterns and what we got is decaying factories in Manchester, brand new plants in Johannesburg and office blocks in Brusssels (TUC 1977, p. 479).

In the face of high levels of capitalist consumption and profits not reinvested, workers have pressed for higher wages. Union leader Terry Duffy told the 1978 Labour Party Conference: 'it is clear that the workers have not benefited from wage restraint...but will they [capitalists] invest? In real terms investment now is less than in 1970. This is despite record profits being raked in by almost every major company in the first three months of this year' (Labour Party 1978, p. 215). In brief, workers' assessments of the appropriate share of wages have differed fundamentally from those of capitalists.

Workers make wage demands in the face of considerable uncertainty and risk. They need to know the likelihood that profits will be reinvested, that any investment will produce dividends, and that present wage moderation will generate satisfactory future incomes. Workers must assess the likely state of the future economy. As a result of such anticipations, workers may have several different strategies by which to maximise wages. Moreover, there will be differences between firms throughout the economy: individual companies with varied profit rates and production costs will bear contrasting wage demands. In many situations workers are likely to be concerned with pushing up their real wages as 'insiders' rather than gambling on long-term payoffs (Lindbeck and Snower 1989).

Workers do not approach wage negotiations concerned purely with future levels of investment. Wage demands do not reflect anticipations of forthcoming economic growth alone. Workers are also likely to take account of such matters as wage drift, inflation, government macroeconomic policy, managerial power, and general working conditions. Within the UK, wage differentials have proved a major issue, one which has severely limited state-sponsored attempts at wage moderation (Taylor 1993). Przeworski's class compromise does not examine the difficulties such schemes encounter as groups of workers attempt to sustain and even widen differentials. A further determinant of wage levels realised through collective bargaining has been the state of the labour market. Where markets have been tight, workers have pushed up wages rather than waited for long-term benefits stemming from higher investment. In the UK in the early 1980s rapidly accelerating levels of unemployment played a part in bringing down wage settlements at a time of high inflation.

Periods of wage moderation in the UK have resulted from political initiatives (Fishbein 1984; Panitch 1976). Various governments have provided the impetus to moderation and the machinery to achieve it, in the form of incomes policy. Przeworski notes the role of the state in sustaining any class compromise (Przeworski 1985, p. 202). In Britain the state has not simply sustained any compromise; rather it has attempted unsuccessfully to initiate it.

The result of this range of factors is that workers may not have such a positive conception either of wage moderation or of the legitimacy of profits. They may be unable to reach agreement with employers over the appropriate share for wages. Having taken other factors into account they may not be inclined towards wage moderation at all. Workers have often concluded that there is scope for wage increases and pressed for their realisation. Capitalists have resisted such pressures, hoping to minimise costs. The postwar experience of collective bargaining in the UK does not indicate any trend towards a permanent class compromise. Pay negotiations have been antagonistic and contentious; strikes and industrial unrest have been commonplace. Workers have challenged capitalist claims about the level of profits required for investment, and historical evidence suggests they may well have been correct in their conviction that there was scope for wages to rise. The share of national income consumed by wages and salaries rose in Britain from 47 per cent between 1860 and 1869 to 70 per cent by 1960 (Van Der Wee 1985, p. 240). Workers have increased their share of national income without the kind of catastrophic damage to investment levels that the class compromise model predicts.

In many countries, workers do not negotiate their wage settlements *en masse*. Instead wage negotiation takes place at several levels, for example at an individual plant or firm and at different times throughout the year. If workers are to restrain their demands, they must know what the wage-setting decisions of other workers across the economy will be, now and in the future. The atomisation of wage negotiation leads to a prisoners' dilemma for workers and unions, raising the question as to whether they are in a position to moderate wage demands (Lange 1984). There are two aspects to the prisoners' dilemma. First, what prevents some workers from free-riding and extracting large wage increases from their employers, in the knowledge that the majority of workers are accepting moderate wage claims? The real income of free-riders will rise relatively as they benefit from the growth (and job opportunities) generated by moderation elsewhere. Second, how can workers be certain that others will conform with a wage moderation agreement? If they are moderate and others are not, then there is a cost to them since other workers' wages will increase while future growth, necessary for future benefits, will not materialise.

The prisoners' dilemma is illustrated by the Labour government's attempt to moderate wages voluntarily after 1974 (Boston 1985). From July 1974, under the Social Contract agreed between the TUC and the Labour Party, workers were to exercise voluntary wage restraint in order to control inflation and support the 'social wage' policies of the Labour government. This attempt at unenforced restraint failed. Each group of workers was forced to better the pay settlement of the last group to settle, so that their real income did not fall as inflation accelerated. The result was a rapid inflationary spiral. Workers did not want this outcome but had little option other than to claim large increases to prevent incurring the costs of wage moderacy at a time when others were not restrained.

Such are the risks of moderation and the potential benefits of militancy, under atomised wage negotiation, that workers may not be able to chance settling for restrained wage increases. As Boston points out, in such circumstances there is a risk that 'unless the vast majority of unions also choose to exercise restraint voluntary pay moderation will be "rewarded" with a loss of real income and a fall in the position of the union's members in the wage hierarchy' (Boston 1985, p. 69). It is difficult for workers to act collectively in promoting the public good of wage moderation. John Bowman has analysed the parallel problems that capitalists face in promoting the collective good of stable prices from which they might benefit (Bowman 1989).

In Przeworski's model, capitalists are extraordinarily sensitive to wage increases when making investment decisions. While wage levels will have an impact on investment it is less apparent that they are as important as Przeworski suggests. In orthodox economic theory capitalists will invest where profitable opportunities exist. The level of investment is likely to be determined by two factors, the rate of return and the rate of interest (or the cost of capital to make the investment – see Backhouse 1991, p. 51). Wage rates are one factor influencing the rate of return; other factors such as production costs and the demand for the finished product are also important.

Investment is not determined by wage levels alone. For a variety of reasons, capitalists may continue to invest despite higher wages. The rate of return may remain attractive if higher wages are offset by lower production costs elsewhere or productivity deals. If the potential investment represents the best return available, capitalists are likely to sustain investment even if profits have fallen somewhat due to higher wages. (Similarly if capitalists can get a better return elsewhere, then they will divert their capital and investment will fall, regardless of wage levels.) Through investment, firms may seek to alter the capital–output ratio and improve the productivity of capital while making themselves less dependent upon labour. Capitalists will also be concerned with the demand for the product they produce. Unless there is adequate purchasing power, profits cannot be realised. In the mid-1980s employers continued to invest in the UK despite rising wages. Employers with different production costs are likely to respond to wage demands in various ways. Moreover, in a competitive market, individual capitalists cannot afford to forgo investment opportunities (provided they are remotely profitable): to do so would be to lose market shares. In sum, there is no straightforward relationship between wages and investment.

The stark conclusions which Przeworski reaches about the rational choices of workers concerning capitalism derive from the assumptions of his model. He assumes that future wages and growth depend upon high investment and profits alone. Alternative models of growth, for example stressing either the role of demand or assuming investment levels less sensitive to rising wages or even accepting a role for public investment, would produce different conclusions about the necessity for wage moderation. The model of the class compromise produces a misleading picture of contemporary capitalism. Capitalists and workers do not agree about the division of national product. The fragmented nature of wage negotiation in the UK has made voluntary coordination by the relevant actors problematic. Wage negotiations, profit levels and investment decisions remain controversial and disputed. Throughout the postwar period, workers have not necessarily opted for either moderation or capitalism. They may see benefits in social democratic reforms which limit capitalist exploitation and result in a more equitable distribution of national product. Capitalism's endurance is due neither to repression nor to false consciousness. But it does not reflect rational endorsement by workers. Consent may be much more passive, more tentative and more contingent that the class-compromise approach implies.

THE FAILURE OF SOCIAL DEMOCRATIC ECONOMIC MANAGEMENT

The third theme to be examined is social-democratic economic management (Przeworski 1985a, pp. 7–46, 239–48; and Przeworski 1990a, pp. 92–6). Przeworski argues that capitalist society imposes major constraints on the freedom of action of social-democratic governments. He notes that the advent of Keynesian economic policy after the Depression of the 1930s appeared to enable social democrats to manage the economy successfully at the same time as they implemented radical reforms. Przeworski goes on to claim that such a social-democratic economic strategy based on Keynesianism was contradictory. Other than in the most contingent of circumstances, it could not reconcile economic growth with social-democratic measures within a capitalist economy. Social democrats attempt to control markets and tax capitalists to fund reforms. At the same time economic growth requires capitalists to have freedom to invest and funds upon which to draw. According to Przeworski, the production of wealth must be given priority and commitments to social democracy jettisoned.

Przeworski's conclusion is reached as follows. Profits are the basis of any future growth (via investment) and social democratic governments, just like workers, are dependent upon them. As noted earlier, Przeworski claims that the well-being of society depends upon the investment decisions of private capitalists and that capitalists enjoy a special position which accords them immense power. Any government, social-democratic or not, requires material growth and a prosperous economy. Policies which might damage economic well-being must be avoided because capitalists would respond to them with disinvestment. In a market economy profits must be protected: 'if profits are not sufficient then eventually wages or employment must fall' (Przeworski 1985, p. 43).

Social-democratic reforms will damage investment: they will require taxation reducing the capital funds available to employers. Far-reaching reforms will create a climate of uncertainty in which capitalists will not take risks or invest. The result of any attempt to introduce social-democratic reforms into a capitalist economy will be that less is available for investment because of lower profits. The rate of investment will fall and growth will decline: 'no government can simultaneously reduce profits and increase investment' (Przeworski 1990a, p. 93). It is likely that an economic crisis will occur as capitalists disinvest to avoid social-democratic reforms.

A social-democratic government must consider carefully the impact reforms will have on investment and the health of the economy. Przeworski states: 'since profits are private, the decisions of individual capitalists concerning the volumes and direction of investment condition the effectiveness of interventions by the state and must be anticipated' (Przeworski 1985, p. 42). Social democrats will be forced to take steps to sustain profits, even if it means forsaking reforms. Przeworski writes: 'when in office they [social democrats] are forced to behave like any other party, relying on deflationary, cost cutting measures to ensure private profitability and the capacity to invest' (Przeworski 1985a, p. 41).

Such is the pre-eminence of capitalists in the economy, reflecting their control of investment, that only policies acceptable to them can be implemented. Governments will not increase taxes if the result is lower investment and poor growth, perhaps even an economic crisis. The implication of Przeworski's model is a negative inverse relationship between taxation and investment. The structural power of capitalists is so great that the state is unable to increase taxation. Przeworski argues that both governments and capitalists recognise this situation. The state knows that it cannot avoid detrimental results if it attempts reforms and therefore does not implement such policies. Capitalists know that they can determine policy outcomes and they make threats to prevent the state from adopting redistributive taxation.

One solution to the structural dependence of the state on capitalists would be for a government to adopt a taxation policy which penalised consumption by capitalists and encouraged, through allowances, investment. Such a policy might encourage capitalists to sustain investment while reforms were introduced. Przeworski accepts that such a strategy may be possible (Przeworski and Wallerstein 1982b). However, he also suggests definite limits to such an approach: capitalists resent such intrusions by the state.

More radical measures, such as nationalisation policies, face the same dilemma as moderate ones. Przeworski states:

measures of nationalisation, distribution of land and monopolization of credit and foreign exchange by the state threaten the very institution of private profit. Under such circumstances, rational private capitalists will not invest. No political organization and no conspiracy is even necessary; rational entrepreneurs do not invest if the return on investment is expected to be zero or negative and when the risk is high (Przeworski 1985a, p. 45).

The state does not have the power to challenge capitalists and lacks the support of workers to do so.

Przeworski is not alone in outlining the theory of the structural dependence of the state. Similar arguments are formulated by Fred Block, Ralph Miliband and Charles Lindblom (Block 1987; Miliband 1969; Lindblom 1977). In an early version Charles Taylor concluded:

> the motor of the system is after all profit, the private accumulation of capital. If we impose very heavy taxes, we are syphoning off the fuel from this motor.... At a certain point we will tax the private sector so heavily that we will affect its capacity (or more important its willingness) to invest (Taylor 1960, p. 11).

Przeworski's conclusion is unequivocal:

> the very capacity of social democrats to regulate the economy depends upon the profitability of the private sector and the willingness of capitalists to co-operate. This is the structural barrier which cannot be broken: the limit of any policy is that investment and thus profits must be protected in the long run (Przeworski 1985, p. 42).

He presents a seemingly unyielding logic as the trajectory of social-democratic choices has unfolded. Social democrats end up attempting to manage the economy in as humane a fashion as possible. Moreover they come to accept such realities: they abandon radical reforms and even moderate redistribution.

MUST CAPITALISTS DISINVEST?

The key questions provoked by Przeworski's analysis are straightforward: first, must social-democratic policies lead to disinvestment by capitalists and economic crisis? Second, will a lower rate of profit always be resisted by capitalists to the extent of provoking an economic crisis? In terms of Przeworski's rational choice assumptions the answer to these questions is yes. Higher taxes mean lower profits and no rational capitalist will accept such an outcome.

Capitalists need not always react in such a way. One of the core features of social-democratic Keynesianism is that it overcomes some of the uncertainty inherent in capitalist economies (Bleaney 1984, p. 130). If there is insufficient demand, Keynesian theory suggests that the state will be able to manipulate demand to boost employment. This commitment by the state benefits capitalists: they are assured of sales, since demand will be maintained. Profits will be reasonably certain. The rate of profit may be lower because of taxes but potential profits are likely to be realised. The element of risk or contingency reserve for the future in high profits can be discounted. Capitalists will not need high profits now to offset lower profits in the future since they are confident about the future. The rate of profit will fall but the absolute volume need not.

The contribution of state spending to the economy should not be underestimated. According to Keynesian theory, state spending generates demand and this demand will encourage investment (see the discussion in O'Connor 1973). By improving the performance of the economy, the state's policy will benefit capitalists. State investment may also contribute directly to growth. There may be limits to the extent that capitalists benefit from public finances but the relationship is more complex than Przeworski suggests. There is no automatic inverse relationship between taxation and investment: state investment and state spending, financed from taxation, can contribute towards growth in a capitalist economy. Consider the opposite situation: when governments deflate, demand falls and firms cut investment, a pattern apparent in the 1979–81 recession in the UK.

In Przeworski's model the capitalist behaves in a predetermined way. However, capitalists have to make decisions in each situation they confront: they must consider the potential powers of the state and its likely behaviour. They must assess the likelihood of any possible outcome. If the state has reserve powers, for example, increased central control or nationalisation, as a threat towards those who disinvest, then capitalists must calculate the probability of the state implementing such measures. If state control or nationalisation is a likely response, capitalists will be careful in deciding to cut investment. Nationalisation means that the capitalist would suffer a much greater loss than would be incurred from higher taxes. It is rational to accept lower profits and avoid appropriation by the state. The capitalist need not be as structurally powerful as Przeworski's model implies.

Disinvestment is costly and will not be undertaken lightly. It may mean abandoning expensive plant and equipment. Depending on alternative investment options, it may result in lower future growth and hence lower profits. The capitalist has to compare slightly lower future profits (from higher taxes) with much lower future profits from disinvestment, lower growth and possibly economic crisis. A rational capitalist will opt for slightly lower profits rather than provoke an economic crisis. The capitalist may look back with fondness to higher profits in the past and regret the reforms but it would be irrational to disinvest as a protest if such actions would lead to even lower profits. Given the cost of 'exit', in Albert Hirschman's framework, many capitalists may resort instead to 'voice' as a means of indicating their discontent (Hirschman 1970).

These possible outcomes arise from strategic decisions by capitalists and by governments of the sort associated with game theory. Under Przeworski's assumptions the game between capitalists and social democrats has only one possible outcome. The capitalists announce their intention to disinvest if the state increases taxes or introduces measures of nationalisation. This declaration (and the possibility of economic disarray) obliges the state to abandon any radical policies. However, it may be possible for the state to announce its taxation increases or nationalisations as binding commitments before the capitalists' investment decisions are known. If the state is resolute, capitalists may feel obliged to maintain investment despite these public policies in order to avoid the worst possible outcome of economic crisis and drastically lower profits. Different outcomes result from the strategic choices of the actors and the power that they exercise. Capitalists may not always secure their preferred outcome.

It is even possible that the worst possible outcome can result because both sides are uncertain about the other's action and call each other's bluff. If capitalists disinvest and the state implements its social democratic policies, economic crisis may result from which all will suffer. Both sides are aware of such an outcome and will seek to avoid it. Rational capitalists will consider such an eventuality before acting: David Vogel concludes that, 'managers and owners are hardly likely to deliberately slow down [sic] the economy or reduce their company's profits so that their lobbyists can become more effective' (Vogel 1989, p. 293). Suboptimal outcomes may occur as the following example illustrates.[10]

Assume the preference orderings shown in Table 8.3 and note the matrix generated from them. In this stylized game, the state and capitalists must set levels of taxation and investment respectively. Capitalists want to ensure tax-free investments, while social democrats want to generate funds for reforms and redistribution. If capitalists and the state both pursue their

Table 8.3 Preference orderings of capitalists and the state

Capitalists' preferences			State's preferences		
Capitalist action	State action		Capitalist action	State action	
Invest	Don't tax	4	Invest	Tax	4
Don't invest	Don't tax	3	Invest	Don't Tax	3
Invest	Tax	2	Don't invest	Don't tax	2
Don't invest	Tax	1	Don't invest	Tax	1

The Matrix

		State	
		Tax	Don't tax
Capitalists	Invest	2, 4	4, 3
	Don't invest	1, 1	3, 2

optimal preference (4) then the solution to the matrix is found in the bottom left quadrant with suboptimal results for both actors (with possible economic crisis). Przeworski's model assumes a dominant solution, in the top right quadrant, where capitalists invest and the state chooses not to tax. Under the assumptions here this outcome is difficult to attain and would be unstable. In such a situation the state could improve its desired outcome by introducing taxation. Different assumptions about the preferences of the relevant actors lead to conclusions different to those of Przeworski. The matrix detailed above has no dominant solution or equilibrium. In order to make a maximising choice, each actor has to make a judgement about the probable choice of the other player. It is not apparent why the capitalists must always win when bargaining with the state. Capitalists' strengths are conditional, not structural: in some situations they may be forced to accept the policies of the state rather than provoke additional losses of profits.

Consider capitalist investment patterns under recent social democratic governments in the United Kingdom. In 1965 the Labour Government introduced corporation tax which reorganised the taxes that capitalists paid on profits. Within a year of its introduction, the revenue raised on profits rose by 250 per cent (Butler and Butler 1986). The rate of profit continued to fall as it had done steadily since the early 1950s. The post-tax rate of profit fell from 6.3 per cent in 1965 to 4.3 per cent the following year (Aaronovitch and Smith 1981, p. 290).

Under Przeworski's analysis, sharp disinvestment should have followed. However, despite falling profit rates, gross investment continued to rise (see Table 8.4). Allowing for the low inflation of this period, investment did not behave in the way that Przeworski anticipates. Historical evidence indicates a steady trend in manufacturing investment, a trend not inversely related to the profit rate (see *Economic Progress Report* 1988). Although capitalists faced lower profit rates, due in part to government taxes, they continued to increase the rate at which they invested. Gross fixed capital formation per head of the labour-force in manufacturing rose from $334 in 1960 to $460 in 1965 and $604 in 1970 (Aaronovitch and Smith 1981, p. 279). Capitalists were prepared to accept lower profit rates because the economy was still growing: the volume or absolute total of profits continued to rise. Despite lower profit rates, investment was not unattractive. This analysis applies to the period since the early 1960s in general: profit

Table 8.4 Profits and investment in the UK

	Pre-tax rate of return	Share of profits in GDP	Gross investment (£ bn, 1975 prices)
1963	11.4	14.9	13.3
1964	11.9	15.0	15.5
1965	11.2	14.5	16.2
1966	9.9	13.2	16.6
1967	10.0	13.2	18.1
1968	10.1	12.9	18.9
1969	9.9	12.8	19.0
1970	8.6	11.9	19.5
1971	8.9	12.6	19.7
1972	9.3	12.6	19.8
1973	9.1	12.5	21.2
1974	6.0	9.2	20.6
1975	5.2	8.3	20.4
1976	5.5	9.0	20.6
1977	6.9	13.0	20.1
1978	7.2	13.5	20.8
1979	5.2	12.6	21.0
1980	3.6	11.5	20.4
1981	2.7	10.7	18.8

Source: J. Backhouse 1983, pp. 209, 223.

rates fell but investment grew from 14.6 per cent of GDP between 1950 and 1959 and 19.3 between 1974 and 1979 (Crafts and Woodward 1991, p. 10; see also Hodgson 1981, p. 156). Capitalists exchanged high but uncertain profits for the stability of Keynesian policy and economic growth.

The 1974–79 Labour government was elected on a far-reaching programme of income redistribution, increased taxes and a radical strategy of public ownership for major profitable firms in the economy. The strategy was intentionally antagonistic to capitalists: alongside public ownership it contained proposals for sweeping interventions in the economy including the introduction of planning agreements between the state and private firms (Holland 1975).

In office, Labour enacted several of these plans. Corporation tax was increased in the first budget of 1974 as was income tax upon higher earnings. The method of payments of corporation taxes was tightened and allowances were reduced. At the same time the government began work on a White Paper outlining its industrial strategy. When published in August 1974, *The Regeneration of British Industry* contained proposals for a National Enterprise Board, planning agreements and increased public ownership. These proposals were intended to shift wealth and power to working people at the expense of capitalists. The government increased taxation and the share of national income absorbed by the state sector. Profit rates fell heavily between 1973 and 1974 and into 1975. The Confederation of British Industry were clearly unhappy with the proposals, attacking the March 1974 budget tax-changes and denouncing the White Paper on industrial strategy (Whitehead 1985). These views were hardly surprising. Did capitalists cut investment as Przeworski's model predicts they would?

There was a small fall in investment in 1974. However, capital investment expenditure in manufacturing rose from £3440 million pounds in 1973 to £3782 in 1974. This rise was offset by a fall in investment in the distribution and service industries (OECD 1980, p. 56).[11] The trend was supported by increased gross fixed capital formation per head in manufacturing industries which grew from $741 in 1973 to $920 in 1974 and $1006 in 1975 (Aaronovitch and Smith 1981, p. 279). Even allowing for inflation, capitalist investment does not represent, in the face of socialist policies, the pattern Przeworski's model predicts. Neither the anticipation of a Labour government nor the rise in taxes by Labour when in office produced any marked disinvestment. The fall in investment that did occur was attributable to the miners' strikes, the three-day week and the general downturn in the world economy after the oil price increase (Artis, Cobham and Wickham-Jones 1992). This pattern is borne out by the investment intentions of business industry. Even in the summer of 1974 investment intentions in manufacturing showed a growth of 5 per cent (see *Economic Trends* during 1974).

Despite a fall in business confidence, capitalists did not disinvest. They recognised that disinvestment would have major costs for them: it would involve the loss of machinery and accentuate the economic crisis from which they would suffer. Capitalists relied on 'voice' rather than 'exit' to express their concerns over government economic policy. They realised the costs of disinvesting and adjusted their actions accordingly. Despite a variety of adverse conditions which affected profits detrimentally, they continued to invest.

CONCLUSIONS

In more recent work Przeworski has modified his arguments about the structural limitations of social democratic governments (Przeworski 1990a, pp. 94–6). Together with Michael Wallerstein, he claims that a strong labour movement, able to control the movement of capital, may be able, through the taxation of uninvested income, to introduce social-democratic reforms without provoking economic crisis. They conclude that 'virtually any distribution of consumption between wage earners and shareholders is compatible with continual private investment' (Przeworski and Wallerstein 1988, p. 24). Elsewhere Przeworski pronounces himself uncertain about the structural dependence of the state: 'My view is that all governments are to some degree dependent on capital but that this dependence is not so binding as to make democracy a sham' (Przeworski 1991, p. 14).

Despite these modifications, Przeworski remains pessimistic about the social democratic prospect. In an open economy, one where governments cannot control capital movements, social democracy remains vulnerable. Przeworski argues that capitalists are likely to anticipate social-democratic reforms in the period before their introduction. They will disinvest either before an election victory or during the drafting of legislation, thereby provoking economic crisis. Only in very specific circumstances might social-democratic reforms be possible. The account presented here suggests, in contrast, that there are more general reasons as to why a social-democratic government prepared to implement reforms may be successful in persuading capitalists who wish to avoid the costs of disinvestment to accept redistributive measures.

Przeworski's analysis of social democracy is stimulating and provocative. His introduction of rigorous argument into discussion of the political economy of Western democracies and of capital–labour relations is welcome. His arguments highlight the serious problems that social democrats face in winning elections and managing the economy. His account outlines the difficult choices that social democrats must confront to achieve even limited reforms. However, Przeworski has not demonstrated the inevitable failure of social democracy. While social democrats encounter dilemmas, modified assumptions within the rational choice framework yield conclusions which are not as pessimistic as those laid out by Przeworski. There are theoretical and historical reasons for rejecting the apparently hopeless and fatalistic conclusions he reaches.

The experience of social-democratic governments in postwar Britain does not fit Przeworski's structural dependence model. The interaction of the state, workers and capitalists has not occurred in the way his model implies. Nor are investment, profits, wages and taxes related in practice as they are in the formal model. Elsewhere the historical record of social democracy is neither as weak nor as indistinct from capitalist societies as Przeworski implies. Social democratic parties have won power in a variety of European countries. In office they have raised living standards and introduced reforms.[12] If social democracy's record was as poor and as structurally dependent upon capitalism as Przeworski claims, social-democratic ideas should have been marginalised as an electoral and political force. That they have not been is testament to the perceptions and choices of workers and others.

NOTES

1. This chapter is a modified version of a paper which appeared as 'Review Article: Social Democracy and Rational Workers', in the *British Journal of Political Science* 20 (1990), pp. 387–413.
2. For example, one other theme central to Przeworski's work is a consideration of Michels' 'iron law of oligarchy' (Przeworski 1985a, p. 14; and Przeworski and Sprague 1986, pp. 19–20).
3. Note Przeworski's definition of workers as those employed in productive industries (Przeworski 1985a, p. 104; Przeworski and Sprague 1986, p. 34).
4. As does the very act of electoral participation (Przeworski and Sprague 1986, pp. 19–21, 50–53).
5. Przeworski and Sprague accept that some policies do not involve a trade-off but do not explore the possibilities of such proposals.

6. Contrast Przeworski and Sprague 'thus the fact of voting.... cannot be treated as a result of a decision made by each individual separately and independently from the past each time' (1986, p. 147), with Przeworski once again on the hypothetical Mrs Jones, 'she has objectives and resources: she chooses to become a worker' (1985a, p. 99).
7. A point made in Michael Burawoy's chapter in this collection, 'Marxism without Micro-Foundations' (see also Kitschelt 1993, p. 322).
8. If Labour had taken 64 per cent of working-class votes in 1979, it would have won over two million more votes. The increase in its middle-class base between 1964 and 1979, from the growing middle-class share of the electorate, brought it under one million more.
9. It is assumed that workers' savings are negligible and that state spending is unproductive (see Przeworski 1985a, p. 179).
10. In this example we assume that capitalists are able to solve the collective action problems they might face and we treat them as a unitary actor.
11. Figures quoted are in 1975 prices. OECD data indicate that a much more severe fall in manufacturing investment occurred between 1979 and 1981 under a Conservative government than between 1974 and 1975. Capital expenditure on manufacturing fell in 1980 prices, from £7495 million pounds in 1979 to £6479 million pounds in 1980 and £4865 million pounds in 1981 (see OECD 1987). Investment remained stable in distribution and services. Przeworski's model does not explain why capitalists were shifting investment from manufacturing to these other sectors.
12. Contrast, for example, the 29 per cent of the aged who lived in poverty in the UK during the late 1980s with the 1 per cent who did so in Sweden (see Anderson 1992, p. 326).

9 Marx and Methodological Individualism
Mark E. Warren

In this chapter I pursue two projects, one critical and one reconstructive. The critical project concerns Jon Elster's influential and controversial argument that methodological individualism guides the acceptable aspects of Marx's thought.[1] Elster's claim is interesting not just because it breaks with the widely held notion that Marx's thinking does not involve methodological individualism in any sense,[2] but also because he uses it to focus on the 'microfoundations' of Marx's claims about social causalities.[3] Marx provides an exemplary account of how to unravel the complex of relations between situated individual actions and their unintended outcomes, relations through which social and historical forces gain their quasi-independent logics. By taking this approach, Elster writes, Marx was able to transform the insight of his predecessors from Vico to Hegel 'that history is the result of human action, but not human design ... from a *Weltanschauung* into a scientific methodology' (Elster 1985, p. 27).

At the same time, Elster argues that Marx did not always follow through on his methodology, often failing to elaborate relations between individual actions and social outcomes. This in part accounts for the fact that so many Marxists use concepts that refer to 'collective actors' such as classes or states, as if these entities had aims and intentions with an autonomous explanatory power.[4] Elster's own project is to provide an account of the implicit microfoundations of Marx's work through rational actor theory, and this is what motivates him to read Marx in light of methodological individualism.

In part because of the intrinsic importance of the problem, in part because of the increasing popularity of rational actor approaches within Marxism,[5] it is worthwhile to look at how Elster conceptualises and defends methodological individualism in Marx, as well as to look at what Marx, and to a lesser extent Max Weber, had to say of relevance to the issue. I argue that although Elster is right to characterise Marx as methodological individualist in *some* sense, he is wrong about the sense for which he argues.[6] His version of methodological individualism fails to relate intentional properties of individuals (in this case, their propensity to rationally maximise) to emergent social properties such as rule-governed languages, cultures, and ideologies. It is also uncritical: because it treats intentional properties axiomatically, it can transform contingent patterns of intentionality into natural ones. For both reasons, Elster misses key and enduring aspects of Marx's method. In contrast both to those who deny methodological individualism altogether and to Elster's version, I argue for a methodological individualism that is critical and compatible with certain kinds of non-reductionist social explanations, while retaining Elster's concern with 'micro-foundations'. I shall also argue that this is the version exemplified in Marx's and Weber's writings.

Part of what is at stake here are different ideas about what counts as an explanation. I want to argue that the issue has been mistakenly conceived as if explanations in terms of social and individual concepts are mutually exclusive.[7] This polarity has had an unfortunate effect when applied to Marx. Commentators who emphasise the irreducibly social aspects of Marx's concepts often reify them in structural concepts. They are then unable to relate their explanations to the historically situated, intentional practices of individuals.[8] In contrast, Elster's attempt to reduce structural concepts to individual ones leaves us unable to explain the intentional properties of individuals, or so I shall argue. Part of the reason that the terms of the debate have been so unsatisfactory is that its participants have failed to relate the methodological issues to questions of social ontology, often implicitly relying on an ontology that abstractly polarises individual and social predicates. One result is that aspects of Marx's method that do not fit this ontology are missed, distorted, or ignored.

The stakes are not only explanatory, however. There are normative dimensions of methodological individualism that are rarely explicated in the literature.[9] I suggest here that different individual-level concepts have different normative implications. I am interested in two different possibilities. Very often methodological individualism seems to involve a belief that an individualistic ontology allows one to salvage conceptually the possibility of free and rational human agency from deterministic views of society (James 1984, pp. 7, 178). Elster's goal is to save the possibility of strategic political action from various kinds of deterministic Marxisms. Whether or not one sympathises (and I do), I argue that his method does not do the job. The reason is that Elster's rational actor approach involves individual properties and capacities in a way that denies an explanatory role to the social relations that make them possible.

But there is a second and more successful way of relating individualistic methods and values to individual agency, implied in the critical dimensions of Marx's method. When, for example, Marx criticises structural concepts (like the English political economists' concept of a market), his aim is to show how they depend on individual activities under specific circumstances, as well as on the ways individuals have been formed by these same structural outcomes and circumstances. In this way, he is trying to produce a kind of knowledge that would, at least in principle, make social outcomes and psychological effects intelligible to the individuals who produce them, thus contributing to their abilities to control their futures. Critical knowledge is a necessary (although not sufficient) condition for exerting human control over social development – necessary in turn for what Marx sometimes calls the 'many-sided development of individuality'. This normative aim underwrites the methodological requirement for relating social processes to individual actions.

Both the explanatory and normative issues depend on a closer specification of what 'individual' means in methodological individualism. I distinguish here between three fundamentally different senses of methodological individualism according to different meanings of the concept 'individual'. First, there is what I shall call a *methodological individualism of events* (MI_e), which is, in effect, a regulative ontology about the material reality of discrete (that is, 'individual') events in time and space. This is a broad sense of the notion, but it is not trivial: it asserts a materialism that rules out spiritual and essentialist notions of causality, and, by implication, holistic and collective concepts that purport to refer to something other than events in space and time. The methodological implication is that good explanations should not refer to things that have no existence in time and space. Most contemporary social thinkers hold this kind of position, including Marx. As I shall argue, the only point in calling this a kind of methodological individualism (rather than simply a metaphysical materialism) is that many, like Elster, draw methodological conclusions from this common sense materialism without distinguishing between ontological problems (what is real?), and epistemological/methodological ones (how do we know this reality?).

The second sense of methodological individualism is more narrow. Here the claim is epistemological, and so more genuinely methodological than the first sense. This claim is about what is *explanatory* of social things, namely, properties of individual humans. A classic formulation is J. W. N. Watkins', who writes that '[t]here may be unfinished or half-way explanations of large-scale social phenomena (say, inflation) in terms of other large-scale phenomena (say, full employment); but we will not have arrived at rock-bottom explanations of such large-scale phenomena until we have deduced an account of them from statements about the dispositions, beliefs, resources, and interrelations of individuals.'[10]

Watkin's methodological individualism stipulates what *class* of phenomena is explanatory by arguing that social realities must be explained in terms of individual properties. In other words, it is a kind of explanatory reductionism. The underlying ontological assumption is that properties of individuals are real, while properties of societies are, at best, heuristic attributes of social theories.[11] I shall call this a *methodological individualism of subjects* (MI_s), because in the form that I want to deal with here, the issue will be how properties of individual *subjects*, especially their intentionality, explain higher level, social concepts.[12] Elster's methodological individualism is a refined and more plausible version of this sense, but, as I shall argue, this sense is not Marx's. Marx regarded similar individualisms as leading to inadequate explanations and ideological consequences because they treat the intentional properties of individuals as metaphysically existent rather than as problematic. For similar reasons, Elster's reconstruction is open to ideological consequences that Marx sought to avoid.

Third, there is what I shall call a *methodological individualism of actions* or practices (MI_a). I shall argue that this methodological individualism is fundamentally different than MI_s, although commonly confused with it. I also argue that this is the sense of methodological individualism one finds in both Marx and Max Weber. MI_a is concerned with the question of what the objects of explanation are like, an ontological question from which methodological consequences follow. The 'individualism' of MI_a involves constituting objects of explanation as the *acts* of individuals, and then showing how properties of both individual persons and society are reproduced by these actions under specific conditions. Explanations refer to the conditions that would be sufficient to explain an act. Unlike MI_s, MI_a can be a non-reductive and critical kind of methodological individualism. MI_a is non-reductive if some of the conditions of actions are irreducibly social, for example, the rules that constitute a language or culture. Thus MI_a does not involve the additional claim, distinctive of MI_s, that individual intentions can only be explained in terms of individual properties. Yet MI_a is not trivial, since it retains the demand of MI_s that social structures, functions, laws and the like have not been fully explained until one shows how they are reproduced by individual actors. This kind of demand is closely related to a notion that one finds in both Marx and Weber, namely, that from a normative perspective, social science is defined by the cognitive interests that individuals have in understanding conditions of action. MI_a thus involves the claim that the significant events for this cognitive interest are the acts – or, in Marxian terms, the practices – of individuals, and that significant explanations are those that, at least in principle, show how capacities for rationality relate to social outcomes. To the extent that Marx's social science is normative in this 'critical' sense, he is a methodological individualist in the senses of MI_e and MI_a, but not MI_s.

METHODOLOGICAL INDIVIDUALISM OF EVENTS

The most general and non-controversial methodological individualism is a methodological individualism of events (MI_e). As suggested, this methodological individualism is a regulative materialist metaphysics that refers laws, structures, functions, systems, languages, and other concepts to the reality of events in time and space. Most social scientists are methodological individualists in this sense, meaning that they regard explanations that refer to real but non-empirical entities (those that do not exist in time and space such as gods and ideal essences) as unscientific. The doctrine is a regulative ontology rather than an epistemology because there can be empiricist, realist, pragmatic, or critical accounts of how one conceptualises events. It is methodological only in the sense that it places a materialist side-constraint on what is to count as an explanation. Nonetheless, within these limits, it is relatively unrestrictive of explanations since it commits one only to something like Kant's view of apperception: phenomena become intelligible insofar as one perceptually synthesises them as events in space and time. Particular notions of causality, mechanism, rule, and so on, are more specific elaborations of these events that in turn require more specific epistemological defences, but which nonetheless ultimately refer to events in time and space.

What do we gain by distinguishing this particular sense of methodological individualism? The distinction is important primarily because of the common (but mistaken) belief that the materialism of MI_e implies the epistemology of MI_s. Elster's assertion that methodological individualism is 'trivially true' is a case in point (Elster 1986a, pp. 66–7). Elster uses the common-sense materialism of MI_e to justify the more specific epistemology of MI_s, which he describes as 'the doctrine that all social phenomena – their structure and their change – are in principle explicable in ways that only involve individuals – their properties, their goals, their beliefs and their actions. Methodological individualism thus conceived is a form of reductionism. To go from social institutions and aggregate patterns of behavior to individuals is the same kind of operation as going from cells to molecules' (Elster 1985, p. 5).

The reason Elster gives for reduction to the properties of individuals is the desirability of referring explanations to sequential events, that is, MI_e, which he elaborates in the epistemology of mechanistic realism:

> The rationale for reductionism can briefly be stated as follows. If the goal of science is to *explain by means of laws*, there is a need to reduce the time-span between explanans and explanandum – between cause and effect – as much as possible, in order to avoid spurious explanations.... [T]hese risks are reduced when we approach the ideal of a continuous chain of cause and effect, that is when we reduce the time-lag between explanans and explanandum. This again is closely associated with going from the aggregate to the less aggregate level phenomena. ... It is not only our confidence in the explanation, but our understanding of it that is enhanced when we go from macro to micro, from longer to shorter time-lags. To explain is to provide a *mechanism*, to open up the black box and show the nuts and bolts, the cogs and wheels, the desires and beliefs that generate the aggregate outcomes (Elster 1985, p. 5).

Among these 'nuts and bolts' are, in Elster's view, the rational intentions of agents, the reasons they do what they do. For Elster, these are, by analogy to natural science, the 'molecules' of social explanation; the ultimate reality to which explanations of intentions ought to refer.

What Elster has done here, however, is transform a regulative ontology into an epistemological doctrine. He has confused what is *real* with what *explains*; he has mistaken the material existence of individual properties for explanation by referring to individual properties.

An example will suggest why this distinction is important. Take the case of language, or for that matter, any symbolic system that is part of social reality. From an ontological standpoint, Elster is right that it is trivially true that language is simply made up of properties of individuals: surely language exists because it is in people's brains, in the sound waves that come out of their mouths, and so on. And it is also true that were we to get rid of all individual speakers of a language, we would also have got rid of the language. There would not be any residual reality, except, perhaps, its physically existent but unintelligible traces in writing.

All of this is true enough, but irrelevant to establishing MI_s: a regulative materialism does not translate neatly into an epistemology. Try as one might, one cannot form a concept of a language that refers only to the empirical existence of individuals: the reason is simply that language is the kind of thing that emerges from social interaction. It gets those structural, rule-like qualities that make up the referents of the concept 'language' in and through social interaction. There is no cosmological mystery to this. It simply means that the speech acts of individuals are intelligible only as part of a shared fabric of rules that govern speech, and cannot be further reduced without loss of intelligibility. As Wittgenstein argued, there can be no 'private language': to know a language is to learn the shared rules of the game. For this reason it is literally nonsensical to aggregate a concept like language, or ideology, or any other symbolic system for that matter, from the properties of individuals. I will return to this issue in the context of discussing Weber's methodological individualism. The point here is that if social phenomena are in part constituted by shared rules such as make up languages and cultures, then the fact that material properties of individuals and their situations are discrete and ontologically real does not determine our epistemological access to them. In such cases, reduction destroys the possibility of explanation. Because Elster confuses ontology and epistemology, he fails to understand that MI_s does not follow from the regulative materialism of MI_e.

If MI_s does not follow from MI_e, does this mean that MI_e is trivial? No. Even when we distinguish its regulative materialism from epistemology, we find that MI_e places more methodological constraints on explanations. For Marx, the materialism expressed by MI_e played a crucial role in dismissing explanations that deduce empirical events from essential, metaphysical realities. For example, he viewed Hegel's concept of history as 'mystical' because it involved seeing human actions as effects of a logically unfolding ideal history.[13] And many of Marx's criticisms of political economy were aimed at the less obviously mystical procedure of deducing explanations of practices from concepts such as 'private property' or 'value' embedded in a theoretical or ideological system.[14] Marx and Engels are quite clear about this in a well-known passage in *The German Ideology*: 'The premises from which we begin are not arbitrary ones, not dogmas, but real premisses from which abstraction can only be made in the imagination. They are the real individuals, their activity and the material conditions under which they live, both those which they find already existing and those produced by their activity. ... The first premise of all human history is, of course, the existence of living human individuals. ...'[15] Contemporary academic practice reified concepts as if they referred to something other than 'real individuals' interacting under specific circumstances. For Marx, the reality of abstractions is in their concrete determinations, that is, in the events they describe. This is why Marx is a methodological individualist in the materialistic sense of MI_e.[16]

The point here is simply that one can subscribe to a regulative materialism in the manner of Kant without subscribing to the epistemological doctrine that only properties of individuals explain. Methodological individualists take this step from a regulative materialist ontology to epistemology because they want to rule out causality by spiritual forces, essences, and other mysterious actors, and in this way increase empirical certainty. Marx did too. What Marx saw, and most methodological individualists miss, is that a materialist constraint on explanations does this all by itself, without added epistemological stipulations about what is explanatory.

ELSTER'S METHODOLOGICAL INDIVIDUALISM OF SUBJECTS

The version of methodological individualism to which Elster subscribes, what I am calling MI_s, conforms most closely to common usage. As I have suggested, it is important to notice that MI_s involves a doctrine of *what is explanatory* of social or individual phenomena, however these are defined as objects. MI_s is a doctrine of what explains, not what is to be explained. In contrast to MI_a (which, as I argue below, posits the possibility of agents as inferred from the meaningfulness of acts), MI_s explains acts as caused by intentions of agents.

Elster's use of MI_s is more careful than most: he does not argue that *everything* about the social outcomes of behavior can be explained in terms of individuals' intentions. He distinguishes between three different types of social explanation, although each is ultimately reducible to some combination of intentional and non-intentional properties of individuals. There is *intentional* explanation, which explains actions by referring to the goals individuals intend to achieve (Elster 1985, pp. 8–18). There is *sub-intentional* causality, which refers to non-intentional psychological properties of individuals that influence behavior (Elster 1985, pp. 18–22). And there is *supra-intentional* causality, which refers to phenomena such as markets which are the unintended outcomes of intentional actions. These social causalities are ultimately the aggregate effects of intentional action, even though they are not themselves intended (Elster 1985, pp. 22–7). It is here, in Elster's view, that Marx made his contribution, by showing how history is the result of human action, but not human design.

The problem, then, is not that Elster simply aggregates society only from intentional qualities of individuals. He is not guilty of psychologism (the view that social phenomena are reducible to psychological ones) or of an atomistic view of society, because he allows for other notions of causal explanation, as well as for the fact that the situations that affect individual actions are not reducible to intentions.[17] Countless sub- and supra-intentional phenomena can and do cause behaviors, actions, and social outcomes to diverge from intentions. On these issues, Elster has some original and interesting things to say.[18] What is at issue here is that when Elster uses intentional explanations, he sees intentions as fully explainable by referring to properties of individuals.[19] Intentions become, by analogy to physical particles like molecules, the rock-bottom referents of intentional explanations, except in this case the particles are instrumentally rational subjects. Elster is a proponent of MI_s (which explains intentions by referring to properties of individual subjects) because of his interpretation of intentionality in rational choice terms. As with all rational actor approaches, an *a priori* conception of agency serves an axiomatic role in the explanation of actions. Elster argues that to be conscious and coherent *as* an intentional actor means 'that given the beliefs of the agent, the action was the best way for him to realize his plans or desires. Hence rationality goes together with some form of maximizing behavior' (Elster 1985, p. 9). For Elster, then, *if* an action is to be explained in terms of intentions, then the explanation will refer to the instrumental rationality of agents. Showing how actions result from maximising behavior is what counts as intentional explanation.

The problem is that Elster can reduce intentional explanations to the properties of individuals *only* by using an axiomatic conception of the agent or subject. He views the individual as a being that acts by relating internal desires to external circumstances through an instrumentally rational process of decision-making. What are historically given and changeable in Elster's model are needs, wants, and preferences. What is axiomatic is the way individuals cognitively relate to internal desires and external constraints. What Elster does, following neoclassical economics, is bifurcate the contents of consciousness into axiomatically-given capacities for decision-making on the one hand, and changeable internal and external contents on the other (see, for example, Elster 1985, pp. 9–10). It would be one thing to argue that this particular model of the subject captures the way individuals are in a particular society or culture – for example, one formed by market rationality.[20] In this case, the model's usefulness is simply an empirical question. But Elster does not historically situate his model in this way: he defines intentions as instrumentally rational, and then attributes this, *a priori*, to individual subjects. The attribution permits him to refer to these qualities of subjects as explanatory. This in turn allows explanation in terms of the properties of individuals, making Elster a proponent of MI_s.

It is true that in other work Elster has entertained the notion that the self may in fact be a multiplicity of agencies and not a unitary agent at all.[21] Elster suggests that much seemingly irrational behaviour – that is, behaviour not consistent with the axioms of rational actor modelling – might be explained as the outcome of competing sub-agencies within the psyche, strategies to maintain continuity of the self over time, and various cognitive devices for transforming immediate desires into long-term strategies. Much of Elster's thinking here is interesting and no doubt explanatory, resonating not only with cognitive psychology, but also with some interpretations of psychoanalysis.

With regard to questions of methodological individualism, however, even these more sophisticated conceptions of subjectivity are equivalent to axiomatic approaches. In both cases, intentional explanation remains a kind of MI_s because what are explanatory of intentions are properties of individuals. The cost is that we are left unable to see how social phenomena – most importantly, culture and language – interact with and enable subjective capacities, including instrumental rationality itself.[22] Thus in *Making Sense of Marx* Elster simply polarises the rational and the social as two, apparently unrelated, kinds of causation: 'Social causation is social causation; rational causation is rational causation' (Elster 1985, p. 476). 'Rational causation' is 'causation' in the special sense that actions are explained by reference to a rational faculty that exists by axiom. And the axiom operates as a metaphysic within the explanation: that is, the axiom is a non-empirical cause of empirical actions. But surely this is an impoverished kind of explanation. As Nietzsche asked, satirising metaphysics of the subject (fully in the spirit of Marx), 'is it not rather merely a repetition of the question? How does opium induce sleep? "By virtue of a faculty, namely the *virtus dormitiva*," replies the doctor in Molière ....'.[23] In rejecting metaphysics of collective actors, Elster transforms what is, in Kant's terms, a regulative ontological materialism into a dogmatic metaphysics of the subject. Clearly, the explanatory defiencies of metaphysics are no less deficient for being individual rather than collective propositions.

MARX'S CRITIQUE

Elster's reconstruction of Marx in terms of MI_s is especially odd since Marx went out of his way to criticize similar, although less careful and sophisticated, stipulative individualisms, not only because they fail to explain individual properties, but also because of their ideological qualities. Central to these approaches, in Marx's view, is a confusion about the conceptual status of the category 'individual'. Liberal Enlightenment thinkers, for example, believed they could guarantee the ideal of the individual by asserting the ontological and actual existence of individuals as explanatory foundations. In the *Grundrisse*, Marx writes that in Rousseau, Smith, and Ricardo, the 'individual appears detached from the natural bonds etc. which in earlier historical periods make him the accessory of a definite and limited human conglomerate. [The Natural Individual now] appears as an ideal, whose existence they project into the past. Not as a historical result but as history's point of departure. As the Natural Individual appropriate to their notion of human nature, not arising historically, but posited by nature.[24] Marx's point is clear: to posit the individual, to treat capacities, interests, or other aspects of the individual as axiomatic, given, natural, or otherwise metaphysically existent is to misunderstand why individuals with specific kinds of properties are possible, and how they develop within social relations.

> Only in the eighteenth century, in 'civil society', do the various forms of social connectedness confront the individual as a mere means towards his private purposes, as external necessity. But the epoch which produces this standpoint, that of the isolated individual, is also precisely that of the hitherto most developed social (from this standpoint general) relations. The human being is in the most literal sense a *zoon politikon*, not merely a gregarious animal, but an animal which can individuate himself only in the midst of society. Production by an isolated individual outside society ... is as much of an absurdity as is the development of language without individuals living *together* and talking to each other.[25]

Stipulative individualisms not only fail to explain, but also function as ideological justifications. Liberal Enlightenment thinkers, for example, would abstract the individual's capacities, needs, desires, and so on from social relations. Then they would make these same attributes into axiomatic foundations of society and deduce necessary attributes of society from them, demonstrating the naturalness and inevitability of a particular kind of society in terms of its own effects.

It is in this way that MI_s can be closely related to ideological justification. Elster's approach does allow one to treat some of Marx's examples as problems of historically variable needs and preferences. But his reification of the instrumental rationality that, on Marx's account, became an attribute of social action only in 'civil society', does not escape this kind of objection.

It is this point that inspired the Marxist structuralism of Althusser and Poulantzas. Their views about the priority of social structures are based on the view that ideologies work in part by constituting specific kinds of self-understandings within specific power relations, in this way producing specific kinds of individuals.[26] Reflexive understanding of the self depends on the attributions of others, on opportunities for actions afforded by power relations, and on concepts of the self embedded in culture. One's view of oneself as an agent with specific capacities for social action (as worker, wife, entrepreneur, citizen, and so on) is an effect of ideological interpretations of one's social position and experience. Because these attributes of subjectivity are, in these senses, social products, they cannot be given a theoretical priority over social relations, nor even conceived outside of them. Whenever theorists do this, their categories of agency become ideological; they veil determinations of subjectivity that are, at least to some extent, defined within power relations. MI_s transforms into non-problems the relationships between ideology and agency to which the structuralists call our attention.

The problem with the structuralists, however, is that they also believe that rejecting MI_s involves rejecting all methodological individualism. They are, as Susan James puts it, 'absolute holists' (James 1984, Chs IV and V). They understand that Marx refused to reify individual needs and capacities – this is clear enough. But they also believe that rejecting MI_s requires the opposite, namely, conceiving individuals as nothing but the effects of social structures. This, of course, confirms the worst fears of those who subscribe to MI_s. By reifying society, Althusser and Poulantzas fail to show how individual capacities are possible, and for this reason fail to engage the critical elements of Marx's social theory. They do not understand that there is an alternative to MI_s, what I am calling MI_a, and which I elaborate below. The confusion shows up, for example, in the fact that they consistently fail to distinguish, as objects of investigation, social structures and collective agents like classes, from practices in the context of social relations. The former were not Marx's problematics and therefore not his primary objects of study, but rather derivative conceptual structures. The latter were his problematics and objects of study. If Elster posits the capacities that define subjectivity, then, the structuralists see every concept of subjectivity as 'ideology'. They cannot make Marx's goal of a socially-enabled individuality intelligible because they hold that *all* references to subjectivity are ideological.

In contrast to both Elster and the structuralists, Marx's position involved seeing attributes of subjectivity – including capacities for rational action – as developed through social interaction. In criticizing Max Stirner's contrast of personal and general interests, for example, Marx writes that 'he should have realized that individuals have always started out from themselves, and could not do otherwise, and that therefore both the aspects he noted are aspects of the personal development of individuals; both are equally engendered by the empirical conditions of life, both are only expressions of one and the same personal development of people and are therefore only in seeming contradiction to each other ....[27]

Marx's theoretical point is that one ought to use concepts that can account for the polarity of self and society, and not treat self and society as axiomatic concepts. To do so would be to treat the results of an historical process of differentiation of self and society as the causes of that process. In statements such as these, it is clear that what Marx is treating as 'real', as the objects of explanation, are human activities. Marx's method follows from the way he conceives these activities – that is, the way he conceptually constitutes 'activities' or 'practices' of individuals as objects of explanation. It will make sense, then, to characterise Marx as a 'methodological individualist' only if one uses the term to capture this aspect of his approach.

METHODOLOGICAL INDIVIDUALISM OF ACTIONS: WEBER

Doing so, however, requires some consideration of what kind of objects human activities are, an ontological question that is always (logically) prior to questions of what explains them. One does not find this kind of investigation in Elster, except as an axiom about rationality which he compares to the regulative metaphysics of mechanism in natural science.[28] Nonetheless, such questions are not outside of what has traditionally been referred to as methodological individualism, specifically, that of Max Weber. One finds in Weber considerations about social ontology that produce what I have been calling a *methodological individualism of actions* (MI_a). A look at Weber's method will allow a characterization of similar features of Marx's.

The notion that Weber's methodological individualism captures the essential features of Marx's method runs counter to the standard view. Most commentators see Marx and Weber as having opposed methodologies, Marx a 'structural' or 'collectivist' and Weber an 'individualist' one.[29] This view, however, rests on a misunderstanding of the distinctive nature of Weber's methodological individualism, as well as a failure to specify the logical relation between social structures and actions in Marx.

A methodological individualism of actions is intrinsic to Weber's social ontology and the conception of social science that follows from it. His well-known beginning of *Economy and Society* defines sociology as 'a science concerning itself with the interpretive understanding of social action and thereby with a causal explanation of its course and consequences. We shall speak of "action" insofar as the acting individual attaches a subjective meaning to his behavior – be it overt or covert, omission or acquiescence. Action is "social" insofar as its subjective meaning takes account of the behavior of others and is thereby oriented in its course.'[30]

Weber is defining here a social ontology of action as a regulative principle of explanation. In doing so he also is defining a certain domain of events as objects of explanation for social science. In this way, MI_a involves a further specification of MI_e. What is 'individualistic' in Weber's method is that he views significant *objects of explanation* as the *acts* (individual or typical) of persons. Actions, rather than persons or social structures, are the ultimate referents of concepts of social science; this what they are about.[31]

By focusing on actions rather than individual dispositions or social structures, Weber implicitly deconstructs the polarity of individual and society from an explanatory perspective, while retaining its normative (as well as existential) significance. For Weber what makes an event in space and time an *action* is its reflexive element, the understandings and goals that individuals attach to their behaviours. He presumes that humans' abilities to evaluate external situations and internal motivations endow them with capacities for agency (Roth and Schluchter 1979, p. 73). This is why explanations must show how agents relate these capacities to their situations – that is, explanations must be sufficient to explain acts of individuals, precisely because these are the events of significance for social science.

Things that are not actions – like natural events, biological stimuli, cultural rules and norms, and even social structures – are not intrinsically interesting for social science; they are not, in the final analysis, what social explanations are about. But this does not mean that such non-individual phenomena are not explanatory, since they are always conditions of action. They mold the intentions, affects, and material possibilities that are combined in actions. Precisely because they are conditions, they can be explanatory of the intentional properties of actions without being properties of individuals. What distinguishes Weber's MIx_a from MI_s is that intentional properties of individuals, including their rational capacities, are problematic rather than axiomatic, and thus are not stipulative of explanations.

This logic of explanation emerges from a careful reading of Weber's most definitive statement of methodological individualism:

> Action in the sense of subjectively understandable orientation of behavior exists only as the behavior of one or more *individual* human beings.

For other cognitive purposes it may be useful or necessary to consider the individual, for instance, as a collection of cells, as a complex of biochemical reactions, or to conceive his psychic life as made up of a variety of different elements, however these may be defined. Undoubtedly such procedures yield valuable knowledge of causal relationships. But the behavior of these elements, as expressed in uniformities, is not subjectively understandable. ... On the contrary, both for sociology in the present sense, and for history, the object of cognition is the subjective meaning-complex of action. ... For still other cognitive purposes – for instance, juristic ones – or for practical ends, it may be convenient or even indispensable to treat social collectivities, such as state, associations, business corporations, foundations, as if they were individual persons. Thus they may be treated as the subjects of rights and duties or as the performers of legally significant actions. But for the subjective interpretation of action in sociological work these collectivities must be treated as *solely* the resultants and modes of organization of the particular acts of individual persons, since these alone can be treated as agents in a course of subjectively understandable action.[32]

This statement, especially the last sentence, is often misunderstood to mean that social structures must be *explained* solely by the beliefs, intentions, and other properties of individuals.[33] If so, this would be an instance of MI_s. But the statement can be read more literally and consistently with Weber's sociology. Social structures must be accounted for in terms of the actions of individuals, but what explains these actions are not simply properties of individual subjects. The individualistic side-constraint applies to showing, for reasons of normative significance, how social structures are reproduced by individual actions. There is no methodological stipulation that sole causes of social structures will be subjective properties, but only that social science involves showing how social laws, structures, and functions are reproduced by the actions of individual persons, since these are the significant objects of cognition.

Put slightly differently, Weber sees an explanation as an account of the conditions of action. Actions are not uniquely explained by subjective properties, simply because not all conditions of action are subjective.[34] Some are intersubjective, such as culture and language, which have their own structural coherence. Others are non-subjective, such as biological capacity, material situation, and material relations of power, violence, and control. This is why Weber emphasises that explanations of actions must be sufficient both at the subjective level of 'meaning', and at the non-subjective level of 'causality'.[35]

Weber's approach has many of the advantages that Elster and others want from methodological individualism: it is materialistic and concrete, since it ultimately is about actions specified by situational relations. Moreover, it avoids the reification that Elster associates with (crude) functional and structural explanations. While Weber believes that social scientists 'cannot afford to ignore collective concepts', they ought to be used heuristically, and above all they should not be treated as if their referents were (metaphysically) real collective actors: 'for sociological purposes there is no such thing as a collective personality which "acts" '.[36] Weber's 'individualism', like Marx's, is directed against reifications of society in the form of social and historical 'laws', Durkheimian functionalism, and legal-institutional explanations divorced from the practices of individuals.

But Weber's approach is different from Elster's on the crucial issue of reductionism in intentional explanations, or explanation at the level of 'meaning'. For Elster, to explain in terms of intentions means to show how instrumental rationality comes to operate on situationally dependent needs, wants and preferences. For Weber, intentions and meanings 'originate' in the subject only in the sense that they presuppose some general needs (such as the need for a meaningful orientation toward one's existence) and some general capacities of subjectivity (that is, the ability to monitor reflexively one's behavior). Intentional explanations that refer only to the properties of the individual *qua* subject are not sufficient. What explains intentions and meanings are, in part, intersubjective (and hence irreducibly social) meaning systems with their own structural coherence. These mold individual intentions and goals, develop or limit capacities, and focus responses to internal affects and external situations. In discussing the historical impact of rationalized religion, for example, Weber writes that '[n]ot ideas, but material and ideal interests, directly govern men's conduct. Yet very frequently the "world images" that have been created by ideas have, like switchmen, determined the tracks along which action has been pushed by the dynamic of interest. "From what" and "for what" one wished to be redeemed and, let us not forget, "could be" redeemed, depended upon one's image of the world.'[37] Although meaning-systems, like the rational religions Weber is discussing here, are reproduced by individuals acting under specific circumstances, they exhibit structural, or rule-like qualities.[38] These are emergent properties of society in much the same way as are languages. Explaining these properties in structural terms is an *epistemological* necessity that is already prefigured in Weber's ontology of social action. There are no 'individualistic' ways of understanding these individual objects of explanation. For Weber, to reduce rule-like phenomena to the properties of individuals would be to dissolve the phenomena, or to mistake the systematic meaning of properties of individual actions for things that emanate only from individual subjects.

This is not a problem of methodological individualism holding only in 'extensional' contexts, and not in 'intensional' ones, as Elster might argue.[39] That is, the issue does not involve a failure to distinguish the factual existence of social phenomena from beliefs about social phenomena that in fact influence actions. Rather, for Weber, intersubjective meanings are only intelligible within languages, systems of ideas, cultures, and religions. These phenomena are not simply aggregates of individual 'beliefs', but rather intersubjective properties sustained only by the (social) interactions of individuals.

To put the point slightly differently, one might argue that these social qualities are nothing other than the beliefs of individuals. As I have suggested, this is not very helpful, since it is true only as an appeal to the regulative materialism of MI_e. It says nothing about our epistemological access to these beliefs. On Weber's account, one can understand (*Verstehen*) how beliefs affect actions only by forming structural concepts ('ideal types') that capture emergent rule-like properties of intersubjective relations.[40] If Elster's distinction between intensional and extensional contexts holds, it does so only for MI_e. It breaks down when MI_e is further specified as MI_a. It is for this reason, of course, that Weber goes to some length to defend the non-reductionist method of *Verstehen* in social science, that is, understanding the structural coherence of the cultural systems of rules that in part determines subjective intentions and thereby the meaning of actions.

As exemplified by Weber, MI_a is consistent with certain kinds of Marxian structural concepts in a way that MI_s is not. In Weber's terms, a social structure is an intersubjective set of rules, often sanctioned in some way, that individuals transform into meanings, and act on according to material circumstances in ways that reproduce structured patterns of conduct – patterns which are very often unintended. For example, in Weber's terms, a Marxist concept like 'capitalist relations of production' would be a second-order concept that explains by combining individual and situational referents. The situational referent would be to material control over property, or exclusions that some individuals enforce with respect to others. The structural referent would be legal and ideological legitimations with rule-like qualities. These rules mold the ways in which individuals conceptualize and act on their material situation as it relates to property exclusions. On this basis, one can develop more complex structural concepts, like classes, markets, a base–superstructure model, and so on, concepts that name emergent social causalities without reifying them from the activities of individuals.[41]

This approach is consistent with situations Elster is especially concerned to explain, those where systematic outcomes are unintended by actors, as in the case of markets. Weber's approach goes beyond Elster's, however, by stipulating that the intentions actors have be explained and related to the systematic outcomes their actions produce. For example, markets may be unintended, but this *particular* unintended outcome is still contingent on cultural rules of maximising behavior that are part of a rationalised consumer culture, and molded by capitalist relations of production. This example suggests that although MI_a is non-reductionistic, it is not trivial: it rules out social concepts that are interpreted in quasi-naturalistic, teleological, or deterministic terms, such as one finds in Second International Marxism, French structuralism, and positivistic social science.

MARX'S METHODOLOGICAL INDIVIDUALISM

Using Weber as a paradigm of MI_a can it be said that Marx is a methodological individualist in this sense, even though he rejects MI_s? Certainly one does not find the explicit articulation of MI_a that one finds in Weber. Moreover, Marx sometimes makes statements that are clearly outside of methodological individualism however one interprets it. In a well-known passage from *Capital* on conceptualizing the relation between capitalists and capitalism, Marx writes that 'here individuals are dealt with only in so far as they are the personifications of economic categories, embodiments of particular class relations and class interests. My standpoint, from which the evolution of the economic formation of society is viewed as a process of natural history, can less than any other make the individual responsible for relations whose creature he socially remains, however he may subjectively raise himself above them.'[42]

Marx is arguing here that the defects of capitalism cannot be reduced to the subjective motives of individuals. It is often read, however, as an assertion that the 'natural laws of movement' of capitalist society determine the individual's practices. Marx's wording here is poor indeed, considering his own extensive polemics against abstract deductions of real events from 'categories', 'laws of political economy', and the like.

The statement seems less serious, however, if we see it simply as a statement critical of psychologism, which aggregates the characteristics of society from the motivations of individuals. Moreover, many other of

Marx's texts are quite consistent with MI_a. We read in the *Grundrisse*, for example, that 'the social character of production is a precondition, and participation in the world of production and in consumption is not brought about by the exchange of labor or the products of labor which are independent of it. It is brought about by the social conditions of production, within which the individual acts.'[43] The social world is neither independent of subjects (as in the case of absolute holism) nor does it reduce to or reflect the properties of subjects (as in the case of MI_s). Both are second-order conceptual abstractions from the practices of individual persons.

The same care is reflected in a passage from *The German Ideology*, where Marx and Engels write that the 'social structure and the State are continually evolving out of the life-process of definite individuals, but of individuals, not as they may appear in their own or other people's imagination, but as they really are, i.e., as they operate, produce materially, and hence as they work under definite material limits, presuppositions, and conditions independent of their will'.[44] Marx is not asserting here that individual subjects are determined 'externally' by their circumstances, or that subjects determine circumstances. Rather, both individual and social properties are outcomes of practices insofar as humans appropriate and transform their circumstances. The perspective is one of actions and conditions of actions that both enable and constrain. This is precisely the perspective that defines MI_a.

Marx's commentators often fail to notice that MI_a is embedded in his elaboration of the object of explanation, 'human activity', and the ontology it presupposes. In this sense, the concept 'activity' (or concepts that Marx uses to denote actions – 'labor', 'practice', 'production', and so on) serves as the primitive concept from which all others follow, and which is a precondition for any explanation whatsoever. Marx's clearest statement to this effect is in *The German Ideology*, where he suggests that the German idealists have not thought through what is conceptually implied in historical activity, and which should therefore enter into explanations.[45] He identifies at least five such implications: the 'first premise of all human existence' is activity oriented toward the material requirements of life – that is, productive activity aimed at external nature according to immediate needs. The second is the 'production of new needs' – that is, a reflexive relation to internal nature.[46] The third set of relations are the rudimentary social relations of the family, relations which must exist to propagate the species. A fourth set are social relations: 'by social we understand the co-operation of several individuals, no matter under what conditions, in what manner, and to what end'. Finally, these relations are conditions for language and self-consciousness, which develop through these historically situated relations to become intrinsic properties of practices.[47]

There are two aspects of Marx's approach that deserve comment here. The first is that Marx, in manner comparable to Weber, has elaborated conceptually his *object of explanation*. The 'premises' of activity are part of the *concept* of activity that Marx is proposing; he is arguing that the notion of activity implies these conditions, and would literally be inconceivable without them.[48] This is what the German Idealists fail to see. These conditions of activity provide criteria for what a sufficient explanation would look like because they suggest what kinds of relations constitute the object, 'activity'.

Second, Marx proposes a conceptual order of derivation: the most rudimentary relations to internal needs, external nature, and other persons precede language and self-consciousness. Marx is arguing that our concepts of external things, our distinctions between self and world, our view of what our needs are and what satisfies them are closely related to the ways we interact with the world; they are sediments of practices. These interactions presuppose needs, language, social relations, nature, and intentionality as conditions of their possibility. But since the characteristics of each of these conditions evolves through activity, none can be treated as an explanatory foundation: one must simply give an account of the process, guided by second-order heuristic concepts that refer to specific historical outcomes.[49]

In the case of Elster, the important implication is that concepts of the self, including selves that behave in an instrumentally rational manner, must be explained as products (not presuppositions) of individual activities situated in specific contexts.[50] A similar point holds, *mutatis mutandis*, with respect to Althusser's and Poulantzas' views that social structures are conceptually fundamental. In contrast, Gramsci's prison euphemism for Marx as the 'philosopher of praxis' makes exactly the right point: praxis, and not maximising behaviour or class structure, is the most encompassing concept in Marx's thinking. These other concepts are secondary elaborations of conceptually entailed relations.

It seems to me that the real difficulty with Marx is that he worked out his ontology of practice in the case of productive activities, but not aesthetic, moral, and linguistic ones.[51] This is what left room within Marx for axiomatic conceptions of the subject, such as one finds in Elster, or misunderstandings about the explanatory status of structural concepts, such as one finds in Althusser and Poulantzas.

THE NORMATIVE DIMENSION

I have also suggested that the stakes of this kind of issue are never strictly explanatory – they are also normative. It is true, as Weber argues, that a normative preference for individualism is not immediately connected with methodological individualism.[52] Yet this is not the whole picture, since what counts as a good explanation often depends on what one wants to do with it. If one is interested in getting a match to burn, one needs only a lawlike generalization about a succession of events that lead up to the match lighting. If one is trying to make a better match, one needs higher standards of completeness – some kind of account of the chemical mechanisms that lead from striking to lighting. Weber points to this sort of thing when he makes his argument for methodological individualism: he argues that sociology should explain actions rather than something else because of its 'cognitive purposes'.[53] Weber is somewhat mysterious about what this cognitive purpose is, but it seems likely from other writings that he thinks that humans have a general cognitive interest in what he calls 'teleologically rational action'.[54] This is why he insisted that sociology explain actions rather than behavior, functions, or some other kind of thing. This also provides his standards of explanatory completeness, *viz.*, his demands for adequacy at the levels of both causality and meaning. Both are necessary for someone to judge their actions according to standards of internal consistency and empirical effectiveness.

In this respect, the normative dimension of Marx's social science is comparable, but not identical. Marx is concerned about the social conditions of freely developing individuality.[55] A fundamental indictment of capitalism, for example, is that the worker 'is no longer the principal agent of the production process: he exists along side it'.[56] Explaining how this could occur, and showing how it might be different, is what makes the action a significant object of social science for Marx. After all, if he had been interested in justifying social order rather than individual development, he probably would have used a different model of social science. For example, in Marx's view, the problem with bourgeois laws of political economy was not their descriptive inadequacy, but that they did not relate markets to human agents, making them seem natural and inevitable. To take another case, Durkheim's organic holism justifies a corporatist order because it distinguishes but does not relate individual intentions and social functions. And Leninist and Stalinist views of history as a law-like process justified the dominion of the party over peasants. Marx's criticisms of abstract holisms – that is, those not elaborated in terms of the practices of individuals – are closely related to his normative interest in the free development of human capacities. In *The German Ideology*, for example, Marx and Engels write that in 'the present epoch, the domination of material conditions over individuals and the suppression of individuality by chance, has assumed its sharpest and most universal form, thereby setting existing individuals a very definite task. It has set them the task of replacing the domination of circumstances and of chance over individuals by the domination of individuals over chance and circumstances.'[57]

In passages such as these, MI_a is a key to the critical aspects of Marx's explanations. By showing how what appear to be natural, lawlike outcomes are in fact outcomes of individual practices under specific circumstances, Marx intended to enlighten a class of people about the conditions of free agency. By altering reflexive understandings of practices, Marx thought he could show how these practices might be changed to produce different social outcomes. In this way, the explanatory concreteness of MI_a is an intrinsic part of Marx's normative and critical projects.

CONCLUSION

The advantages of reconstructing Marx in terms of a methodological individualism of actions are real. They involve strictures on concreteness: explanations should ultimately refer to the practices of historically-situated individuals rather than to non-empirical collective actors, laws of history, spiritual causalities, or axiomatic subjects. The advantages are also critical and normative: a methodological individualist reading highlights the interest Marx had in showing how humans can develop as free, rational agents by showing how this interest relates to his critical method, that is, relating seemingly independent social determinations to the activities of individuals. Marx's normative goals could be served only by making society transparent to individuals in this way. However, these advantages attach to MI_e and MI_a, not to MI_s: the methodological individualism of subjects merely substitutes metaphysical individual actors for metaphysical social actors. The advantages that Elster would like to capture through MI_s are better represented by MI_a, which entails neither the reductions nor the metaphysics of MI_s. Moreover, MI_a provides a more consistent and plausible interpretation of Marx's method.

NOTES

1. See Elster (1985), p. 4: 'the principle of methodological individualism, not infrequently violated by Marx, [underlies] much of his most important work'. For criticisms of Elster's reading of Marx, see a symposium in *Inquiry* 29/1 (1986). Elster is not the first to have interpreted Marx in this way; his position is put forward in substance, although less convincingly, in Tucker (1980).
2. With a few exceptions (see below, n. 5) Marxists and non-Marxists tend to agree on this point. For an example of the former, see Miller (1978), and for an example of the latter, see Popper (1966), pp. 323–4, and Agassi (1960), pp. 249–50.
3. Cf. Levine, Sober and Wright (1987). For comments on this see below, n. 10.
4. Elster (1985), esp. pp. 27–37. Elster is especially concerned with 'unelaborated' functional explanations, those that explain the existence of some social phenomenon (such as a class or a capitalist state) in terms of the consequences of its existence for reproducing the social system of which it is a part. According to Elster, if one fails to show how both the functions and the phenomenon stem from individuals, then one must depend on concepts of collective actors (e.g. the 'state guarantees the conditions of reproduction of the capitalist class', or 'the capitalist class uses the state as a means of guaranteeing private property') which have no ontological existence as *actors*. The question of functional explanation in Marxism is explored in a special issue of *Theory and Society* 11/4 (1982).
5. See also e.g. Roemer (1986), and Przeworski (1985b). Cf Tucker (1980).
6. The arguments of this chapter also apply, without revision, to Roemer (1986), pp. 191–201, and to Tucker (1980), Ch. 1.
7. I agree with Anthony Giddens's comment that '"structural sociology" and methodological individualism are not alternatives such that to reject one is to accept the other .... The point is to discard some of the terms of the debate while elaborating others further than any of its contributors have done. What the "individual" is cannot be taken as obvious. The question here is not that of comparing predicates but of specifying what human agents are like ...' – and, I would add, how they are possible (Giddens 1984, p. 220). For similar comments in relation to Marx, see Avineri (1971), pp. 94–5, Gould (1978), pp. 33–8, and Cunningham (1973), pp. 236–9.
8. This is especially clear in the writings of the French structuralists Althusser and Poulantzas.
9. The normative implications of methodological individualism are often denied. Max Weber writes, for example, that 'it is a tremendous misunderstanding to think that an "individualistic" *method* should involve what is in any conceivable sense an individualistic system of *values*' (Weber 1978, p. 18). Cf. Elster (1985), p. 8.
10. Watkins (1968), p. 271. This version of methodological individualism does not require the more restrictive *definitional* methodological individualism, a doctrine usually associated with the positivist requirement that valid social concepts be translatable into a language referring only to observable

properties of individuals. Levine, Sober and Elliot (1987, pp. 77–8) misunderstand this when they characterise methodological individualists (Elster included) as 'type reductionists'. They intend 'types' to refer to collective concepts in a theory, such as the notion of the 'fitness' of a species in the theory of natural selection, or 'class' in Marxism. Levine *et al.* argue that methodological individualism requires that such concepts be reduced to individual ones. What methodological individualists such as Watkins argue, however, is that concepts such as 'fitness' must ultimately be explicable, in principle, in terms of individuals and their environments. What is at issue for all but definitional methodological individualism is not whether holistic theoretical terms have a place in explanations, but rather the ontological status of their referents. Since Elster is not a definitional methodological individualist, the criticisms of Levine *et al.* miss the point.

11. Watkins (1968), p. 270. Cf. Popper (1972), p. 341.
12. There is, however, a crucial confusion of individual and social categories when these methodological individualists allow 'interrelations of individuals' an explanatory status. Such statements are individualistic in the sense of MI_s only if these relations are the sum of the properties of individuals. If not, they are not 'rock-bottom'. If so, methodological individualism includes residual social relations with intersubjective properties such as language, and would therefore allow explanatory status to structural concepts. On this issue, see Miller (1978), pp. 388–91.
13. See, for example, Marx (1977) *Economic and Philosophical Manuscripts*, 'Critique of Hegel's Dialectic and General Philosophy', pp. 96–108.
14. See Marx (1977) *Economic and Philosophical Manuscripts*, pp. 77–8, and Marx (1975) 'Notes on Adolph Wagner', pp. 190–1.
15. See Marx (1977) *The German Ideology*, p. 160.
16. Cf. the methodological portion of Marx (1973) 'Introduction', pp. 100–8.
17. Elster's position here is comparable to that in Popper (1966), Vol. 2, Ch. 14. Cf. Watkins (1968), pp. 272–4; Jarvie (1972), p. 156; Agassi (1960).
18. See, for example, Elster's comments on the importance of cognitive mechanisms (cognitive dissonance, framing , etc.) in explaining ideologies (Elster 1985, pp. 29–31, 487).
19. Michael Taylor correctly notes that Elster's 'three-tiered framework for explanation is a form of methodological individualism [my MI_s] only *if* the causes of the attitudes and beliefs which cause action are themselves nothing but the actions and properties of individuals' (Taylor, M. 1986, p. 4).
20. See Taylor, C. (1980) for comments to this effect on Elster's *Logic and Society*.
21. See Elster's introduction to his edited volume *The Multiple Self* (Cambridge: Cambridge University Press, 1985).
22. Contrast Jürgen Habermas's move away from purely instrumental conceptions of instrumental rationality in *The Theory of Communicative Action*, Vol. 1, trans. Thomas McCarthy (Boston: Beacon Press, 1984).
23. Friedrich Nietzsche, *The Basic Writings of Nietzsche*, ed. and trans. Walter Kaufmann (New York: Random House, 1968), pp. 208–9.
24. See Marx (1973), p. 83.
25. See Marx (1973), p. 84.
26. See Althusser (1971), and Poulantzas (1978), pp. 63–75.

27. Marx (1977) *The German Ideology*, p. 183.
28. Elster (1985), p. 5. Cf. the similar analogy in Watkins (1968), p. 270.
29. See for example Miller (1978), pp. 391–6; Slaughter (1986), pp. 45–56. For a standard reading of Weber's methodological individualism, see Lukes (1973), p. 111. See also Lukes (1977), Ch. 9.
30. See Weber (1978), p. 13.
31. See Weber (1949), p. 107.
32. See Weber (1978), p. 13.
33. See, for example, Miller (1978), p. 392; Slaughter (1986), p. 47; Lukes (1973), p. 111.
34. Steven Lukes's failure to make this distinction accounts for his confusion about Weber's methodological individualism. After categorising Weber with methodological individualists such as Hobbes, Saint-Simon and Comte (my MI_s), Lukes writes in a note that 'Fortunately, Weber did not systematically follow this methodological principle in his substantive work', where 'structural factors' carry some of the explanatory burden (see Lukes 1973, p. 111). In contrast, my account suggests that Weber did follow his principles, but these were not the same as those of Hobbes *et al.* Cf. the similar confusion in Agassi (1960), pp. 259–61, where Weber is portrayed as caught between 'psychologism' – reduction of society to individual beliefs, and 'institutionalism' – determination of individual beliefs by institutional norms.
35. See Weber (1978), p. 11.
36. See Weber (1978), p. 14.
37. See Weber (1946), p. 280.
38. For Weber's concept of a rule, see Weber (1977), pp. 98–126.
39. Elster (1985), p. 6. Weber makes this distinction in (1978), p. 14.
40. Elster considers this objection in Elster (1985, p. 460) as it might be put by Charles Taylor in Taylor, C. (1985), but he misunderstands its force: he defends his view that 'the theory of ideologies is in acute need of microfoundations', about which he is quite right. 'To this assertion some will respond by saying that the web of social beliefs is in principle irreducible to individually acquired and individually held beliefs.' He interprets this objection as meaning that 'the full set of conceptual or linguistic practices may appear as a supra-individual entity that dominates and constrains the individual members of society'. Against this, he points out that there are cracks in the structure, and these appear when individuals cannot work within it, and set out to change it, but Elster is responding to objections such as Taylor's with a social ontology that polarises individual and society, and thus rules out the phenomena *a priori*. Thus his only response can be that if one allows social explanation of intentions, it must lead to an Althusserian spectre in which agents are entirely determined by supra-individual structures. The real alternative is a Wittgensteinian view of language and culture. Wittgenstein made explicit what Weber presupposes in his sociology: the meaning of rules is a question of how they are used within specific situations, forms of life. Individuals can, and do, use systems of symbols and roles in different ways, especially under changing material conditions, social relations, and so on. The issue is not whether individuals are fully determined by external structures, but rather whether language and other

symbolic systems can be in any sense intelligible as 'beliefs' that are reducible to properties of individuals. To argue that language cannot be reduced to its individual users does not mean that it can be conceived apart from them, but only that communication makes sense only as an intersubjective phenomenon, a system of rule-following that exists only when there are groups of individuals. A 'belief' certainly is 'in' the mind of the individual as a psychic property. But the point is trivial by itself: these psychic properties are completely unintelligible, and therefore useless for social scientists, apart from intersubjective systems of meanings in terms of which they have social significance. On the continuity between Weberian social science and Wittgensteinian ordinary language analysis, see Bernstein (1976).

41. Weber in fact held that Marx's concepts *ought* to be interpreted in terms of MI_a, what he refers to here as 'ideal types' of actions: 'all specifically Marxian "laws" and developmental constructs – insofar as they are theoretically sound – are ideal types. The eminent, indeed unique, *heuristic* significance of these ideal types when they are used for the *assessment* of reality is known to everyone who has ever employed Marxian hypotheses and concepts. Similarly their perniciousness, as soon as they are thought of as empirically valid or as real (i.e. truly metaphysical) "effective forces", "tendencies", etc. is likewise known to those who have used them' (Weber 1949).

42. Marx (1977) *Capital*, p. 417.
43. Marx (1977) *Grundrisse*, p. 361.
44. Marx (1977) *The German Ideology*, p. 164.
45. Marx (1977) *The German Ideology*, pp. 165–8.
46. With respect to needs and preferences, for example, we read in Marx (1973), p. 92 that 'production thus not only creates an object for the subject, but also a subject for the object. Thus production produces consumption (1) by creating the material for it; (2) by determining the manner of consumption; and (3) by creating the products initially posited by it as objects, in the form of a need felt by the consumer.' Cf. Marx (1977) *The German Ideology*, p. 166.
47. Marx (1977) *The German Ideology*, pp. 165–7.
48. By 'conceptually implied' I do not mean logically implied, but rather *universally* implied. The difference is that Marx's claims are not *necessarily* true, and thus are non-trivial claims. Yet they are not claims that are appropriate for empirical investigation since they conceptually constitute the kind of object that is being investigated.
49. Cf. Marx (1975) 'Notes on Adolph Wagner', pp. 190–2.
50. Where Elster quotes passages from Marx that indicate the contingent social development of rational capacities, he is invariably interested with issues that do not relate to the axiomatic status of instrumental rationality in his typology of explanations. For example, in Elster (1985), pp. 71–3, Elster quotes passages that refer to the development of species capacities, but his interest is only whether the subjects of this development are individual men, or Man. Elsewhere, on pp. 62–4, Elster is concerned only with whether Marx's distinctions between capacities of humans and those of animals are accurate.

51. The broader suggestion in Marx – one that emerges especially in his critique of Hegel – is that one should account for *all* activities that define species-being in terms of potentials of specific practices. To date, Jürgen Habermas's *The Theory of Communicative Action* is the most systematic attempt to work out the logic of practices in language, ethics and politics.
52. See above, n. 9.
53. Weber (1949), p. 13.
54. See Max Weber, *Roscher and Knies: The Logical Problems of Historical Economics*, trans. Guy Oakes (New York: The Free Press, 1975), p. 192. Cf. Weber (1946), pp. 151–3. I am indebted to Wolfgang Schluchter's essay 'Value Neutrality and the Ethic of Responsibility', in *Max Weber's Vision of History*, ed. Wolfgang Schluchter and Guenther Roth (London: George Allen & Unwin, 1982), pp. 45–6; and E. B. Portis, 'Max Weber's Theory of Personality', *Sociological Inquiry* 48: 113–20.
55. Elster insists that 'methodological individualism is a doctrine about how social phenomena are to be explained, not about how they should be evaluated' (1985), p. 8. He is certainly correct if he means that methodological and ethical individualism are distinct positions, but wrong if he means that methodological individualism has no normative significance. Elster himself draws out one normative implication on pp. 117–18, where he points out that interpretations of Marxism as a theory of collective actors and functions helped to justify the 'disregard for individuals' from 'Stalin to the Red Guards'.
56. Marx (1977) *Grundrisse*, p. 380.
57. Marx continues by noting that this task cannot be achieved by every individual acting on their own, but only by the cooperative organisation of communist society (Marx 1977, *The German Ideology*, p. 190).

10 Philosophical Foundations of Analytical Marxism[1]
Graeme Kirkpatrick

MARXISM AND HISTORY

Marx's theory of history contains at its core a dialectic between inherited material circumstance and its incessant social transformation by contemporary human agency. In the now classic statement of this idea Marx wrote:

> Men make their own history, but they do not make it just as they please; they do not make it under circumstances chosen by themselves, but under circumstances directly encountered, given and transmitted from the past.[2]

On the received wisdom of Marxist orthodoxy, the dialectic whose rudiments are sketched here derives its momentum from 'praxis': creative human agency which grows in self-awareness as it shapes the future through labour.

In at least one early work, however, Marx explicitly connected his own ideas on historical process with the Enlightenment tradition which incorporates both philosophical rationalism and the materialism of the eighteenth-century encyclopaedists. In so doing he suppressed the central role of labour and laid much more emphasis on the role of consciousness operating against a background of material constraint.

In *The Holy Family*, Marx stressed the expansion of human knowledge, especially self-knowledge, as the creative-emancipatory side of his dialectic. The constraints on this were the the inherited material conditions and social relations, understood in the conventional way:

> There is no need of any great penetration to see from the teaching of materialism on the original goodness and equal intellectual endowment of men, the omnipotence of experience, habit and education, and the influence of environment on man, the great significance of industry, the justification of enjoyment etc. how necessarily materialism is connected with socialism and communism (Marx 1956, p. 176).

258

Concentrating on this early text, then, it is plausible to align the revolutionary impetus of Marx's thought with that of Condorcet, who in 1795 already understood that:

> force cannot, like opinion, endure for long unless the tyrant extends his empire far enough afield to hide from the people, whom he divides and rules, the secret that real power lies not with the oppressors but with the oppressed (Condorcet 1795, p. 30).

The goal of a scientific theory of history would be to make this fact about power visible, to enlighten.

In previous epochs, however, the masses had made history only to remain spellbound and enslaved by their own products (in thrall to those whom they themselves made rich, made into kings, lords, etc.). Under capitalism the producers could, for the first time, become aware of themselves as the real creative force behind the apparently independent processes of history. This knowledge would enable them to take control of those processes, and enjoy the benefits of their productive power themselves, rather than through the proxy of an exploiting class. For this reason Marx believed that the industrial working class had a historic significance which was first elaborated in his theory, and that its existence was a condition of possibility for the elaboration of his theory.

Traditionally, this thesis on the historical significance of the working class has been read as deriving from the polyvalent centrality of praxis mentioned previously. The impending universality of the proletarian condition was held to equate its perspective as a class with the omniscience of Hegel's God, while through its labour the working class daily produced the world anew, making it omnipotent as well. In *The Holy Family*, however, Marx offers a rather different explanation of the unique capacity of the working class to arrive at this level of self-understanding:

> To... communist criticism corresponded immediately in practice the movement of the *great mass* against which history had so far developed. One must be acquainted with the studiousness, the craving for knowledge, the moral energy and the unceasing urge for development of the French and English workers to be able to form an idea of the *human* nobility of that movement (Marx 1956, p. 113).

Here Marx attaches great significance to the burgeoning tradition of working-class self-education, its thirst for enlightenment.

A reconstruction of Marx's theory which is motivated by the desire to infuse it with the highest possible standards of 'clarity and rigour' (Cohen 1978, p. ix) is, then, far from alien to the spirit of Marx's own understanding of his project. The attempt to make the underlying dynamics of historical and social processes visible to the rational consciousness which apprehends them 'from within' is fully in line with at least one of the many strands in Marx's thought.

Other questions do arise, though. There may be disagreement over what it means to make an argument clear. We may want to reflect on why we value clarity as much as we do, and on whether the same standards of clarity hold for any theoretical discourse, regardless of the nature of its object or objects. In particular: Is clarity in the conception we hold of a political philosophy to be assessed and valued in the same way as clarity in the exposition of a mathematical theorem or a hypothesis of natural or physical science?

ANALYTICAL MARXISM

Analytical Marxism (AM) is positivist, which is to say that its answer to the last question is in the affirmative. The same critical standards inform the assessment of all theoretical discourses, regardless of the disciplinary field within which they are located. G. A. Cohen, who founded AM with his *Karl Marx's Theory of History: A Defence*, insists in that book that Marx 'did not deviate' from a 'rather simple', nineteenth-century conception of science, and argues that

> The fashionable effort to enlist him in the ranks of recent anti-positivist (Kuhn, Feyerabend, etc.) philosophy of science is entirely misguided (Cohen 1978, p. 46).

Furthermore, Cohen maintains that this unified conception of science remains defensible today, and can be retained in the contemporary attempt at reconstruction.

Despite his conservative polemical tone, however, Cohen's attempt to reconstruct Marx is not based exclusively, or even largely, on an old-fashioned attitude to science. On the contrary, AM is very much the product of a novel, and in some circles quite fashionable, school of philosophy. Analytical philosophy identifies with the rationalist conception of science as differentiation of its object according to rules whose paradigm case is philosophical logic. Faithful to positivism, its first move is to transpose this conception of theoretical practice into the characteristic domain of philosophy in the second half of the twentieth century: language. Given the association observed above between Marx's thought and the rational materialism of the Enlightenment, analytical philosophy has an obvious appeal.

For Cohen, then, the project of reconstructing Marx follows the path of a break with epistemology rather than that of imputing an 'epistemological break' (Althusser 1977). In his work the emphasis is on getting the various propositions in the Marxist theory clear in relation to one another, and on showing how these propositions can be used to offer valid explanations of historical development. In short, Cohen prioritises the logical scrutiny of Marx's formulations over the issue of their empirical validity. Whether they actually have a bearing on real history is not rendered irrelevant by Cohen, but it is marginal to his main concern.

Reading Marx in this way, Cohen reproduces the founding moment of analytical philosophy within Marxist theory. Michael Dummett attributes this move within philosophy in general to Wittgenstein, who 'reinstated philosophical logic as the foundation of philosophy, and relegated epistemology to a peripheral position' (Dummett 1973, p. xv). Wittgenstein did this by restricting philosophical reflection to the analysis of language and insisting on the absolute inscrutability of anything beyond it. Philosophy, he argued, must first struggle for clarity of expression, it must attempt to make language make sense. It cannot stray beyond this because the limits of language are the limits of the intelligible world.

The attempt to infuse philosophical language with the clarity associated with mathematics commits philosophy to a Leibnizian search for logically exclusive singularities, or 'fixed points':

> so long as we do not distinguish what is genuinely a complete entity, or substance, we shall never have any fixed point at which we can stop; and such a fixed point is the one and only means of establishing solid and real principles (Leibniz 1973, p. 71).

The terms which constitute the 'singularities' of AM, however, are not fixed in any ontological sense, but only by virtue of their logical exclusivity in relation to the rest of the system of descriptions which constitutes the theory. Only when each word functions with the most rigorous specificity will the required clarity be attained.

In the *Philosophical Investigations*, however, Wittgenstein (1958) drives the pursuit of philosophical clarity headlong into the problem that words seem to 'mean' different things in different contexts. His solution is to terminate the preoccupation with philosophical, or ultimate, ideas about meaning, and to argue that it should be replaced by analysis of the use to which terms are put in restricted contexts. The further philosophical analysis of language should focus on 'language games', within which each term has a singular sense which is confirmed by patterns of consistency in the behaviour of those who use and respond to it in this limited context.

Accordingly, Cohen's use of analytical philosophy to reconstruct Marx casts his theory as a set of descriptions operating within a restricted area, in a manner thoroughly analogous to Wittgenstein's conception of 'language game'. In Cohen's work the emphasis is on establishing a set of definitions which will constitute the groundfloor of the discourse of the theory of history, by virtue of their rigorously circumscribed analytical integrity. For analytical philosophers, a pristine layer of definitions constitutes the outermost limit of any theoretical discourse – it sets its explanatory range.

COHEN AND THE LIMITS OF HISTORICAL DISCOURSE

Cohen's defence of his version of the theory of history must therefore begin by insulating historical descriptions from other, related discursive fields. On such a defence, the theory of history is subject to limitations of scope which would have been alien to Marx, who frequently makes the use of the idea of history as an all-encompassing 'totality' (e.g. Marx, 1973, p. 105). This point is readily conceded by Cohen in his foreword. By contrast with Marx, Cohen declares that his intention is to provide a theory of history to the extent that history will allow itself to be theorised, 'which is neither entirely, nor not at all' (Cohen 1978, p. 27). It is only at such limits that the finite units of an analytical science can be established.

Cohen develops the case for the analytical prioritisation of description within the finite limits of a given discourse in the following way:

> All phenomena may be described more or less specifically, and an explanation of a phenomenon succeeds or fails relative to some finitely specific description of it, not irrespective of how it is described (Cohen 1978, p. 163).

Historical phenomena are described by the theory of history, and these descriptions may only be rivalled by descriptions which are also recognisably of history, and more or less specific in relation to this object.

Cohen locates historical-type descriptions on the boundary between the accounts of material phenomena which make up natural science and descriptions of the human interaction which comprises society. Natural objects, such as rocks, water, sea, etc. enter the theory of history under descriptions that bring out their relation to human social reproduction, as 'raw material' or, 'means of production'. Similarly, social phenomena only enter the theory of history under descriptions which emphasise their general and constant categorial status rather than their more limited, epoch-specific aspects. Hence, the modern family and the feudal religious community enter the theory of history as 'relations of production', for example.

Each theoretical discourse explains phenomena as they appear from the standpoint of the theoretical discourse itself:

> Each standpoint on a thing reveals a distinct set of properties, but the thing has all of them (Cohen 1978, p. 91).

Since historical theory must be limited to a single field of explanation it cannot stray into neighbouring zones whose most specific layers of description are different. Hence, while the objects described in historical theory and natural science may sometimes be the same, each discourse describes and explains what are essentially the same phenomena in a completely different way.

The theory of history, then, has as its most basic level of description the account of how objects of natural scientific provenance and social phenomena come together in human reproduction. Cohen clarifies the distinction between them with the aid of a 'thought experiment':

> Being capital and being a slave are ... relational properties of means of production and men. More specifically, they are social relational properties, whereas being means of production and being a man are not. The latter are possessed independently of the social form. Remove the social form in thought experiment, and those properties persist (Cohen 1978, p. 90).

The theory of history uses descriptions of natural and social phenomena to generate a level of discourse whose elements hold for all societies, and offers a ground of possible explanation which is not conjuncturally specific. Marxist social theory is then similarly limited to the analysis of social phenomena from a standpoint which brings out their place in the patterned movement of history, and must tend to elide those aspects which are characteristic of particular societies at determinate points in their development. Cohen argues that

> a description is social if and only if it entails an ascription to persons – specified or unspecified – of rights or powers *vis-à-vis* other men (Cohen 1978, p. 94).

On this account, historical materialism limits the range of Marxian social description to include only those relations of ownership and control which are determinant moments in the historical pattern. The attempt to limit social description in this way derives from the thesis that any logically plausible explanation operates on the basis of a finite conception of its discursive field.

The identification of a finite discursive space, though, is not as unproblematic as Cohen seems to take it to be. Why should it be accepted that there is such a region within science as the theory of history, and how does the meaning of the term 'history' differ in its scientific use from that which it has in ordinary language? More particularly, how much discrepancy is permissible between the two uses before they are held to conflict unacceptably? As will be seen below, Cohen's theory seems to draw heavily on conventional usage to get off the ground, only to subject this usage to extensive mutilation in the interests of theoretical precision and logical structure.

THE THEORY OF HISTORY

Cohen presents a version of historical materialism which takes Marx's 1859 'Preface' as its point of departure. In this work Marx gave the following, distinctive formulation of the essential dialectic identified above:

> In the social production of their life, men enter into definite relations that are indispensable and independent of their will, relations of production which correspond to a definite stage of development of their productive forces. The sum total of these relations of production constitutes the economic structure of society, the real basis, on which rises a legal and political superstructure and to which correspond definite forms of social consciousness. The mode of production of material life conditions the social, political and intellectual life process in general.[3]

In this presentation of his view, Marx affords clear priority to 'circumstances transmitted from the past', these latter conceived primarily in terms of productive power.

In accordance with his method, Cohen first defines the elements of the thesis advanced in the 1859 preface. He begins by defining a productive force as follows:

> To qualify as a productive force a facility must be capable of use by a producing agent in such a way that production occurs (partly) as a result of its use, and it is someone's purpose that the facility so contribute to production (Cohen 1978, p. 32).

The analytical method of eliminating possible sources of confusion by establishing a foundational and unambiguous level of discourse is clearly in evidence in Cohen's rigid exclusion of the productive forces from the economic structure, on the basis that they are not analytic with production relations:

> the productive forces are not part of the economic structure. ... they could be part of it only if they were a subset of production relations (Cohen 1978, p. 28).

Cohen later qualifies his apparently quite empirical definition of the productive forces, with the following:

> that definition is neither so precise nor so authoritative as to leave no role for other considerations in assessing an item's claims to productive forcehood. On the contrary: when asking whether x is a productive force, we must have regard to the place of the concept in historical materialist theory (Cohen 1978, p. 41).

It is on the basis of its compatibility with four theses of historical materialism, which he goes on to list, that a described object is screened for its admissibility to the category. Being a 'productive force' situates an object within a determinate theoretical system. The category of productive forcehood denotes an exclusive place within this system; it says 'nothing about the ontology of the object' (Cohen 1978, p. 47).

On the basis of his purification of Marx's terms, Cohen clarifies the 1859 Preface into a distinctive explanatory thesis, namely the primacy of the development of the productive forces in the explanation of historical change. Cohen formulates this thesis as follows:

> The primacy thesis is that *the nature of a set of production relations is explained by the level of development of the productive forces embraced by it* (to a far greater extent than vice versa) (Cohen 1978, p. 134).

For Cohen, this is the core argument of historical materialism. Its explanatory power depends upon rigour in the specification of its causal dynamic.

The kind of argument entailed by the primacy thesis is, on Cohen's defence of it, based on the use of functional explanation. Functional explanations are valid in the field of historical science (just as they are in biology) because they offer logically satisfying descriptions. Cohen defends this in the following way:

> On the view to be developed here, a functional explanation is *logically* in order in answer to any why-question. It could explain why a certain event occurred, why a particular thing has a certain property, why something regularly behaves in a certain manner, and so on, without

restriction:... only the facts decide whether a question has a functional answer, not the structure of the question itself (Cohen 1978, p. 256).

It is in connection with his defence of functional explanation that Cohen writes of his 'escape from the issue of meaning' because, his reference to the facts[4] notwithstanding, the epistemological question of its relation to actual events is not here at issue. The key to the validity of a functional explanation lies in its logical coherence as a description. 'Does it make sense?' has priority over the question of its empirical truth.

For Cohen, the terms of the theory of history derive their meaning from the intentions of the human agents represented in it. These agents are the anchor points for Cohen's reconstruction, the only category of which, he writes, simply 'need no further explanation' as elements in a scientific account. Within analytical philosophy, this thesis of the primitiveness of persons originates with P. F. Strawson. In his work, the argument that the existence of persons has logical priority has two, related functions. First, the presence of individuals in the theoretical discourse gives it 'identificatory force', transforming it from a disembodied shell into a concrete description with a definite connection with the real. Second, the primitiveness of persons permits a whole class or predicates in philosophy, predicates which attribute properties to people in this pristine state.

The significance of the second of these points lies in its claim to be a counter-argument to Wittgenstein's assertion that meaning is inextricably tied to specific behavioural contexts. For the latter, words lack constancy of meaning from one 'language game' to another. Grandiose discourses like philosophy are aberrations arising out of the natural tendency to overlook this propensity of the meaning content of language to alter dramatically, while its discursive form remains the same. Strawson argues that this argument cannot apply to the term 'persons' in his sense of it since, if no continuity of meaning adhered to this term, even the most mundane forms of discourse and life would become unthinkable – the effect could not be limited to philosophy.

Intentionality first emerges as a pivotal category in analytical philosophy when Strawson presses himself for a non-trivial answer to the following question: 'What is it that given this concept 'person' its quasi-universal intelligibility?' Strawson concedes the difficulty of the question, but argues,

> I think a beginning can be made by moving a certain class of P[person]-predicates to a central position in the picture. They are predicates, roughly, which involve doing something, which clearly imply intention or a state of mind... (Strawson 1959, p. 111).

The ultimate importance of Strawson's argument is to move analytical philosophy towards a position where the theoretically unreflected individuals which anchor philosophical discourse can nevertheless enter it as determinate moments in meaningful descriptions.

We are expected to identify with the primitive persons in the theory; their history is ours. This is particularly important for a theory like Marxism, which has always been associated with a distinctive practical relation to the real. Cohen's actors, however, populate a history whose horizons are much narrower than our own. They exist in history only in so far as the latter is susceptible to logical explanation. In AMist social science they are themselves seen to be similarly cut short as representations of human life.

PHILOSOPHICAL FOUNDATIONS OF ELSTERIAN METHODOLOGY

Jon Elster adopts essentially the same approach to the reconstruction of Marxist social science as Cohen does to the theory of history. However, Elster does not accept the limit of social scientific discourse as laid down by Cohen. Instead, he draws on the work of Donald Davidson (1980) to specify the range of the theory somewhat differently. The relevant innovation with which Davidson is associated is his argument that physical phenomena cannot be adequately explained in terms of the physical states that are coterminous with them. Elster cites him to this effect:

> If a certain psychological concept applies to one event and not to another, there must be a difference describable in physical terms. But it does not follow that there is a single physically describable difference that distinguishes any two events that differ in a given psychological respect (Elster 1983a, p. 22).

On this basis, Elster argues that the explanation of human actions (and therefore of social phenomena) must take place on distinctive terms, terms which are irreducible to those of the physical sciences.

It follows from this that the most specific level of description available to social science is of individual actors. Elster's first thesis, then, is methodological individualism (MI). He defines this as:

> the doctrine that all social phenomena – their structure and their change – are in principle explicable in ways that only involve individuals – their properties, their goals, their beliefs and their action (Elster 1985, p. 9).

Following Cohen, then, Elster exploits the theoretically unreflected unity of the individual of theory and the cognitive subject. However, the individuals of MI are as severely mutilated in relation to any normal conception of empirical human beings as was Cohen's notion of history in relation to its ordinary language origins. MI 'involves' those aspects of individuals which Elster designates as 'internal relations'. Internal relations are those aspects of individuals which can be inferred from the fact of social interaction. Elster points out that: 'Any relation of interaction is also an internal relation, but ...the converse need not hold' (Elster 1985, p. 95). In other words, a great many internal relata may make up the inner structure of the individual psyche, but they are not all accessible from the standpoint of social description. Only those internal relata which also describe facts of social interaction are accessible to such descriptions.

Elster contrasts this approach with that of empirical social science in the following way:

> in the analysis of society one cannot... begin by describing isolated individuals and then go on to define the (comparative) relations between them, since an (interactional) relation must be present from the outset. In the study of society, relations are prior to predicates. An empiricist methodology of social science is one that rests on the opposite priority (Elster 1985, p. 95).

A predicate attributes a property or properties to things or people. It is to be distinguished from 'internal relata', which only describe the same thing or person in relation to some other person or thing. To illustrate, predicates of a person take the form A is civil, charming, kind, etc., while relata would have the form A intends, chooses, desires x.

Elster's argument is that, in offering determinate descriptions of individuals, social science is limited to describing them in terms of their relation to other people and things. The point of this manoeuvre is to insulate the boundary of social science against other disciplines also concerned with irreducible properties of mind. By excluding descriptions which are not inherently relational Elster eliminates the possibility that the study of society based on MI could regress into an endless series of predicates describing the infinitely various characteristics of each individual.

The 'fixed points' of social scientific discourse, then, are the individuals of MI, described exclusively in terms of internal relata. In itself, however, this does not constitute a very robust heuristic device. Given that human individuals can be described in this way we still cannot see how to construct explanations of human action merely on the basis of descriptions of them which are refined to exclude non-relational data. Explanations operating on this level would amount to fairly useless propositions of the type: A did x because she chose to. What is needed to strengthen the explanatory power of MI is a further assumption about its individuals, one which will facilitate their integration into more complex accounts. For social science to get started it is necessary to be able to show why, having certain relationally defined dispositions, individuals act in certain ways. This is the basis upon which Elster introduces the assumption that individuals are rational.

Elster's version of Marxist social science is based on the idea that rational choice models of behaviour constitute the most secure ground for the explanation of human action. The methodological individual's actions are to be explained as follows:

> A rational choice explanation involves showing that the action was rational and that it was performed because it was rational. That the action was rational means that given the beliefs of the agent, the action was the best way for him to realize his plans or desires. Hence, rationality goes along with some form of maximising behaviour (Elster 1985, p. 76).

Elster's assumption of strategic or 'maximising' rationality on the part of his methodological individual, like the individual itself, derives from the theoretical requirement that it must fit into the most logically satisfying account. It has little or nothing to do with the empirical observation that this is how individuals 'are'. In short, the individual of social science must conform to this standard if we are to be able to construct logical explanations of social phenomena at all. In this sense, the individual of MI mirrors the Leibnizian monad, serving as a condition of possibility of coherent knowledge.

It is as a result of the same logical necessity that parsimony is to be preferred to generosity in the most rigorous accounts of individual choice and action:

> Not all rational actions are selfish. The assumption that agents are selfishly motivated does, however, have a methodological privilege, for the following reasons. For non-selfish behaviour, e.g. altruism, to be possible, some other agents must be selfishly motivated but not vice versa. Non-selfish behaviour is logically parasitic on selfishness, since there can be no pleasures of giving if there are no selfish pleasures of having. Or again, if I am concerned about your welfare the latter cannot solely be made up of your concern for mine (Elster 1985, p. 9).

The focus of explanations on individuals, the rationality assumption and the priority of selfishness constitute an ascending hierarchy in Elsterian terms. The best explanations draw on all three assumptions, and integrate them into the explanatory description of social phenomena. All are derived from a rigorous extension and development of the same foundational principles as are found in Cohen: the primitiveness of persons; the stress on a precise economy of descriptions, and the emphasis on logical structure as the sole guarantor of scientificity.

However, Elster's development of Cohen's argument shows that it already contained the germ of an essentially non-corroborative field of discourse. On Elster's methodology propositions drawn from the theory of history can only assume explanatory significance for social science if they are compatible with MI. This precludes a privileged role for many of the major theses associated with historical materialism. In particular, it prohibits explanations based on generations which impute pattern, direction or an ultimate goal to social processes, while these are irreducible to the intentions of individuals. The notion, long associated with Marxism and defended by Cohen, that productive power expands over the historical long term, for instance, must now be defended with reference to the rational intentions of human individuals that it be so. In more recent work Cohen has found himself obliged to defend this, somewhat implausible view (Cohen 1989, Pt II Ch. 9).

In the absence of an explanatory role for the theory of history no question of social interactions can have priority over any others. Marxism's traditional emphasis on labour and productive activity, for example, retained and reworked by Cohen as 'the intentional structure of the labour process', is no longer justified. In short, Marxist social science loses its distinctive problematic. Rational choice theory and its concomitant 'game scenarios' can be applied to any question of social science whatsoever, having no inherent connection with the Marxist agenda.

Reconstructing Marxist social theory on the basis of Elsterian MI also denies any practical meaning to the theory of history. On the best descriptions of the methodological individuals, that is those descriptions which have analytical priority and are therefore theoretically determinate, the individuals are primarily, even exclusively self-interested. It follows that more abstract beliefs held by them, for example in the principles of historical progress, are denied any salience in the explanation of social change. The mutilated individuals of MI are deprived of historical consciousness and of a practical-moral orientation to future events.

On the AMist defence, the reader of the theory of history is engaged in an essentially solipsistic exercise from the point of view of Marxist social science. Nothing gained thereby is liable to modify the explanation of social events which, as has been shown, is based exclusively on the imputation of logically scrutible intention.

CONCLUSION

Orthodox Marxism was philosophically anchored in the notion of praxis. Praxis 'made history', it 'reflected on what it had made' and came to 'self-realisation' through political activity guided by this reflection. Praxis is a highly compounded notion, fusing various aspects of the Marxist theory of agency and obscuring the complexities of the various areas of the theory they represent in the process. In the praxis-based conception the productive, the cognitive, the practical-moral, and the communicative aspects of human agency are all rolled into one.

Like Althusserianism, AM breaks this unity up and lays exclusive stress on its cognitive aspects. Hence, the theory is propelled in its construction by the search for logical clarity, and in this search it generates descriptions of human agents under which rationality is their most salient feature. In this sense, AM represents an attempt to align Marxism with an Enlightenment-type conception of human liberation.

To achieve this realignment, however, AM enlists the central doctrine of contemporary analytical philosophy, which is that clarity of expression equates with logic in the formulation of propositions. Historical and social theory are then obliged to posit logical continua of their objects so that explanations of them can approximate as closely as possible to the rigours of mathematics.[5] Their descriptive 'singularities' are pressed into the homogenising and static thought medium of purely rational cognition. The pursuit of mathematical clarity abolishes time, purges historical and social theory of their temporal dimension.

This chapter has attempted to show that AM results in a theory of history which is implicitly undermined by the rigours of a logic it opens up against itself. Henri Bergson pointed out long ago the inherent contradiction of any attempt at a purely logical conception of human affairs.

> A consciousness unable to conserve its past, forgetting itself unceasingly, would be a consciousness perishing and having to be reborn at each moment: and what is this but unconsciousness? When Leibniz said

of matter that it is a 'momentary mind', did he not declare it, whether he would or no, insensible? (Bergson 1920, p. 5).

Elsterian social science is a free-floating device for the random mathematising of bits of social reality, whose severing of itself from its original moorings in the theory of history was a logical inevitability. Once set loose, however, it poses a threat to any attempt to understand individuals in terms of their development through time, and how else are individuals to be understood?

The inherently self-subverting nature of Cohen's philosophical method is the root cause and ultimate significance of Elster's criticisms of his use of functional explanation, and of Brenner's (1977) criticisms that the theory of history cannot explain epochal transitions. Alan Carling's (1991) attempts to reconcile the two are motivated by the desire to retain a practical role for the theory of history by making historical transitions appear 'rational', and to impose some kind of a limit on the subversive range of rational choice methodology by refounding the latter on other, unspecified terms. The argument presented here, however, shows that he can only succeed at the price of the philosophical integrity of the AM paradigm. The theory of history and AMist social science are irreconcilable, and this contradiction within AM is a direct consequence of the more basic antagonism between AM's peculiarly logical positivism and the practical-moral intention which must motivate any effort of Marxist reconstruction.

The AMist annulment of time precludes the possibility of a normative dimension within historical and social theory. Despite much talk in analytical circles of a 'theory of justice' and of the moral virtues of 're-centring' Marxist theory on the individual, Marx's 'ethical individualism (EI)' (the phrase is Elster's) never surfaces within AMist discourse. This is because passage from the methodological to the ethical individual is essentially a journey through time.

The decision that it is worthwhile to reflect on the historical past and the social future already takes us beyond the boundaries set by AMism, which is moving in the opposite direction. AM prioritises radical inwardness (into private space) over critical reflection and mediation in real time. In so doing it achieves inner clarity at the price of any hope in the outside world. The extent to which the future is describable in the finite and specific terms of AM is in inverse proportion as it has the capacity to elicit hope.

Marx argued that 'even the most abstract categories... are... a product of historic relations and possess their full validity only for and within those relations' (1973, p. 105). The tendencies toward specialisation perennial to capitalism demand that Marxists constantly reassess the categories of Marxist theory against the background of real events in real time. Jürgen Habermas (1971) has analysed some of the real historical stresses on the notion of praxis, and there is no need to rehearse them here. Much hinges, however, on how we break the idea down, and on the philosophical presuppositions which govern this operation. Adherence to the AMist method entails the liquidation of its practical-moral side, and AM is unable as a consequence to preserve the vitality of Marxist theory.

Immanuel Kant argued that while practical reason could not offer the same epistemological security for the study of history as the critique of pure reason could for science, it was able to generate 'regulatory' ideas which would make reflections on history meaningful (1972, pp. 655–6). Reconstructing Marxism it is necessary to establish a Kantian position between the Leibnizian rigidities of AM and the Hegelian simplicities of praxis Marxism. Such a position would acknowledge and endorse the drive to analyse Marxist concepts and make them clear which is the hallmark of AM.

At the same time, however, it would aim to temper this drive with practical considerations whose terms are inherently 'synthetic' in that they elude strict integration into the monadic frame of reference of Elsterian science. These transcendental concepts would be derived from critical reflection on the notion of praxis, reflection based on the prioritisation of the practical-moral over the cognitive dimension of subjective agency. The regulatory concepts of this thoroughly moralised, but still essentially rationalist, Marxism could be deduced from a study of the constitutive processes which are conditions of possibility of the continued existence of any society.

The notions of solidarity and respect for other persons represent transcendental and practical norms implicit in the coming-to-be of any society. At the same time, their content is inherently resistant to inclusion as monadic 'internal relata' of the kind required by MI. As necessary conditions for all societies they would be equally resistant to the relativising flux of Hegelian historicism, and would constitute a permanent injunction against repetition of the Stalinist aberration. Above all else, the task of Marxist reconstruction must proceed on the basis of a thoroughgoing critique of our Marxist past, as it is in the shadow of this that we are now all condemned to labour. The influence Marxism is to have upon the future will be in direct proportion as it is open to permeation by, and reflection on its own past:

> The balloon set free takes the position in the air which its density assigns it (Bergson 1920, p. 28).

NOTES

1. I am grateful to Sarah-Jane Bey-El-Araby, Peter Benson, Alan Carling and Alex Callinicos for their comments and criticisms of an earlier version of this paper, which prompted extensive rewriting.
2. Marx (1977) *The Eighteenth Brumaire of Louis Bonaparte*, p. 300.
3. Marx (1977) 'Preface' to *A Contribution to A Critique of Political Economy*, p. 389.
4. Cohen (1978), p. 257. Habermas (1983) refers to modern positivism's deference to the world of facts as the 'ironic' revenge of metaphysics, since, as we have seen, these are a constantly vanishing point on the horizon of analytical philosophy's linguistically constituted world.
5. I do not mean here to align AM with the 'ideal language' school of philosophy, but refer to Elster's remark (1983a, p. 24) to the effect that systems of differential equations come closest to providing the canonical form of explanation. He, of course, acknowledges that no such canonical form has actually been accomplished.

11 The Limits of Rational Choice Theory
Michael Goldfield and Alan Gilbert

INTRODUCTION

In recent years rational choice approaches have come to be a major paradigm, perhaps the central emerging theoretical framework, within the political science profession.[1] Its proponents and practitioners can be found within virtually every subfield of research, including in the most unlikely of places, e.g. among those who think of themselves as Marxists and even in one recent book which purports to explain the development of the 1950s and 1960s civil rights movement in the United States. Many of its adherents claim that rational choice theory is the basis for a new science of politics (although a few of the leading practitioners are remarkably modest in their claims; note in this regard Fiorina and Shepsle 1982; Hardin 1982; although in contrast, see Ordeshook 1986). Most proponents, however, make a strong claim that rational choice models are the only valid basis for doing rigorous work in the social sciences. Rational choice theory is, thus, not merely posed as an alternative to other theories or as an attractive, emerging research program, but as a universally applicable, superior orientation – the only one a *reasonable*, serious social science researcher ought to choose.[2] This chapter examines these claims, making some preliminary remarks.

Our plan will be as follows: We will first examine the most prominent, narrowly circumscribed, mathematically tractable neoclassical version of rational choice theory. We will indicate the kinds of cases in which neoclassical models are most persuasive and those where they break down. We will then examine those modifications that relax some of the more troubling neoclassical assumptions, assessing what is gained and what is lost in the less 'economic' versions of rational choice. We will next attempt to see if even the more nuanced formulations run into insurmountable problems in explaining certain important types of social phenomena. Finally, we will look at arguments that are counterposed, not only to the universal explanatory claims of rational choice theory, but also to a philosophical criterion of methodological individualism as an important requirement for constructing rigorous social science explanations. In contrast, we will invoke contemporary philosophy of science insights about the role of contending theories in generating scientific advance.

THE NEOCLASSICAL APPROACH

Rational choice theory in its traditional, noeclassical form begins with a series of assumptions:

(1) All fundamental social explanations are explanations about individual actions and behavior. Explanations that cannot be reduced to such terms are suspect or wrong. Those that have not been reduced are incomplete. J. W. N. Watkins states a philosophical principle of methodological individualism shared by virtually all varieties of rational choice proponents in political science:

> According to this principle, the ultimate constituents of the social world are individual people who act more or less appropriately in the light of their dispositions and understanding of the situation. Every complex social situation, institution, or event is the result of a particular configuration of individuals, their dispositions, situations, beliefs, and physical resources and environment. There may be unfinished or half-way explanations of large-scale social phenomena (say, inflation) in terms of other large-scale phenomena (say, full employment); but we shall not have arrived at rock-bottom explanations of such large-scale phenomena until we have deduced an account of them from statements about the dispositions, beliefs, resources, and inter-relations of individuals (Watkins 1968, pp. 270–1).[3]

(2) Individuals have relative fixed or constant preferences, i.e. their preferences are invariant and exogenous. These preferences are ranked in a consistent, hierarchical preference structure. An individual's preferences are expressions of her perceived self-interest, measurable in material terms, almost always in money.

(3) Individuals act to maximise their preferences or self-interest, i.e. they carry out individual decisions. The parameters of choice which involve preference structures, the feasible set of alternatives, and the available means and costs can often be represented by a neoclassical utility function. To understand human activity as rational is

to understand it as activity by individuals to maximize their utility functions. To act otherwise is irrational; virtually all humans behave rationally. Behaviour that appears irrational is usually found to be rational upon closer examination.[4]

(4) Individuals attempting to maximise their self-interest compete and cooperate, in order to achieve their ends with other similarly materialist individuals (who have their own well-defined self-interest). This complex web of interactions forms an equilibrium.

There are a number of additional assumptions that are important in many formulations, but which are not as central:

(5) Individuals have complete (or at least extensive) information about alternative courses of actions and consequences of their actions. Virtually all the neoclassical formulations assume complete information. Dropping this assumption voids much of the neoclassical technical apparatus, although some political scientists attempt to maintain the neoclassical framework while looking at choices under uncertain conditions.

(6) Many consider the use of game theory in social explanation to be central to rational choice theory. Yet there is no necessary connection between game theory and methodological individualism. For game-theoretical approaches could be used by those interested in the structure of class conflict or the strategy of the capitalist state, problems that could be formulated, for instance, by envisioning states or classes (and their representatives) as actors, without a commitment to methodological individualism.

MERITS OF THE NEOCLASSICAL FRAMEWORK

There has been debate over whether the neoclassical assumptions have more than limited applicability to non-capitalist societies (whether conceived as traditional, tribal, feudal, etc.). It should surprise no one, however, that this framework has some initial plausibility in explaining many social and political activities in developed capitalist societies. Gary Becker, for example, gives quite useful models for illuminating some of the contours of racial discrimination in the United States and under apartheid in South Africa. Neoclassical economists have also predicted a number of important relationships that have been confirmed by empirical studies. Becker also successfully predicts that families will have fewer children as the market value of a mother's time increases.[5] He also highlights many economic aspects of the marriage relationship, including the greater likelihood of divorce, the more money a married woman earns, a prediction also suggested a century ago by Friedrich Engels, a decidedly non-neoclassical social scientist. Few would find it unusual to see that monetary factors play such a large role in the personal and social lives of people in capitalist societies. The young Karl Marx, for instance, a harsh critic of egoistic economic analysis, argued incisively in the *1844 Manuscripts* that the cash nexus of the capitalist market frames and ultimately undermines all traditional values, including love, beauty, intelligence, strength, personal worth, and virtually everything else. According to the *Communist Manifesto*, capitalist development 'has left no other nexus between man and man than naked self-interest, than callous "cash payment". It has drowned the most heavenly ecstasies of religious fervor, of chivalrous enthusiasm, of philistine sentimentalism, in the icy water of egotistical calculation. It has resolved personal worth into exchange value ....' (1977, p. 223; see also Gilbert 1984, 1990).

The central question, however, is not whether economic calculations are important to individual behaviour in modern capitalist societies, but whether, as the proponents of neoclassical rational choice theories argue, they are ubiquitous, generalisable, i.e. whether they can explain everything or at least everything important. Becker asserts:

> I have come to the position that the economic approach is a comprehensive one that is applicable to all human behaviour, be it behaviour involving money prices or imputed shadow prices, repeated or infrequent decisions, large or minor decisions, emotional or mechanical ends, rich or poor persons, men or women, adults or children, brilliant or stupid persons, patients or therapists, businessmen or politicians, teachers or students (Becker 1976, p. 8).

Without argument against competing interpretations, however, such 'findings' seem little more than prejudice. For a series of counter-examples suggests that alternative assumptions or perhaps alternative theories are necessary. As Kristin Monroe's analysis shows, the neoclassical rational choice framework cannot explain the motivation of heroic persons who rescued Jews from the Nazis. Since cost–benefit calculations are almost always irrelevant to these activities, none of the cases can be subsumed under standard neoclassical accounts of altruism. Neoclassical rational choice explanations of voter apathy which purport to explain why roughly only half of eligible adults vote in American presidential elections explain too much. They show why it is irrational for anyone, except for a handful with special incentives, to vote at all. Similarly, Olson's analysis of the logic of collective action, while perhaps useful as an indicator of one type of constraint in the development of large-scale organisations and movements, leads one to predict the impossibility or at least the unlikelihood of very common phenomena such as strikes (see, e.g. Sabia 1988). And, to take a rather extreme case, privileging a single standard of rationality (i.e. the maximisation of money) can lead to some pretty bizzare, counter-intuitive results. We speak in common terms of 'crazy' people and 'rational' people, rationality often having to do with whether people's actions are predictable, with whatever values or standards they choose. Very few people would think it 'rational' to set their ailing grandmothers on a main thoroughfare and run away so as to avoid the financial strain. While neoclassical approaches may help us focus our attention on certain important monetary and self-interest constraints, they do not always help us understand why individuals act as they do or what actions they are likely to take. Thus, a number of theorists, committed to the general rational choice framework, have attempted to modify certain neoclassical assumptions, while preserving what they see as important aspects of the rational choice model.

ATTEMPTS TO MODIFY THE ASSUMPTIONS

Robert Frank attempts to shore up the neoclassical rational choice (or as he calls it the 'self-interest') model. He argues that

> many people do not fit the me-first caricature. They give anonymously to public television and private charities. They donate bone marrow to strangers with leukemia. They endure great trouble and expense to see justice done, even when it will not undo the original injury. At great risk to themselves, they pull people from burning buildings, and jump into icy rivers to rescue people who are about to drown. Soldiers throw their bodies atop live grenades to save their comrades (Frank 1988, p. ix).

Frank also gives examples of people who tip waitresses and waiters in distant cities and of workers who endure the loss of income associated with strikes and lockouts rather than suffer what they see as an unjust settlement. Yet the self-interest model of rational choice considers all these examples and many more merely as irrational behaviour. From an explanatory standpoint, one might wonder whether it is rational to have a theory of 'rational' behaviour which obscures so much important activity.

Frank contends that the emotions that lead us to act in ways contrary to the neoclassical model are ones that we are socialised into having. They are part of our upbringing, education, and training. More important, however, these so-called irrational actions (at least from the standpoint of neoclassical theory) confer long-term advantages. They are thus in the end rational, in a person's long-term self-interest. This is so, according to Frank, in two closely related ways:

First, they confer advantages by gaining trust and friendship, leading others to see one as the type of person who can be trusted in a business relationship, in loaning money, etc. Second, they allow one to have self-respect, coincident with those personal values which society values and respects. These two points, of course, are not unrelated.

Even when they know what is in their long-term self-interest, people do not automatically do it. Thus, the emotions, according to Frank, play what he labels as a strategic role in reinforcing one's tendency to act in such a manner. People who have strong feelings about fairness often feel terrible if they cheat someone. Such feelings also help us reject a favourable deal if the other person seems to be making an unfair gain. They also help us attempt to remedy injustices or obtain refunds even when the expenses of doing so far exceed our original losses. Such activities are part of the character-building that establishes us as the type of people not only who can be trusted by other people, but who should not be trifled with. Frank's qualifications thus preserve the centrality of self-interest after all, but the resultant conception is devoid of the powerful (and mathematically tractable) tools of cost–benefit analysis, based as they are on immediate economic considerations. Frank's argument is analogous in philosophy to Mill's rule-ultilitarianism – the adoption of moral rules without calculation is justified when they maximise happiness in the long run. This view is distinct from act-ultilitarianism which, like narrow neoclassical models, requires cost–benefit calculations about each decision (Brandt 1979).

Yet, individual behaviour is often more complex than Frank suggests. Emotional responses are often not 'strategic'. Pride, stubbornness, and insecurity lead people to act irrationally in ways that provide no benefits, short-term or long-term. Weakness of will, sour grapes, and a host of other common psychological phenomena subvert rationality and self-interest.

In addition, several of Frank's examples are both less and more compelling than at first sight. A social class analysis of tipping, for example, may show it to be more rational both for the upper classes (given their long and short-term self-interests) and for workers (given certain moral or solidaristic feelings of decency and compassion). Thus, people of a higher economic strata often give tips as part of *noblesse oblige* or withhold them to express displeasure, and thus reaffirm their class dominance, a form of authority 'rational' at home or away. For this stratum, Frank's critique of self-interest model of rational choice fails; models sensitive to social meanings and class interests look more promising (Kratochwil 1989). On the other hand, as a consequence of such upper-class behaviour, workers often regard enforced dependence on tips (itself generally a consequence of low-wage service employment) to be demeaning. Thus, unionised workers have sometimes had tipping abolished in favour of either higher wages or a standard charge for service as part of the bill. Such demands, however, illustrate workers' concerns to be treated as equals, not as servants. They speak to the mutual regard which is part of genuine individuality, but which is belied by rational choice conceptions. In addition, workers as customers often regard the tips they give differently. When Goldfield worked on the midnight shift as a teamster, he and his partner would stop for lunch at 4:00 a.m. at a diner. The partner usually drank a single cup of coffee, but would leave a tip many times its price. Eventually Goldfield questioned him about this. He responded matter-of-factly that he took up a seat and that the waitress had to feed her family, too. For these cases, moral concerns – part of substantive, not merely formal, rationality – play a central explanatory role. This solidarity and compassion, which would rate high on the Kohlberg scale of putting oneself 'in another's shoes', contrasts with the calculating one of most middle- and upper-class people, with its upward or downward adjustments based on assessment of quality of service.

Frank's praise of people who don't disconnect anti-pollution devices on their cars also reveals the limits of the rational actor model (keeping such devices supposedly reflects a concern for the environment, and of the world in which the individual must live), but still have unexplored class aspects. For the skills and motivation – lower disposable income, conjoined with the supposed costs of higher fuel consumption generated by the devices – to do the disconnecting reside predominantly with working-class people. It must first, of course, be noted that for those with more disposable income, the relative price for being socially responsible is less. In contrast to rational choice analyses, the behaviour of working people need not be seen as narrow and selfish. For a distinction may be drawn between narrow self-interest – always seeking additional monetary reward – and the broader, Aristotelian interest in being a self – which would include the environmental concerns above. A poor person may have priorities, for instance feeding a family or providing other support for children, which might take precedence over the use of anti-pollution devices. Thus, on a subtler account of conflicting goods, even those who disconnect might sometimes prove a counterexample to theories of narrow monetary self-interest.

In a different direction, Jon Elster goes further than Frank in emphasising the psychological sources of 'irrationality' that undermine neoclassical rational choice theory. Like Frank, he rejects the economic material self-interest basis of much important human activity. Yet he is less sanguine than Frank about the ultimate rationality of many emotions. He provides interesting analyses of altruism, *akrasia*, i.e. weakness of will, and sour grapes, i.e. the modification of preferences when their attainment proves to be difficult. He finds many more fundamental, problematic, and less strategic violations of rational self-interest than does Frank. Elster locates the terrain of analysis of these violations of the neoclassical model in individual psychology.[6]

Amartya Sen offers a still more radical critique of neoclassical versions of rational choice theory. In a pithy example, Sen argues that individuals do not just give answers to questions that will maximise their gains.

> 'Where is the railway station?' he asks me, 'There,' I say, pointing at the post office, 'and would you please post this letter for me on the way?' 'Yes,' he says, determined to open the envelope and check whether it contains something valuable (Sen 1989, p. 9).

Sen argues that a good deal of our behaviour is governed, not by gains-maximising goals, but by our commitment to public norms and rules. He suggests that many of our actions are neither totally egoistic, i.e. only concerned with maximising one's own gains, nor totally non-egoistic (only concerned equally with the claims of all). Rather, according to Sen, much of our behaviour is concerned with the claims of 'family, friends, local committees, peer groups, and economic and social classes' (Sen 1989, p. 85). Sen concludes that these concerns are at the core of rational behaviour or what we have called concern for being a self including a concern for one's relationships with others. Thus, Sen concludes that 'The *purely* economic man is indeed close to being a social moron.' Or, in his more poignant phase, a 'rational fool' (Sen 1989, p. 104).

Sen's analysis is highly suggestive about the limits of neoclassically-rooted rational choice theory. He does not, however, answer the question of whether some alternative rational choice model, e.g. one like Elster's, is needed or whether such a model itself is too limited to provide the basis for good social science explanations.

THE APPEAL TO METHODOLOGICAL INDIVIDUALISM

Even the analyses of Elster and Sen (to the extent that the latter retains the rational choice perspective) have their problems. Many of these difficulties arise from the rooting of rational actor explanatory models on the philosophical principle of methodological individualism. Yet most authors who hold to the latter assumption merely assert methodological individualism as a first principle without argument.[7] Some couple this assertion with a claim that a denial of methodological individualism leads to mysticism or irrationality. Such, for example, is the stance of the economist Kenneth Arrow who states:

> A full characterization of each individual's behaviour logically implies a knowledge of group behaviour; there is nothing left out. The rejection of the organism approach to social problems has been a fairly complete, and to my mind salutary, rejection of mysticism (Arrow 1968, p. 164).

It is quite common to offer the vacuous tautology that all social entities (e.g. families, governments, bureacracies, corporations, economies) are solely composed of individuals. Though true, this claim gains less than its advocates usually think. Certainly Marx and perhaps Hegel would agree with this assertion. Once one accepts the importance of social relations, ideology, and complex psychological phenomena, virtually no types of explanation are excluded by invoking individualist principles.

A further problem is that Arrow's assertion offers no legitimate explanation of why social scientists should confine their reductions to individual human beings. For all individuals are composed solely of flesh and blood, organic matter, cells, nothing more or less, i.e. there is nothing left out. So why not say, as empiricists or physicalists often have, that descriptions and explanations of individual activities must be reduced to descriptions and explanations of organic matter?[8] Or to take an alternative tack, we might reduce the actions of individuals to the physiological, electrical stimuli and responses of the nervous system. And, one need not stop here either. Organic matter, cells, as well as physiological processes, are composed solely of physical matter and processes, ultimately reducible, not merely to molecules and atoms, but to those atomic components (no matter how hypothetical and problematic) that are currently regarded as the basic building-blocks of the universe. There is nothing left out. Thus, the most popular arguments for methodological individualism provide one with no clear rationale for standing pat with a reduction to individual human beings.[9]

Among the few people who address this question explicitly are Donald Davidson (1986) and following him Jon Elster (1983a, p. 22). Davidson argues that all human actions or behaviour can only be described in terms of intention (Davidson 1980, pp. 229), i.e. an aspect of an individual's psychological state. One the one hand, Davidson maintains as a premise that psychological events 'are describable, taken one by one, in physical terms, that is, they are physical events' (Davidson 1980, p. 231). On the other hand, such events are not fully describable in physical terms, since they require reference to broader psychological aspects, to the 'holistic character of the cognitive field', which itself has no direct correlate in physical terms.

> Any effort at increasing the accuracy and power of a theory of behaviour forces us to bring more and more of the whole system of the agent's beliefs and motives directly into account. But in inferring this system for evidence, we necessarily impose conditions of coherence, rationalitiy, and consistency. These conditions have no echo in physical theory, which is why we can look for no more than rough correlations between psychological and physical phenomena (Davidson 1980, p. 231).

This argument, echoed in Elster, denies that human actions can be completely described and explained by sub-intentional causality.

A similar type of argument, however, might be directed against methodological individualism itself – that there might be broader social entities, e.g. the state, families, the market and the like, that cannot be perpicuously explained solely by references to the actions of individuals. In fact, one might argue that a full theory of human identity and personality (and our ability to predict certain aspects of individual behaviour) might require a fuller reference to other individuals and the social entities to which they belong. We will in due course suggest that this is most likely the case.

Further, even if individualism were correct, how do we know which specifications of individual intentions are relevant or sufficiently concrete? If one is attempting to provide an adequate explanation, for example, of why the 1917 Russian Revolution occurred, how do we decide which individual actions are most relevant? What importance do we give to Lenin's strategic arguments with other Bolsheviks about the insurrection? To what the tsar did the morning or the week before being deposed? How do we choose the proper framework for causal selection and weight? We will explore the import of such questions later.

First, however, we wish to discuss the characterisation of the methodological debate offered by Arrow in the previous citation and emphasised by Elster. They propose a dichotomy between methodological individualism and methodological collectivism, holism, or even mysticism. This claim seems not just wrong, but highly ideological. A more nuanced epistemological and ontological view might suggest that social entites (institutions, groups, or structures) have various levels. These levels include physical, biological, mental, and emotional aspects of individuals, as well as social or relational aspects. The so-called higher levels presuppose and are based on the lower levels, with much interaction and mutual penetration (in the language of contemporary philosophy, particular levels supervene on others, without reductionism). But this more dialectical perspective does not entail holism, for instance the claim of some British idealists and in certain writings of Bertell Ollman, that everything is highly related to and dependent on everything else. From an explanatory point of view, how important various substrates and levels are will depend on the particular question to be answered or explanandum to be assessed. In some cases, an account appealing to straightforward individual intentions (How did you get to work this morning? I drove.) will be evidently the best; at other times, such accounts will be insufficient. In many important research cases, it may be indeterminate (so far) as to which aspects or levels are most important. For example, consider the ongoing debate about the basis of some psychological diseases. Is there a chemical or physiological basis for some psychoses? Alternatively, or as a supplementary hypothesis, do any have broad social roots? To what extent in these instances are we dealing with social artefacts about 'deviance', e.g. cases of blaming the victim (Gilbert, 1990; Chorover, 1975)? Sometimes, analysis at the level of various aspects of the individual is relevant, sometimes larger social relationships and ideologies are central.

METHODOLOGICAL INDIVIDUALISM AND BAD SOCIAL SCIENCE

We will explore three major arguments about social science explanation that undermine methodological individualism. We will refer to them as the ontological, the structural, and the epistemological.

The Ontological Argument

The ontological argument is traceable to Aristotle, who argues that humans are *zoon politikon*, i.e. fundamentally political (and hence social) animals, who cannot be understood as isolated, autonomous individuals. Aristotle's ontological claim about what we might call social individuality is also an explanatory one, focused on how to achieve the most reasonable explanation of the relevant pehnomena among (potentially) competing philosophical or scientific opinions. Dispositions (what the neoclassicists refer to as preferences) and the potential for moral character are themselves social products, the results of one's upbringing in a particular family, one's formal education, wider relationships, and the polis in which one is raised, including the laws that govern it. This social experience gives rise to individual's valuing diverse intrinsic goods (friendship, political community, science, art, contemplation, virtues and the like) which shape ethical deliberation (i.e. substantive rationality). Within his conception of a polis, Aristotle includes culture (and what moderns think of as national character). His theory focuses primarily on two modes of social interaction: the family (which for Aristotle includes both the hearth or *Gemeinschaft*/biological relationships and the locus of economic activity) and the political association.

Both the skills needed to achieve one's ends and the ends themselves that one actually pursues in particular situations are a social product based on lengthy habituation. While individuals can engage in moulding their character to some degree, i.e. choose to act in ways to develop the type of habits and virtues that would make one the type of person one wants to be, the range of choice is often quite restricted. Proper socialisation is much more important, and in any case, a necessary prerequisite.

Contrary to Elster's claims which suggest a complete dichotomy between either individual choice or complete social determinism, the recognition of the constraints and limits on choice does not necessarily eliminate choice. It would be foolish to think of the Aristotle of the *Nicomachean Ethics* and *Politics* as a methodological collectivist, or as a social determinist. To fully understand an individual, however, is to understand her as a social product. To ask why people act in certain ways, i.e. why Americans don't vote, why individuals commit crimes, why people divorce, why individual civil rights activists in the 1960s risked arrest, beatings, and death, is to ask social questions whose explanations and answers are not always best achieved by reducing them merely to questions about individuals.

Empiricists have long complained about the allegedly vague claims of 'collectivists'. But to what extent does Aristotle's argument actually conflict with individual-level analysis? Since the views, intentions, and deliberative possibilities people acquire as a result of experiences in the family and the polis are held by individuals, Aristotle's explanatory emphasis on the practical and theoretical primacy of the polis is consistent with the most compelling aspects of methodological individualism. Aristotle's theory differs from neoclassical theory mainly in its insistence on and specification of formative social experiences and in providing clear and coherent moral characterisations of the deliberators. Once Aristotle's views on natural slavery, women, and the alleged deficiencies of artisans are abandoned, his theory of deliberation is ironically internally more consistent and coheres better with a worked out, modern theory of individuality than does neoclassical preference theory (see Gilbert 1990, Ch. 1). In contrast to the asocial, exogenously determined preferences, and hence character, envisioned in neoclassical theory, and the reduction of even interactive versions of individualism to these allegedly naturally-based preferences, a contemporary version of Aristotle's political theory would *prima facie* provide a better framework for investigating the social relationships within which individuality emerges (see Gilbert 1990, Chs 1,7, for further comments along this line).

When looking at the assumptions of classical economics, Marx makes a similar argument:

> Individuals producing in a society – hence the socially determined production of individuals – is, of course, the point of departure. The individual and isolated hunter or fisherman, with whom Adam Smith and Ricardo begin, belongs among the unimaginative conceits of the eighteenth century's Robinsonades ....It is, rather, the anticipation of 'civil society'. ...In this society of free competition the individual appears detached from natural bonds etc. which in earlier historical periods make him the accessory of a definite and limited human conglomerate. The human being is in the most literal sense *zoon politikon*, not merely a gregorious animal, but an animal which can individuate itself only in the midst of society (Marx 1973, pp. 83–4).

The substance of the ontological argument is that the abstraction of individuals from their roots or social relationships is misplaced, missing the real issues of individuality, which have to do with particular deliberations in a definite setting over a lifetime, not with the predication that every choice is an achievement of individuality or freedom. Denying substantive rationality, views which emphasise 'freedom of choice' distort the actual diversity of ethical goods (friendship, attention to the environment, political commity, and the like) which mark genuine deliberation and moral conflict. Further, certain 'choices' – for instance, choosing to be enslaved – conflict with the maintenance of a free regime, individuality, or even the consumer sovereignty which neoclassicists extol. Technically, the argument for absolute freedom of choice is, thus, self-refuting. An Aristotelian view of social individuality contrasts with the arbitrary individualism of rational choice theory which systematically underestimates various aspects of the social relationships and social rootedness of individuals and downplays any notion of substantive rationality.[10]

The Structural Argument

A central claim of methodological individualism is that an explanation is not complete until it has micro-foundations at the level of individual human beings (see Elster 1983a, p. 23 as well as the previous quote from Watkins). In contrast to the question whether micro-foundations provide a deeper level of explanation, we answer the following : sometimes yes, often no. Sometimes micro-explanations are useful, sometimes diversionary, besides the point, or wrong. We will emphasise two points here: First, as we suggested earlier, many initially plausible explanations suggest structural accounts; yet, methodological individualism leads researchers to artificially exclude these very explanations from the outset, and consider only 'individualist', i.e. preference-based ones (we label this stance the *a priori* exclusion of alternate theories). Second, the methodological individualist insists on different levels of analysis, arguing that the reduced one – the level of individual intentions – is primary and deeper. We suggest that this perspective is often misleading. In many important cases, structural claims are primary; the specifying mechanisms, including those provided by game theory, are many times parasitic on the relevant structural explanation. Thus, the appropriate individualist explanation often follows from the structural insight rather than vice versa. Here some examples are appropriate.

The 1929 Stock Market Crash
Much discussion has taken place since late 1929 over the origins of the Great Depression. Many see it as having been precipitated by the stock market crash on Wall Street in late 1929. What caused the crash? On the micro-level, it was precipitated when the first trader panicked and sold cheap, followed by others. Does it help us to know who these individuals were, what was on their minds, what were their reasons and intentions for panicking? Probably not. Of the standard analyses of the depression, monetarist, underconsumption, overproduction, declining rate of profit, Kindelberger's suggestion that no hegemonic international power existed, none focuses on the role of the particular individuals who actually brought about the crash, nor have analysts felt that further information about these individuals would aid in a deeper explanation.

Weber on the 1848 Berlin Uprising
Max Weber (1949) discusses the difference between historical situations in which individual actions and decisions (i.e. the micro-level) are decisive for an explanation and those where they are not. In this respect he examines a

number of contentions by the nineteenth-century German historian Eduard Meyer. Meyer believes that the decision of Bismarck led to the war of 1866 (Weber 1949, pp. 181). Without Bismarck's decision, according to Meyer, the war in all probability would not have happened. Weber does not challenge the claim that sometimes political decisions, taken by individuals, have great explanatory weight. Instead, he puts forward the following counterfactual rule in analyzing the causes of historical events:

> The assessment of the causal significance of an historical fact will begin with the posing of the following question: in the event of the exclusion of that fact from the complex of factors which are taken into account as co-determinants, or in the event of its modification in a certain direction, could the course of events, in accordance with general empirical rules, have taken a direction in any way different in any features which could be *decisive* for our interest? (Weber 1949, p. 180).

By applying this rule, Weber offers a 'non-micro' analysis of the causes of the February Berlin workers' uprising, which triggered the 1848 German revolution. The micro-explanation and narrative sequence for the Berlin uprising are, according to Weber, as follows: a crowd assembles, soldiers appear, two shots are fired by the troops, rumours spread throughout the city that peaceful demonstrators are being killed, the revolution begins. But, the particular sequence of events was not that causally significant. According to Weber, the grievances were such, the degree of social unrest so high, that a wide variety of incidents could have triggered the revolution. A deeper causal analysis, thus, would look at the broader social and structural features of German society and politics before March of 1848. A micro-explanation would at best be secondary and at worst be diversionary.

Capitalist Development
Marx gives a structural analysis of the dynamics of capitalism. He argues that the system compels individual capitalists and firms to attempt to maximise profits, to increase their production, to search for broader markets on pain of extinction. Capitalists are in a life-and-death struggle with other capitalists. Although there may be respites and truces, each capitalist tries to gain a greater share of the market, to produce his or product more cheaply. Capitalists must also try to lower labour costs, both by technical innovation and by getting more work for less money out of their labourers. Individual capitalists like Robert Owen who try to treat their employees humanely, to pay them much more, or not to compete with other capitalists on the world market are irrelevant to capitalist development. Either

they occupy a small niche which takes up a decreasing share of production and the market or they are simply driven out of business as unprofitable producers. Either way, the particular motives of individual capitalists, aside from the compunction they feel to maximise profits, are largely irrelevant. Thus, capitalism as a system cannot be understood at its deepest level at the micro-level. It must be understood structurally.

The Development of the African-American Freedom Movement
There is a vast literature on the development of the civil rights movement in the United States in the 1950s and 1960s. Among the important questions that have concerned investigators are two types : (1) What caused the existence of the patterns of racial discrimination that existed before they were challenged by the movement? Why was this discrimination so draconian, especially in the South? (2) How did the movement for social equality develop? Why was it successful in undermining many of the barriers to social and political equality?

The most insightful analysts have focused on a number of structural factors which they claim explain the existence and strength of the system of white supremacy. In turn, they argue that it was the weakening of these factors which allowed for the possibility of the system's defeat, if not its elimination. These commentators point to the importance of cotton to the southern economy for much of the nation's history, and of the need of southern planters to maintain a cheap, coerced supply of agricultural labour. While racism developed a life of its own, while all classes of whites participated in sustaining and enforcing the system of white supremacy, it was the economic interests of southern planters and their control of southern politics – and hence their influence in the Democratic Party and Congress – which was its bedrock.

Thus, it was the changing economic environment which provided the crucial context for the success of the civil rights movement. As Piven and Cloward state succinctly, 'political modernization in the South followed from economic modernization' (1979, p. 182). Several important economic changes had taken place in the South in the decades before the 1950s: there was a decrease in the importance of cotton within the southern economy, especially after the 1930s; combined with this trend, mechanisation had diminished the importance of agricultural labour; other important economic sectors developed that may have supported and benefited from segregation, but whose survival did not require it.

Secondly, a number of external factors emerged which raised the cost of the system of white supremacy for those outside the South: the increasing numbers of northern African-Americans, particularly in large cities in large industrial states, pushed many Democratic Party politicians to become more forceful in demanding civil rights for Blacks, creating something of a crisis within the Democratic Party; after the Second World War, the moral (and hence political and economic) costs of the system of racial discrimination increased within the world arena in which the United States was attempting to play a leading role in the conflict with the Soviet bloc. Finally, the increased urbanisation of the African-American population in the South gave greater independence and strength to organisations within the black community, especially the Black church.

Now certain of the factors might be reduced to and analysed in terms of individual decision-making, although in many cases this would not be very illuminating. Even in those cases most illuminated by discussions of decisions and individual actions, an exclusive focus on rational choice can lead one in the wrong direction. In a recent book, for example, Dennis Chong focuses on how individuals decide to participate and 'how these individual decisions translate into collective outcomes' (1991, p. 1). Despite a number of interesting insights about collective action and civil rights tactics, his analysis is obtuse to the broader context which other writers have seen as crucial. Further, his insistence on formulating all questions of group action in terms of rational choice logic, leads him at times to do violence to social reality. An example is the following claim: 'In the civil rights movement, membership in the NAACP (National Association for the Advancement of Colored People) during its formative years brought solidarity and financial rewards. Association meetings gave middle-class blacks an opportunity to socialize and provided a convenient forum in which black professionals could advertise their services to prospective clients.... Clearly if the value of these incentives exceeds the cost of membership, then it is in the self-interest of the rational individual to join' (pp. 31–2). Which clearly misses the striking fact, confirmed by numerous empirical accounts, that even NAACP membership in the Deep South during the 1950s carried with it the risk of violence and death.

Finding the Best Explanation
Returning to the empiricist's worry, we may note that these two types of explanation, structural and methodological individualist, are not, as Weber's account suggests, mutually exclusive. Rather, the question of which level is primary or not can only be determined by empirical examination of a particular question, not by *a priori* stricture. Sometimes a reduction to the level of individual decisions helps get at the fundamental explanation. Thus, Bismark's calculated belligerence in initiating the war

of 1866 may be decisive. Often such a reduction is a useful analytic exercise that helps one identify more important causal structures. But the role of Bismarckian statesmanship might conceivably be said to arise from political *possibilities* determined by German capitalist development, the tradition of Junker militarism, the failure of the revolution of 1848, and specific social features of rival European powers. To appeal to his decision and character in explaining fundamental choices about war and peace presupposes a structural account and is not necessarily 'reduction' to individual preferences. Rather, this appeal answers a specific well-formulated structural question about possibilities. Thus, from an explanatory standpoint, Bismarck's preferences for Frühstuck the morning of the invasion are probably not as important as his penchant for conquest. Similarly, whether Bismarck made his calculations five months, five minutes, or four minutes and 53 seconds before – Elster's suggestion that the more specific the information, the better the explanation notwithstanding – is probably misguided (Elster 1985). Thus, the individualist standpoint can sometimes divert from or obfuscate important questions and relevant responses.

In what is probably the most careful study of levels of explanation, Alan Garfinkel (1981) puts forward the following criterion for whether a reduction is successful:

> one realm of discourse is reducible to another if the reduction theory gives us all the explanatory power of the theory being reduced.
>
> This give us a criterion for assessing a reduction. Look at the explanations that are possible in one realm of discourse and see whether we can explain the same phenomena in the other. If we can, the reduction is successful (Garfinkel 1981, p. 50).

Garfinkel proposes a notion of redundant causality in looking at ecological systems. He considers a system which contains rabbits and their predators, foxes (something like an isolated forest). When the level of rabbits is high the foxes find plenty to eat and have a high survival rate. As the fox population grows, it tends to diminish the rabbit population, thus providing less food for foxes. The foxes then diminish in number, giving the rabbits a chance to prosper. When the fox population is high, the likelihood of an individual rabbit being caught and eaten is great. Thus, it would be reasonable to say that the cause of the death of a particular rabbit was the density of the fox population. The less illuminating micro-explanation would simply be that the rabbit passed through the capture space of a particular fox. Garfinkel concludes:

The problem of reductionism is therefore: Do microexplanations such as this enable us to dispense with macroexplanations?

Garfinkel concludes that they do not. 'The microexplanation, therefore, contains much that is irrelevant to why the rabbit got eaten and does not really answer that question at all' (p. 56). Thus the search for micro-explanations and the assumption that they are always superior, 'deeper', more fundamental, is misguided. The rabbit could have died in numerous ways. As with the stock market crash and the Berlin workers uprising, we have a case of *redundant* causality. When redundant causality operates, the actual cause at the micro-level will be inadequate to explain the deeper cause located at the macro-level. The error of always searching for explanation at the micro-level, Garfinkel labels *hyperspecificity* or *hyperconcreteness*. The microreduction gives us a false sense of the sensitivity of the situation to perturbations at the micro-level (p. 62). Garfinkel concludes that the best way to test whether a structural property exists, i.e. requiring a macro-explanation, over and above or independent from the micro-explanation, is to pose a counterfactual question. If the micro-situation had been different – if the rabbit had not been at place x, at time t – would the outcome have been different (would it necessarily have avoided being eaten?)? 'Whenever a global property is not simply the sum of N individual properties ... the explanation of that global property will involve [structural] presuppositions' (p. 72). In such cases, from the outset, theorists will need a different level of analysis, a structural one, to highlight the important issues. Thus, the methodological individualist assertion that the deepest explanations are never structural, that a micro-explanation is always superior, is false.

The Epistemological Argument

In philosophy of science over the past twenty-five years, the empiricist arguments that underpin methodological individualism, e.g. Popper's and Watkins', and that survive in today's political science and economic literature, have been largely discredited. Neo-Kantian and realist historians and philosophers of science have underlined the importance of contending theories in research design. Scientific investigation does not progress, as political science empiricists have it, through gathering data (observations) and constructing single hypotheses ('theory building') which are then tested against 'the data'. Rather the data to be explained are shaped by the questions characteristic of a branch of scientific investigation as it begins to mature or 'become internalized' (Shapere 1984). The important questions that guide research are determined by plausible, fairly stated, competing theories or hunches (usually no more than two) which specify the relevant 'theory-saturated' observations or what empiricists sometimes call 'crucial experiments'. The choice among contending theories occurs not by deduction but by what Gilbert Harman (1965) calls 'inductive inference to the best explanation' across a range of important cases. Thus, a complex theoretical conversation occurs in a given field to get the best (most refined) statement of the relevant alternatives and assess them across a range of important cases. On this view, Darwin's *Origin of Species*, which takes the examples most favorable to creationism, including the complexity and beauty of the human eye, explores novel evidence, and provides case-by-case reasons for the superiority of natural selection, is a paradigm: yet empiricist or Popperian reconstructions often allege Darwin's view to be a borderline case of science or even unscientific. For despite its great explanatory power, it provides no direct predictions of new species.

In recent years, sophisticated empiricists or falsificationists (Imre Lakatos, for example), have acknowledged the central role of conflicts of theory and the complexity of scientific research. Thus, Lakatos suggests that the progressiveness or degeneracy of a whole theoretical research programme, including the relevant auxiliary statements, must be assessed against others; that no theory gets falsified merely by a particular factual counterexample (Lakatos 1970, Shapere 1984, Boyd 1984, Gilbert 1984, 1990). That these controversies have been unexamined in political science methodology is an interesting anomaly.[11]

This approach, exhibited in recent philosophy of science discussions, allows us to reinterpret and assimilate the grain of truth in methodological individualism. What it will not allow is the easy dismissal of broader types of explanations by 'rational choice Marxists' and others who often pick extremely weak examples to criticise. The object of attack is often a type of inappropriate and crude functionalism, e.g. that capitalists supposedly always get their way under capitalism even when one cannot imagine any mechanism for their doing so, or that even protests against the system, including militant strikes, somehow are functional in strengthening the capitalist system. We certainly agree that such crude examples should be ruled out. No philosophical or scientific progress is ever made, however, by concentrating one's arguments on the weakest examples and formulations of one's opponents. Such examples can be ruled out by following the simpler, *a posteriori* criterion or research guideline suggested by Gilbert (1990, pp. 234–5). Given the relevant contest of theories in a field, we place a low research priority on badly stated, empirically implausible, theoretically uninteresting hypotheses.

The *a priori* exclusion of theoretical alternatives leads to bad social science, because of its harmful effects on the refinement of major theoretical alternatives. An example from recent literature may clarify the distinction between controversial explanatory individualist proposals and misguided philosophical individualism. A major question for those political scientists who analyse voting behaviour is explaining why some people vote, why others do not, and what determines the proportions of each. The rational choice tradition tends to begin with neoclassical assumptions, looking at the costs and benefits that accrue to individual voters (explanatory individualism). Much discussion starts with Downs' model (1957). Downs argues that the likelihood of an individual's vote influencing an election outcome is infinitesimal, at least above a certain minimal number of votes (say, several thousand), for those voting in Congressional, Senate, and Presidential elections.Thus, the benefits that one gains from seeing one's candidate win are unlikely to be affected by whether or not one votes. On the other hand, there are certain costs to voting which are real, minimally the time and energy it takes to vote. Thus, the narrow calculus of voting shows it to be an irrational and therefore unlikely act, not in anyone's self-interest. Yet many people do vote.

Thus, the analysis of voting which focuses on individual decision-making must supplement the simple model by other supposed interests or concerns that a voter might have. Riker and Ordeshook (1968) propose a whole list of additional individual 'satisfactions' from 'affirming allegiance to the political system' to 'affirming one's efficacy in the political system' (p. 28). Ferejohn and Fiorina (1974), unhappy with these considerations, propose a new calculus of 'minimax regret', as an alternative to utility maximization: a voter supposedly casts her ballot to minimize the feeling of utter dispair she would feel if she did not vote and her candidate lost by a single vote.

Hardin (1982) and Uhlaner (1989) both propose additional criteria, even farther removed from the Downsian neoclassical paradigm. Hardin (1982, pp. 108–9) suggests that people often participate in collective actions from elections to 'world-shaping historical events' out of 'the desire to be there, to take part in history, to ... develop through participation...' Uhlaner argues that participation brings individuals 'relational goods', goods that allow one to be accepted and recognised as a member of a group to 'reaffirm my sense of self' (1989, p. 258). While we believe that Hardin and Uhlaner's arguments move in the right direction, their proposals probably fit more easily with a paradigm other than rational choice, for instance, a more robust psychological and sociological conception of individuality.

We do not maintain, however, that even the neoclassical models of voting based on individual decision-making are completely uninformative.

Quite the contrary. After discussing the various costs of voting, e.g. Downs argues:

> At first glance, all these costs may appear trivial, and biases in ability to bear them seem irrelevant. However, the returns from voting are usually so low that tiny variations in its costs may have tremendous effects on the distribution of political power. This fact explains why such simple devices as holding elections on holidays, keeping polls open late, repealing small poll taxes, and providing free rides to the polls may strikingly affect election results. (Downs 1957, p. 266).

Downs' analysis also provides the basis for understanding why changes in the weather (e.g. a warm and sunny day versus a cold and rainy one) have such a large effect on election turnout, allowing us to pinpoint anti-democratic features of American electoral laws.

Within political science, there is an alternative tradition of explanation of voting behaviour that does not take the preferences of individuals or the framework of choice as fixed, but sees them as the main object of study. This tradition looks at the election process in comparative and historical perspective. While perhaps complementary, it implicitly claims to provide deeper explanations for turnout rates in the US than the individual-level analysis.

Walter Dean Burnham (1979), whose work along with that of V. O. Key, exemplifies this approach, e.g. begins with three aspects of voting in the United States: (1) the decline in turnout in the United States over the last century; (2) the low percentage of voter turnout compared to Western Europe at the present time; (3) the class skew of non-voting, i.e. non-voting is highest among the lower classes in the US, a skew that does *not* exist in Western Europe.

Burnham, along with Piven and Cloward (1988), attributes these factors in part to the greater difficulties in registering to vote in the US – largely obstacles to working-class voting. Burnham, following Hartz, also argues that there is an '*uncontested hegemony*' in the United States about 'the nature of the political economy, the organization of the political system, and the role of religion in public life which was and is quite absent in any European context, even the British, (1982, p. 117). In contrast to Hartz, however, who glorifies this situation, Burnham sees it as an unfortunate consequence of the lack of an influential labour, social-democratic, socialist, or communist party in the US, that is, a class-based party to represent working-class people; this absence diminishes the political efficacy of lower-class voters.

The structure of political choices offered the electorate in the United States, and the major decisions made by political elites, have together produced more and more baffled ineffective citizens who believe that chance rules their world. This not only implies the long-term paralysis of democracy, but also a rapid speed-up of this paralysis in the most recent period of history (p. 134).

Now it might seem that rational choice analysts could try to assimilate the insights of Burnham and Piven and Cloward into their standard individual decision-making model of voting. But even this attempt would make the abstract rational choice model *parasitic* on the comparative class theory to which Burnham appeals. It would make the rational choice model explanatorily interesting *only* by conceding that another theory – one focusing on social relationships – is in fact an inference to the best explanation. For the latter looks at the American pattern of voting and non-voting as the result of a lengthy historical collective action problem faced by lower- class voters. Thus, voting (along with political party activity, union membership and activism, company bowling leagues, and other forms of working-class group participation) is not best seen as the product of decisions of isolated individuals. Rather, one must look historically at how group identities and allegiances have been forged, the ties, commitments, obligations, expectations, patterns of activity, habits, and ways of life that have developed along various classes and substrata. In particular, we may rightly explain voting participation and non-participation in the US as a product of the undeveloped state of working-class consciousness and organisation in comparison to that in Western Europe, a result of the working-class organisational fragmentation and the 'uncontested hegemony' pinpointed by Burnham. Following a group rational actor model, we might then view voting as part of a much broader collective action problem.

Burnham's argument about the stifling of political alternatives may be supplemented by looking at the rich historical literature. Mention might be made of the frequent emergence of incipient radical movements in American history and of the extent and comparative effectiveness of political repression of these movements: from the 1919 Palmer Raids against the Industrial Workers of the World and the fledgling Communist Party to the post-Second World War expulsion of eleven Communist-led unions, the firing and blacklisting of thousands of rank-and-file union organisers and others, including academics during the McCarthy period (Goldstein 1978; Schrecker 1986). An even broader explanation might appeal to historical factors in the United States which have held back the development of working-class political alternatives: the special intensity of racial and ethnic divisions among working people; the strategic decisions of communists, radicals, and labour activists at critical junctures, particularly during the 1930s; the overwhelming hegemony of the US economy in the post-Second World War period (Prickett 1975). The importance of radical strategic decisions, especially during the 1930s, arises, as in the case of Bismarck, in a particular structural-political context of possibilities. The theory-governed, comparative, historical, structural line of argument appears richer in examining these questions than the more abstract, 'universal' analysis of costs and benefits to every individual. Much of the tenor of post-Second World War social science in the United States, at least until recently, has refused to assess or even acknowledge the evidence for alternative perspectives. Despite the considerable merits of particular neoclassical studies, adherence to methodological individualism as an a priori dogma has legitimized the exclusion of alternative explanations, particularly radical ones, from consideration by otherwise fair-minded researchers.[12]

In sum, we argue that individualist explanatory proposals should remain an important pole in research and debate in the contemporary social sciences. We also argue that the exclusive focus on such explanations, the methodological individualist banning of alternative explanatory perspectives, necessarily leads to bad social science.

CONCLUSION

In summary, we have argued:

Neoclassical versions of rational choice theory run into severe problems, in good part because of the narrow, egoistic assumptions they make about human behaviour. These assumptions often diverge dramatically from real human conduct, thus making neoclassical models unable to account for important social phenomena.

Most of the criticisms of neoclassical rational choice theory, for instance those offered by Frank, Elster, and perhaps Sen maintain a good deal of the basic neoclassical framework and are legitimised by appeal to methodological individualism. Elster's willingness, however, to examine phenomena that are difficult to explain within the rational choice framework has led him to abandon many of the positions for which he is best known.

Most rational choice proponents assert methodological individualism, providing little argument. On those rare instances when arguments are given, they are weak and often beside the point.

Proponents of rational choice wrongly conflate philosophical, explanatory, and moral individualisms. But there is no necessary connection between explanatory rational actor models and philosophical individualism.

Ontologically, social entities are often constitutive of individuals (and, of course, vice versa, as methodological individualists often claim). The importance of that ontology is revealed by the best explanations of important phenomena, historically, as Marx argues, and in the life of the individual, as Aristotle claims, and in the formation of preferences, by the role of social norms and group welfare, as Sen suggests.

Philosophical methodological individualism often rejects *a priori* comparatively plausible, and upon examination, deep explanations for those social activities where causal redundancy exists. In those cases, structural causes play a central role in explanation; individualist arguments often take the slippery slope to irrelevant hyperconcreteness.

An epistemological criterion which emphasizes the importance of fairly stated, competing theories in guiding scientific research can exclude the same bad arguments that methodological individualism wishes to exclude. In contrast to methodological individualism, however, it ensures the fair and courteous consideration of plausible alternatives.

Our arguments cast doubt on the currently popular claims of rational choice theory to be a superior overall framework to all other alternatives for analysing politics scientifically. The argument, however, leaves room for interest in much rational choice research, either individual or collective, where proponents advance more modest claims.

NOTES

1. The term, of course, encompasses a diverse range of orientations. Here, we include those views which refer to themselves as rational expectation, rational politics, rational choice, and rational actor theories, including many aspects of strategic, individual-based analysis.
2. One of the few 'rational choice' theorists who rejects the primacy of rational choice explanations over other types of explanation is Michael Taylor, making him virtually unique among adherents. Our criticisms do not, of course, apply to his work. It is important to note that he is an exception in this respect who stands alone.
3. Ordeshook (1986) and Elster (1982a, 1985) state this principle explicitly. Interestingly, Becker (1976) is less committed to methodological individualism since he is willing to look at the preferences and maximising behaviours

of firms, households, unions, government bureaus, and even nations, without reducing these activities to those of individuals.

4. While many practitioners insist on the element of conscious choice, a few economists such as Becker feel that it is only necessary to assume that people act *as if* they were making such choices.

5. Becker's explanation, of course, suggests that production of children is centrally linked to their monetary value to a family. A deeper and subtler explanation of these phenomena, however, might focus on the dynamic of gender roles and different forms of domination within marriage as well as the competing aspects of self-realization versus status achievement outside the home. This point is linked to what we call below the ontological criticism of methodological individualism.

6. Elster's early work (1983a, 1986b, 1987) has provided the entry into rational choice theory for many political scientists, and it is, thus, on this work which we concentrate. In more recent writings, however, Elster has abandoned many of the arguments for which he is best known.

7. Levins and Lewontin (1984) give some suggestions about why this might be the case.

8. Ironically, sociobiologists like E. O. Wilson claim that social science can only be scientific when based on biology. This view was responsible for part of the organisation of the National Science Foundation until recently, as the social sciences were a subset of biology, to the funding detriment of the former.

9. We find it especially ironic for a view that styles itself in being empiricist that it rejects other arguments and perspectives without empirical examination. Thus, we find its practitioners engaging in the *a priori* exclusion of alternative theories.

10. For a discussion of modern liberal and radical views of social individuality focused on Montesquieu, Hegel and Marx, see Gilbert 1990, Ch. 1. For examples of similar issues which focus on the labour movement, see Goldfield 1989, passim and esp. pp. 160–2.

11. For exceptions, see the arguments in Goldfield (1989b, 1990) about the importance of testing and comparing alternative theories about the causes of the passage of New Deal labour legislation. See also Gilbert (1990a, Ch. 3).

12. It should, of course, be emphasised, in contrast to those who assert its value neutrality, that methodological individualism was popularised by Popper and Watkins as a principle which would specifically exclude Marxism and other radical approaches.

12 Rational Choice Marxism and Postmodern Feminism: Towards a More Meaningful Incomprehension
Alan Carling

A funny thing happened to me at the Annual Meeting of the American Political Science Association in San Francisco in 1990 (some pretty strange things had happened when I was last in San Francisco, in 1968, but I won't go into those here). The bus in from the airport was set high enough to see behind the billboards, into what looked like vast sales lots for mobile homes, but which I soon realised were permanent housing for the San Francisco poor, tucked away out of sight behind the commercial façades, exactly as Engels had recorded the journey into Manchester in 1844. I felt uneasy, too, stepping over the beggars on the sidewalk to enter the Hilton Hotel, but you have to hand it to US academics: they sure know how to organize a conference that feels like a serious business convention. There were actually men and women there in suits, especially those silver-sheeny ones in a mottled semi-reflective material that looks as if they descend from a job-lot of curtain lengths delivered by UFO somewhere over Colorado circa 1955. (Baudrillard might well call them crystalline.) By dressing below this level, it was possible to regard oneself as a marginally dangerous intellectual presence, or at any rate a marginal one. (In the UK, by contrast, it is physically impossible to dress so low as to be the worst-dressed person present at the Annual Conference of the British Sociological Association.)

Because it was so big, so open-hearted, and so much in San Francisco, the conference catered even to the most exotic tastes, and so I tried to attend all and only those sessions devoted either to Marxism or to feminism. And this is the funny thing that happened to me at the APSA. The sessions on Marxism were preoccupied with analytical

Marxism (not all advocating it, but consistently oriented towards it); the sessions on feminism were preoccupied with postmodernism (not all advocating it, but consistently oriented towards it). Not just class on the one hand, gender on the other; but two distinct sets of theoretical preoccupations, and two quite different kinds of language to describe them. How come?

MARXISM AND FEMINISM

It is a commonplace that from a strictly theoretical point of view, second-wave feminism in its early stages borrowed heavily from Marxism. The thought seems to have been: if they (the men, the Marxists) can have capitalism (or 'the mode of production – the distinction between the two is not at issue here), then we (the women, the feminists) can have patriarchy; and the ways in which patriarchy was initially conceived owed a great deal to the then-prevailing conceptions of capitalism. Two basic positions arose fairly spontaneously regarding the relationship between patriarchy and capitalism, and the two positions went on to stake out their characteristic theoretical-political territory, partly in opposition to each other, and partly in opposition to orthodox Marxism, in the course of the classic debates of the 1970s.[1]

In gross description, the two positions were dual systems theory on the one hand, with its associated programme of socialist feminism, and the dialectic of sex on the other, whose politics inclined towards radical feminism. Dual systems attempted to set patriarchy alongside capitalism; the dialectic of sex to replace capitalism with it. The logic of the radical position led it towards questions of personal and institutional violence, sexuality, and a discourse of difference. In its most unexpected twist the dialectic of sex biologised, or at any rate essentialised, gender difference, in a move which has no formal counterpart to my knowledge within the Marxian tradition. (No one ever argued that the proletariat was essentially different, in an analogous sense of essentialness.)[2] On the socialist feminist side, the focal concerns included domestic labour, the social history of gender – class interrelationships, and a discourse of equality. If one takes Heidi Hartmann's synthesis as a benchmark for socialist feminism in the late 1970s, there is also envisaged what might be called a divisionist perspective – one compendious enough to embrace all manner of structured social inequality. For if dual systems theory had already been established securely via the interaction of feminism with Marxism, why not move on out to multiple systems, via the inclusion of race and ethnicity, sexual orientation, age, and disability?[3]

MULTIPLE SYSTEMS AND POSTMODERNISM

Poised at the outset of the 1980s to carry all before it, multiple systems crash-landed soon after the launch. Far from extending its scope and influence, it was hard-put to maintain its viability as a research programme even within its heartlands of Marxism and feminism, class and gender.

I am still perplexed as to why this occurred – it doesn't seem to me to have much to do with the intrinsic merits of the programme as such.[4] No doubt it has to do partly with the sensitivities of broaching the connection with race – there was I think no lack of good faith, but the attempt foundered quickly on the reaction of a number of women of colour, castigating white feminists for presuming to speak for all women.[5] It cannot have helped either that at about the same time second-wave feminism's original birth attendant was undergoing an intellectual implosion. Consider the sequence: Althusser, Poulantzas, Hindess and Hirst, the dead-end of classical value theory, the faltering of the great English tradition of Marxian historiography evident in Edward Thompson's magnificently futile outburst against the French. These developments must have made it seem that Marxism was a theoretical companion offering less than reliable means of support. On the one hand postmodernism in the early 1980s shook up an already troubled and disoriented dual systems research programme, since it seemed to articulate the inadequacy of the latter's overall design; on the other hand, it offered a positive way out for some feminist writers, since it projected an alternative perspective from which social difference might be addressed.[6]

Somewhat innocent of the significance of these events, I had attempted to effect a juncture between what I took to be the most promising variant of contemporary Marxist theory – rational choice Marxism (RCM) – and the divisionist perspective opened out by Heidi Hartmann. I argued, in particular, that John Roemer's models of class exploitation could be generalised to provide a rational choice account of all the major social divisions. This attempted generalisation might be represented as yet another dreary colonising manoeuvre directed at feminism and anti-racism by Marxism; unsurprisingly, I do not see the matter in that light. Since rational choice had in my view already colonised Marxism to outstanding effect, why not spread the good news in every other direction? The thought was to use a theoretical paradigm which was neutral as between the social divisions (or at least defined as external to any one of them) as a way of drawing them all together, thereby establishing a fruitful discourse of comparison between them.[7]

I may well remain almost the only person who has ever thought this, since the people who believed in rational choice never believed in multiple systems; the people who believed in multiple systems never believed in rational choice; and not many socialists or feminists these days seem to believe in either multiple systems or rational choice.[8] It was certainly a combative move to declare in 1986 that RCM represented 'the reinstatement of the subject', intending of course both Marxist topic and individualistic method (see above, pp. 31–78). But this description of the project unwittingly discloses its vulnerability to the postmodern critique. Postmodernism does for RCM because it demands the fragmentation of the subject, in the same two connotations of discourse and person; it does for socialist feminism because it ostensibly excludes *grandes narratives* (than which *rien* – not even Marxism – is le *plus grande* than Heidi Hartmann's prospectus for a multiple systems theory), and it does for radical feminism because it rules out essences.[9] Perhaps its deepest achievement *vis-à-vis* feminism (and therefore the too-few parts of Marxism alive to gender issues) was the conviction it managed to generate that the very forms of language in which social theory had been conducted were implicated in male supremacy. If we had to invent a whole new way of speaking – perhaps even a whole new way of relating – in order to cope with social difference, how could we expect to leave unchanged all the old ways of doing politics and social science?[10]

But this isn't quite good enough. It is natural to reconstruct the impact of postmodernism (as I have done above), as the intrusion of an external force, which introduced in the early 1980s a new torsion into the whole field of received social theory, unsettling all its carefully-crafted relationships.[11] Such a description will serve, but only up to a point, since it tends to suppress the Marxian provenance of postmodernism itself. I do not refer only to the intellectual biographies of the leading figures: Baudrillard, Lyotard, Deleuze and Guattari, Jameson, Mensonge – you name them, they have a Marxist past (and in at least one case – Jameson – a Marxist present);[12] I mean that they bring to their work a continuing preoccupation with classic Marxist themes in the analysis of society and culture. To hear postmodern feminism talking past rational choice Marxism at the APSA is to hear two Marxian dialects which apparently no longer speak the same language; one speaking through class, the other speaking through gender.

So do they really speak the same language, or have they diverged irreconcilably from a common Marxian root?

THE TROUBLE WITH MODERNISM

> All fixed, fast-frozen relations, with their train of ancient and venerable prejudices and opinions, are swept away, all new-formed ones become antiquated before they can ossify. All that is solid melts into air, all that is holy is profaned, and man is at last compelled to face with sober senses, his [sic] real conditions of life, and his relations with his kind (Marx 1977, p. 224).

The reference to the sweeping away of fast-frozen relations makes clear how acutely Marx and Engels anticipated in this passage from the *Communist Manifesto* the development of techniques of instant cryogenesis for departed kinfolk, and 'all that is solid melts into air' has become a slogan – indeed, a cliché – of postmodern culture.

Marx and Engels are describing a culture in a chronic state of flux, which both undermines received or established forms ('ancient and venerable prejudices and opinions') and refuses stability – or at least refuses continuing legitimacy – to new-fangled ones ('antiquated before they can ossify'). The question is: are they describing a modernist culture or a postmodernist culture? If they are describing a modernist culture, then a new criterion must be introduced in order to distinguish postmodern culture from modern culture, despite the fact that the banishment of fast-frozen relations is as handy a capsule definition as any of what many critics take to be the essence of postmodern culture (insofar as postmodern culture is allowed to have an essence). If they are describing a postmodern culture, then they are doing so with great prescience, almost 30 years before the advent of the epoch Toynbee would later call Post-Modern, and almost 80 years before the first currently-recorded sighting of the word 'postmodern'.[13] More importantly, they are doing so by drawing a straightforward contrast with a preceding traditional culture ('ancient and venerable prejudices and opinions'), without bothering to notice any intermediate term. But if modernism does not exist because there is no space to sandwich it between traditionalism and postmodernism, then postmodernism cannot exist either, because there is nothing relative to which it can count as post. So what's modern and what isn't?

One sense of the 'modern' is simply 'that which is most recent'. Such a designation of an artefact, theory, value, attitude, etc. is not merely chronological; it comes freighted with the presumption that what is modern is somehow more worthy of note than what preceded it, and that past manifestations are in some sense subsumed under their current representations, so that the past must be understood in relation to the present. In this respect it is probably fair to say that the designation of the modern is tied to a conception of progress, and is a quintessentially Enlightenment cultural project. It also models culture after an ideal type of scientific knowledge, wherein each scientist stands on the shoulders of all his or her predecessors.

Yet, since, as Marx and Engels say, it is inherent in each temporary manifestation of the leading edge of cultural progress that it will be superseded ('it becomes antiquated'), the problem arises of how one designates something that was once modern but now no longer is. The leading-edge conception of the modern begins, in other words, to press against another conception, according to which the modern designates artefacts, theories, etc. credited with specific aesthetic conventions and effect, techniques and materials of construction, theoretical assumptions and modes of expression which have come to encapsulate (what was once known as) 'the modern'.[14]

As time goes on for any culture conceiving itself as modern, this hiatus begins to yawn embarrassingly wide. What counts as modern in the leading-edge conception necessarily constitutes a tiny proportion of the sum total of cultural activity – roughly, what the (self-identified?) avant garde happens to be watching, reading, inhabiting,...eating?... at any given moment – whereas the stock of artefacts and representations which have counted as modern at some stage in the past is necessarily increasing. Indeed, this stock could grow in principle to cover the whole cultural field, whereby absolutely everything had some claim of title to be modern, and all possibility of cultural discrimination would be lost to the term.

Perhaps the wildfire acceptance of the idea of the postmodern owes something to the release of this endemic tension between the in-fact-long-established modern and the ever-newly-fangled modern, whereby the modern can at last be held more comfortably in retrospect – as a now-completed phase, and a final cultural stock – whereas the postmodern figures as something that is not just new, but completely different.

Yet this release of tension (if this is what it is) merely creates fresh occasions for new tensions. The postmodern must be it. The modern becomes like a fast-running stream discharging into an enormously capacious vat of the postmodern. This vat must accommodate absolutely everything that is capable of being produced *from now on*; I mean, to the year dot. What could possibly come *after* the postmodern, and what on earth would it be called?[15]

But once culture finds itself discharged from the dizzying stream of the modern into the deep waters of the postmodern, certain changes occur; it slows down, and begins to turn around. Everything now is evidently defined looking backwards rather than forwards – in relation to the last cultural artefact rather than the next. The connotation of intellectual progress is also inevitably lost: we stand in the shadows of great predecessors – via nostalgia or pastiche – and not on their shoulders, via emulation and incorporation.[16]

It needs to be borne in mind, however, that this change of perspective on culture has occurred largely by means of an operation internal to cultural criticism – an operation that follows through the logic of endorsing the idea of the postmodern in relation to its predecessor – and not by any change either in the prevailing social conditions or, initially, in cultural production itself. Could one construct the following sequence? (to parody, or is it pastiche, the elliptic form in which postmodern theory tends to be presented): cultural critics find it unbearably boring to be still stuck in the modern (and when one thinks of high-rise council flats, who can blame them – why don't we all get mobile homes?); but since this generation grew up under the sign of the modern ('sign' in the sense, *natürlich*, of both signifier and signified; indeed, in the always already conjunction of the sign's two component parts) they cannot bring themselves to break completely with modernism's linear notion of time. Whatever replaces the modern must thus be conceived to follow after it, and not just be different from it: not just unmodernist, but postmodernist.

But the unhappy critic now gets carried away by the unexpected implications for critical attitudes of the notion of the postmodern. It becomes mandatory to see everything back-to-front: no longer the past understood in the light of the present, but the present understood in the light of the past – out with Marx, in with Nietzsche. The critic therefore casts around for artefacts, theories, buildings, bits of music etc. which exemplify the new attitude, and whose presence reinforces the conviction that the seachange from the modern to the postmodern is already well-established in the culture. Pretty soon artists themselves – who are, of course, critics in another guise – begin producing artefacts, etc. self-consciously imbued with the new mentality, not least because these types of product will very likely find approval from the critics. (Parents in the UK will immediately think in this connection of any children's TV programme produced by Janet Street-Porter, which requires an ability to process pictures at the speed of light, an attention span measured in nano-seconds, and an IQ of - 300.)[17] Surrounded by self-consciously postmodernist works, the critical critic senses that a cultural change of extraordinary importance is taking place. And the more momentous the aesthetic change seems to be, the more it must be related to some equally important underlying causes of social change (the postmodernist retains a lingering attachment to Marx in this respect at least). Thus the critic who began merely being worried by high-rise buildings comes to think that we are in the midst not just of postmodernism, but of post-Fordism, post-industrialism and Post Office Counters.[18] When allied to a parallel political crisis, and a failure of direction on the left, the whole caboodle can be parlayed into a completely novel era of social development: 'New Times' (Hall and Jacques, 1989).

HOW NEW ARE 'NEW TIMES'?

It is difficult to believe that the situation addressed by postmodernism derives from some fundamental change in the nature of capitalism itself. Marx and Engels had already described the tendency of capitalism to hollow out received cultural forms, and to subordinate them to the relentless dictates of commodity production. Since it is part of the distaste expressed by critics that postmodernism undermines all non-commercial criteria of value, and since we are in any case allegedly passing through the final triumph of capitalism on a world scale, it is difficult to imagine that postmodernism involves any essential discontinuity in economic development. Subcontracting? one thinks of putting-out, the butty system or the chainmakers of Cradley Heath (Keating 1976, pp. 174–84); dual labour markets? one thinks once more of Engels on Manchester (1987, pp. 111–26); part-time employment, low wages and casualization? one thinks of Charles Booth, family life and the London docks (Keating 1976, pp. 112–41); intensification of work? one thinks of *Capital*, Vol. 1, and the filling of the pores of the working day; new technology? read one of the sentences just prior to those quoted above, which gives Marx and Engels's explanation why culture under capitalism is subject to constant flux: 'the bourgeoise cannot exist without constantly revolutionising the instruments of production, and thereby the relations of production, and with them the whole relations of society (Marx 1977, p. 224).

Post-Fordism is at most a return to Victorian values rather than a new phase; flexible accumulation involves (locally important) local variation in the strategies of profit maximization available to individual firms; just-in-time manufacturing systems exploit information technology to economize on buffer-stocks (what could be more traditional than economization as a capitalist strategy?)(Sayer and Walker 1992, pp. 162–90); decentralization of production is hardly ever postmodernist fragmentation of production, since institutional control apparently relinquished at the periphery is usually recouped, and indeed intensified, in more compact and fiercer central units – holding companies, head offices, banks, and so on (and the same pattern is repeated in the state: in the UK, out with local government, in with Treasury control); robots are introduced when and because they are more reliably productive than assembly-line workers, just as power-looms were introduced when and because they were more reliably productive than hand-loom weavers (indeed, what is a power-loom but a robot weaver?); internationalisation of finance via new information systems enables the imperatives of the market to be registered more swiftly, more brutally and more completely. Far from changing its spots, capitalism is every day revealing them.[19]

POSTMODERNISM OF THE AUTHOR-POSITION

Since there is little scope for discovering postmodernism within the socio-economic development of capitalism itself, it may be more fruitful to seek it in the author-position from which capitalism is described. Recall that the passages from Marx and Engels cited above contain three elements: (i) a description of a culture – 'all that is solid melts into air' (ii) an explanation of why the given culture takes the (lack of) form it does – 'the bourgeoisie cannot exist, etc.' and (iii) the announcement of an author position from which this culture may be apprehended in this way – 'and man is at last compelled to face with sober senses, his real conditions of life, and his relations with his kind'.

Notice the determinism in Marx and Engels's account of the critical response to capitalism. A person immersed in all the frenetic confusion of a capitalist culture is bound sooner or later to react against it, as if awaking from a drunken stupor ('at last compelled to face with sober senses'), and then, in that reaction, somehow to achieve a critical vantage-point from which to ascertain the truth about that culture ('real conditions of life, and relations with his kind'). We might ask – what compels anyone to undergo this sequence of critical responses? Perhaps it is humanly intolerable to experience the level of uncertainty about social relationships that capitalism tends to create. But it looks also as if this level of uncertainty is a precondition for attaining to a correct appreciation of social relationships: by casting everything into question, capitalism serves to demystify everything, including, even especially including, demystifying capitalism itself ('all that is holy is profaned'). Yet this demystification can (only?) be achieved from a position which is at odds with the constantly-revolutionising culture of capitalism itself: a position which is 'sober', in contrast to the intoxication normally induced by life under capitalism. This is a prototypical expression of what feminist theorists came to regard as a standpoint theory – i.e. not just a theory which articulates the interests of those at the sharp end of an invidious social process, but an articulation which could not have been achieved without the lived experience of the process.

It is not always clear in Marx and Engels precisely which experiences of capitalist society and culture generate the requisite anti-capitalist standpoint, but there is little doubt that, once attained, the standpoint is a thoroughly stable one: 'sober senses' are the rock on which an analysis rests which does not melt into the thin air of capitalist metaphysics.[20] What happens, then, if the insight about the character of the society is made to reflect back on those who would write society's script: if the presuppositions of Marxist cultural theory are among those things which capitalism causes to melt into air?

ENTER LYOTARD

It has been common practice at this point to nod sagely, announce the death of Marxism, and plead Lyotard in aid. According to Lyotard, the author-positions of the Enlightenment are the first casualties of the postmodern era. He defines Enlightenment discourse as a quest for consensus 'cast in terms of a possible unanimity between rational minds' (a meeting of minds like the confrontation of commodity owners across the floor of the exchange). He notes that science in the Enlightenment tradition aims to set itself apart from, and above, the narratives of everyday life, seeking to 'legitimate itself with reference to a metadiscourse ... making reference to some grand narrative, such as the dialectics of spirit, the hermeneutics of meaning, the emancipation of the rational or working subject, or the creation of wealth' (Lyotard 1984, p. xxiii).[21] These grand narratives arise out of the *narratives petites* of secular culture, and continue to exist amongst them, but there is an asymmetry in the relationship between the discourses of science and the discourses of the life-world: secular discourses tolerate the scientific, and even accord them an honoured specialised role, but the scientific discourses despise the secular, claim an exclusive access to truth, and pretend to believe they can get along on their own. These attitudes are institutionalised in the Encyclopaedic arrangement of the modern University, beginning in the 1820s with Berlin, and its fixing of the map of knowledge by faculty and discipline.

For Lyotard, 'simplifying to the extreme', the postmodern is defined by contrast as 'incredulity toward metanarratives', and he is clearly on the side of the oppressed discourses against their oppressors (Lyotard 1984, p. xxiv). In view of what he has said before about modernism, the postmodern stance immediately implies a loosening of the boundaries of the academic disciplines, a reappraisal of the relationship of secular to scientific culture, and a scepticism towards the truth claims of science – in short, a legitimation crisis for the knowledge institutions of the West. If we ignore the impact of all this on university budgets (postmodernist scepticism would come as music to the ears of the Department for Education in the UK), Lyotard commends the playfulness of unanchored intellectual creativity ('paralogy'), and the proliferation of language games without a single centre, free of domination by any master discourse, such as that imposed in a modernist culture by one of the grand narratives – Marx, Freud, the hermeneutics of meaning, and so on.

One can appreciate how this vision of an open discourse would resonate with feminists reaching similar conclusions by a different route: not just that new voices were given permission to speak, but that permissions to speak were no longer required.[22] Yet Lyotard's conclusion depends on particular arguments in the sociology of knowledge. Leave aside the criticism that Lyotard's recapitulation of science since the Enlightenment places him squarely in the grand narrative business,[23] if Lyotard's argument is right, what does it show? In line with Bachelard, Feyerabend and Kuhn, he draws attention to the fact that science is a social activity conducted within a community of scientists by means of linguistic devices – rhetoric, metaphor, fable, as well as specialised vocabularies and techniques – which bear no necessary relationship to any 'truth of the matter'. This is insufficient, however, to dispose of science's special claim to truth: the defence would be that, unlike vernacular discourses, the institutions of scientific practice – publication, citation of evidence, forms of argument, intellectual competition, mutual reference, etc. – mobilise rhetoric, interest and status behind a particular, potentially cumulative, goal conventionally called 'the pursuit of truth', where 'the truth' is provisionally recognizable partly on cognitive, partly on procedural and partly on pragmatic grounds.

This defence may or may not be valid, but it requires a much closer attention to the practices of science than Lyotard provides.[24] Sometimes he seems to be saying that science never deserved the privileges it has given itself since the Enlightenment, at other times he assays a new, specifically postmodern, phase of scientific practice bound up with the communications revolution: 'knowledge in the form of an informational commodity indispensable to productive power is already, and will continue to be, a major – perhaps the major – stake in the worldwide competition for power'. This suggests a belief that the conduct of science has changed, and not just our understanding of the way it has always worked in practice. He goes so far in this emphasis as to prescind entirely from science as a social process. He 'expect[s] a thorough exteriorization of knowledge with respect to the "knower", at whatever point he or she may occupy in the knowledge process. The old principle that the acquisition of knowledge is indissociable from the training (*Bildung*) of minds, or even of individuals, is becoming obsolete and will become ever more so' (Lyotard 1984, p. 4).[25] So meaning now bypasses human subjects, and inheres instead in mechanical systems?[26]

This nonsense alerts us to a curious feature of the postmodern debate: on the one hand postmodernism is the most extreme culturalism – it takes off from Marx's analysis of commodity fetishism, and then tries to convert the relative autonomy of the superstructure into the absolute autonomy of the superstructure (a move made most shamelessly by Baudrillard). On the other hand, extreme culturalism consorts with the crassest expressions of technological determinism, in which the silicon chip transforms the basis on which any human knowledge can be gained: the typewriter gives you society with Virginia Woolf; the PC society with Janet Street-Porter. (At this point, and in an access of populist enthusiasm, I thought I should ask my computer for its opinion, so I have typed in 'what do *you* think?', and recorded the answer in a footnote).[27]

POSTMODERNISM EATS ITS TAIL

In one plain sense, the postmodern stance is self-defeating. If the challenge to the conventions of reference are taken too far within a discourse which relies for its meaning on those conventions, then one is left with a sequence of signs without signification. One could presumably (and within another discourse relying on those conventions) point to the sequence of signs as a manifestation of postmodern culture, but the theory of it would be modern, since such a description would necessarily rely on the very conventions which the postmodern manifestation had sought to deconstruct. But then the manifestation itself would count as modern rather than postmodern, since the distinguishing characteristic of the modern is, by hypothesis, the availability of such a vantage point beyond cultural flux from which the manifestations of cultural flux may be described. (Marx and Engels's capitalist culture is modern because their perspective on it is.) If a theory of the postmodern is possible, in other words, it cannot be a postmodern theory, and, in view of this, it cannot be a theory of the postmodern.

Case in point: Warhol's *Diamond Dust Shoes* is important enough as an image for Jameson to display it on the front cover of his book – for him it enjoys iconic status. In the text, he compares it to *A Pair of Boots* by Van Gogh (shall I compare thee to a pair of boots?). Whereas Van Gogh's peasant's downtrodden boots *express* alienation, Warhol's flat surface shoes *are* alienation. This is the key move from the modern to the postmodern sensibility. 'Appropriate readings of *The Pair of Boots* may be described as *hermeneutical*', says Jameson, 'in the sense in which the work in its inert, objectal form is taken as a clue or as a symptom for some vaster reality which replaces it as ultimate truth... Andy Warhol's *Diamond Dust Shoes* evidently no longer speaks to us with any of the immediacy of Van Gogh's footgear; indeed, I am tempted to say that it does not really speak to us at all. Nothing in this painting organizes even a minimal place for the viewer, who confronts it .. with all the contingency of some inexplicable natural object... a random collection of dead objects hanging together on the canvas like so many turnips, ... shorn of their earlier life world.'

And, he goes on, there is also 'the emergence of a new kind of flatness or depthlessness, a new kind of superficiality in the most literal sense, perhaps the supreme formal feature of all the postmodernisms... we must come to terms with the role of photography and the photographic negative, ... which confers its deathly quality to the Warhol image... It would be inaccurate to suggest that all affect, all feeling or emotion, all subjectivity, has vanished from the newer image. Indeed, there is a kind of return of the repressed in *Diamond Dust Shoes*, a strange, compensatory, decorative exhilaration, explicitly designated by the title itself, which is, of course, the glitter of gold dust, the spangling of gilt sand that seals the surface of the painting and yet continues to glint at us (Jameson 1991, pp. 8–10).

This is considerable eloquence on behalf of a painting which does not speak for itself. Imagine Jameson's book hung on the wall of the Museum of Postmodern Art in New York, between *Diamond Dust Shoes* and *A Pair of Boots* (better still, imagine it propped up on the sidewalk between those two pictures in the Postmuseum of Postmodern Art in Ex York). The surface of the learned tome is flat, indeed photographically negative, since it reproduces *Diamond Dust Shoes*, but the cover of the book refers sideways both to the left and to the right: on the left, from the image on its cover to (what it seems inevitable to call) Warhol's original, and, to Van Gogh's *Boots* on the right, via the relationship between modernism and postmodernism fathomed in the text beneath, to a depth of 438 pages in my edition. To make Warhol's art speak, and to establish its relationship to a modernist precursor, entails the treatment of it as a 'clue to a vaster reality'. And that is the point: why Jameson's procedure, if not his icon, reduces to a modernist endeavour.[28]

JAMESON'S SOCIAL THEORY

I have criticised postmodern theorists for combining extreme culturalism with crude technological determinism: they move directly from forces of production to superstructures without passing through the relations of production.[29] Jameson – who remains the most sophisticated of the postmodern social theorists – also avoids this trap, but he is arguably caught in another – that, having decided postmodernism is a qualitatively new cultural phase, and wanting to remain a Marxist, he has to find a phase in the development of capitalism corresponding to it. For this purpose he lights upon Mandel's *Late Capitalism*, despite the fact that paralogical *jouissance de texte* and Mandel make rather strange bedfellows: not for nothing is the latter nicknamed Deadly Ernest.

Jameson relates three phases of culture – realist, modernist, postmodernist – to three phases of capitalist organisation – market, imperialist, late multinational – which are in turn related to the three phases of technological development attributed to capitalism (slightly idiosyncratically) by Mandel. The beginnings of these phases involve the onset of the building by machines of the machines which supply the predominant motive power in the relevant phase, which Mandel dates to 1848 (steam engines); 1890 (electric motors and internal combustion engines); and 1940 ('machine production of electronic and nuclear-powered apparatuses') Jameson 1991, p. 35). If we re-assemble these components into their respective phasal entities, we find capitalism periodised as a steam-powered realist market economy (1848–90), followed by modern electric imperialism (1890–1940), and thence a nuclear-powered multinational postmodernism (1945 to date).

We may gloss over the historical infelicities implied by this scheme: what technology was capitalism using before 1848?; why was the most imperialist country in the imperialist Phase 2 – Britain – an imperialist country already by 1650, 200 years before it entered its pre-imperialist laissez-faire Phase 1?; how is it that the thing which lends its name to the characteristics productive organisation of Phase 2 – the Ford – achieves its greatest fame as symbol only later on, in the postmodernist, post-Fordist Phase 3?

Jameson is not generally concerned with such details. He tends to proceed by hinting at the critical affinity between some phenomenon allegedly characteristic of postmodern culture – schizophrenia, depthlessness, the evaporation of a sense of history, 'the transformation of reality into images, the fragmentation of time into a series of perpetual presents', etc. – and a list of allegedly parallel ('consonant') features of late capitalism – 'new types of consumption; planned obsolescence; an ever more rapid rhythm of fashion and styling changes; the penetration of advertising, television and the media generally to a hitherto unparalleled degree throughout society; the replacement of the old tension between city and country, center and province, by the suburb and by universal standardization; the growth of the great networks of superhighways and the arrival of automobile culture' (Jameson 1985, pp. 124–5).

For the rest, and for the most part, he leaves the economic base largely in the hands of Ernest Mandel, despite the fact that he has grafted on to Ernest's Phase 3 base a postmodern construction quite alien to the late capitalist superstructure designed by Ernest himself. It is true that Mandel, like Jameson, emphasises the 'industrialization of superstructural activities', so that 'Pop-art, television films and the record industry are in this respect typical phenomena of late capitalist culture', but the emphasis in his discussion of the ideology of late capitalism falls not on the fragmentation of discourse but on the totalising presence of 'technological rationalism'. This is an all-encompassing creed which creates a 'social prison', and 'all that is left is the dream of escape – through sex and drugs, which in their turn are promptly industrialized ' (bit-part for the misguided hippies of '68?). And then in terms which echo the *Manifesto*, Mandel affirms that 'the ideology of "technological rationalism" can be exposed as a mystification which conceals social reality and its contradictions, at four successive levels' (no half-measures here). Technologically rationality is first, reified; second, incomplete and internally incoherent; third, 'overestimates the ability of late capitalism to achieve the integration of the masses' and is finally, and in italics '*a contradictory combination of partial rationality and overall irrationality*' (Mandel 1975, pp. 502–3).

Mandel thus appeals, in a traditional, indeed a modernist, Marxist vein, to a higher rationality which can transcend the narrow limits imposed by the second-rate bourgeois version. The cultural lesson he reads into late capitalism is not intertextuality, but good old central planning. Mandel thus argues in orthodox vein that socialism is the completion of the project of modernity, and the very cultural forms which he says late capitalism creates are the ones that Jameson claims it has already left behind, even though Jameson gestures towards Mandel to lend his claim authority.

CULTURAL EXPLANATION

The problem is: how does one fit cultural phenomena into social explanations; what controls the ascription of superstructures to bases? I take it, first, that many cultural manifestations are likely to be epiphenomenal from the Marxist point of view. That is, since their occurrence is neutral with respect to the phenomena on which Marxian explanations bear, they are inexplicable from the Marxian point of view (see Cohen 1988, pp. 155–82). Second, that cultural manifestations are explicable within Marxism (where they are explicable at all) by their effects, and not by any intrinsic artistic, ideological or aesthetic characteristics. This point is of some importance, since it means that the criteria by which cultural manifestations are grouped together involve commonality of effects, rather than necessarily commonality of form. The unity criterion for cultural manifestations is not critic-centred, so to speak, but socially oriented.

But what effects count, in counting together? In static terms, the effect that counts for Marxist theory is the effect of stabilizing the relations of production. In more dynamic terms, I would argue that the effect which counts is the effect of enhancing the reproduction of one set or type of productive relations over another set, within some socio-economic field of play.

In 1986, we are told, David Lynch's film *Blue Velvet* 'was one of the most talked about of the year,... drawing around-the-block lines in New York for three weeks'. This is on the Richter scale of cultural impact. I doubt, if the Holy Bible were published for the first time, it would detain Manhattan for a week. *Blue Velvet* divided audiences into 'those who love[d] it and [found] it brilliant and bizarre, and those who hated it and [found] it sick and disgusting'. The audience could select their critical interpretation of the film from a list including 'pornography, parable of sin and redemption, like religious art, a cult film, gothic, coming-of-age film, trash, mindless junk, *film noir*, murder-mystery, small-town film, dream film, comedy, surrealism' as well as 'pastiche, and parody, an effacement of the boundaries between past and present, a presentation of the unpresentable derogatory of women, an assault on nostalgia, and a threat to safe, middle-class life' (Denzin 1988, pp 468–9, partly citing the *New York Times*). What effect would such an event have on either the stability or the reproducibility of relations of production?

Suppose first that members of the audience were utterly certain in their reaction to the film, though their reactions differed. Then one would establish the effect of the whole event by tracing the effects of the different reactions taken one at a time. Are the 10 percent of the audience who definitely see the work as a parable of redemption thereby reconciled to the social order, or more inclined to question their social roles within it?; Does dreaming by film make one more or less of a complaisant employee, or have no effect whatsoever, and what is the balance of these outcomes in the lives of the escapists who constitute, say, 25 percent of the audience? This type of analysis raises no issues specific to postmodernism, beyond an emphasis on the fact that any given work may strike consumers in different ways. More genuinely postmodern are the consumers who carry all possible interpretations within their heads; who are so sensitive to the multiplicity of viewpoints that they finally abstain from judgement.[30] Perhaps they have taken Jane Flax's feminism to heart, and learned 'to tolerate and interpret ambivalence, ambiguity, and multiplicity as well as to expose the roots of our needs for imposing order and structure no matter how arbitrary and oppressive these needs may be' (1987, p. 643).

Suppose that the audience is 100 per cent like this. Would a postmodernist consciousness at this level unleashed into the public domain stabilise or undermine capitalism? It all depends on how far it goes – confined to the cultural domain, disorienting politics, it would tend to disable opposition, hence stabilise the status quo. It would only destabilise the status quo if it spread with corrosive effect to the real master discourses, not Marx and Freud, but market, state and law. Yet this seems unlikely; New Yorkers queued round the block to pay to get in, and there is no evidence that postmodernists have given up shopping, even if they hardly know what to buy. Perhaps, though, there is some hollowing out of institutions; people purchase goods benumbed, without absorbing the promises of the good life which attend the sale; they seek the external credentials of knowledge no longer believing in the value of education. Cynicism is the keynote. But it is very hard to tell whether scepticism towards values has actually accelerated in the postmodern era, and as a consequence of a Lyotardian shock.

In more dynamic vein, the promulgation of a postmodern sensibility might soften up discourses of resistance to commodity relations, thereby facilitating the penetration of capitalism into new areas of culture and society, or new societies. But this again depends empirically on the balance between the disorganising and the recuperating elements in the relevant discourse – does rap merely disarrange existing language and music, or is it a ground-clearing operation on behalf of the Coca-Cola corporation, allowing US business to move in on a wasted zone and clean up? Likewise normatively – one's attitude to the subversive effects of paralogy will depend on one's attitude to what it subverts. Depthlessness directed against oppressive traditions and institutions, fine; schizophrenia infecting established forms of popular resistance and control, not so good.

Above all, if it is said that postmodernism reflects a new phase of capitalist development, it must be shown why the simulacrum serves capitalist consumerism better than the cult of the new, and how this advantage explains the preferential reproduction of postmodernist forms and attitudes at the expense of their modernist precursors; what are the mechanisms of social selection for cultural phenomena? Jameson, who remains the postmodern social theorist with his feet closest to the ground, has not even begun to address this question, or even show much awareness that it needs to be addressed.

POSTMODERNISM AND FEMINISM

Postmodernism, then, is sustainable neither as epistemology nor as social theory. In so far as it does not lapse into self-contradiction, its methodological stance reduces to modernism. There is no reason to believe that the social and cultural changes linked with postmodernism represent a qualitative departure for capitalism ('New Times'). This is not to underestimate the need to explain the character of the changes we are living through, only to suggest that we do not need a philosophical revolution to accomplish the result.

As a socio-cultural phenomenon in its own right, the take-up of postmodernism may be analogous to runaway selection in the theory of evolution, whereby signals between writers and their audiences were allowed to precess to an extreme, in a situation where certain restraints on discourse, especially those customarily expressed by the requirements of truth, were deliberately relaxed. This may be all there is to it, though one might attempt an anterior sociological explanation of postmodernism as the revenge of the disillusioned Situationists of '68 (Callinicos 1989), or the sigh of the downwardly mobile professoriat (Bauman 1988; Collins 1992).

But one would miss the political significance of postmodernism if one ignored its conjunction with feminist theory.[31] Postmodernism was taken up in the States enthusiastically by Donna Haraway and Jane Flax, and with greater caution by Sandra Harding, at a moment when its promise of open discourse must have seemed music to feminist ears.[32] Yet the reaction of feminists seems always to have been tempered by a sense of proportion derived from their political concerns (perhaps feminist politics supplied the discursive moorings which mainstream postmodernism had thrown off). Harding (1986, pp. 246–7), Fraser and Nicolson (1988, pp. 390–1), Hutcheon (1989, p. 168), Hekman (1990, pp. 188–90), Blake

(1990), concurring with Gallop (1987) and Braidotti (1987), Springer (1991, p. 323) – indeed, nearly all the feminists who have given the question sustained attention – have distanced themselves from postmodernism pure and simple.[33] This has been flirtation, not infatuation (nor of course seduction, which Baudrillard says no longer exists). The point is that a space for different voices can be opened up in unpostmodern ways, and the multiplication of identity does not entail a postmodern episteme. Nancy Fraser has written most recently that 'social identities are discursively constructed in historically specific social contexts; they are complex and plural; and they shift over time. One use of a theory of discourse for feminist politics, then, is in understanding social identities in their full socio-cultural complexity, thus demystifying static, single, variable, essentialist views of gender identity' (Fraser, 1992, p. 52).

It would be too much to say that there is a convergence here with current preoccupations of rational choice theory, but there is a certain mutual movement inwards from two extreme positions: the non-subject on the one hand, versus the unitary subject on the other. The endemic problem for rational choice is how to cope with norms and values, once it is conceded, as even Elster (1989, p. 128) must, that 'the power of norms derives from the emotional tonality that gives them a grip on the mind'.

One can distinguish the strong programme from the weak programme within rational choice. According to the strong programme, norms and values, with their corresponding aspects of the self, should ultimately be explicable in rational choice terms. Gambetta (1994), for example, has applied this approach to the case of the Mafia: in order for a mafioso's threats to be effective, the victim must believe that they are credible, which requires in turn that the mafioso is thought to be a true mafioso who will not eschew violence, as opposed to a civilian merely posing as an extortionist. Certain presentations of the self, and conceptions of honour, are therefore seen as part and parcel of a strategy in an exploitation game. The weaker programme does not seek to explain norms or values in rational choice terms, but sees them as internalised constraints on feasible sets, alongside the external constraints of the social situation which generate the incentive structure under which the actor acts.[34] This in effect contextualizes rational choice to social identity, just as Fraser's post-postmodern feminism contextualizes gender history and social locale. These positions are by no means the same, but they share a view of recent intellectual history: to be dynamic, divisionist, and non-essentialist, one need not be postmodernist. The task of theory is to comprehend variety, not to embrace ambiguity.

NOTES

1. I used to think that feminist theory went through socialist feminism *before* reaching the radical stage. Sarah Perrigo has put me right on this point, and I am generally indebted to her for discussions over the years on the issues raised in this chapter. I owe a similar debt of gratitude to Beryl Spink, Ann Walker, Ken Smith, Ed Reiss, Clare Snook, and Graeme and Sarah-Jane Araby-Kirkpatrick. Paul Thomas was most generous in his hospitality in San Francisco for the APSA conference.
2. 'Firestone invoked biological differences between women and men to explain sexism. This enabled her to turn the tables on her Marxist comrades by claiming that gender conflict was the most basic form of human conflict and the source of all other forms, including class conflict' (fraser and Nicolson 1988, p. 382).
3. See especially the closing paragraphs of Hartmann's rejoinder to criticisms of her 'Unhappy Marriage', where racism and heterosexism are singled out (Sargent 1981, p. 372).
4. I would however criticise the conceptual treatment of the multiple systems as parallel, rather than integrated. In Hartmann's work this comes out in the notion of 'empty places', according to which patriarchy or racism create the individuals to fill the roles available within the economic structure. The question though, is whether the economic roles would exist in the absence of the kind of people who are as a matter of fact constructed to fill them. Could the roles of slave, say, or housewife, exist independently of the systems of white racism or patriarchy which determine which individuals fill the roles?
5. An especially pointed attack on Hartmann along these lines was delivered by Gloria Joseph in 'The Incompatible Menage à Trois: Marxism, Feminism and Racism' (Sargent 1981, pp. 91–106).
6. 'There is nothing about being "female" that naturally binds women.... Painful fragmentation among feminists (not to mention among women) along every possible fault line has made the concept of *woman* elusive, an excuse for the matrix of women's dominations of each other.... The recent history for much of the U.S. left and U.S. feminism has been a response to this kind of crisis by endless splitting and searches for a new essential unity. But there has also been a growing recognition of another response through coalition – affinity, not identity' (Haraway 1985, pp. 72–3). Haraway's 'Manifesto for Cyborgs' is by way of being a Manifesto for Postmodern Feminism.
7. Though this approach can be criticized for reproducing the parallel treatment of social division evident in Hartmann (see n. 4 above)–the application of rational choice is made to class issues, then gender issues, then race issues. One way this problem might be overcome is sketched in n. 34 below.
8. This is less true of some of the academic disciplines than it is of their more engaged participants; rational choice has made a good deal of headway into political science on both sides of the Atlantic, and to a limited extent within sociology. Philippe van Parijs is the figure most sympathetic to the divisionist perspective among the major contributors to Analytical Marxism (see e.g. Van Parijs 1989, pp. 222–6).

Notes 321

9 For a critique of the residual essentialisms in a range of writers including Chodorow, Gilligan, Ferguson and Folbre, Hartsock and MacKinnon, see Fraser and Nicholson (1988, pp. 384–7).

10 Sandra Harding (1986, p. 29): 'how (can) a science apparently so deeply involved in distinctively masculine projects ... possibly be used for emancipatory ends?', and cf. Fax (1987, p. 633).

11 Think for example of the impact of the postmodern sensibility, waiting just around the corner, on the careful arrangement of feminist theories achieved by Alison Jaggar in her 1983 compendium Feminist Politics and Human Nature.

12 Callinicos (1989, p. 170) describes the political stance of the first four as 'on the spontaneist, anti-Leninist wing of the post 1968 far left'; Bradbury's painstaking reconstruction of Mensonge's biography for the same period leaves a similar impression (1987, p. 32). I am grateful to Roger Fellows for introducing me to Mensonge.

13 In Spanish in 1934, according to Hassan (1984, p. 120), also citing Toynbee.

14 I don't say it is an easy matter to establish the substantive content of the modern, when Joyce both is and isn't in, and when Hassan (1984, p. 119) regards Habermas as postmodern even though every one else (including Habermas, vehemently) regards Habermas as modern. On this, see especially Callinicos (1989, pp. 9–28).

15 Featherstone (1988, p. 195) mentions a 1977 occurrence of 'post-post-modernism', but my question has perhaps answered itself by the appearance of works with titles including the phrase 'after postmodernism': (Fekete 1988) and (Woodiwiss 1990).

16 'The postmodern eye looks fearfully into the future and it sees technology, uncontrolled sexual violence, universally corrupt political systems. Confronting this vision, it attempts to find safe regions of escape in the fantasies and nostalgia of the past. Dreams are the postmodern solution to life in the present' (Denzin 1988, p. 471). I thank Ann Walker for this reference.

17 'A literary taste always begins on some decent reason, but once started, it is propagated as a fashion in dress is propagated; even those who do not like it read it because it is there, and because nothing else is easily to be found' (Bagehot 1896, pp. 89–90).

18 Note to readers outside the UK: Post Office Counters Ltd is the government agency in the UK which receives cheques for private road users' annual licence tax. (Does having to explain a joke negate it? Probably not when it's as bad as this one.)

19 In all this I agree very much with Callinicos (1989, pp. 132–44).

20 Harding (1986, p. 26) acknowledges the Marxian provenance of the standpoint concept, although its application to the feminist case is somewhat clearer cut than in the anti-capitalist case. Feminist sobriety *vis-à-vis* patriarchy clearly arises from (and ultimately only from) the experience of being a woman (though there are some analogous difficulties, e.g.: is the experience of motherhood essential to feminist consciousness, or only the potential for it?) Within the Marxian tradition, the experiences deemed necessary to attain the correct anti-capitalist standpoint range from the mainly intellectual (a bourgeois education and a thorough exposure to the Hegelian dialectic)

through the intellectual-practical ('the philosophers have only interpreted the world; the point however is to change it') to the mainly sociological, whereby proletarian experience is a *sine qua non* for proletarian awareness. What is interesting about Marx and Engels' standpoint proposition above is that the relevant experiences are not class-specific, since they relate to the universal features of a dynamic commodity culture. Hence the coalition disposed by its direct experience to an understanding of modernism (and thence postmodernism) would be broader than the coalition so disposed by its experience of, say, alienation in factory employment.

21 I am grateful to Graeme Kirkpatrick for leaving his copy of Lyotard on my desk for so long that I was eventually forced to read it.

22 '... within feminist theory a search for a defining theme of the whole or a feminist viewpoint may require the suppression of the important and discomforting voices of persons with experiences unlike our own. The suppression of these voices seems to be a necessary condition for the (apparent) authority, coherence, and universality of our own' (Fax 1987, p. 633), and see the very strong closing statement: 'Feminist theories, *like other forms of postmodernism*, should encourage us to tolerate and interpret ambivalence, ambiguity, and multiplicity as well as to expose the roots of our needs for imposing order and structure no matter how arbitrary and oppressive these needs may be' (p. 643, emphasis added).

23 '... despite his strictures against large, totalizing stories, he narrates a fairly tall tale about a large-scale social trend' (Fraser and Nicholson 1988, p. 379).

24 There is plenty of scope here for radical critiques of science, especially feminist critiques of scientific practice) – but there is also the dilemma that feminist theorists have addressed: is there an alternative feminist knowledge-practice which grounds a (necessarily special) claim to truth without inviting a self-defeating feminist critique?

25 This line of thought is carried even further in his 'Can Thought Go on Without a Body?'. Indeed, the argument there is alarmingly loopy: because the Sun is going to explode in 4.5 billion years, we should 'manufacture hardware capable of "nurturing" software at least as complex (or replex) as the present-day human brain, but in non-terrestrial conditions' (1988, p. 79). This is apparently in order that we – or at least some emanation from us – will live after the death of our solar system. It is difficult to caricature postmodernism when it does such a good job on itself.

26 In spite of its severely reduced – indeed, almost Lyotardian – budget, the University of Bradford has recently disbursed an enormous sum of money on an optical character reader designed to encode the vast number of feedback forms on academic staff performance now required from students by the DfE. It occurred to me that one could short-circuit this procedure by hooking up the output of the OCR directly to the lecturer, thereby ensuring instant quality assurance, and responsiveness to consumer demand. I thought of this device as TIM (short for Teaching Improvement Monitor). I then wondered why we needed teachers at all – why not hook up TIM directly to the students? I now see that even in this suggestion I was fatally wedded to the bourgeois problematic of the subject. Who needs students? Why not hook up TIM's output to TIM's input and cut out the troublesome human factor completely? The University would certainly be much easier to manage.

27 [There was no reply.]
28 I have tried to illustrate Jameson's self-contradiction from his cultural criticism, but it can be done also from his epistemology. Consider the following: 'it would therefore be inconsistent to defend the truth of (postmodernism's) theoretical insights in a situation in which the very concept of "truth" itself is part of the metaphysical baggage which poststructuralism seeks to abandon. What we can at least suggest is that the poststructuralist critique of the ... depth model is useful for us as a very significant symptom of the very postmodernist culture which is our subject here' (Jameson 1991, p. 12). But what is 'usefulness as a very significant symptom' except a type of truth-claim for the relationship of a statement of cultural criticism to its socio-historical object?
29 Even in the very compressed statement of their position quoted above, Marx and Engels are careful to avoid this mistake: technological change impacts on the relations of production and only 'with them the whole relations of society'.
30 This doesn't apply to Denzin on *Blue Velvet*, interestingly enough, since he does venture an unequivocal verdict on the film, that in the end it reproduces bourgeois individualism and 'sustains[s] the key elements of a conservative political economy' (1988, p. 472).
31 This is my main quarrel with Callinicos (1989), who manages to avoid mentioning any of the feminist postmodernists (or indeed any of the French feminist post-structuralists) in a book-length study devoted to the political character of postmodernism! But one can record the same depressing oversight in the non-Marxist sociological treatments of Bauman (1988), Collins (1988), and e.g. the recent text-book survey by Smart (1993).
32 This was a precisely identifiable moment: compare Harding (1983) with Harding (1986) – the first article argues for a 'reflexive theory' which 'requires both inquiry and organizing to make visible to all of us the politics of our differences as well as of the commonalities in our lives' (p. 40). The sentiment is (what became called) postmodernist, but the vocabulary and the reference-apparatus are not. By 1986, Harding had taken postmodernism on board as a vehicle for the expression of difference, and a fully-fledged strand within feminist theory.
33 Some hewing back from the brink is also evident in the recent Lawrence and Wishart collection *Principled Positions*, significantly subtitled *Postmodernism and the Rediscovery of Value* (Squires, 1993).
34 The weak programme obviously requires supplementation by non-rational choice explanation for the norms and values which constrain choice. The most promising approach involves explaining the complex of norms-plus-rational-choice-behaviour-on-the-basis-of-norms in terms of social selection, as a unit of social interaction with preferential survival-value in a given larger environment, such as that supplied by e.g. market for inter-state competition. This approach conforms naturally to the evolutionary bent of Marxist historical theory (Carling 1993).

References and Select Bibliography

Aaronovitch, Sam, and Smith, Ron (1981) *The Political Economy of British Capitalism*, New York: McGraw Hill.
Abrams, M, and Rose, R. (1960) *Must Labour Lose?*, Harmondsworth: Penguin.
Agassi, Joseph (1960) 'Methodological Individualism', *British Journal of Sociology* 11:244–70.
Althusser, Louis (1971) 'Ideology and the State', in *Lenin and Philosophy and other Essays*, trans. Ben Brewster, London: New left Books, pp. 121–73.
Althusser, Louis (1977) *For Marx*, London: New Left Books.
Anderson, Perry (1976) *Considerations on Western Marxism*, London: New Left Books.
Anderson, Perry (1980) *Arguments within English Marxism*, London: Verso.
Anderson, Perry (1983) *In the Tracts of Historical Materialism*, London: Verso.
Anderson, Perry (1992) *English Questions*, London: Verso.
Arrow, Kenneth (1968) 'Mathematical Models in the Social Sciences', in *Readings in the Philosophy of the Social Sciences*, ed. May Brodbeck, New York: Macmillan, pp. 635–67.
Artis, M., Cogham, D., and Wickham-Jones, M. (1992) 'Social Democracy in Hard Times', *Twentieth Century British History* 3:32–58.
Aston, T. H., and Philpin, C. H. E. (eds) (1985) *The Brenner Debate*, Cambridge: Cambridge University Press.
Avineri, Shlomo (1971) *The Social and Political Thought of Karl Marx*, Cambridge: Cambridge University Press.
Backhouse, Roger (1983) *Macroeconomics and the British Economy*, Oxford: Martin Robertson.
Backhouse, Roger (1991) *Applied UK Macroeconomics*, Oxford: Blackwell.
Bagehot, Walter (1896) *Politics and Physics*, London: Kegan Paul.
Ball, Terence, and Farr, James (eds) (1984) *After Marx*, Cambridge: Cambridge University Press.
Barrett, Michèle (1985) 'Weir and Wilson on Feminist Politics', *New Left Review* 150:143–7.
Bauman, Zygmunt (1988) 'Is there a Postmodern Sociology?', *Theory, Culture and Society* 5:217–37.
Becker, Gary S. (1976) *The Economic Approach to Human Behaviour*, Chicago: University of Chicago Press.
Benton, Ted (1984) *The Rise and Fall of Structuralist Marxism: Althusser and his Influence*, London: Macmillan.
Bergson, Henri (1920) *Mind Energy*, trans. H. Wildon Carr, London: Macmillan.
Bernstein, Richard J. (1976) *The Restructuring of Social and Political Theory*, Philadelphia: University of Pennsylvania Press.

Bhargava, Rajeev (1992) *Individualism in Social Science: Forms and Limits of a Methodology*, Oxford: Oxford University Press.

Bhaskar, Roy (1978) *A Realist Theory of Science*, Hassocks: Harvester Press.

Bhaskar, Roy (1979) *The Possibility of Naturalism*, 2nd edn 1989, Hassocks: Harvester Press.

Blake, Pamela (1990) 'Directions in Feminist Theory: Displacing Postmodernist Panache', unpublished paper presented at the APSA Annual Meeting, San Francisco.

Bleaney, Michael (1984) *The Rise and Decline of Keynesian Economics*, London: Macmillan.

Block, Fred (1987) *Revising State Theory*, Philadelphia: Temple University Press.

Boston, J. (1985) 'Corporatist Incomes Policies, the Free Rider Problem and the British Labour Government's Social Contract', in *Organised Interests and the State*, ed. Alan Cawson, London: Sage, pp. 64–84.

Bowles, Samuel, and Gintis, Herbert (1986) *Democracy and Capitalism*, New York: Basic Books.

Bowles, Samuel, and Gintis, Herbert (1990) 'Contested Exchange', *Politics and Society* 18:165–222.

Bowman, John R. (1989) *Capitalist Collective Action*, Cambridge: Cambridge University Press.

Boyd, Richard (1984) 'The Current Status of Scientific Realism', in *Scientific Realism*, ed. Jarrett Leplin, Berkeley: University of California Press, pp. 41–82.

Bradbury, Malcolm (1987) *Mensonge*, London: Arena.

Braidotti, Rosi (1987) 'Envy: Or with your Brains and my Looks', in *Men in Feminism*, ed. Alice Jardine and Paul Smith, New York: Methuen, pp. 233–41.

Brandt, Richard B. (1979) *A Theory of the Right and the Good*, Oxford: The Clarendon Press.

Brenner, Robert (1977) 'The Origins of Capitalist Development: A Critique of Neo-Smithian Marxism', *New Left Review* 104:25–92.

Brenner, Robert (1985) 'The Agrarian Roots of European Capitalism', in Aston and Philpon (1985), pp. 213–327.

Brenner, Robert (1986) 'The Social Basis of Economic Development', in Roemer (1986), pp. 23–53.

Brenner, Robert (1989) 'Bourgeois Revolution and Transition to Capitalism', in *The First Modern Society*, ed. A. L. Beier, David Cannadine, and James M. Rosenheim, Cambridge: Cambridge University Press, pp. 271–304.

Burawoy, Michael (1985) *The Politics of Production*, London: Verso.

Burawoy, Michael (1987) 'The Limits of Wright's Analytical Marxism and an Alternative', *Berkeley Journal of Sociology* 32: 51–72.

Burawoy, Michael (1989) 'Should We Give Up on Socialism?', *Socialist Review* 19/1:57–76.

Burawoy, Michael (1989) 'Reflections on the Class Consciousness of Hungarian Steelworkers', *Politics and Society* 17: 1–34.

Burnham, Walter Dean (1982) 'The Appearance and Disappearance of the American Voter', in *The Current Crisis in American Politics*, New York: Oxford University Press, pp. 3–21.

Butler, David, and Kavanagh, Dennis (1980) *The British General Election of 1979*, London: Macmillan.

Butler, David, and Kavanagh, Dennis (1984) *The British General Election of 1983*, London: Macmillan.
Butler, David, and Kavanagh, Dennis (1988) *The British General Election of 1987*, London: Macmillan.
Butler, David, and Kavanagh, Dennis (1992) *The British General Election of 1992*, London: Macmillan.
Butler, David, and King, Anthony (1965) *The British General Election of 1964*, London: Macmillan.
Butler, Gareth, and Butler, David (1986) *British Political Facts*, London: Macmillan.
Callinicos, Alex (1976) *Althusser's Marxism*, London: Pluto Press.
Callinicos, Alex (1988) *Making History: Agency, Structure and Change in Social Theory*, Ithaca NY: Cornell University Press.
Callinicos, Alex (1989) *Marxist Theory*, Oxford: Oxford University Press.
Carchedi, Guglielmo (1987) *Class Analysis and Social Research*, Oxford: Blackwell.
Carling, Alan (1986) 'Forms of Value and the Logic of *Capital*', *Science and Society* 50: 52–80.
Carling, Alan (1987) 'Exploitation, Extortion and Oppression', *Political Studies* 35: 173–88.
Carling, Alan (1988) 'Liberty, Equality, Community', *New Left Review* 171: 89–111.
Carling, Alan (1990) 'In Defence of Rational Choice: A Reply to Ellen Meiksins Wood', *New Left Review* 184: 97–109.
Carling, Alan (1991) *Social Division*, London: Verso.
Carling, Alan (1993) 'Analytical Marxism and Historical Materialism: The Debate on Social Evolution', *Science and Society*, 57: 31–66.
Carver, Terrell (1989) 'Marx, Engels and Dialectics', in *Approaches to Marx*, ed. Mark Cowling and Lawrence Wilde, pp. 49–60, Milton Keynes: Open University Press.
Carver, Terrell (1992) 'Putting your Money where your Mouth Is: The Social Construction of Individuality in Marx's' *Capital*', *Studies in Political Thought* 1: 19–41.
Chong, Dennis (1991) *Collective Action and the Civil Rights Movement*, Chicago: University of Chicago Press.
Chorover, Stephen (1975) *From Genesis to Genocide*, Cambridge MA: MIT Press.
Coates, David (1975) *The Labour Party and the Struggle for Socialism*, Cambridge: Cambridge University Press.
Cohen, G. A. (1978) *Karl Marx's Theory of History: A Defence*, Oxford: Oxford University Press.
Cohen, G. A. (1981) 'The Labour Theory of Value and the Concept of Exploitation', in Steedman (1981), pp. 202–23.
Cohen, G. A. (1983a) 'Reconsidering Historical Materialism', in *Nomos* XXVI, *Marxism*, ed. J. Roland Pennock and John W. Chapman, New York: New York University Press, pp. 227–52; repr. Cohen (1989), pp. 132–54.
Cohen, G. A. (1983b) 'Reply to Four Critics', *Analyse und Kritik* 5: 195–222.
Cohen, G. A. (1986) 'The Structure of Proletarian Unfreedom', in Roemer (1986), pp. 237–59.

Cohen, G. A. (1989) *History, Labour and Freedom*, Oxford: Oxford University Press.

Cohen, Joshua, and Rogers, Joel (1983) *On Democracy*, New York: Penguin.

Collins, Randall (1992) 'On the Sociology of Intellectual Stagnation: The Late Twentieth Century in Perspective', *Theory, Culture and Society* 9: 73–96.

Condorcet, Marie Jean Antoine Nicolas de Caritat (1795) *Sketch for a History of the Progress of the Human Mind*.

Crafts, N. F. R., and Woodward, N. (1991) 'Introduction and Overview', in *The British Economy since 1945*, ed. N. F. R. Crafts and N. Woodward, Oxford: Oxford University Press, pp. 1–24.

Crewe, Ivor (1983) 'The Disturbing Truth behind Labour's Rout', *The Guardian*, 13 June.

Crewe, Ivor (1987a) 'A New Class of Politics', *The Guardian*, 15 June.

Crewe, Ivor (1987b) 'Tories Prosper from a Paradox', *The Guardian*, 16 June.

Crosland, Anthony (1960) *Can Labour Win?* London: Fabian Tract 324.

Cunningham, Frank (1973) 'Practice and Some Muddles about the Methodology of Historical Materialism', *Canadian Journal of Philosophy* 3: 235–48.

Davidson, Donald (1980) *Essays on Actions and Events*, Oxford: Oxford University Press.

Denver, D., and Hands, G. (eds) (1992) *Issues and Controversies in British Electoral Behaviour*, Brighton: Harvester/Wheatsheaf.

Denzin, Norman K. (1988) 'Blue Velvet: Postmodern Contradictions', *Theory, Culture and Society* 5: 461–73.

Downs, Anthony (1957) *An Economic Theory of Democracy*, New York: Harper & Row.

Dummett, Michael (1973) *Frege*, London: Duckworth.

Dunleavy, Patrick (1991) *Democracy, Bureaucracy and Public Choice*, Brighton: Harvester/Wheatsheaf.

Dunleavy, Patrick, and Husbands, Christopher (1985) *British Democracy at the Crossroads*, London: George Allen & Unwin.

Elster, Jon (1978) *Logic and Society*, New York: John Wiley.

Elster, Jon (1979) *Ulysses and the Sirens*, Cambridge: Cambridge University Press.

Elster, Jon (1980) 'Cohen on Marx's Theory of History', *Political Studies* 28: 121–8.

Elster, Jon (1982a) 'Marxism, Functionalism and Game Theory', *Theory and Society* 11: 453–82.

Elster, Jon (1982b) 'A Paradigm for the Social Sciences', *Inquiry* 25: 378–85.

Elster, Jon (1982c) 'Roemer versus Roemer', *Politics and Society* 11: 363–73.

Elster, Jon (1983a) *Explaining Technical Change*, Cambridge: Cambridge University Press.

Elster, Jon (1983b) 'Exploitation, Freedom and Justice', in *Nomos XXVI*, pp. 277–304.

Elster, Jon (1983c) *Sour Grapes*, Cambridge: Cambridge University Press.

Elster, Jon (1984) 'Historical Materialism and Economic Backwardness', in Ball and Farr (1984), pp. 36–58.

Elster, Jon (1985) *Making Sense of Marx*, Cambridge: Cambridge University Press.

Elster, Jon (1986a) 'Reply to Comments', *Inquiry* 29 : 65–77.
Elster, Jon (1986b) *Ulysses and the Sirens*, New York: Cambridge University Press.
Elster, Jon (1987) *Sour Grapes*, New York: Cambridge University Press.
Elster, Jon (1989) *The Cement of Society: A Study of Social Order*, Cambridge: Cambridge University Press.
Engels, Friedrich (1987) *The Condition of the Working Class in England*, Harmondsworth: Penguin.
Esping-Andersen, Gosta (1984) *Politics Against the Markets*, Princeton: Princeton University Press.
Featherstone, Mike (1988) 'In Pursuit of the Postmodern: An Introduction', *Theory, Culture and Society* 5: 195–215.
Fekete, John (1988) *Life after Postmodernism*, London: Macmillan.
Fiorina, Morris P., and Shepsle, Kenneth A. (1982) 'Equilibrium, Disequilibrium, and the General Possibility of a Science of Politics', in Ordeshook and Shepsle (1982), pp. 49–64.
Fishbein, Warren H. (1984) *Wage Restraint by Consensus*, London: Routledge & Kegan Paul.
Flax, Jane (1987) 'Postmodernism and Gender Relations in Feminist Theory', *Signs* 12: 621–43.
Frank, Robert H. (1988) *Passions within Reason: The Strategic Role of the Emotions*, New York: Norton.
Fraser, Nancy (1992) 'The Uses and Abuses of French Discourse Theories for Feminist Politics', *Theory, Culture and Society* 5: 373–94.
Fraser, Nancy, and Nicholson, Linda (1988) 'Social Criticism without Philosophy: An Encounter between Feminism and Postmodernism', *Theory, Culture and Society* 9: 373–94.
Freeman, John R. (1989) *Democracy and Markets*, Ithaca NY: Cornell University Press.
Frerejohn, John A., and Fiorina, Morris P. (1974) 'The Paradox of Not Voting: A Decision Theoretic Analysis', *American Political Science Review* 68: 525–36.
Fulcher, J. (1987) 'Labour Movement Theory versus Corporatism', *Sociology* 21: 23–52.
Gallop, Jane (1987) 'French Theory and the Seduction of Feminism', in *Men in Feminism*, ed. Alice Jardine and Paul Smith, New York: Methuen, pp. 111–15.
Gambetta, Diego (1994) 'Inscrutable Markets', *Rationality and Society*, 6: 353–68.
Garfinkel, Alan (1981) *Forms of Explanation*, New Haven: Yale University Press.
Gay, Peter (1970) *The Dilemma of Democratic Socialism*, New York: Basic Books.
Geras, Norman (1983) *Marx and Human Nature: Refutation of a Legend*, London: Verso.
Geras, Norman (1985) 'The Controversy about Marx and Justice', *New Left Review* 150: 47–85.
Giddens, Anthony (1979) *Central Problems in Social Theory: Action, Structure and Contradiction in Social Analysis*, Berkeley: University of California Press.
Giddens, Anthony (1984) *The Constitution of Society*, Berkeley: University of California Press.
Giddens, Anthony (1985) *The Nation State and Violence*, Cambridge: Polity Press.

Gilbert, Alan (1984) 'Marx's Moral Realism: Eudaimonism and Moral Progress', in *After Marx*, ed. Terence Ball and James Farr, Cambridge: Cambridge University Press, pp. 154–83.

Gilbert, Alan (1990) *Democratic Individuality*, Cambridge: Cambridge University Press.

Goldfield, Michael (1989a) *The Decline of Organized Labor in the United States*, Chicago: Chicago University Press.

Goldfield, Michael (1989b) 'Worker Insurgency, Radical Organization, and New Deal Labor Legislation', *American Political Science Review* 83:1257–82.

Goldfield, Michael (1990) 'Explaining New Deal Labor Policy', *American Political Science Review* 84: 1304–15.

Goldstein, Robert Justin (1978) *Political Repression in Modern America*, Cambridge MA: Schenkman.

Gould, Carol C. (1978) *Marx's Social Ontology*, Cambridge MA: MIT Press.

Gramsci, Antonio (1971) *Selections from the Prison Notebooks*, New York: International Publishers.

Habermas, Jürgen (1971) 'Introduction: Some Problems in the Attempt to Link Theory and Praxis', in *Theory and Practice*, London: Heinemann, pp. 1–40.

Hall, Stuart, and Jacques, Martin (eds) (1989) *New Times: The Changing Face of Politics in the 1990s*, London: Lawrence & Wishart.

Habermas, Jürgen (1983) *Knowledge and Human Interests,* Cambridge: Polity.

Haraway, Donna (1985) 'A Manifesto for Cyborgs: Science, Technology and Socialist Feminism in the 1980s', *Socialist Review* 80: 65–107.

Hardin, Russell (1982) *Collective Action*, Baltimore: Johns Hopkins University Press.

Harding, Sandra (1983) 'Common Causes: Toward a *Reflexive* Feminist Theory', *Women and Politics* 3: 27–42.

Harding, Sandra (1986) *The Science Question in Feminism*, Milton Keynes: Open University Press.

Harman, Gilbert (1965) 'The Inference to the Best Explanation', *Philosophical Review* 74: 88–95.

Hassan, Ihab (1984) 'The Culture of Postmodernism', *Theory, Culture and Society* 2: 119–31.

Hekman, Susan J. (1990) *Gender and Knowledge: Elements of a Postmodern Feminism*, Cambridge: Polity.

Hilton, Rodney (1976) *The Transition Debate*, London: Verso.

Hilton, Rodney (1985) 'Towns in English Feudal Society', in *Class Conflict and the Crisis of Feudalism: Essays in Medieval Social History*, London: Hambledon, pp. 102–13.

Hindess, Barry (1984) 'Rational Choice Theory and the Analysis of Political Action', *Economy and Society* 13: 255–77.

Hindess, Barry (1985) 'Actors and Social Relations' in Wardell, M., and Turner, S. (eds) *Sociological Theory in Transition*, pp. 113–26, London: Allen & Unwin.

Hindess, Barry (1986) '"Interests" in Political Analysis' in Law, J. (ed.), *Power, Action and Belief: A New Sociology of Knowledge*, pp. 112–31, London: Routledge & Kegan Paul.

Hirschmann, Albert (1970) *Exit, Voice and Loyalty*, New Haven: Yale University Press.

Hodgson, Geoffrey M. (1981) *Labour at the Crossroads*, Oxford: Martin Robertson.
Holland, Stuart (1975) *The Socialist Challenge*, London: Quarter.
Hutcheon, Linda (1989) *The Politics of Postmodernism*, London: Routledge.
Jagger, Alison (1983) *Feminist Politics and Human Nature*, Brighton: Harvester.
James, Susan (1984) *The Content of Social Explanation*, Cambridge: Cambridge University Press.
Jameson, Fredric (1985) 'Postmodernism and Consumer Society', in *Postmodern Culture*, ed. Hal Foster, London: Pluto Press, pp. 111–25.
Jameson, Fredric (1991) *Postmodernism, or the Cultural Logic of Late Capitalism*, London: Verso.
Jarvie, I. C. (1972) *Concepts and Society*, London: Routledge & Kegan Paul.
Kamolnick, Paul (1988) *Classes: A Marxist Critique*, New York: General Hall.
Kant, Immanuel (1972) *Critique of Pure Reason*, trans, N. Kemp-Smith, London: Macmillan.
Keating, Peter (1976) *Into Unknown England 1866–1913: Selections from the Social Explorers*, Glasgow: Fontana/Collins.
Kieve, Ronald A. (1986), 'From Necessary Illusion to Rational Choice? A Critique of Neo-Marxist Rational-Choice Theory', *Theory and Society* 15: 557–82.
King, Desmond (1987) 'The State and the Social Structures of Welfare in Advanced Industrial Societies', *Theory and Society* 16: 841–68.
Kinnock, Neil (1986) *Making our Way*, Oxford: Blackwell.
Kitschelt, Herbert (1993) 'Class Structure and Social Democratic Party Strategy', *British Journal of Political Science* 23: 299–339.
Kolakowski, Leszek (1969) *The Alienation of Reason*, trans. Norbert Guterman, New York: Doubleday/Anchor.
Kolakowski, Leszek (1978) *Main Currents of Marxism*, trans. P.S. Falla, 3 vols, Oxford: Oxford University Press.
Korpi, Walter (1983) *The Democratic Class Struggle*, London: Routledge & Kegan Paul.
Kratochwil, Friedrich (1989) *On Rules, Norms and Decisions*, Cambridge: Cambridge University Press.
Labour Party (1978) *Annual Conference Report*, London: Labour Party.
Lakatos, Imre (1970) 'Falsification and the Methodology of Scientific Research Programs', in *Criticism and the Growth of Knowledge*, ed. Alan Musgrave and Imre Lakatos, Cambridge: Cambridge University Press, pp. 91–196.
Lange, Peter (1984) 'Unions, Workers and Wage Regulation: The Rational Bases of Consent', in *Order and Conflict in Contemporary Capitalism*, ed. John Goldthorpe, Oxford: Oxford University Press, pp. 98–123.
Lash, Scott, and Urry, John (1984) 'The New Marxism of Collective Action: A Critical Analysis', *Sociology* 18: 33–50.
Leibniz, Gottfried Wilhelm (1973) *Philosophical Writings*, ed. G. H. R. Parkinson, London: Dent.
Levine, Andrew (1984) *Arguing for Socialism*, London: Routledge & Kegan Paul.
Levine, Andrew (1987) *The End of the State*, London: Verso.
Levine, Andrew (1989) 'Rationality and Class Struggle', in Callinicos (1989), pp. 17–47.

Levine, Andrew, and Wright, Erik Olin (1980) 'Rationality and Class Struggle', *New Left Review* 123: 47–68.
Levine, Andrew, Sober, Elliott, and Wright, Erik Olin (1987) 'Marxism and Methodological Individualism', *New Left Review* 162: 67–84.
Levins, Richard, and Lewontin, Richard (1984) *The Dialectical Biologist*, Cambridge MA: Harvard University Press.
Lewin, L. (1988) *Ideology and Strategy*, Cambridge: Cambridge University Press.
Lindbeck, Assar, and Snower, Dennis J. (1989) *The Insider-Outsider Theory of Employment and Unemployment*, London: MIT Press.
Lindblom, Charles (1977) *Politics and Markets*, New York: Basic Books.
Lukes, Steven (1973) *Individualism*, New York: Harper & Row.
Lukes, Steven (1977) *Essays in Social Theory*, London: Macmillan.
Lyotard, Jean-François (1984) *The Postmodern Condition: A Report on Knowledge*, Manchester: Manchester University Press.
Lyotard, Jean-François (1988) 'Can Thoughts Go without a Body?', *Discourse* 11: 74–87.
Marx, Karl (1956) *The Holy Family*, Moscow: Progress.
Marx, Karl (1973) *Grundrisse*, ed. and trans. Martin Nicolaus, Harmondsworth: Penguin.
Mandel, Ernest (1975) *Late Capitalism*, trans. Joris de Bres, London: New Left Books.
Marx, Karl (1975) *Texts on Method*, ed. and trans. Terrell Carver, Oxford: Blackwell.
Marx, Karl (1977) *Selected Writings*, ed. David McLellan, Oxford: Oxford University Press.
Marx, Karl (1986) *Capital*, Vol. 1, trans. Ben Fowkes, Harmondsworth: Penguin Books.
Massey, Doreen (1984) *Spatial Divisions of Labour*, London: Macmillan.
Miliband, Ralph (1969) *The State in Capitalist Society*, London: Weidenfeld & Nicholson.
Miller, Richard W. (1978), 'Methodological Individualism and Social Explanation', *Philosophy of Science* 45: 387–414.
Miller, Richard W. (1984) *Analyzing Marx: Morality, Power and History*, Princeton: Princeton University Press.
Miller, William (1990) 'Voting and the Electorate' in *Develoments in British Politics 3*, ed. Patrick Dunleavy et al., London: Macmillan, pp. 42-68.
Miller, William et al. (1991) *How Voters Change*, Oxford: Oxford University Press.
O'Connor, James R. (1973) *The Fiscal Crisis of the State*, New York: St. Martin's Press.
OECD (1980) *Economic Survey UK 1980*, Paris: OECD.
OECD (1987) *Economic Survey UK 1987*, Paris: OECD.
Ordeshook, Peter C. (1986) *Game Theory and Political Theory*, New York: Cambridge University Press.
Ordeshook, Peter C. and Schepsle, Kenneth A. (1982) *Political Equilibrium*, Boston: Kluwer-Nijhoff.
Panitch, Leo (1976) *Social Democracy and Industrial Militancy*, Cambridge: Cambridge University Press.

Parkin, Frank (1979) *Marxist Class Theory: A Bourgeois Critique*, London: Tavistock.
Parijs, Philippe van (1981) *Evolutionary Explanation in the Social Sciences: An Emerging Paradigm*, Totowa NJ: Rowman & Littlefield.
Parijs, Philippe van (1984) 'Marxisms' Central Puzzle', in Ball and Farr (1984), pp. 88–104.
Parijs, Philippe van (1989) 'A Revolution in Class Theory', in Wright (1989), pp. 213–41.
Pimlott, Ben (1992) *Harold Wilson*, London: HarperCollins.
Pitkin, Hanna Fenichel (1990) 'Slippery Bentham', *Political Theory* 18: 104–31.
Piven, Frances Fox, and Cloward, Richard A. (1979) *Poor People's Movements*, New York: Vintage.
Piven, Frances Fox, and Cloward, Richard A. (1988) *Why Americans Don't Vote*, New York: Pantheon.
Popkin, Samuel (1991) *The Reasoning Voter*, Chicago: Chicago University Press.
Popper, Karl (1966) *The Open Society and its Enemies*, Vol. 2, London: Routledge & Kegan Paul.
Popper, Karl (1972) *Conjectures and Refutations*, London: Routledge & Kegan Paul.
Poulantzas, Nicos (1978) *State, Power, Socialism*, London, Verso.
Prickett, James R. (1975) *Communists and the Communist Issue in the American Labor Movement 1920–1950*, Ann Arbor: University Microfilms.
Przeworski, Adam (1980) 'Social Democracy as a Historical Phenomenon', *New Left Review* 122: 27–58.
Przeworski, Adam (1985a) *Capitalism and Social Democracy*, Cambridge: Cambridge University Press.
Przeworski, Adam (1985b) 'Marxism and Rational Choice', *Politics and Society* 14: 379–409.
Przeworski, Adam (1986) 'Material Interests, Class Compromise, and the Transition to Socialism', in Roemer (1986), pp. 162–88.
Przeworski, Adam (1990a) *The State and the Economy under Capitalism*, Chur, Switzerland, and New York: Harwood Academic Publishers.
Przeworski, Adam (1990b) 'Marxism and Rational Choice', in *Individualism*, ed. Pierre Birnbaum and Jean Leca, Oxford: Oxford University Press, pp. 62–92.
Przeworski, Adam (1991) *Democracy and the Market*, Cambridge: Cambridge University Press.
Przeworski, Adam, and Sprague, John (1986) *Paper Stones*, Chicago: University of Chicago Press.
Przeworski, Adam, and Wallerstein, Michael (1982a) 'The Structure of Class Conflict in Democratic Capitalist Societies', *American Political Science Review* 76: 215–38.
Przeworski, Adam, and Wallerstein, Michael (1982b) 'Democratic Capitalism at the Crossroads', *Democracy* 2: 52–68.
Przeworski, Adam, and Wallerstein, Michael (1986) 'Popular Sovereignty, State Autonomy, and Private Property', *Archives of European Sociology* 27: 215–59.
Przeworski, Adam, and Wallerstein, Michael (1988) 'Structural Dependence of the State on Capital', *American Political Science Review* 82: 11–30.
Przeworski, Adam, and Wright, Erik Olin (1977), 'Proletariat into a Class: The Process of Class Formation from Karl Kautsky's *The Class Struggle* to Recent

Controversies', *Politics and Society* 7: 343–401; repr. in Przeworski (1985a), pp. 47–98.

Resnick, Stephen, and Wolff, Richard (1987) *Knowledge and Class*, Chicago: University of Chicago Press.

Riker, William H., and Ordeshook, Peter C. (1968) 'A Theory of the Calculus of Voting', *American Political Science Review* 62: 25–41.

Robertson, David (1984) *Class and the British Electorate*, Oxford: Blackwell.

Roemer, John (1982a) *A General Theory of Exploitation and Class*, Cambridge MA: Harvard University Press.

Roemer, John (1982b) 'Property Relations vs Surplus Value in Marxian Exploitation', *Philosophy and Public Affairs* 11: 281–313.

Roemer, John (1982c) 'Methodological Individualism and Deductive Marxism', *Theory and Society* 11: 513–39.

Roemer, John (1983) 'Unequal Exchange, Labour Migration and International Capital Flows: A Theoretical Synthesis', in Desai, Padma (ed.), *Marxism, the Soviet Economy and Central Planning*, Cambridge MA: MIT Press, 1983, pp. 34–60.

Roemer, John (1985) 'Should Marxists be Interested in Exploitation?', *Philosophy and Public Affairs*, 14: 30–65. Reprinted in Roemer (1986), pp. 260–82.

Roemer, John (ed.) (1986) *Analytical Marxism*, Cambridge: Cambridge University Press.

Roemer, John (1988) *Free to Lose: An Introduction to Marxist Economic Philosophy*, London: Radius.

Roth, Guenther, and Schluchter, Wolfgang (1979) *Max Weber's Vision of History*, Berkeley, University of California Press.

Sabia, Daniel R., Jr (1988) 'Rationality, Collective Action, and Karl Marx', *American Journal of Political Science* 32: 50–71.

Sanders, D. (1992) 'Why the Conservative Party Won – Again', in *Britain at the Polls 1992*, ed. Anthony King, London: Chatham House, pp. 171–222.

Sargent, Lydia (ed.) (1981) *The Unhappy Marriage of Marxism and Feminism: A Debate on Class and Patriarchy*, London: Pluto Press.

Sarlvik, Bo, and Crewe, Ivor (1983) *Decade of Dealignment*, Cambridge: Cambridge University Press.

Sayr, Andrew, and Walker, Richard (1992) *The New Social Economy: Reworking the Division of Labour*, Oxford: Blackwell.

Schrecker, Ellen W. (1986) *No Ivory Tower: MacCarthyism and the Universities*, New York: Oxford University Press.

Sen, Amartya (1989) 'Rational Fools', in *Choice, Welfare and Measurement*, Oxford: Oxford University Press, pp. 84–106.

Shapere, Dudley (1984) *Reason and the Search for Knowledge*, Dordrecht: Reidel.

Slaughter, Cliff (1986) 'Making Sense of Elster', *Inquiry* 29: 45–56.

Smart, Barry (1993) *Postmodernity*, London: Routledge.

Springer, Claudia (1991) 'The Pleasure of the Interface', *Screen*, 32: 303–25.

Squires, Judith (1993) *Principled Positions*, London: Lawrence & Wishart.

Strawson, P. F. (1959) *Individuals: An Essay in Descriptive Metaphysics*, Oxford: The Clarendon Press.

Steedman, Ian (ed.) (1981) *The Value Controversy*, London: Verso.

Stephens, John D. (1979) *The Transition from Capitalism to Socialism*, London: Macmillan.

Taylor, Charles (1960) 'What's Wrong with Capitalism', *New Left Review* 2: 5–11.
Taylor, Charles (1980), 'Formal Theory in Social Science', *Inquiry* 23: 139–44.
Taylor, Charles (1985), 'Interpretation and the Science of Man', *Philosophical Papers*, Vol. 2, *Philosophy and the Human Sciences*, Cambridge: Cambridge University Press, pp. 15–57.
Taylor, Michael (1976) *Anarchy and Co-operation*, Chichester: Wiley.
Taylor, Michael (1982) *Community, Anarchy and Liberty*, Cambridge: Cambridge University Press.
Taylor, Michael (1986), 'Elster's Marx', *Inquiry* 29: 3–10.
Taylor, Michael (ed.) (1988) 'Rationality and Revolutionary Collective Action', in Taylor, Michael (ed.), *Rationality and Revolution*, Cambridge: Cambridge University Press, pp. 63–97.
Taylor, Robert (1993) *The Trade Union Question in British Politics*, Oxford: Blackwell.
TUC (1977) *Annual Report*, London: TUC.
Tucker, D. F. B. (1980) *Marxism and Individualism*, Oxford: Blackwell.
Uhlaner, Carol J. (1989) '"Relational Goods" and Participation: Incorporating Sociability into a Theory of Rational Action', *Public Choice* 62: 253–85.
Van der Wee, H. (1985) *Prosperity and Upheaval*, Harmondsworth: Penguin.
Vogel, D. (1989) *Fluctuating Fortunes*, New York: Basic Books.
Watkins, J. W. N. (1968) 'Methodological Individualism and Social Tendencies', in *Readings in the Philosophy of the Social Sciences*, ed. May Brodbeck, New York: Macmillan pp. 269–79.
Webb, N., and Wybrow, R. (1981) *The Gallup Report*, London: Sphere.
Webb, N., and Wybrow, R. (1982) *The Gallup Report*, London, Sphere.
Weber, Max (1946) *From Max Weber*, ed. Hans Gerth and C. Wright Mills, New York: Oxford University Press.
Weber, Max (1949) *The Methodology of the Social Sciences*, New York: The Free Press.
Weber, Max (1977) *Critique of Stammler*, trans. Guy Oakes, New York: The Free Press.
Weber, Max (1978) *Economy and Society*, Vol. 1, ed. Guenther Roth and Claus Wittich, Berkeley: University of California Press.
Whitehead, Phillip (1985) *The Writing on the Wall*, London: Michael Joseph.
Wittgenstein, Ludwig (1958) *Philosophical Investigations*, Oxford: Blackwell.
Wood, Allen (1981) *Karl Marx*, London: Routledge & Kegan Paul.
Wood, Allen (1986) 'Marx and Equality', in Roemer (1986), pp. 283–303.
Wood, Ellen Meiksins (1981) 'The Separation of the Economic and the Political in Capitalism ', *New Left Review* 127: 66–95.
Wood, Ellen Meiksins (1984) 'Marxism and the Course of History', *New Left Review* 147: 95–107.
Wood, Ellen Meiksins (1990) 'Explaining Everything or Nothing?' *New Left Review* 184: 116–28.
Woodiwiss, Anthony (1990) *Social Theory after Postmodernism*, London: Pluto Press.
Wright, Erik Olin (1978) *Class, Crisis and the State*, London: New Left Books.
Wright, Erik Olin (1982) 'The Status of the Political in the Concept of Class Structure', *Politics and Society* 11: 321–41.

Wright, Erik Olin (1983) 'Giddens' Critique of Marxism', *New Left Review* 138: 11–36.
Wright, Erik Olin (1985) *Classes*, London: Verso.
Wright, Erik Olin (1989) 'The Comparative Project on Class Structure and Class Consciousness: An Overview', *Acta Sociologica* 32: 3–22.
Wright, Erik Olin (ed.) (1989) *The Debate on Classes*, London: Verso.

Index

Analytical Marxism (AM)
  and formal models, 19–23
  and realism, 15–16, 29 n. 5,
  and science, 15–18, 27–8
  concepts of, 18
  definition of, 1–3, 12–14, 30–3, 70 n. 8, 137–9, 164, 168
  relation to Marxism, 23–7, 271–3

Brenner, Robert,
  and transition to capitalism, 106–9, 134 n. 19
  theory of history, 109–11

capitalism, 308–9
Cohen, G. A.
  and functional explanation, 3–4, 19, 23
  and rational choice Marxism, 111–12
  'development thesis', 3
  invents Analytical Marxism (AM), 1–2, 260–2
  on exploitation, 73 n. 35
  on Marx's theory of history, 17, 20–1, 33–5, 108–9, 259–60, 262–4

electoral politics
  and social democracy, 202–4
  in Britain, 207–13
  micro-foundations of, 147–50
  see also Przeworski, Adam
Elster, Jon
  and class, 95–8
  and functional explanation, 253 n. 4
  and methodological individualism, 5–6, 112–13, 231–2, 257 n. 55, 267–71
  criticizes functional explanation, 4–5
  criticizes historical materialism, 5

definition of Analytical Marxism (AM), 1–2
  see also methodological individualism
Engels, Friedrich, 5
explanation, 212, 233–4, 244–5, 250, 291–3, 316–18
  see also, Cohen, G. A.; Elster, Jon

historical materialism, 264–7
  general theory of, 37–8, 84
  special theory of, 37–9, 72 n. 19, 84
  see also Marx, Karl

individualism, methodological, see methodological individualism

Kolakowski, Leszek, 1, 2

Marx, Karl
  and methodological individualism, 240–3, 248–50, 252
  and praxis, 271
  and teleology, 114–15
  conception of history, 5, 113–14, 258–60
  critique of political economy, 9, 39–42, 114
Marxism
  and culture, 309–10, 314–15
  and feminism, 301–3, 320 n. 4, 321–2 n. 20
  and gender domination, 25–6, 29–30 n. 18, 303
  and modernism, 305–8
  crisis of, 11–12, 136, 162–3, 310–12
Marxism, Analytical, see Analytical Marxism (AM)
Marxism, Rational Choice, see Rational Choice Marxism (RCM)
methodological individualism, 285–7
  and empiricism, 293–4

Index

and microfoundations, 7–8, 9, 22, 80–1, 86, 138–9, 161–2, 231–3, 288–91
and Rational Choice Marxism (RCM), 2–4, 5–6, 21–2, 87–8, 282–5
normative dimensions of, 232, 251–2
of actions (MI_a), 234–5, 238, 243–8, 252
of events (MI_e), 233, 235–8, 244, 247, 252
of subjects (MI_s), 233–4, 235–7, 238–40, 241–2, 244–5, 252
see also electoral politics; Elster, Jon; Marx, Karl; Roemer, John; Przeworski, Adam

positivism, 2
postmodernism, 312–14
and feminism, 318–19, 323 n. 32
Przeworski, Adam
and class compromise, 150–3, 155, 169, 215–20
and class formation, 89–91, 170–3, 177–8, 206
and class interests, 150–1, 175–6
and class struggle, 140–2, 144, 155, 170
and consent, 153–4, 213–15
and economic crisis, 222–6
and electoral politics, 169, 174–5, 200–2, 206–7
and exploitation, 121–4, 141
and ideology, 165 n. 6
and individual identity, 145–7, 170, 172
and Labour Party policies, 227–8
and methodological individualism, 160, 164
and micro-foundations, 143–4, 168
and Rational Choice Marxism, 159–60
and the state, 154–7
and theory of history, 139

and social democracy, 19–21, 26, 144–5, 157–9, 163–4, 200–2, 220–2, 228–9
and socialism, 159, 167–8
and transition to socialism, 8, 134–5 n. 25, 140, 147
and voters, 204–7

Rational Choice Marxism (RCM)
and individual choice, 93–5
and determinism, 130–3
and ethnicity, 65–8
and game theory, 88–91
and gender, 62–4
and history, 99–102
and Marxism, 124–5
and moral argument, 118–21
and microfoundations, 98–9
and postmodernism, 129–30, 132–3, 302–5
and socialism, 68–9, 116–18, 127–9
and teleology, 115–16
and voting, 6–7, 295–8
definition of, 2–3, 9, 21–2, 33, 70 n. 8, 79–83
politics of, 82–3, 125–7
relation to Marxism, 35–7, 61–2
Rational Choice Theory, 298–9, 299 n. 1
critiques of, 279–82
limitations of, 277–9
neo-classical, 276–7
Roemer, John
and capitalism, 104–6
and class relations, 91–3
and coercion, 50–2
and definition of Analytical Marxism (AM), 1–2
and exploitation, 7, 17, 22, 42–4, 52–3, 59–60, 80–1, 83–5
and historical materialism, 55–7, 58–9
and history, 102–4
and methodological individualism
and power relations, 48–50

and property relations, 47–8, 85–6
'Class Exploitation Correspondence Principle', 44–7, 53–5, 75 n. 50
feudal exploitation, 58, 86

socialist exploitation, 57–60, 76 n. 60
status exploitation, 58–60, 63, 76 n. 60

Weber, Max, 243–8